NOV 1995

D0338696

HAPPY DAYS

SHANA ALEXANDER

HAPPY DAYS

MY MOTHER, MY FATHER,
MY SISTER & ME

———

DOUBLEDAY / NEW YORK LONDON TORONTO SYDNEY AUCKLAND

PUBLISHED BY DOUBLEDAY

a division of Bantam Doubleday Dell Publishing Group, Inc.
1540 Broadway, New York, New York 10036

DOUBLEDAY and the portrayal of an anchor with a dolphin are trademarks of
Doubleday, a division of Bantam Doubleday Dell Publishing Group, Inc.

Book Design by Gretchen Achilles

Library of Congress Cataloging-in-Publication Data

Alexander, Shana.
    Happy days : my mother, my father, my sister and me / Shana
Alexander.
        p.   cm.
    Includes index.
    1. Alexander, Shana.   2. Journalists — United States — Biography.
3. Ager, Milton, 1893–1979.   4. Musicians — United States — 20th
century — Biography.   I. Title.
PN4874.A44A3   1995
070'.92 — dc20   95-36398
[B]   CIP

ISBN 0-385-41815-9
Copyright © 1995 by Shana Alexander
All Rights Reserved
Printed in the United States of America
November 1995

1   3   5   7   9   10   8   6   4   2

FIRST EDITION

For

LAUREL AGER BENTLEY

CONTENTS

ACT II

WAR SONGS

ACT III

HAPPY DAYS

ACT I

POLES
APART

INTRODUCTORY NOTE

Children, we know, can never understand their parents. But no child misunderstood her parents more than I did. Or so I think now. The idea began creeping up on me when I started trying to write about them, a decade after their deaths. Fortunately I have a three-years-younger sister, Laurel Bentley, and Laurel did, at least somewhat, understand them.

Without Laurel's hand sometimes on the tiller, sometimes the oars, and always firmly clasped in my own (if this makes us a pair of three- or four-handed sisters, that is not the only anomaly in our family) I would not have dared set out on this voyage of memory, and certainly could not have stayed with it. Laurel has been at different times my lamp, my translator, my star, and my scourge, and I bless her for every minute of it.

Our parents were Milton and Cecelia Ager, an unusually accomplished pair and, by common consent, the most interesting people on either side of our large family. Each one had left home at the earliest opportunity and come straight to Manhattan. One a born creator, the other a born critic, they met and thrived in the Jazz Age. He was a master of music, she of words. In the twenties, Milton Ager was one of the nation's most successful composers of popular music, writer of more than three hundred published songs, many still played today. In the thirties and forties, Cecelia Ager's stiletto-sharp takes on the fashionable and fatuous — a column in *Variety*, a stretch in Hollywood, a decade as a Manhattan movie critic, and forty years of occasional pieces in snooty magazines — were considered by discerning readers the best things of their kind. Unlike Milton, she never found the wide audience she deserved. But today her work is studied in film schools.

One other oddity should be mentioned. Words and music are rarely so mutually exclusive as they were in our household. Cecelia, virtuoso of the *mot juste*, was not the least bit musical. Indeed, she seemed to me nearly tone-deaf, though I cannot be sure; like my mother, I can barely carry a tune. Laurel has an excellent ear, and a passion for music, but she has virtually devoted her life to her family and to the abstruse aerospace proposals on which she serves as writer and editor. As for Milton, he was an exceedingly literate and well-read man, yet near incapable of writing lyrics. Like almost every other songwriter of his period — Irving Berlin and Cole Porter being the great exceptions — he required a collaborator.

Each parent reached the top fast; they peaked while Laurel and I were very young. By the time we were in college, their own professional lives were tapering off. But they carried on without complaint, without compromise, and without comment through the fifties, sixties, and seventies, fierce with honor, crisply witty, personally reticent, and totally indifferent to the opinions of others.

Despite their individual gifts, it was as a married couple that Cecelia and Milton Ager were most interesting. They were not like anyone else's parents, and nothing like the couples one meets in books. Their eccentricity, so distressful to me for so many years, never appeared to bother them. Nor were they at all interested in justifying their prickly entente to anyone, least of all their own children.

Physically, they were much alike — brisk, blue-eyed insomniacs of small stature. At five feet three, he was taller by an inch or two. But their temperaments were entirely different. He stayed up all night, she rose at dawn. He was sweet-natured, she tart. He was intensely analytical; she navigated by dead-eye instinct. He was generous, she withholding, yet he was righteous and puritanical and she far more free-thinking and forgiving.

Each of them had a distinctive speaking voice. Hers was low and cello-like, though capable on occasion of descending to bass viol level. His retained a Chicago twang. *Dji-GAH-ge*, he called the place; spuds were *buh-DAY-duhs*. If I now wish to write about them, I can hear each voice telling me, I am free to do so; we are, after all, a family of writers. But they have no intention of letting their hair down just because we happen to be related. Navel-gazing is odious. Full confession, today's fashion, is also its pathology.

As Laurel and I were growing up, we watched Cecelia and Milton growing more and more apart; we were eyewitnesses, virtually the only ones. No one else got close enough. To call them "private people" understates the matter. "Sharing," an obligation now seen by some as right up there with faith, hope, and charity, would have been anathema to both of them. Sharing is for egg rolls.

What held two such dissimilar and fiercely independent people together for so many years was always, to their children, and to a relatively small number of intimates, the central mystery of their lives. By the time their close friends had dwindled down to a precious few, these people were still asking one another—and occasionally asking the Agers directly—the same questions that now preoccupy me. Why did they stay together fifty-seven years? Why keep on? Why never chuck it, as so many of their friends did? Certainly they were sophisticates, two people ahead of their time, independent free thinkers, each one well equipped to go it alone, and neither one at all religious. So what was the magic glue, or the unleapable barrier? It was not us, their daughters, it was definitely not money, and it never looked like love.

As an eyewitness to Acts I and III of Milton's and Cecelia's lives, I feel reasonably comfortable telling what I saw of their story. But I was scant witness to Act II. Once I made my escape from parental clutches via matrimony, the easiest route in those days, I was more or less estranged from the Agers for twenty years. I saw them occasionally, but they made me uncomfortable. For one thing, they had little use for either of my husbands, and the ill feeling was reciprocated. More important, I was focused on my own life, professional and personal, on my work as a journalist, and on trying to raise a family as different from my own as I could possibly manage. Hence I can offer only a bare scaffolding to span the Agers' story between Acts I and III. Fortunately, Act II appears to have been a relatively fallow and featureless time for them.

Somehow or other, all four of us made it through this middle passage, Laurel with the inestimable help of her husband, Wray Bentley, an engineer and computer programmer, and their delectable daughter, Hannah, today a solo-practice environmental lawyer in San Francisco. For me, things worked out differently. I lost the two husbands, not in the least unwillingly, to divorce, and then, more than a decade later, I lost my one great love to death and desertion (mutual). A decade after that I lost my beloved daughter, Kathy, at the age of twenty-seven.

But this book is about the Agers and me, and Act III of the Agers' lives — their last ten or fifteen years — was a very good time for all of us, even though Cecelia and Milton were suffering the pains and humiliations of aging and I was riding the ups and downs of a hard-to-handle love affair. During this period my difficult parents — the former foe — became my closest friends, the many pleasures of their sophisticated company eclipsing the memory of the miserable childhood that had driven me away from them. More than friends, we were by then the mutual sculptors of one another, each of us over time having patterned and eroded the other in multitudinous, overlapping, uncountable ways.

Of course this book is for my sister, Laurel, without whom I could not have written it, nor lived it, nor savored it, nor survived it. And I couldn't have got it right either. The Good Fairy endowed me at birth with a great many gifts, but scrupulous memory was not among them. So on top of everything else, I thank Laurel for helping me get things straight, even though the cost at times — as Eliot reminds — was not less than everything.

"Children don't ask to be born," Milton used to say to his wife and daughters. There were periods in our long lives together when he seemed to say it every day. I never fully understood what he meant until I was middle-aged and the man I was so much in love with, a playwright and poetry critic, asked me to think about some lines of Housman's:

> *The night my father got me,*
> *His mind was not on me.*
> *He did not once consider*
> *The thing you see.*

CHAPTER ONE

THE NEST

The first moment I remember is holding his hand and walking down the long, white-tiled hospital corridor. We are going to see my new sister. My eyes follow an inset band of blue tiles level with my father's shoulders. I am three years old today. It is his birthday too.

The first sound I recall is the scratch, scratch of his razor blade on music manuscript paper scraping out wrong notes. He writes late at night by candlelight on a fold-up Salvation Army organ that Cecelia bought him and put in our bedroom. We can't hear the music because he doesn't need to pump the pedals. He hears it in his head. The scratching goes on for hours, a pleasant sound in the near darkness.

What else? Three bad tastes: oysters, rhubarb, milk of magnesia. The awful German frauleins who cared for us. All the wonderful closets to explore. In the hall closet are stacks of records of Milton's songs, his piles of symphony and opera scores, his collapsible silk hat, our Christmas tree ornaments, and, on the bottom, our bootleg whiskey. Sime Silverman, the burly, rough-voiced editor of *Variety*, where Cecelia works, brings the whiskey, and never forgets to bring Laurel and me a quart of Louis Sherry ice cream, hand-packed, with little black specks in the vanilla.

Our own closet holds all our smocked English dresses and high-laced shoes, and the beloved Oz books that Grandmother Fanny sends twice a year from Hollywood. My child-size golf bag and clubs hang from a hook. Out of reach on the top shelf is a beautifully dressed French doll as tall as I am. Fanny sent her too, but Cecelia says she is "too good" to play with. We don't like dolls anyhow. We like our big blackboard, our child-size, simple American furniture: two chairs, work bench, the big revolving globe.

The linen closet outside our parents' bedroom holds their bed sheets stacked in scented piles tied with ribbon. Their towels are peach color or turquoise, monogrammed in lowercase letters, *cra*: Cecelia Rubenstein Ager.

How glamorous our mother is to me, and scary, especially in the mornings, when she wakes up in her black eye mask and reads the papers and sips her café au lait and smokes a Chesterfield while Milton is still sleeping in the other bed. In the evenings, I cannot wait for them to go out so I can investigate her big closet stacked floor to ceiling like a milliner's shop with boxes upon boxes of silk flowers from Paris in every color and variety. Alongside are piles of soft leather gloves in every shade and belts of every material and hue. At the very back in a special bag is her crimson silk velvet evening wrap trimmed with ermine tails, and a thin gown of white silk sprigged with tiny flowers, and a pair of winged sandals woven of gold and silver strips. Over everything floats the fresh, ferny scent of New Mown Hay, from J. Floris, in London.

New Mown Hay was the only perfume she ever wore. Years later, when I visited the shop and tried to buy her some, I was told they no longer made it. All the hay in Europe had been cut down during the war.

*   *   *

About my birth I know only that it started gaily and ended badly for everyone. On the evening of October 4, 1925, Cecelia and Milton had gone with their friend Lou Clayton, Jimmy Durante's manager, to the Club Durante on West 58th Street to catch the new act. When Durante began smashing up his piano and hurling pieces of it at his own orchestra, Cecelia laughed so hard she started going into labor. Milton rushed her to the select Lying-In Hospital off Gramercy Park where Cecelia's favorite cousin, Hannah Stone, M.D., was on the obstetrics staff. For the next two days Hannah and Sylvia Yellen, the wife of Milton's lyricist partner Jack Yellen, took turns at Cecelia's bedside. Nearly forty hours passed before I was finally born. Sylvia was right there in the delivery room holding Cecelia's hand, just as Cecelia had done for her when the Yellens' first son was born two years before.

I finally made it with the assistance of a pair of wicked, long-handled surgical spoons, standard tools for a high forceps delivery, that left me with permanent scars under my left eyebrow and along the right side of my neck, and a lifetime sense of having a huge head. The ordeal left Cecelia half-dead, and perhaps not feeling entirely cordial toward her firstborn, or so it was much later suggested independently, by different psychoanalysts, to each of us.

My parents lived then at 157 West 57th Street. Cecelia was in thrall to a fashionable Park Avenue pediatrician who decreed that a bottle is the only sanitary way to feed a baby and that crying is nature's way of developing an infant's lungs. Hence a crying baby should never, repeat never, be picked up, hugged, or rocked, and so far as I know, she never did it.

After Laurel was born, I remember hearing my parents arguing over these matters. My information about their lives before her birth is next to nil. About all I know is that Cecelia's favorite brother, Laurence, two years younger, was killed in a car crash a few months before Laurel's birth, and she was named for him. Although our parents were professional writers, neither one kept a journal or diary or scrapbook. They didn't save desk calendars. They didn't keep letters or other memorabilia. No family photographs were on display. Cecelia seemed pathologically disinclined to talk about herself or her early life, at least to her children. Milton loved to reminisce, but not about the person I was most interested in hearing about, George Gershwin.

"I knew George Gershwin up close," Milton said to me when he was over eighty and we were discussing the book we intended to write together about Tin Pan Alley. "But I won't talk about him. Because unless you're a fellow musician, you won't understand what I'm saying." He had talked about him, of course, from time to time over the years, but always in a guarded and extremely protective way.

However, Cecelia and Milton had been good friends of George and Ira Gershwin and the rest of the family. And the Gershwins — early aware that they were harboring a genius in their midst — had kept meticulous records and saved everything. Old check stubs, theater tickets, calendars, doodles, and every scrap of paper ephemera has since been catalogued. Much of the little I know about the Agers' early years comes from tidbits pieced together from the extraordinarily well documented Gershwin saga.

My first sighting of Cecelia and Milton as a married couple is in June of 1926, when they appear in a well-known photograph of the Gershwins and a couple dozen of their pals at a beach hotel on the Jersey Shore. Their hosts were Albert and Mascha Strunsky, prosperous Greenwich Village landlords and restaurateurs. Soon the Strunskys' daughter Leonore, known as Lee, would marry Ira Gershwin or, as Cecelia always put it, would "finally get Ira to marry her."

The occasion for the Strunsky photograph was a house party celebrating the sixth wedding anniversary of Lee's older sister Emily and Lou Paley, an erudite English teacher and sometime lyricist. The showbiz guests were posed by George, who reclines odalisque-like in the foreground, the Young God recumbent. The couple not exactly snuggling on the top step, left, are Milton and Cecelia.

Did either parent ever mention this picture to me? Not once. I came across it quite by accident nearly a half century later, in a new book lying on the coffee table of their Wilshire Boulevard apartment. The writers were Edward Jablonski and Lawrence D. Stewart, Gershwin's biographers. Jablonski lives in New York, and Stewart, an attractive, easygoing man about my age, in California. I'd met Stewart once or twice visiting my parents. Twenty years after that, desperate to increase my meager store of data on Cecelia and Milton, I'd taken a chance and called him up. It was like stumbling across the Lost Dutchman's Gold Mine. He kept a journal, I discovered, a lifelong habit he picked up while writing his doctoral dissertation on one of the many eighteenth-century litterateurs who buzzed around Dr. Johnson. Over the years Stewart had become as fascinated as I by the Agers and their unique relationship, and each time he'd seen them, singly or together, he'd noted the occasion in his journal. Furthermore, Stewart is a lifelong musicologist, historian, archivist, and connoisseur of contemporary arts. I can count on the fingers of one hand the people who were a friend of both Cecelia and Milton, and appreciated them equally, and Lawrence Stewart is one. He had also been a close friend of Ira and Lee, at the hub of their extensive Hollywood social circle, and had worked fourteen years on the Gershwin archives. He had helped Ira write his little 1959 masterpiece, *Lyrics on Several Occasions*, produced a few record albums of contemporary music, and contributed erudite liner notes for many more. His readiness to share with me his Ager notes and recollections made me feel like Winnie the Pooh falling into the honey pot.

It was from Stewart, not my father or mother, that I learned that Milton had spent years trying to teach George Gershwin orchestration. My father gave Stewart the text they'd used, as a memento. It was an 1889 German classic, *The Material Used in Musical Composition: A System of Harmony Designed Originally for Use in the English Harmony Classes of the Conservatory of Music at Stuttgart*, by Percy Goetschius. Milton's copy was the twentieth edition, published in 1914, which would have been about the time he and Gershwin met as young fellows trying to break into the music business. Fifteen-year-old George had just quit high school to become "the world's youngest piano pounder" at J. W. Remick's, music publishers, and twenty-year-old Milton was doing the same thing a few blocks away at Waterson, Berlin, and Snyder, Inc.

Unfortunately, Stewart's Goetschius has no handwritten marginal notations, but it does bear the same MILTON AGER stamp in violet ink that I remember seeing as a child on all my father's opera and symphonic scores in our hall closet, and on the miniature scores that Milton read in bed while waiting for his latest brand of sleeping pill to kick in. Milton was both a perpetual student and a tireless, gifted, sometimes compulsive teacher of certain complex subjects which interested him. His technical knowledge of harmony and orchestration, of the behavior of spheres in motion, golf balls and billiard balls in particular, and of the permutations and combinations of playing cards was phenomenal. Of other people's tolerance for being instructed in these matters, he was thought at times insensitive.

Early in 1928, Cecelia again found herself pregnant, and Milton, appalled by her ordeal the first time, insisted on a change of doctors and hospitals. The baby was not due until September, and in the spring Milton planned to accompany George and Ira and Lee to Paris and call on Maurice Ravel. They had met the French maestro on his American concert tour early that year, when he astounded the music world with his newest composition, *Bolero,* a tour de force tornado of orchestration which Leonard Bernstein later termed the bible of the craft.

Gershwin was already celebrated as a composer of concert works as well as of pop and show tunes. The thrilling *Rhapsody in Blue,* orchestrated by Ferde Grofé, had had its premiere four years earlier. But he was fundamentally a pianist, a brilliant pianist in a hurry, and it was relatively late in his career — not until after the *Rhapsody* — that he found time to master a craft which Milton, among many, had been urging him to study more deeply for a decade. Private instruction from Ravel would be ideal.

Nor did I know that Milton had spent the same decade methodically attempting to teach George Gershwin to play better golf. I did not become aware of this burst of frustrated pedagogy until 1979, when my father's obituary was published in *The New York Times* and the paper forwarded to me a condolence letter from a retired bank president who had started out in life as Milton and George's caddie. He had helped put himself through law school on the extra-lavish tips he'd received from Milton during the several seasons the Gershwin golf lessons endured. George was a good natural athlete, and almost twice Milton's size, but he had never *studied* golf the way Milton had. Teacher and pupil would arrive at Milton's golf club at twilight, said the ex-caddie, and each night as the moon rose he had to lug two golf bags around nine holes while Milton patiently explained and demonstrated the finer points of the overlapping grip and the backswing.

For reasons unknown to me, not one of these plans bore fruit. At the last minute, Milton abruptly decided to skip the trip to France and remain with his wife. Gershwin took up tennis, about which Milton knew nothing. And when the Gershwins arrived in Paris, Ravel firmly rejected his would-be pupil. "Why be a second-rate Ravel," he said, "when you can be a first-rate Gershwin?"

Laurel's birth on September 29, 1928, turned out to be no trouble at all. But for some reason Milton thereafter adamantly refused to accompany Cecelia to Paris, or any other place she wanted to visit, for thirty-five years. Our hardworking parents took vacations, but only separately. Several times a year Milton went to Miami Beach or Palm Springs for a few weeks of golf and bridge with his best friend, the bandleader Ben Bernie. Ben was a joyous, amusing, handsome Hungarian with velvety eyes, smooth tan skin, white teeth, and an ever-present cigar. The advent of network radio in the twenties had made him one of the most popular dance-band leaders in the nation, and Ben spent the rest of his life touring the country's ritzier watering holes with his orchestra and a retinue of after-hours pals and admirers of both sexes. Ben called Milton "the

Little Professor," because of his compulsion to instruct, and Milton called Ben "the Mice," short for *maestro*. They were so fond of each other that their friends called them Damon and Pythias.

Cecelia vacationed in the Bahamas in winter and toured Europe in summer with her best friend, Gerry Morris, a gorgeous, green-eyed blonde. Gerry had the flamboyant manner of a Broadway star, but was in fact the recent wife of Bill "Junior" Morris, son of the founder of the William Morris theatrical agency. She formerly had been married to a doctor and had an endearing son about my age called Nicky. Though Milton himself wouldn't budge, he was somewhat critical of Cecelia's jaunts around the Continent with Gerry. He considered her "fast company," and often compressed his lips in silent disapproval. By the mid-thirties he had got to compressing his lips so often that Ben stopped calling him the Little Professor and started calling him "Tiss." Tiss stood for tissue paper, which was how thin Milton's lips got when he thought about Cecelia rollicking through the capitals of Europe with the stunning Geraldine.

Laurel was a small, pretty baby with a profound sense of injustice, seemingly inborn. She could not have been more than three the day she cried out, in response to one of Cecelia's latest dietary edicts, "I never get enough *English* filet of sole!" Doubtless her feelings were spurred by the accident of being the second child and by the peculiarities of our parents' child-raising theories. A second child rarely gets enough of anything, and in Laurel's case the indignities were compounded by continually being told by Milton how equal we were. "We treat you and Shana as *adults*. We love you *equally!*" He said it every day. I can see him telling it to Laurel when she was barely old enough to stand. "We treat you as adults. We love you equally. You and Shana are equally wonderful. Equally beautiful. Equally smart." He wears a sharply tailored suit and is bent way over so he can get his gray-blue eyes down near the level of

Laurel's own. She stares gravely back at him, swaying a little in her high-laced, plain brown Indian Walk shoes.

Equal! To me the word clanged like an anvil. Each time I heard it, I knew it was a lie. I knew I was considered a wunderkind, and the favorite, and I was acutely aware of my father's hypocrisy and the helpless unfairness of Laurel's position. Cecelia, unlike double-talking Milton, made no effort to hide her preference, and Laurel saw the situation clearly at a very early age. But I was made so uncomfortable by their obvious favoritism that it took me half a lifetime to admit the truth of its existence.

From 1928 to 1934, when Laurel was five and I was eight, we lived with our parents and a series of nannies in a magical tenth-floor corner apartment at 171 West 57th Street directly across from Carnegie Hall. James Reynolds, a gifted Irish stage designer infatuated with Napoleon, loved my parents and had contributed the apartment's elaborate decor as a sort of house gift. Jimmy had painted the walls and ceiling of the apartment's very long and windowless entry corridor to suggest that one was walking through a great tent. He'd done freehand murals of swagged canvas, ropes, and flags, hung about with painted pikes and sabers, with a flaming torch at each light fixture. All were fakes, of course, but to a child the illusion was overpowering. As one approached the living room, the tent gave way to outdoors, and an entire cavalry charge came pounding down one wall.

Pushing on, one saw a living and dining room with lavish silk-and-wool draperies, real ones, looped around fake javelins and sword points. Framed prints of French helmets and cuirasses and regimental insignia lined the walls, and a large eighteenth-century map of Paris hung over the sofa. The pair of coffee tables in front of the sofa were actual drums, with crossed flags and regimental insignia painted on their sides, though the "rawhide" that bound the drum skins together was clothesline, stained to look like leather. Atop each drum — about my height when I first saw them — were a little cloisonné ashtray and a crystal urn containing a spray of white pasteboard English-made cigarette holders with gold rims and goose-quill mouthpieces. Alongside these was a brightly painted miniature drum with more fleurs de lis, tiny swords, and crossed banners proclaiming *Liberté* and *Fraternité*, which turned out, when you lifted the blue-and-red harlequin lid, to be full of cigarettes. Never can tobacco have been more alluringly presented.

At either end of the sofa were two beautiful lamps, deliberately unmatched, designed by Jimmy. One had a tapered oval shade of white parchment that appeared to hang suspended in air above a classic white plaster scallop shell. The other had a perfectly square base and shade on which Jimmy had painted a single graceful green stalk of wheat. He would have found a pair of matching lamps banal; Cecelia would have agreed.

Because of my parents' diminutive stature, the excellent old French and Italian furniture which Jimmy chose was of very small scale. Everything was carefully and dramatically lit. A somewhat out-of-period note, above the fireplace, was a copy of Gauguin's painting of Tahitian women seated on a bench. The overall effect was stunning.

The Napoleonic theme eased up a bit in the dining room, where our tall Philco with a phonograph on top stood adjacent to some bookshelves. A small drop-leaf mahogany table occupied the opposite corner. In the evenings, our cook unfolded it and set it in the middle of the room, under the chandelier, lit the candles, and served our parents dinner. Jimmy had thoughtfully provided a couch along one wall so that Laurel and I, by now bathed and wearing pajamas and bathrobes, could sit and converse with them as they ate. They didn't believe in "baby talk," and we were taught to address them as "Mother" and "Father." Terms like "Mommy" and "Daddy" were forbidden. We were little adults. If we had to go to the bathroom, we said we needed to urinate.

Cecelia talked about new movies or stage show acts she had just seen and written up in *Variety*. Laurel and I had never seen a movie. Movies were "not good for children," Cecelia said, evidently not even for children who were adults.

Milton talked a great deal about his digestion. His stomach was an unusually delicate and sulky organ, and he was always taking something new to placate his undependable and cranky digestive tract. All the talk about his digestion mystified me and clearly bored Cecelia. She and I had been born with stomachs of iron, perhaps to compensate for ears of tin.

Laurel and I must have been about three and six years old when we discovered the marvelous forbidden book on top of the Philco, too high, it was thought, for us to stumble upon. A slim, tan volume translated from the German and titled *The Culture of the Abdomen*, it had drawings of a naked man sitting on a toilet, showing the proper and improper postures for making stool.

The only big thing in the entire apartment was Milton's grand piano, which he had bought from George Gershwin when we moved in. It filled one corner of the living room, and the area underneath it was Laurel's and my playhouse. I loved lying there in my nightclothes watching Milton's feet pumping the brass pedals. When guests came for cocktails, we children, already dressed for bed, were allowed to remain under the big Steinway and listen to the grownups. I remember the surprise on some of these occasions of seeing Gershwin's feet at work, so long and slender in comparison to Milton's short, stubby ones.

I am concerned that I can remember only Gershwin's feet. Gershwin and his family were an important part of our lives then, but my memory does not contain the whole man — the ax-blade profile, long head, lank body, the legendary magnetism mentioned by all who met him.

The playwright S. N. Behrman noted "the rush of the great heady surf of vitality" any time Gershwin sat down at the piano. "The room became freshly oxygenated; everybody felt it, everybody breathed it." In the course of researching his biography, Stewart read Behrman's comment to Cecelia.

"That *is* the word!" she exclaimed. "For forty years I have been looking for the word that would describe George's effect upon a room, and that is it. You cannot imagine what a party was like when he was expected and he did *not* appear."

But of *my* Gershwin I retain only small fragments. First, those narrow shoes of shiny black calf. Second, the ugly, green-faced oil portrait of Cecelia that Gershwin painted. After we had left the magic apartment — been cast out, as it seemed to me — that hideous painting tagged along with us ever after, from hotel to hotel, like a stray cat. A third Gershwin fragment is not an image, just a tag line that Milton and George liked to repeat in front of other people, and that Milton kept saying long after the Gershwins had passed out of our lives.

"We steal," they would each say with a grin. "But we only steal from the best."

Today I build back my memory of Gershwin from these fragments the way a paleontologist with only bits of jawbone and vertebrae is able to reconstruct an entire dinosaur. It helps that I can still see everything in the magic apartment with extreme clarity. The brightly flowered Indian cotton covers on our parents' twin beds; the Chinese red lacquer box that sat on Cecelia's early American chest of drawers; the tiny telephone table in the hall with its veined gray marble top and delicate pierced brass gallery; the tall telephone with its brown silk cord. The telephone number: Circle 6-2660.

Cecelia was a terrific snob, for all the best reasons. A key element of her intense chic was her worship of the plain, or the seeming plain. She liked English, not French, children's clothes. She preferred hard-to-find plain Chinese household furniture to the more common, ornately carved teak stuff. Her Mr. John outfits were made with the fabric deliberately inside out. Her favorite American painter was Edward Hopper. The one unplain object of her affection was her brassy friend Gerry. Birds of a very different feather, Geraldine a gorgeous bird of paradise, Cecelia a chic little minimalist wren, they were a striking combination.

Another aspect of my mother's reverence for the unadorned was her distaste for jewelry, and she wore almost none. The exception was a large emerald-cut diamond ring which made a major impression on me at an extremely young age. Even *I* could tell it was a very big stone, and beautifully, simply set. It was not an engagement ring, she said. She disdained such symbols as "bourgeois." But I knew the diamond had been a gift from Milton.

Save for Gerry, Cecelia's taste was remarkably consistent. Each choice showed her preference for austere elegance, a carefully thought-out perfection. My mother's hairstyle changed only once in all the years I knew her. She had very long, perfectly straight, fine yellow hair shiny as satin, and she wore it like a gleaming helmet, looped in smooth semi-circles over the temples and knotted at the back of her neck. In the mid-thirties, the knot moved up to the top of her head, in a kind of baroque little French twist, where it remained.

I almost never saw Cecelia with her hair down. When she came home from work and relaxed, she put on one of her Chinese silk robes with high, stiff collars and slit sides. The robes and her sleek hairdo gave me the idea very early that my mother was a blonde Chinese.

Her special chic extended to more than her wardrobe. We had a lovely old triangular corner cabinet of Italian walnut that supported a "malachite" urn, faked by Jimmy. She decreed that the urn could be filled with "lemon leaves" only. These were not the leaves of lemon trees, but a common swamp plant with beautiful, opposite-set leaves of dark, glossy green that florists gave you free to surround and enhance their more expensive cut flowers. Cecelia said that only ordinary people liked flowers. Lemon leaves lasted longer, were cheaper, and had more style. She was right.

In the enchanted realm I have described, we children lived a rather brutal existence. Our clothes, the special food we ate, the very language pertaining to our lives, not Theirs, seemed to us harsh and hateful. The regimen decreed by our parents, and fanatically obeyed by the sequence of German frauleins they employed, was at times absurdly adult, at other times needlessly infantile. By day, we were expensively dressed in Liberty cotton dresses, scratchy tweed coats, felt hats with chin elastics. Our shoes were sensible, high-laced brown leather. We were forced to wear these until we were seven or eight, to guard against "weak ankles." Until about the same age, we slept in one-piece Dr. Denton pajamas, with a back flap that had to be lowered before getting on the toilet. This garment, I later learned, had been designed by the vigilant Dr. Denton to discourage masturbation.

Because Cecelia considered jewelry vulgar, we were permitted none, and my lust to own something precious grew overpowering. The day I discovered in Milton's desk a slender silver-and-gold fountain pen, initialed MA and tarnished almost black, I stole it, kept it hidden for years, and was in my thirties before I finally lost it and forgot about it. In 1994, Lawrence Stewart identified it. George Gershwin had bought the pen for Milton to thank him for his orchestration lessons. Stewart had found the receipt, from Cartier's.

All the rules for our daily lives were set by a fashionable Park Avenue pediatrician, Dr. William St. Lawrence, he of the mandatory baby bottles and the edicts against hugging, kissing, lap-sitting, and all forms of cuddling. We were fed only specially nourishing children's foods. "Hamburger" had to be made from scraped prime sirloin. Unpasteurized Walker-Gordon milk came from a famously spotless dairy in New Jersey. Any fraulein who let a sip of ordinary Borden's pass our lips could expect to be sent packing. Only hot cooked cereal was permitted. Puddings and baked apples were the only sweets. Coca-Cola was deemed poisonous.

Every morning before she dressed to go to work, Cecelia did the day's marketing from her bedside telephone, and gave two different grocery orders. Everything "for the children" was disgustingly whole-grain, rough-textured, light on sugar. No snacks, no eating between meals. No jam, only honey, and brush your teeth for five minutes three times a day. Only *sweet* butter. Only *loin* lamb chops. Only *English* filet of sole. It got a little mad. Having to count out exactly ten grains of sugar to put on our cereal each morning cannot have been the pediatrician's idea; it must have been some German nanny's lunatic improvement on his regimen. But Laurel and I both remember having to do it, just as we remember having to go to Central Park every single day when it wasn't actively raining or snowing, walking backwards up Seventh Avenue on windy days so germs could not blow into our mouths. The fear of polio was great, and once we got to the park the nannies had strict orders never to let us go near other children.

The doctor's rules for feeding children went thus:

1. Sit child in high chair and put her food dish and utensils in front of her. The dish was divided into three sections and had a hot water compartment beneath. The utensils were a child-size fork and spoon and something shaped like a silver snowplow called a "pusher."

2. Leave child and food together for a closely watched twenty minutes. Do not speak. Do not attempt to feed the child. At the end of twenty minutes, remove child from high chair, remove bib, put food dish containing remaining food in icebox, wash utensils.

3. At next meal, put child back in high chair, tie on new bib, remove dish with uneaten food from icebox, warm (slightly) with new hot water, and repeat previous procedure.

In a surprisingly short time, Dr. St. Lawrence promised, the child would learn to feed herself and would eat without complaint whatever food was offered.

The regulations for bathing and bedtime were equally severe. After being bathed separately, never together, buttoned into Dr. Dentons by the nanny, and carried to our parents for a goodnight hug, we were brought back to our room and Laurel was placed in her crib. My bed was against the wall, protected from light and drafts by a folding screen, another of Jimmy's fancies, painted as if one were looking down through tall Paris windows at children flying balloons in the park below. A light was left burning, but we knew that in a few minutes Milton would come in, kiss us both, and stand in the doorway to say "Guten Abend, Schlafen Sie gut!" before turning out the light.

Milton had grown up in a large working-class family and must have seen the harshness and absurdity of the regime. But Cecelia, believing it to be "scientific," was insistent. She had an additional concern that I was not aware of. Before Laurel was a year old, Cecelia had taken a full-time job at Variety, and her household orders had to be carried out in absentia. The nannies' zeal was remarkable. It was only long after I had grown up that it occurred to me what "good Germans" they were. Quite possibly the fundamental Bad Guy of our childhood was not Cecelia, but the frauleins so zealously carrying out her orders.

Cecelia behaved toward her children like a conscientious officer to his men: she was remote, preoccupied, and stern, but scrupulously fair. The frauleins were her noncoms. I doubt she understood how completely the regime isolated us from the rest of humanity, including one another. Her concern was to leave us in a safe, germ-free world while she was away. If Cecelia had heard of the Skinner Box, she would immediately have arranged to install a couple in our apartment, and considered them the perfect solution to her needs as a working mother.

Modern as she was in many matters, Cecelia was also strict, judgmental, and rigid, like her Polish-born father, Zalkin. She seemingly disliked touching or being touched. She took no enjoyment in children *as* children. She saw them not as people but as lesser beings in need of training. Until recently, surgeons convinced themselves that infants did not feel pain, and routinely operated on them without anesthetics. Cecelia's attitude was similar. In fact, despite the repeated assurances that "we treat you as adults," we were treated as neither children nor adults. The entire regime and attitude — no kissing, no rocking, no picking up a crying baby, no talking at mealtimes, no playmates, no baby talk — was in essence antichild.

Milton understood children far better than Cecelia did, but sometimes he let his intellectual ideas about how to deal with them get in the way. Once we started school — in my case before I was three — our parents' rules about language were acutely embarrassing in front of other children. We soon refused to call these strange people Mother and Father, and started calling them Cecelia and Milton instead. In so doing we achieved distance, we felt, if not retribution. Our parents didn't understand our rebellion. They *liked* being addressed by their first names. They wanted us to talk like adults, and act like adults, at the earliest possible age. All we wanted in the world was to be treated as children.

We were lonely children. Until we started school, the only other child we knew was Gerry's son Nicky. After we started school, we were never permitted to accept invitations to play at schoolmates' apartments.

"You have a perfectly good playroom of your own." Nor were pets allowed. Dogs and cats were creatures we knew only from books. Cecelia said that dogs didn't belong in city apartments and cats aggravated her hay fever. There was no appeal from her edicts, and we knew it. But we were desperate and Milton finally came through. One year at the circus, vendors sold live chameleons attached to lapel pins. You were supposed to fasten the little green lizard to your jacket and see him change color according to what you were wearing. Milton bought us one, and we put it in a cage with some shreds of carrot. It didn't change color. It didn't eat or move. We switched to lettuce, but still nothing happened. It just got thinner, and when it actually began to shrivel, the fraulein said it was lonely and needed to get back into the woods with other animals, so we trudged to Central Park and let it go.

"Yah? Iss gut now?"

Laurel was too young, but I knew it was going to die.

Although Milton talked continually about treating us as adults, he was also the parent who treated us as the small children we were. Patiently he taught us to tie our shoes, button our coats, brush our teeth, and always wash our hands before leaving the bathroom. He never showed impatience or anger, and had unshakable faith that, given a chance, he could teach anything to anybody. He had bought me the little golf clubs the summer before Laurel was born, and sought to imbue two-and-a-half-year-old me with correct form by standing behind me and patiently rearranging my chubby fingers on the shaft into the correct grip before guiding my arms through a proper backswing.

Milton enjoyed spending time with us. He brought us up to the Polo Grounds to watch Carl Hubbell pitch, across the street to hear Paderewski play for Poland, down to his friend Billy Rose's *Jumbo* at the Hippodrome. We sat with him in the front row at the Metropolitan Opera House to hear *The Mikado* or *Iolanthe* when the D'Oyly Carte players came to town. Laurel was too young, but sometimes I went with him and Ben to Glen Oaks and walked around a few holes as "assistant caddie."

I could not have been more than four or five when I first accompanied Milton to his office at Seventh Avenue and 49th Street above the

Brass Rail. Having recently learned to read, I was thrilled by the tall, gold-lettered sign AGER, YELLEN & BORNSTEIN, INC. that wrapped around the corner of the building. The same words in gold were on a door leading into a small reception area with cuspidor, potted palm, leather couch, and motherly secretary. Behind her was a warren of cubicles with frosted glass doors, each containing a man playing the piano. Ben Bornstein, the professional manager, was a thin man with a tight vest, floppy watch chain, derby hat, and yellow-tooth smile. I must have known Jack Yellen too — I have clear mental pictures of his wife Sylvia and their two sons — but Jack's image has disappeared entirely from my memory. Laurel doesn't remember any of these people. By the time she was a year old, Jack's family had returned to Buffalo to live.

The best outings were our annual visits with Milton to the circus at Madison Square Garden. He explained everything, took care we missed nothing, and seemed to enjoy each act as much as we did. He took us downstairs to the freak show, and up into the bandstand to meet his friend the conductor. He bought us hot dogs, ice cream, peanuts — all forbidden foods at home. Our favorite act was the lion tamer Clyde Beatty. Clad in white jodhpurs, he faced a cage full of snarling lions and tigers and put them through their paces protected only by a kitchen chair and a long, crackling bullwhip.

One evening Cecelia came home from work and said she had spent the afternoon interviewing Beatty for *Variety*. I was awestruck. "How big is Clyde Beatty?" I asked.

"Not big at all," she said. "In fact, he's very small. Just a little bigger than your father."

Milton chuckled with delight each time he repeated this story. He was almost always good-humored, and one of the rare small men I've known with no insecurity about his height.

Cecelia had little time to spend with us. For me, the best moments were when she taught me how to knit and crochet, seated side by side on the dining room couch in a faint cloud of New Mown Hay. I was left-handed, and she had to figure out how to do everything backwards before putting the yarn and needles in my hands and manipulating my fingers through the proper motions. Her hands were warm and silk-soft. I had never felt anything like them until the day someone brought a puppy to school. The puppy's belly felt like my mother's hands.

We also sat together on the couch while Cecelia listened to football games on the radio. As a graduate of the University of California at Berkeley, she followed the big games with passionate concentration, diagramming plays on a yellow legal pad in her strong handwriting. When Laurel grew older, she and I were placed on the same couch after baths to follow the nightly radio adventures of Buck Rogers and Jack Armstrong. But the sweet-smelling, New Mown Hay times with Cecelia are what I recall most, because they were precious and rare.

Our mother placed great importance on appearance — the necessity for good posture, a pleasant voice, impeccable manners, proper speech. She taught me to stand up straight by rapping me sharply between the shoulder blades. Today I have the posture of a field marshal, as did she. She taught me never to pipe or lisp or squeak. "Lower your voice," she said very softly, over and over, in a soft basso rumble. Just as critical was the need to avoid any trace of a New York accent. "Not *New Yawk*. New *Yor-r-k*. Not *awrenge*; it's *orange*. *O-range*." She could utter the word so lightly, it sounded like a soufflé.

Cecelia believed above all that children had certain responsibilities which must not be ducked; to *duck* was her only four-letter word. They must never duck their responsibilities to adults, especially to their parents; she never had. As soon as she noticed that her little brother Victor's teeth were crooked, she demanded that her parents take him to an orthodontist for braces; she insisted on it. "I didn't *duck* my responsibilities."

Cecelia ruled by the awful power of her withering scorn. She never raised her voice; for emphasis, she lowered it. This, and the baleful basilisk stare, were all it took to bring me to heel. Laurel, the braver daughter, talked back occasionally, me never. Like most kids, she sometimes enjoyed being bad for the hell of it. She led the way in our six A.M. forays through the living room after parties, draining the dregs from all the cocktail glasses before anyone else was afoot. One night when our parents were out, she broke all the English cigarette holders in half. Another night she threw all our brushes and combs out the window.

"Who did it?"

"*I did it!*" said the defiant four-year-old. Laurel never ducked.

By the time we were four and seven, Laurel and I were served weekend lunches in the dining room, seated at opposite ends of the drop-leaf table, bibs firmly tied on. Since we had to clean our plates, we invented the game of tying up particularly disgusting foods like spinach and liver with black sewing thread and leaving them to dangle out the window. This worked until the Japanese servant next door spotted the stuff and rang our back doorbell to report us.

This individual, a mystery to us for some time, was the manservant to the occupant of the one other apartment on our floor, a leonine-looking man whom we seldom saw, not even in the elevator. But very often, on our way to and from the park, we saw other men ringing his doorbell. Our neighbor, I later learned, was Dr. Leo Michel, a thriving urologist whose convenient location across from Carnegie Hall kept him very busy as clap-doctor-in-chief to the entire classical music profession.

Our parents believed in reason and intellect above all things, and their children's behavior must often have baffled them. Sometimes it baffled us. Once Laurel was sent home from kindergarten for having put a pussy willow up her nose. "Now, Laurel," Milton said in his most reasonable voice, "*why* did you put a pussy willow up your nose?"

"It *fell* up my nose," she replied. He couldn't talk her out of it.

My style was different. One evening about bath time the nanny, who had been sewing in our room, gave me a handful of pins to return to the sewing box in her room, which was off the butler's pantry. I liked to linger there when it was time for the cook to set the table and admire the goblets, the wooden French pepper mills, the salt in little green glass swans from Venice which she had set out on the counter. This particular evening, I noticed a lovely yellow block of butter also on the counter. Dreamily, I pushed the pins into the butter, one by one, and carefully smoothed over the sides.

The cook served dinner, we children looking on from the couch, and the butter was soon discovered to be mined with buried pins. Milton was horrified, and I confessed. But when he asked me *why* I had done it, I could give no sensible answer. I still can't. The lovely butter was simply *there*, unguarded, and I'd had a handful of pins.

Another evening Cecelia came into our room, thunder-browed. "We have *told* you that you may not write on the walls." God knows this was true. The urge to add our own ornamentation to Jimmy's murals could be irresistible, and we had been cautioned many times, "Write on your blackboard only!" But again today, she said, while she had been away at work, somebody had drawn a pencil line all the way through the Napoleonic wars. "Who did it?"

We both denied the crime. Cecelia marched us out into the hall and pointed out a long, wobbly pencil line running the entire length of the corridor. Only then, seeing it, did I remember the exquisite pleasure I'd felt when committing this marathon defacement. Horrified, I kept silent. But I knew she knew. Cecelia knew everything.

One awful morning she summoned me to her bedside. Her unpinned hair was still down, lying around her shoulders in Medusa coils. Lately she had often heard me using the word *okay*, she said. "*Okay* is a slang term," she began. "It is common slang. It is not interesting slang. It is hackneyed and boring slang."

I was accustomed to being spoken to this way, and I knew what her words meant. *Hackneyed, ordinary* and *boring* were among her most common terms of opprobrium. I listened attentively, determined to improve my speech in the manner she wished. The lecture went on and on. I wanted to go to the bathroom. I stared at her hair.

At last it ended. "I never want to hear you use that word again." Her voice dropped at least an octave. "Do you understand me, Shana?"

I nodded and, turning to go, in horror heard my own voice reply, "Okay."

My blood froze. I fled.

But that was only the second-worst thing that happened in the magic apartment. The worst was a night late in 1929 when Laurel was still too young to sit on the couch with me while our parents were eating dinner. I was there alone, a polite little adult of four or five, and I asked when we were going to get to see the two Yellen boys again. I had a dim memory of playing soldier with two boys in Jimmy's fake tent while Laurel was still a baby.

At my question, Milton sprang to his feet. He was choking and red-faced with fury. "I never want to hear that name spoken again by ANY-ONE IN THIS HOUSEHOLD!" he shouted.

I wet my pants and burst into tears. That my father too was in tears, tears of heartbreak as well as of rage, would take me nearly fifty years to learn.

CHAPTER TWO

VARIETY

Tin Pan Alley is the generic term for American popular music. It was coined around the turn of the century, when almost all the nation's music publishers were concentrated in a single New York City block, West 28th Street between Sixth Avenue and Broadway. In summer when windows were open and the song demonstrators were going full blast, hawking new tunes for the fall vaudeville season, sixty or eighty pianos might be heard playing at one time. Later the publishers moved uptown to the fringes of Times Square, but the term Tin Pan Alley endured, with particular reference to the songs written in the first quarter of this century, before the advent of talking pictures. Talking short subjects had come out in 1926, and Al Jolson's feature-length *The Jazz Singer* the following year. Hollywood moguls immediately saw the value of placing all revenues from the fabulous new product under their own control, and by 1929 the new dinosaurs of Hollywood had bought out the old dinosaurs of the music publishing business and the Alley was no more.

The moment talkies were invented, word had gone out from Hollywood to corral every available songwriter and set him to churning out movie musicals. Eventually all the songwriters went west: the Gershwins, Kern, Arlen, Harburg, Mercer, Porter, Berlin. Among the earliest to arrive were Milton Ager and Jack Yellen. They were hot, they were fast, they had "the common touch," and, unlike some of the others, they were not preoccupied with Broadway book shows. They had always been most successful with "popular songs," new material for immediate use by vaudeville, revue, and radio performers.

In 1928 and 1929 Ager and Yellen wrote and published scores for four movie musicals and two Broadway shows — about thirty songs in all — and another twenty pop tunes. The partners made the long cross-country train trip a dozen times a year, but traveled separately, and I remember the period as a time when Milton was perpetually singing and humming and whistling on the telephone to Jack, from either our home in New York or the one in California.

Since Cecelia's parents, Fanny and Zalkin Rubenstein, lived in Hollywood, it was a relatively simple matter for the Agers and their small daughters to move back and forth, and for a few years all four of us did, traveling first class on the Twentieth Century Limited to Chicago, and on to California on the Chief or, later, the Super Chief. Indeed, we spent so much time on luxurious cross-country trains that Laurel and I were familiar with the uses of finger bowls and lump-sugar tongs and fold-up toilets before we were five years old; we even knew individual stewards and porters.

In those days, nobody who was anybody went all the way to Union Station in downtown Los Angeles. The smart folks got off at Pasadena, and there on the open platform stood Cecelia's mother Fanny, stout, short, and smiling, clad in rippling navy blue silk, arms outstretched. Fanny and Zalkin Rubenstein had both come to this country as children and spoke English with pronounced Polish accents. Fanny drove us back to Hollywood from Pasadena in her big Packard, always stopping en route to buy a live chicken at a kosher market — not that she thought its poultry godlier, merely fresher.

Zalkin, a stocky, silent man who owned a men's clothing business downtown, didn't come home until dinnertime, and he left the house immediately after to play pinochle or attend a meeting of his Masonic lodge. Fanny had a nose for real estate, and the Rubensteins had done well in the twenties Hollywood land boom. They lived in a ground-floor apartment in a two-story stucco apartment house on the corner of Sunset Boulevard and Hobart which they had built in the flush twenties. After the crash of 1929, they always had a vacant apartment available for us.

Among the few people I knew, the tenderest and kindest was Cecelia's mother, our plump, black-haired, ever-adoring grandmother. Life in Fanny's sunny apartment house was a tropical idyll. Our family usually occupied an upstairs apartment around the corner on Hobart, but Laurel and I spent our days with Fanny in her big downstairs apartment on the Sunset Boulevard side, where the two sky-high palm trees grew. Instead of snowsuits, we wore sunsuits. We could go outdoors at will, unsupervised. A crop of poinsettias for the Christmas trade grew in the empty lot next door, and at the rear was a sprawling fig tree that produced sweet, ripe fruits. We could eat as many as we liked. We could have sugar and cream on them.

California would have been a complete idyll for us were it not for the horrid Carl Curtis athletic school farther west on Sunset, where Cecelia enrolled us for morning gymnasium and swimming lessons to which Fanny drove us. My life brightened when I found out that Carl Curtis also taught tap dancing to would-be movie moppets, and Fanny let me switch from gym to tap lessons without telling Cecelia, who would assuredly have disapproved. Our mother loathed "cute" little tots who danced or sang for grownups, and what with the recent phenomenon of six-year-old Shirley Temple in Baby, Take a Bow, there were suddenly a lot more of these around. She also had enormous contempt for "stage mothers," whom she viewed as monstrous exploiters of helpless children, and she used to mimic Shirley's mother standing behind the camera exhorting, "Sparkle, Shirley, sparkle!"

Fanny was always beautifully dressed, smelled wonderful, and spoke with a strong accent. "Shan, dollink, go tell de Jap to turn de spreenkles." A stocky Japanese gardener in pith helmet and perfectly pressed khakis was eternally to be found somewhere on the lawn hosing the path, mowing the grass, or wielding the long, metal key that activated the sprinkling system.

In the afternoons Fanny often drove Laurel and me to Grauman's Chinese Theater, or another of the Hollywood Boulevard movie palaces nearby, always with a stop afterwards at C. C. Brown's for homemade ice cream. Movie outings began with Fanny seated at her dining table with a glass of tea and the newspaper neatly folded back to the page that listed what was playing at various theaters. "Look up!" she directed us. She was so proud that already we could read and write, and even tell time from the wonderful, upside-down crystal ball watch suspended by a black silk cord over the great shelf of her corseted bosom.

"Look up!"

It did not occur to us that we could read English better than she.

The best of my transcontinental train rides occurred in the early autumn of 1928, only days after Laurel was born. Milton needed to get to work right away on *Glad Rag Doll* with Dolores Costello, so he and I went west together, accompanied by his friend Jack Pearl; Cecelia and Laurel would follow in a few weeks. Jack was radio and vaudeville's Baron Munchausen, teller of colossal, outrageous lies, and I spent most of that trip sitting on my father's lap on the rear-facing observation platform, fussed over by a couple of elderly porters and listening to the Baron spin special tall tales for three-year-old me as we watched America unreeling behind us.

By the time Cecelia and Laurel arrived, we had rented a house on the beach in Malibu. In the following year Ager and Yellen wrote scores for four more movies; a Broadway revue, John Murray Anderson's *Almanac*; and a musical, *Rain or Shine*, starring the brilliant comic Joe Cook, that ran for 360 performances at the George M. Cohan Theater. One of the four movies, *Road Show*, was notable only for a rowdy scene between Marie Dressler and Polly Moran as two drunken actresses. The picture was so bad MGM decided to shelve it in favor of *They Learned about Women*, a weird baseball-vaudeville amalgam starring the vaudeville team of Van & Schenck. The third picture was *Honky Tonk*, starring Sophie Tucker.

As soon as everybody got back to New York, Sophie threw one of her famous formal dinners complete with liveried butlers, silver candelabra, and rough talk. Cecelia, twenty-seven and by far the dewiest person at the table, found herself seated next to the lusty Sime Silverman, the founder, owner, and editor of *Variety*. She'd only discovered the publication after meeting Milton, and was "absolutely crazy about it. It had its own *lingo!*" she told an interviewer many years later.

> I had just married a songwriter and encountered this lingo and was fascinated by it. It was unique, so *alive*. . . . I got high, because I was so scared, sitting beside the editor. Emboldened by wine, I told him what a miserable paper he was running. "You have so many opportunities to do this and that," I said. "And instead you let them fly by." I knew nothing about show business. I was a provincial from California, and couldn't have been more of a twerp. But he was a great, wonderful person. And he said, "All right, little girl. If you're so smart, show up for work tomorrow."

Among his other distinctions, Sime was famous for spotting talent in the bud. By the time Sophie seated him next to Cecelia, he had discovered Buster Keaton in a third-rate vaudeville act, Chaplin in an obscure English comedy group, Jolson in a minstrel show, and Durante in a grubby nightclub. Cecelia had never had a job in her life, nor dreamed of having one. "All I knew was that I enjoyed reading *Variety*, and then this was *thrust* at me. It was a dare."

And Cecelia grabbed it. She was on *Variety*'s doorstep the next morning. The whole enterprise was jammed into a sixteen-foot-wide brownstone on West 46th Street off Broadway. Sime had bought the five-story walk-up from Madame Frances, a hoity-toity dressmaker for stars like Fanny Brice, and Sime's only change had been to paint *Variety* in large green letters across Madame's front show window. The famous logo was reflected in the grimy mirrors which still lined the walls. Sime's desk occupied the raised platform at the rear from which the models used to descend. Their runway was now an aisle dividing rows of desks leading from the front door up to Sime's shabby throne.

The editor's big jaw and handsome, crooked smile gave him the look of a successful politician. Large and untidy, in suspenders and shirt-sleeves, he had a stubby pencil in one hand, a phone in the other, and a cigar in his mouth. Cecelia started up the aisle. Sime looked up, put the phone against his chest, said, "Hiya, kid. Your desk is over there," and went back to work. Cecelia sat down and looked around. At the other desks, hefty Underwoods and Royals clacked amid piles of newspapers, back issues, press releases, and miscellaneous documents held in place by overflowing ashtrays. Behind each typewriter sat a hunched-over, blue-jowled man holding the phone to his ear with his shoulder while typing furiously with two fingers. The place was noisy as a factory floor and blue with smoke.

Variety's editor didn't give assignments, Cecelia learned. Reporters were expected to *know* what was important in showbiz that week and go out and cover it. It was sink-or-swim journalism.

> You had to find out what to do by seeing what *ran*. I remember sitting in the office and seeing *grown men* go up to Sime's wastebasket when he wasn't around, and go through the trash to see what he had torn to shreds, what copy was rejected.
>
> It was the kind of place that, while you were doing your work, the Marx Brothers would come in and do their new act.

And you paid no attention, because you were too busy writing your new story. It was a great place. . . . I was the only woman on the paper at the time.

Cecelia's copy wound up in Sime's wastebasket for weeks, until the day it struck her that tea dancing was the latest showbiz rage. Constance Bennett was leading tea dances at the Plaza, and "on Broadway there were new little soda fountains that wanted to be chic, and they had tea dancing too." Cecelia visited one, wrote up the story, and, the following week, found it on the front page, with byline.

Cecelia adored her boss, and he was nuts about her. Milton liked him too. The man was free-spending and smart. He maintained his own fleet of open cars, two full-time chauffeurs, and a private speakeasy that never closed on the office's top floor. Sime's many showbiz buddies, from Mayor Jimmy Walker on down, each had his own key. Champagne and scotch flowed nonstop, and the party often spilled over to a nearby nightspot, or uptown to the Silvermans' big Central Park West apartment where Hattie Silverman presided until dawn.

Sime Silverman was the first I remember in a long series of louche, roughneck types — "diamonds in the rough" as Cecelia and Milton called them — whose company my tidy, mannerly little parents hugely enjoyed.

Cecelia soon learned that "Sime saw women as cooks, recipe people, and curfew-receivers — that was it. They were not supposed to know anything." She also discovered that the paper did have another woman staffer who was required to write under the nom de plume "The Skirt." In reality she was Sime's wife. A small, tough-talking, affectionate woman with dyed red hair and enormous vitality, Hattie Silverman lived to be one hundred years old.

Sime soon gave Cecelia a weekly column, on the women's page alongside "The Skirt," headed "Going Places . . . by Cecelia Ager," and he put no limits whatever on the places she could go. Burlesque, nightclubs, vaudeville, circuses, prize fights, legit, movies, stage shows all were her domain. But to avoid trouble with Hattie, and with the paper's regular reviewers, he told Cecelia she had to cover everything from "the woman's angle," which to Sime meant covering what showbiz women *wore.* Sime's attitudes about women were somewhat Victorian, and the day Cecelia described the magnificent leopard skin worn by the beautifully muscled *untershtander* who anchored the pyramid of acrobats at Loew's State, Sime summoned her to his desk to remind her that, as a married woman, writing about what *men* wore was out of bounds.

Although beautiful clothes and exquisite dressmaking had always been matters of passionate interest to Cecelia, she had no difficulty transcending Sime's limitations. Of an early Ann Harding movie, she wrote, "Ann Harding scared to death is all right. It's Ann Harding natural that's so harrowing." In an oft-reprinted tribute to the Marx Brothers' great straight woman, she wrote,

> There ought to be a statue erected, or a Congressional Medal awarded, or a national holiday proclaimed, to honor that great woman, Margaret Dumont, the dame who takes the raps from the Marx Brothers. For she is of the stuff of which our pioneer women were made, combining in her highly indignant person Duse, stalwart oak, and Chief Fall Guy — a lady of epic ability to take it, a lady whose mighty love for Groucho is a saga of devotion, a lady who asks but little and gets it.

The week Josephine Baker moved from a Broadway stage to her own nightclub, write Baker's latest biographers, Jean Claude Baker and Chris Chase, she danced in a way she hadn't been permitted before.

> She worked almost naked, flanked by two white men who maneuvered around her in a wildly suggestive adagio. And the press, which had seemed to turn on her, was beguiled again. "The Baker bumps got going," wrote journalist Cecelia Ager, "in a costume which amazed even her press agent."

The paper's staffers referred to themselves proudly as "*Variety* muggs." The practice had begun in response to an admiring piece on

Variety's literary style by H. L. Mencken in *The American Mercury*. "Aw shucks, we're justa buncha muggs," Sime is said to have responded to Mencken's praise. The sole female muggs in my mother's days on *Variety*, from 1929 to 1937, were "The Skirt," Cecelia, and, briefly, Ruth Morris, Bill's sister. All three women smoked and worked with their hats on.

What Sime had spotted in Cecelia was that, ladylike as she may have behaved, she had one of the savviest, least reverent eyes around. Soon her little "fashion" stories became wicked mini-reviews notorious among cognoscenti for their sly command of scorn and putdown.

> "Burlesque today," said Ann Corio, gravely thinking it over in her dressing room at the Apollo on 42nd Street while she deftly removed even her makeup, "is just strip, strip, strip."
>
> Acknowledged by burlesque house box-office grosses the country over as the supreme strip teaser of them all, Miss Corio had just come off the stage at the finish of her number — just as she finishes her number — in all her natural glory. Meeting the *Variety* reporter in the wings, she murmured a formal Emily Post "How'd you do. . . . Perhaps we can talk better in my dressing room." . . .
>
> First Miss Corio pulled on long dark stockings, then tiny white net panties. Now a peach satin garter belt with "Ann" embroidered in a dainty flourish in front; next a robin's egg blue chiffon chemise. Then a pink silk slip, and now over this decently complete underpinning a sober black dress with long sleeves and a high neck primly faced with white. Now a black hat, a black coat, a silver fox cape and black kid gloves. Thus does a strip artist, in her private life, get even.

Pausing to reflect upon some of the perils of her craft, Cecelia wrote:

> Interviewing is a series of upsets, a revelation and a disillusionment. Serious actors become cut-ups, romantic actors turn into heavy thinkers; great lovers are hen-pecked. Only the comics call their souls their own.

Picture producers are wild for publicity and lady picture stars the most indifferent. In between, in order, come stage actors, stage actresses, waning picture players making personal appearances in film houses and vaude, picture "types," film directors, male picture stars and film writers.

Stage actors have the best manners and foreign stage actors lead the field in suggesting to any woman interviewer she is charming and uniquely sympathetic. All stage actors are disappointments in their dressing-room dressing-gowns. . . .

Western (riding) stars are strong and silent because they can't help it. Practicing to be quick on the draw . . . had left them little time for the study of world affairs. The painstaking breaking of an idea over their manly faces is like the slow dawn on the mesa.

Soon places like *Vanity Fair* and Random House were bidding to publish Cecelia's work. But greater prestige and money didn't interest her. She was never conventionally ambitious, and *Variety* was too much fun to give up. She never lost her affection for showbiz and its "lingo," and all her life her conversation was studded with words like "straight man," "ham," and "small-time," verbs like "stooge" and "fold." Cecelia's friend S. J. Perelman, another aficionado of *Variety* lingo, once told me admiringly that my extremely chic and elegant little mother had coined the term "flash act."

Alistair Cooke remembers, in 1934 as a Harvard graduate student, getting so hooked on Cecelia's writing that back in London he rushed each Saturday morning to Selfridges only "to pick up *Variety*. I certainly would never have bought it if it hadn't been in anticipation of Cecelia Ager's . . . column. I thought her at the time a deliciously funny writer — the funniest, most brilliant woman writer of her day."

On *Variety* Cecelia swiftly worked out, on her own, the interviewing techniques her readers so enjoyed. Fifty years later she described her methods to her nephew Steve Rubenstein's journalism class at the University of California, Berkeley.

Cecelia: It turned out that I had a knack for interviewing. Or so they thought. My method was to scare hell out of the interviewee, accost him, by saying something that would unsettle the poor thing. And that always worked. Something important would come forth and make entertaining reading.

The point was: everybody wanted something. The interviewees wanted some publicity . . . they knew what they were doing there. I knew what *I* was doing there. Nobody was fooling anybody. So it was — on the level, but crooked.

Steve: Did you scare the hell out of them at the beginning or the end of the interview?

Cecelia: I opened with it [because] that's a good way to get a rise out of somebody. An interview is not supposed to be something to just . . . just *lie there*. Something's supposed to *happen*. That was my technique. I'd had absolutely no training of any sort, so this was all sheer cussedness on my part.

Steve: Didn't you find yourself getting off on the wrong foot with whoever you were talking to?

Cecelia: If I did, it didn't bother me.

Student: What are some of your other techniques? Suppose the person you are interviewing is rather dull? How would you go about it?

Cecelia: (laughing) I think I'd just walk out. You see, none of this was urgent, had to be done. The only thing I thought was required was that the copy be entertaining. Because I was writing for a showbiz paper, not a fan magazine.

Student: Tell us how you prepared for an interview.

Cecelia: I *didn't* prepare an awful lot. Something would just strike me about the person I was going to see . . . or it might be something I may have seen in a picture, some little quirk. . . .

Steve: What happened if you didn't know anything about your subject?

Cecelia: I never went to a subject like that. They were all in showbiz, and I knew my stars. So there was always something to talk about. Like — why was business so bad on her last picture?

One of Cecelia's favorite subjects over the years was Joan Crawford. In *A Woman's Face*, Crawford played a woman the camera sees only in profile, the other half of her face having been hideously destroyed in an accident. When the studio set up yet another Ager/Crawford interview, the actress, in a last attempt to disconcert Cecelia, conducted the interview stark naked while undergoing a series of dress fittings in her hotel suite.

Cecelia retaliated by not mentioning the encounter in her story and instead writing an entire article about Crawford's *other* eye, the one not destroyed in the accident. "It had so much mascara on it that I thought this was worth discussing," Cecelia told the students.

"Damn you! Nothing gets by you!" Crawford hissed when she saw Cecelia later at the movie's opening night party.

"But she said it very gently," Cecelia assured the journalism class. "And I took it gently."

Air conditioning was nonexistent before World War II, and nobody spent the summer in Manhattan who could afford to leave town. The Agers spent every summer before Laurel was born in California. The summer Cecelia was pregnant again and Milton stayed home from Paris, they rented a house in Great Neck, a community near his golf club favored by artists and writers.

In 1929, I was sent off for part of the summer to Fort Ethan Allen, near Saratoga, New York, the cavalry post where Cecelia's Uncle Bill was then stationed. Since Bill was still unmarried and presumably living in bachelor officers' quarters, I've no idea how he managed the care of a four-year-old. The next summer Laurel and I were sent to stay with Cecelia's Uncle Harry. Bill and Harry Mayer were my grandmother Fanny's two youngest brothers, exceptionally sweet-natured men, only ten and twelve years older than Cecelia and, like Clyde Beatty, only a few inches taller than our father. Both had been born in Manhattan shortly after the family arrived from Poland in 1893 and, unlike their older brothers and sisters, they did not seem foreign and did not speak with accents. Gentle, bespectacled Uncle Harry, as Laurel and I called him, though he was really our great-uncle, had been a mathematics prodigy who'd attended Columbia University on scholarship and later taught mathematics at both Cornell and UC Berkeley. But his real passion was the Communist Party, and by the time I knew him he'd settled in Brooklyn as a math teacher at James Madison High School in order to have sufficient time for political activity.

The summer I remember best was the one Laurel and I spent in a Vermont farmhouse near Arlington with the wildest of Cecelia's relatives, her red-haired Aunt Anzia, about two years younger than Fanny, but older than Harry and Bill. Anzia Yezierska, a writer, dressed in peasant denim and sandals and spoke with a strong accent. The simple life in rural Vermont, where a farmer brought us fresh milk and butter and eggs each day, and vegetables from his garden, should have made our histrionic great-aunt easier to be around. But Anzia decided that this summer was to be a working vacation for her two spoiled and overcoddled nieces, ages three and six. We would be taught to wash dishes, scrub floors, and do other things working-class children do, the hated domestic chores Anzia had had to do as a child. Quite naturally, we hated it too. But Anzia was firm. She even made us pitch hay and, after our day's chores, she forced us to take cold baths in a tin tub in the kitchen.

But each evening she cooked a delicious rice pudding in a white enamel washbasin, and after supper she read to us from one of her favorite authors—Oscar Wilde, Washington Irving, Mark Twain. When she put us on the train home, in the care of a conductor, she embarrassed me anew by providing a fresh basin of rice pudding for the journey.

At one time or another, Anzia embarrassed everybody. She was a firebrand, a socialist, a breast-beater, a hair-puller, perpetually upset, and upsetting to everyone around her. A consequence of her temperament was a weak stomach. In New York, she lived alone in a room in Greenwich Village where she seemed to subsist solely on tea, soda crackers, rice, and the bottle of milk she kept on the windowsill. She was in constant rebellion against all middle-class values, and totally contemptuous of money and its comforts. These were not unknown to her. Anzia had a past I was not then aware of. After years of rejection slips, in 1919 she had written a short story, "The Fat of the Land," which was named Best Short Story of the year in the distinguished series of books edited by Edward J. O'Brien, and made its unknown author a celebrity overnight in a way that seems to happen only in America.

"Probably as romantic a figure as American literature affords," said the *New York Tribune* of November 19, 1922, "is that of Anzia Yezierska, who landed at Ellis Island as a frail, young Polish-Jew immigrant girl, and who has now won her way through dreary hours in sweatshop and scullery to a place among the successful authors of the day." Her first two books were bought by Hollywood, and major magazines clamored for her work. But by the time I knew her, all this was in the past. Anzia was again struggling with grinding poverty, and with a glacial writer's block that would hold her in its frigid grasp for eighteen years. In one of many frantic efforts to break free, she had impulsively rushed off to Arlington upon learning that Dorothy Canfield Fisher lived there. Anzia doubtless envied Fisher's smooth, polished prose, so unlike her own hectic, half-strangled outpourings.

"She arrived weeping and distraught," Fisher later wrote of Anzia's desperate search for new people and places to write about that might free her frozen pen. The kindly Fisher and her friends found Anzia the twelve-dollar-a-month farmhouse, planted a vegetable garden, and donated their own cast-off furniture, thus joining a long string of benefactors who yielded to Anzia's nose-pressed-against-the-glass method of securing underwriting for her literary life, her only life.

Anzia was one of ten children, and all but Fanny cordially loathed her at one time or another, some of them nearly all the time, as did Milton. Cecelia was the member of the family who respected Anzia most. Though she and Anzia stopped speaking for long periods, their attachment was deep and lifelong. Laurel and I were far too young to realize it, and would have been horrified to hear it, but Anzia Yezierska had been Cecelia's mentor when she was a precocious youngster growing up in Hollywood, captive to and bored by her uneducated immigrant parents, and later in New York, both before and after her marriage to her successful songwriter husband.

As Anzia's daughter Louise Levitas Henriksen put it in her 1988 biography, *Anzia Yezierska: A Writer's Life*, despite a difference of eighteen or twenty years in their ages, and a vast gulf separating their social positions, Cecelia was unquestionably "the confidante who best understood Anzia." Their understanding must have been to some degree mutual; Anzia more than anyone must have held the key to enigmatic, silent, unhappy, untouchable Cecelia. How I wish now that I had not sided with my bourgeois-minded father, a man who saw Anzia as a noisy, penny-pinching, troublemaking egomaniac to be avoided whenever possible. To him, she probably represented the irrational, emotional Old World ways he had tried so hard to put behind him. To me, she represents the insoluble mystery of my mother that still holds me in its thrall.

The summer I was nearly eight and Laurel not quite five, Cecelia sent us off to summer camp. Laurel was so little she couldn't sleep alone and had to share the room of the smelly camp directress, but not so young she cannot still remember the jolly song we had to sing every day, to the tune of "There Is a Tavern in the Town." "We're down at Housatonic Camp—*tonic camp!* And there we run and play and scamp—*play and scamp!*" The worst of the playing and scamping were the coed swimming periods in the Housatonic River, everybody stark naked. Laurel was young enough not to mind, but I was already modest and mortified. My salvation was a saucy nine-year-old, Gloria Stone, who taught me to shriek with laughter at all the naked boys. Gloria, whom I did not recall meeting before, turned out to be my second cousin and, by the end of summer, she was my first friend.

Gloria was the daughter of Cecelia's gynecologist cousin Dr. Hannah Stone and Hannah's urologist husband, Dr. Abraham Stone, selfless physicians who spent their lives crusading for birth control. Dr. Hannah, as she was known, was nine years older than Cecelia, and in addition to being on staff at the prestigious Lying-In Hospital, she also served without pay as medical director of the Margaret Sanger Clinic and Research Bureau, the first place in the United States to openly dispense birth control information and supplies.

Contraception in the twenties was more than illegal; it was literally unmentionable. Terms like *birth control* were not even permitted in novels, let alone in newspapers and magazines. Hannah was jailed twice for her activities in connection with birth control, and finally forced to choose between discontinuing her work at the Sanger Clinic and giving up her hospital affiliation. She chose the latter, and thereafter practiced with Abe in an office on lower Fifth Avenue.

Hannah was a daughter of Max Mayer, the eldest of a brood of ten, of whom the four youngest were, in order, Fanny, Anzia, Harry, and Bill. I knew these four people very well, the older six not at all.

My cousin Gloria, freckle-faced and always laughing, was happy to let me help her tend the family frog farm in the fireplace of the Stones' West 12th Street apartment. The fireplace housed a terrarium of tiny African tree frogs smuggled through customs in the pockets of Hannah's and Abe's raincoats for use in birth control experiments, or perhaps pregnancy tests.

The Stones reminded me of people in books. They were the first happy family I actually knew. Hannah was beautifully serene, with wide-set gray eyes, and Abe's small, bearlike Ukrainian eyes twinkled out over an enormous mustache. Their book-lined apartment was hung with cartoons made by friends at *The New Yorker* of lecherous sperms chasing after shy, demure ova. As an only child, Gloria sometimes thought of herself as the family mistake.

Although Abe and Hannah had limited incomes as dedicated physicians to the poor and pregnant, they were also coauthors of the era's best-selling sex book, A *Marriage Manual*. Cast in a simple question-and-answer format, the book had established Abe and Hannah as the Jazz Age Masters and Johnson, and in the thirties it was still earning royalties that would help pay for Gloria's own years at medical school, and remains in print today. After the Stones had completed their first draft of A *Marriage Manual*, they had asked Cecelia to edit it and put the authors' stiff and formal medical prose into colloquial English.

The Stones owned a small farm in Bound Brook, New Jersey, and I spent many joyful weekends there playing with the animals and reading for profit. Hannah and Abe paid Gloria and me two cents a page to read *The Story of Mankind*, by Hendrik Willem Van Loon, and *The Story of Philosophy*, by Will Durant. Both writers were friends of the Stones and frequent guests at their farm. I knew that Cecelia and Milton would have disapproved of these fee arrangements. "So don't tell them," said Hannah and Abe, a brilliant solution that would never have occurred to me.

Although I was not aware of Gloria before she rescued me from the ignominy of naked swimming lessons, she was already attending an advanced-thinking progressive school as unique in its own way as Housatonic Camp. The Lincoln School of Teachers College at Columbia University was on West 123rd Street, between Morningside Park and Harlem, and as soon as I became old enough for kindergarten, Cecelia enrolled me, and Milton brought me uptown in a taxi. Lincoln prided itself on teaching reading in kindergarten, and when the teachers discovered I could already read — thanks to Milton — they sighed and said I was ready to start first grade, even though I was not quite five years old. In retrospect, it was a serious mistake, with far-reaching consequences that nobody foresaw.

Lincoln was different from all other schools of its time, a coeducational private day school which went all the way up through twelfth grade. Nothing like it exists today. Students were deliberately chosen from diverse backgrounds, and many had scholarships. Intellect and promise were important. There was a heavy sprinkling of faculty children from Columbia's various colleges, of children from upper-middle-class families of progressive bent, many of them Jewish. Nearly all the boys and girls who went there, no matter their age or background, considered Lincoln the most exciting, enriching part of their lives. No other educational experience I had subsequently ever came near it.

The school served Teachers College as an experimental laboratory for new ideas in education and teacher training. Classes were small, and the plant magnificent—a handsome brick building with spacious classrooms, wide terrazzo corridors, beautifully equipped labs in which to teach science and biology, studios for painting and sculpture and music, rooms fully outfitted for classes in cooking and sewing and shop. A theater and auditorium was available for student productions, a vast and comfortable library overlooked the park, marvelous indoor and outdoor gymnasiums were on the roof, and in the basement was an Olympic-size swimming pool.

I loved Lincoln from that first day. Since I could already read, I was immediately given the run of the library, a holy place presided over by Miss Eaton, a librarian so passionate that at Christmas she sat the kindergarten children on her lap, one by one, and read an individual Christmas story to each in her low and musical voice. She lived to be over ninety, and I read in her obituary that dozens of writers whom she had been the first to infuse with the love of words had dedicated their books to Dorothy Eaton.

Lincoln being a "progressive" school, Latin and Greek were deemed "dead languages" and banned from the curriculum, and the new science of social studies was the focus of classroom work. Each class worked together on a year-long "homeroom" project. In second grade it was New York City, and we began by moving our chairs and desks out into the hall and painting a map of Manhattan Island that covered our entire schoolroom floor. By the end of that year, we had actually visited all the museums, neighborhoods, and monuments we had identified, not omitting a six A.M. field trip to the Fulton Fish Market.

Report cards took the form of frequent, thoughtful letters from teachers to parents, and all of my teachers, from kindergarten onward, said exactly the same thing: Shana does well, but she could do much better. The difficulty is that she is too interested in the other children, and spends more time hanging around them than attending to her own schoolwork.

Cecelia and Milton insisted on discussing these letters with me at great length, and I had to be careful never to reveal their real meaning. Yet I was amazed that my all-knowing parents couldn't see it. The truth was that I was utterly desperate to be "popular," to "belong." I could not bear to be so different from all the other children and to have such freakish parents — a mother who worked, in show business, a father who stayed up all night and seemingly played the piano for a living. I longed only to, please God, be exactly like everyone else. Lincoln encouraged parents to visit classes, but I was delighted that mine stayed away. Cecelia's chic embarrassed me. She did not look or dress like any other Lincoln mother, nor like any of my beloved teachers.

In second grade, I discovered "popular music." Until then, the only songs I knew, or thought I knew, were the ones we sang at Lincoln: "America," "Adeste Fideles," and the like. Then, for the first time, I got to visit another child after school. I believe that Cecelia approved this particular child not because her father was a judge, but because her half-brother was the cartoonist Peter Arno. My classmate had a marionette theater, and her mother looked exactly like a Peter Arno dowager, down to the black dress and three ropes of pearls. For the finale of the impromptu show we put on for her mother that afternoon, we drizzled silver dust from the flies while my friend sang "Stars Fell on Alabama," a different kind of song than any I had heard before. I liked it so much she sang me another, "Shuffle Off to Buffalo," and taught me a dance to go with it. She said these tunes were known as "popular songs."

I could hardly wait to tell Milton about my thrilling discovery. "Did you know there's a whole other kind of song from the ones we have to sing at Lincoln?" I said the instant he got home. "It's called a 'popular' song. 'My heart beats like a hammah, . . .'" I piped. Milton gave me a bleak look.

In third grade, the boys learned to make things in shop, and we girls learned, really learned, to cook and sew. At age eight I could make lump-free white sauce. In sewing, I made a blue sateen Marie Antoinette shepherdess dress with a silver lamé inset panel, and a hoopskirt with a real wood hoop that I also made.

In fourth grade, when I was eight, we were allowed to use the school theater for the first time. Our class play was *Thumbelina*, by Hans Christian Andersen, and by then we were expert enough to build our own stage sets. I was assigned to the scene crew until the evening Miss Enright called my parents at home. The girl who was playing Thumbelina had come down with measles. Could Shana learn the part in time? The next thing I remember about this is my entrance, from stage left. Thumbelina was a tiny fairy who had been born in a walnut shell. So, when the time came, I was towed out in front of everybody on a painted lily pad, curled up in my shell, costumed in — only — a leaf, a mortifying garment stitched from two wisps of green gauze.

Then I heard the applause. Other children and their parents roared approval. I thanked God my own parents were not on hand to witness my total embarrassment. I did not know until the punch and cookies party afterwards that Anzia had watched me from the balcony. Teachers, parents, and children were crowding around me, and smiling. I had become, at last, *popular*. It was the happiest moment of my life.

Shortly after my triumph in *Thumbelina*, the Visigoths arrived. Laurel was in kindergarten by then, and one day the two of us got home from school to find our apartment thronged with burly men from the Manhattan Storage and Warehouse Company. The long, painted entrance corridor, now harshly lit with work lights, was stacked with cartons, excelsior, and raw lumber out of which men were pounding together crates and barrels. Though we did not realize it, the entire contents of our fanciful habitat, every single thing we owned but our clothes and a few books, was about to disappear from our lives. The pounding resumed the next morning. No one would explain anything. Laurel and I were hustled off to the school bus. When we returned, the corridor was piled high with crates, boxes, and barrels all nailed shut. Dirty canvases were thrown over the piles. Shreds of excelsior littered the floor. We would not see our belongings again in toto for more than forty years.

CHAPTER THREE

AFTER THE VISIGOTHS

When we awoke the next morning, our family occupied a glum suite of rooms with tan walls and dull green upholstery in the Hotel Salisbury down the block. Laurel and I still shared a bedroom, but each parent now had a private bedroom and bath. We still had a living room, but dining room, kitchen, and cook had vanished. Children's meals were cooked on a two-burner stove; our parents dined out. Our beloved child-size furniture and all our games and books had disappeared along with everything else.

Clothing aside, our Salisbury apartment contained only three familiar objects. Milton's piano stood at the far end of the living room near the two windows. A bookcase sat between them, and the portrait of Cecelia by George Gershwin was propped on top. It had been painted in the style of Gershwin's favorite artist, Georges Rouault, the face heavily lined in muddy purples and greens, and I did not understand why the thing had been awarded such a place of prominence. The visage haunted me, and I was gratified to read many years later that so eminent a critic as Alexander Woollcott considered Gershwin's paintings "god-awful."

Save for these three items, our family now occupied an entirely impersonal, rented habitat. Our parents said that the arrangement was temporary. But "temporary" is not a concept readily graspable by the eight-year-old mind. To me it seemed as if someone had performed a cosmic magic trick. In those Depression days, itinerant street pitchmen used to sell hot neckties, three for a dollar, which were displayed inside a cheap suitcase opened flat atop a folding stand. At the approach of a policeman, the vendor was able to slam shut his array of bright silks and instantly disappear into the crowd. It has always seemed to me that, on the day the Visigoths arrived, the bright box of my childhood slammed closed and vanished in the same way.

We lived in the Hotel Salisbury more than three years. When we moved there, Laurel was a slender, smiling five-year-old with long braids down her back. I was eight, much chubbier, with curly hair and a grave expression. It was a painful part of my childhood, and I have a partial amnesia about what the place looked like. I remember just the front hall where the phone and message pad were, and the window end of the living room. I know that our parents ordered individual breakfasts at different hours from room service. Someone must have cooked our supper and got us up and dressed and fed and onto the Lincoln School bus each morning, but it wasn't either parent. Milton slept in the mornings, and Cecelia read the papers in bed. She was irritable and curt, struggling out of a night of insomnia which she treated with sleeping pills and endless English mystery novels rented from Womrath's, the bookstore downstairs.

Sometimes I awoke in the night and heard Cecelia and Milton shouting, a noise I hated, but I don't know what they fought about. Had they fought in the magic apartment too? I don't recall hearing it there, but I was younger, and the floor plan was different. Very likely the sounds that occasionally woke me were just ordinary domestic quarreling. Who knows? The DMZ is no place from which to analyze a battle, and the egocentrism of childhood distorts the image of one's parents. The bicker in the bedroom is heard as the clash of giants, and it takes years of living for the truth of Housman's lines to sink in: "The night my father got me / His mind was not on me." Or as Milton now started saying over and over, "Children don't ask to be born."

Cecelia and Milton were now thirty-one and forty. A fashionable pair, they wore mostly custom-made clothing, a consequence not just of their demanding tastes but of their uncommonly small size. Even hats and shoes were made to order. The hotel closets were too small to hold everything, and in each of their bedrooms stood an open theatrical trunk, ranks of little suits and dresses hanging neatly on the special wood hangers and expandable metal rods, oddments and accessories spilling out of the partially open drawers.

It did not take me long to discover that Cecelia's scarlet cape had vanished, along with the diamond ring and Milton's top hat and tails. The ring was in the vault, to save on insurance, Cecelia said, and she found the sorts of occasions that required formal dress — charity dinners and ASCAP banquets — tedious in the extreme. True, she was an excellent dancer, and would surely have enjoyed an occasional twirl around somebody's private ballroom. But our parents were strictly showbiz; they didn't move in the starchy circles where people gave dinner dances. Besides, Milton didn't dance. His dinner jacket and dress shirts were on hand for the occasional night he was called on to attend a professional dinner or play his songs at an ASCAP affair, and my happy duty on such evenings was to insert his sapphire shirt studs and handsome octagonal cufflinks of beaten gold. His stud box also contained a beautiful gold signet ring that he never wore. A girl named Rayna had given it to him long ago, he said. She was dead now.

Each evening around dusk our parents came home, changed for dinner, met in the dark, narrow living room for a drink and a chat with us, and a ritualized discussion that never varied.

"Where would you like to eat tonight, Cecelia?" Milton asked as he poured his second whiskey.

With a sigh of exhaustion, Cecelia replied, "I don't care where we go." Milton then named eight or ten or twelve of Manhattan's best restaurants. Eventually a choice was agreed upon, one of them telephoned for a reservation, and they bid us goodnight and sailed out the door. Milton soon decided that on Friday nights, when there was no school the next day, Laurel and I would go to dinner with them. He wanted us to know and appreciate all types of cuisine, he said, and "not have any childish food prejudices." But we knew he also wanted to spend more time with us.

Before I was nine, and Laurel six, we were well known by name to the owners of the finest eateries in Manhattan. We taxied each Friday to Moore's or Lindy's or the Oak Room of the Plaza Hotel for American food, or down to Luchow's German restaurant on 14th Street for *Knackwurst mit Sauerkraut*. Or we drove farther downtown to Canal Street, and climbed a narrow flight of red-painted stairs to Lum Fong's. On other Fridays we taxied down to a street off Washington Square for the Parisian elegance of the Café Lafayette, or down the West Side to Mama Leone's where huge-breasted Mama herself led us to a prime table near the piano. Laurel and I were encouraged to read the menu and order for ourselves. We knew the difference between lasagna and ravioli before non-Italian children our age had even heard of spaghetti. After thirty minutes of "Ciribiribin" and "Funiculi! Funicula!" the pianist reached the high point of his act. He stood up, removed his dinner jacket and shoes and socks, rolled up his trouser cuffs, went into a kind of yoga headstand, and played the piano with his toes. Laurel and I were enchanted. We were also avid readers of the funny papers, and followers of "Bob Ripley's Believe It or Not!" in the *Journal-American*, and the day our own upside-down pianist was featured in "Believe It or Not!" was the joyful moment we realized we knew our first celebrity. That our parents and their many restaurant friends, the people with whom they exchanged pleasantries and ordered drinks sent back and forth, were also frequently in the newspapers was a matter of which Laurel and I were unaware.

I remember all the restaurant interiors clearly, much better than I do the Salisbury, because restaurants were now the only places we were still together as a family. The favorite restaurant of all four of us was Moore's, on West 46th Street, a closed, immaculate, white-tiled universe of polished brass and mirror ruled absolutely by the Old Man. Everyone called him "the Old Man," including his family. To his face, he was "Mr. Moore," or "Jim." Nobody ever risked calling him "Dinty," not even the cartoonist George McManus who had immortalized him in his comic strip "Bringing Up Father." I can still see him clearly: a wobble of chins, a shirtfront of creamy pongee, a fine London suit with a cuff of long underwear peeking out, a pink, just-barbered face, and a few long strands of hair plastered on gleaming scalp. Mr. Moore and his restaurant were so Irish that years later, when I first visited Dublin, Ireland seemed a larger, much-diluted, outdoor Moore's.

The Old Man had inflexible rules about everything important in life — food, sex, death, and deportment — and many of my own values, I can see now, were formed in his restaurant. Its effect on me was so powerful that today when I think of it, the whole place comes floating up out of my past, all its lights ablaze, a gala, ghostly cruise ship bearing my childhood back to me. I can still smell Mr. Moore's briny oysters and taste his corned beef and cabbage, the "nose-warmers" of oxtail soup, the rice pudding nonpareil. I still feel the ionized, charged atmosphere of the place. Anything might happen in this closed world of delicious food and fierce emotions, where once a customer was literally heaved out the door for ordering his hamburger without onions, and out on the sidewalk enraged rabbis in black hats and beards picketed because the menu listed "Kosher calf's liver with Irish bacon."

The white-tiled kitchen in the rear was wide open to public view, and for a time Cecelia arranged for Laurel and me to go there after school for cooking lessons. Our teacher was the Old Man himself. While our classmates were wearing white gloves and learning the right way to fox-trot, we wore big white tablecloths tied around us, waiter-style, and learned the right way to cook carrots and peas (rapidly, with a pinch of sugar) and potatoes (unpeeled, with a handful of salt).

Mr. Moore had rigid standards. Leaving your mother and gambling were the two unforgivable sins. Larceny was lower down the scale. When Cecelia once protested that Jim should not waste his time and energy making up elaborate food hampers to send to Laurel and me at summer camp, he told her it was no trouble. He had to do the monthly baskets anyway "for the boys up the river."

George McManus was right about the long-smoldering warfare of the Irish household. In the Moore family, no one talked to anyone else if he could avoid it. Mr. Moore and his wheelchair-bound wife occupied separate floors above the restaurant and had not spoken in years. The children rarely spoke either, except to borrow money or plot against one parent or the other. Willie Moore, the only son, had committed some infraction, probably at the racetrack, that had got him barred for life from entering the restaurant proper. He stood outside on 46th Street, even when it was raining, until he spotted his chance to dart inside and enter the tiny elevator behind the coat check racks that brought him to sanctuary with his mother upstairs.

The two maiden daughters, Annie and Cora, took turns running the cash register until the day they wagered the restaurant on the horses, and Mr. Moore had to buy it back from the bookmakers. I'm not sure who ran the cash register after that. Not Mr. Moore. His role was to roam his domain, keep an eye on waiters and busboys, and occasionally sit down for a drink and a chat with favorite customers. We thought of him as part of our family, and he sat with us every time we came in.

Laurel and I saw our parents during their cocktail hour and on Friday nights. The other nights, when they went to dinner without us, Milton put Cecelia into a taxi afterwards, paid the driver to take her wherever she was going, and walked over to the Friars Club, which in those days occupied a shabby suite of rooms in the Edison Hotel on Eighth Avenue and 46th Street. We heard a lot about the Friars, but never saw the place. It was a men-only club founded by convivial Jewish show business people who were barred because of their race, or religion, or whatever it was, from joining the older actors' hangout, the Lambs Club. By the time Cecelia got home, we were asleep.

As time went on in the dowdy but expensive hotel suite, it was hard to miss seeing how separate Cecelia's and Milton's lives had become. They lived and worked in different rooms, and came and went at different hours of the day and night. She arose at dawn, which was about when he went to sleep, and bathed and dressed after we had gone off to school. Milton awoke and rang for his room service breakfast at about eleven, dropped by his music publishing office, and in fine weather managed to get to the golf course nearly every day.

He worked at the piano at all hours, usually playing a two-or-three-note phrase, or variations of the same chords or chord changes, over and over and over. Sometimes he spent an hour or two at the piano before leaving in the morning, or we'd find him there in the afternoon, when we came home from school, or hear him late at night, long after we had gone to bed. I was so used to his piano that I didn't really hear it except when he broke off his eternal tinkering and let a strong melodic phrase, perhaps an entire chorus, pour forth. But this happened rarely; the melody, save for minor adjustments, was already set. The tinkering was an attempt to improve the verse, or to adjust chord progressions and harmonics.

Cecelia spent most of her working time in the dark, watching movies and vaudeville and nightclub acts, and usually wrote them up at her office. If we heard her typewriting at home, it was always behind her firmly closed bedroom door. In the thirties, critics were still reverent about movies; Cecelia read like no one else. Her comments were consistently terse, witty, and devoid of pretense, and it could take her a long, agonizing time to get it right. Entertaining reading, not culture or uplift or doublethink, was all Cecelia ever sought to provide.

Bette Davis in *Parachute Jumper* seems convinced she's become quite a charmer. Slowly she raises her eyelids to sear the hero with devastating glances, then satisfied, she smiles a crooked little Mona Lisa smile. Unfortunately, this procedure takes place while Miss Davis is wearing a curious pill-box hat that perches on her head at an angle slightly comic. The hat, and her own self-satisfaction, interfere with the effect.

Our little Mae West, with her sunny ways, her elegant refine-
ments, her classy accomplishments, has come back to us —
come back to us in *I'm No Angel*, a bigger, better, and bolder
broad.

Like Eadie, everything Miss West does, she does elegant. . . .

What was the real reason we had moved to a hotel? They would never
say. But the move marked a permanent change in the way we lived. Now
we were together only in public, in restaurants. They too were together
only in public, only at times when they looked their best, and were on
their best behavior. Why would they not discuss it? Why did these sophisticated, modern people who told us we were adults, who sometimes embarrassed us frightfully by walking around naked to demonstrate that
there were no taboos in our family, refuse to discuss the question uppermost in our minds, or even to acknowledge that something had happened? Laurel and I discussed it in whispers after lights out, and at any
other opportunity, for many years. We talk about it still. Had one of them
fallen in love with someone else? Perhaps. But which one? And with
whom? Or was there some other reason?

I'm not sure when I came to the conclusion that most probably Cecelia had become involved with George Gershwin. Sime Silverman was
a second, more remote possibility. But what the involvement was, and
how far it went, or if indeed it went anywhere, I had no clue, save for
the fact that our parents had stopped seeing the Gershwins. They were
not among the few who sometimes dropped by the Salisbury for cocktails in the late afternoon.

Sime had died suddenly earlier in the same year that we moved, and
the paper was now owned and published by his son Syd and edited by
Abel Green. But Sime's faithful secretary, Betty Brown, still ran the
switchboard and acted as den mother to the muggs. Cecelia called her
"Snoo," and the first thing she did when she came home from work in
the late afternoon was flop onto her bed, kick off her expensive, Belgian-

made shoes, light a cigarette, and pick up the telephone. "Snoo? What's noo?" she'd giggle, and Sime's old secretary would whisper the latest, hottest showbiz gossip.

Whatever had happened, the reason for putting our world into storage, our lives on hold, became the central mystery of Laurel's and my existence, and long after we were grown and had children ourselves, the family belongings were still in storage and we were still trying in vain to get our parents to say why. The motivation could not have been economic. Living in a sedate apartment hotel like the Salisbury was drab but costly. The rent and phone bills must have been more than twice as high, and the room service and restaurant bills enormous. Milton also had to pay the storage company every month. I say Milton because, though our parents had a joint bank account, he was its only depositor. Cecelia banked her earnings in her own account. Milton insisted on it. When a man married, he believed, one of his ineluctable responsibilities was the full support of his wife and children and household.

Beneath Gershwin's muddy-faced portrait were shelves holding our few books – a half dozen items of nonfiction, plus the complete works of Milton's once-favorite novelist, James Branch Cabell. Cecelia must have preserved Cabell's thirty-odd novels as a last-minute gesture of appeasement to her husband's outraged household gods, before entombing everything else in the Manhattan Storage and Warehouse Company. Our beloved collection of Oz books having disappeared, I tried hard to like Cabell, but found him unreadable.

Between the ages of eight and eleven, I reread our few non-Cabell books many, many times. There were six: the 1928 one-volume edition of *The Golden Bough* by Sir James Gordon Frazer, *Microbe Hunters* by Paul deKruif, Carl Sandburg's *American Songbag*, a first edition of *The Joy of Cooking* by Irma S. Rombauer, the 1934 Modern Library edition of Bulfinch's *Mythology*, and a copy of *Webster's Dictionary* which I actually *read* for sheer lexical pleasure; it was my personal *Joy of Words*. I also valued it because it said "College Edition," and because my mother had given it to me and inscribed my name on the flyleaf in her strong hand. When I got sick of rereading the books, I picked out on the piano with one finger all the folk songs in what I came to think of as *The Sandbag*, and memorized even unto fifth and sixth verses the words to the few tunes I knew I could sing on key, even away from the piano, simple airs like "The Streets of Laredo" and "Down in the Valley."

Many years later I came to realize that absolutely everything I know and care most about is based on these six books. They are the fundament of my entire imaginative and professional life. *The Golden Bough*, my favorite, since it discussed things like circumcision, tattooing, and fertility rites, is responsible for my majoring in anthropology in college, and also for my life as a reporter. Anthropology and journalism have much in common; both require one to observe and record the scene in detail, yet take pains not to allow one's own presence to contaminate the field.

The deKruif book, a solid work of popular science, prefigures my own fascination with such abstruse subjects as kidney dialysis, elephant breeding patterns, and modern medical ethics, all of which I have written about at length. Bulfinch's sections on Greek and Roman mythology have informed my life, peopled my fantasies, and very much helped me as a writer to find some of the necessary metaphor I continually sought. This need was a particularly urgent one for me, as our parents were nonbelievers, and we children received no religious training of any kind.

As for the Rombauer, I didn't read her for the recipes. Thanks to Lincoln School, I already knew how to cook. But her tables of equivalents were valuable, and her calorie tables unique and invaluable, as I was already ashamed of being overweight. Mostly I was fascinated by Rombauer's advice on formal dinner parties and proper table settings, now that our own beautiful china and silver had disappeared. Reading her gave me a sense of how "normal" families lived. I had no idea. We never visited other families and had no nearby relatives but Great Uncle Harry in Brooklyn, Great Aunt Anzia in Greenwich Village, and the decidedly not "normal" Doctors Stone.

In most families, a Bible would have been among the few books saved from storage. But the Agers had no Bible. Religion was a matter of utter disinterest to them both. In the magic apartment, we used to have a Christmas tree, but I expect Jimmy Reynolds was responsible for that too. Our parents were artists and intellectuals. They did not believe in burdening their offspring with what Milton called "mumbo jumbo." But though they had no interest in God, they developed a growing determination as Hitler rose to power to make it clear to the world, and incidentally to their children, that we were Jews. This new insistence involved a certain amount of backtracking on their part in what had been a determined march toward total emancipation from their Old World origins. Suddenly, loyalty to their roots compelled them to reemphasize certain aspects of their heritage from which they had been happily moving away. All this became an area of great bafflement and fuddle to their children, triggering a religious or ethnic identity crisis never entirely resolved.

About the time people in the United States first heard that Hitler was forcing the Jews of Germany to sew yellow stars onto their clothing, Cecelia's dear friend Mr. John gave her a small, chic solid gold Star of David that hung on a supple, snakelike gold chain. I had never seen such an object before. She tried to explain its meaning to me, but I had no idea what she was talking about. Though my mother had no religion and professed to despise jewelry, she wore the little Jewish star at her throat or wrist every day for the rest of her life.

Mr. John was the designer partner of John-Frederics, Inc., New York's most expensive and fashionable milliner. A liquid-eyed man of enormous charm and taste, he had been born Hansi (John) Harburger in Berlin, and had run off to Paris to design hats at an early age. His devoted business partner, Mr. Fred (Hirst), was another sophisticated former Berlin Jew. Their millinery salon and workshops were done up entirely in gray velvet, mirrors, and gold leaf, a monochrome background against which to display the hundreds of hats, as elegant a roost as that of any Paris couturier.

Cecelia and John and Fred had become close friends back before the men had opened their salon, when they were still anonymous wholesale milliners. The moment they met her, they recognized her special chic, her perfect eye, just as she did theirs. John-Frederics' clientele were wealthy society women of taste, titled Europeans, and movie stars. Like Cecelia, Laurel and I had the run of the salon and workrooms, and Greta Garbo, Beatrice Lillie, Ilka Chase and Marlene Dietrich were among the frequent customers whose faces we saw distantly reflected in the salon mirrors.

John and Fred were warmhearted men, and their favorite children were Laurel and me. They never came to the Salisbury without a box of Viennese chocolates or other forbidden sweets. If I was sick in bed, John brought me two or three perfectly made miniature hats created solely for me to play with. They had tiny veils, silk ribbons and flowers, and inner hatbands of gold lace, just like the $100 originals. My favorite was a tricorn in shades of bronze and green with a pert, swallow-tail ribbon at the back, a miniature of a hat he had just finished designing for Vivien Leigh to wear in *Gone With the Wind.*

One day a strange set of visitors turned up — a man and wife, their two-year-old son who spoke only Chinese, and his Chinese amah. The father turned out to be the youngest of Fanny's brothers, the man I'd been boarded with at the cavalry post, Cecelia's Uncle Bill. For a decade, Captain William Mayer had been stationed in Peking. It was he who had sent Cecelia the Chinese silk robes. Only ten years younger than Bill, Cecelia was his favorite niece. His wife was Isabel Ingram, the daughter of a heroic medical missionary and veteran of the Boxer Rebellion. Born in China and educated at Wellesley, Isabel was an art historian schooled in Chinese court etiquette, and had spent several years as tutor to Wan Jung, the "Little Empress," and Xuang Tong, concubine of the "Last Emperor."

Cecelia told Laurel and me the highlights of Bill's military career. The immense scar that creased his bald head front to back like the dent in a fedora was a souvenir of his service in Colonel Billy Mitchell's air force. It had happened when he failed to duck in time after starting a plane by tugging down sharply on its wood propeller blade. The dent in Bill's skull was a source of great fascination to anyone who sat on his lap, but being only nine years old, it did not occur to me to marvel at the size of an airplane that could crease the skull of a man no taller than five feet six.

Despite his accomplishments, Bill would never make a higher army rank than colonel, Cecelia explained, because he was a Jew.

"What's a Jew?"

"We're Jews. Most people don't like us. But we're better than they are. Marx, Freud, and Einstein all were Jews." Cecelia was a woman of few words.

Bill was the first person in the family to marry outside the Jewish faith, Cecelia went on. I decided not to like Isabel, but she was beautiful, with glossy black hair parted in the middle, and a hard, slim, warm body under her supple Chinese silks, and soon I liked her very much.

At about the same time that Cecelia began wearing her gold star, Milton started taking piano lessons. Although he had played piano professionally since boyhood, and could play anything, by sight or by ear, and transpose instantly into any key, he was entirely self-taught and lacked proper fingering technique. He had small hands, and as a youth had broken several fingers playing handball. Having overcome his various handicaps, he hoped now to acquire a more classical keyboard technique.

His piano teacher was Eddie Fink, a small, bald man who wore a dome-shaped emerald on the little finger of his left hand. Laurel and I knew Eddie as the piano player in the quartet at Luchow's. He sat in a tuxedo four hours a night amid potted palms on an elevated platform playing Strauss waltzes and other high-class dinner music. (The crowded restaurant was on multiple levels, and one night we saw a customer lose control of the *Knackwurst* he was trying to cut. It squirted off his plate, whizzed amid the startled string players, sailed above several tables of diners, and impaled itself on the antlers of an elk mounted on the opposite wall.)

Like Mr. John and Mr. Fred, Eddie Fink had been born in Berlin, but to me he was far more German than Jew. Milton soon decided that since Eddie was going to be coming to the Salisbury anyway, he might as well give piano lessons to the children too. Eddie put us, ages seven and ten, on the same daily piano practice regimen he prescribed for Milton: half an hour's limbering up by playing scales, followed by a second half hour of classical drills from *The Duvernoy School of Mechanism*, and *Carl Czerny's Exercises for the Left Hand*. The teacher of Franz Liszt, Czerny was the inventor of the so-called rigid-finger technique, which decreed, among other strictures, that the thumb must never be used to strike a black key. Czerny's fingering was so arduous to master, Oscar Levant later wrote, that as a young pianist his right thumb regularly bled after his daily practice.

During our twice-weekly lessons, Eddie held a ruler in his right hand and rapped us sharply across the offending knuckle each time we hit a wrong note or hit the right note with a wrong finger. Sometimes he added a sharp jab with his ring into ribs or kidney. We were not taught to play a single tune, and all in all the lessons and practice sessions were sheer hell. Any faint musical aptitude I may have had was permanently beaten out of me by Eddie's ring and ruler, though it could never have been much. It was some years before I discovered that Luchow's had fired its string quartet because they were Jews and that Milton had been trying to keep Eddie's head above water financially by throwing him whatever clients he could, even seven-year-olds. And it was many years after that when I got to know the classical music mandarin Schuyler Chapin and his wife, Betty, a witty woman about my age. She had been born Betty Steinway, she told me, and had also grown up on 57th Street, in Steinway Hall, down the block from the Salisbury.

"Do you play the piano?" I inquired politely.

"Not one note," she said firmly.

"Eddie Fink?" I said.

"You betcha."

In between practicing piano, I practiced typewriting on a special typewriter Cecelia gave me. Save for the two books, it is the only childhood present from her that I can remember, though I remember every key. They were tinted pink, green, yellow, and blue, and decorated with bunnies, piglets, ducks, and chickens to help one remember which fingers to use on which keys. In a short time I was a good touch typist, like my mother.

The strict and mysterious rule about not uttering Jack Yellen's name was still in force, but life in the Salisbury was so boring that sometimes when Milton was working at the piano, one of us rushed into the living room, shrieked the forbidden words, and dashed out. It was a cruel sport, and we had no idea what it meant, but it broke the after-school monotony of park, homework, piano practice, bed. We were not unhappy, just lonely. School was fun, home was not.

Cecelia had inflexible attitudes about family gift-giving. Her birthday in particular was so set about with rules and taboos as to be worthy of inclusion in *The Golden Bough*, and the approach of it filled us with dread. The only acceptable present to her was something you made yourself, preferably in a package you made yourself, accompanied by a homemade card. A bought present or commercial greeting card was cast aside unopened, not even glanced at, and the disdain it evoked filled the room with its stink.

The succession of nannies and maids on whom Laurel and I were dependent for shopping for art supplies at Woolworth's on Sixth Avenue, under the El, couldn't understand the seriousness of this taboo, and sometimes urged us to buy her a pair of mittens, or some other ready-made item. "It's the thought that counts," they said, and sometimes I let myself be persuaded they were right. Frightful scenes resulted, maids and children all in tears under Cecelia's basilisk eye. Cecelia's birthday was like a medieval ordeal, an occasion of such anxiety that I blanked out on the date, and was in my thirties before I knew whether it was January 21, 22, or 23. Why did she make such a big deal of it? Neither parent celebrated any other holiday; Thanksgiving, Hanukkah, Christmas, and Easter all passed unobserved. We never went trick-or-treating; they never went out on New Year's Eve.

A good example of Cecelia's unsparing nature occurred one night at Moore's. The savory moment of ordering was at hand. Moran, the big waiter, stood at our father's elbow, pencil poised, as we scanned the shiny white menu cards. Should it be baby scallops with Irish bacon? Irish lamb stew with fresh peas? Milton gave Cecelia's order first, then glanced at us. We named our choices.

"Don't these children ever read the right-hand side of the menu!" Cecelia snapped.

At first I was baffled. After I figured out that it was all those numbers, the *prices*, I knew she was right. I never *had* looked. No one had ever mentioned the numbers. From then on, I read that side first, and tried to order only the cheaper foods.

Cecelia had several variations on this theme. "Don't you *ever* think of the other person!" she would ask, with maximum scorn. Children walked behind their elders. Children opened doors for older people. They carried their packages, ran their errands, took their messages, helped out with household chores. Children were willing servants of their elders. In sum: contrary to the prevailing mood at Lincoln School, and among the families of our friends there, and the repeated assertion by Milton that we were adults, children usually came last.

What I wanted most in the world was to be exactly like a particular group of my Lincoln classmates, all of whom lived on the Upper East Side. This meant having velvet dresses and patent leather pumps and attending Miss Viola Wolff's Saturday dancing classes for the children of well-heeled Jewish families. Cecelia said she would not have her daughter in a class of children of German Jewish descent hot-bent on assimilation and hoped-for disappearance into British-aping airs and ways. She had no doubt she was better than everybody else. Her loving mother had made the matter quite clear from birth. She had always been the center of her family's attention, and did not understand her daughters' feelings of isolation. Her children were automatically superior to other children, she believed; the danger was letting them slip back into the common herd.

The Agers belonged to no organizations or clubs. One of the few places they went together, besides restaurants and theater, was the supper room of the Taft Hotel whenever Ben Bernie and his orchestra were playing there, and on Fridays we came along. Sometimes Cecelia danced with Ben or one of his brothers. She was as graceful and light-footed as Sally with Tony DeMarco, or Yolanda with Veloz, who were also on the bill. Ben's immediate family, which was like a part of our own, consisted of his brothers Herman, Dave, and Jeff, and his girlfriend Wes. The brothers' father had been a blacksmith in New Jersey. Wes had been Dorothy Wesley, a champion Olympic swimmer who excelled in the breaststroke; Ben preferred her to say the chest stroke. Her best friend, Eleanor Holm, had recently moved in with Billy Rose, also a part of the Ben Bernie gang when he was in town. Herman Bernie was a theatrical agent referred to affectionately within the family as "Herm the Worm," and Jeff was everybody's bookmaker. Dave Bernie, who played piano, also had a dance band. His relief piano player had been Oscar Levant, who later moved over to Ben's band before his emergence as a classical pianist.

Ben and his gang were the type of self-educated, stylish, smoothie, witty "diamonds in the rough" whom both Agers appreciated. The gang membership changed slightly and moved around frequently, something like a floating crap game, between New York and Chicago and Florida, depending where Ben's orchestra was booked, with stops in Hollywood and Hot Springs, Arkansas, and other centers of racing and high living. For a while Laurel and I speculated that Trudy, a vivacious, ever-present friend of Wes Bernie (as she was known), of whom Milton and all of us were very fond, might have been the cause of our sudden move to the Salisbury.

Often the gang gathered at the old Lindy's restaurant, at 50th Street and Broadway, for Jewish foods and endless gags about Lindy's waiters. Around the corner was a tiny Cuban cigar store where a man sat in the window rolling handmade cigars on his knee. Ben and Milton both loved "heaters," and one day they bought the store. After that they could call up any time they ran out of cigars and a boy would run over with a fresh box at no charge. They thought it a wonderful economy.

I knew Ben was a bandleader, but little more. His longtime radio sponsor was Pabst Blue Ribbon beer, and it is a measure of my worldliness that each week when the announcer said, ". . . brought to you by

Pabst Blue Ribbon," I thought Ben sold ribbons. That he was separated from an enraged wife, that Wes was his mistress, that he had packed a son off to military school, were among the things I had yet to learn.

Ben loved classical music, and he and Milton had a running argument about the greatest ten minutes of music ever written. After a great deal of discussion and educated humming, they usually settled on Wagner's *Liebestod*. A few years later, when Capehart marketed the first home phonograph that could turn the records over, the way a jukebox does, Ben sent us one of the vastly expensive machines, loaded with eight sides of *Tristan und Isolde*.

Ben was a mine of anecdotes. Himself a fiddle player, he loved to tell the story of Heifetz on the road doing one-nighters in hick towns for Hurok. One night during the Mendelssohn violin concerto, Heifetz glanced at his watch and gave the conductor a wink, meaning: cut to the coda.

"'Plunk, plunk, plunk,' Heifetz plays, and a voice from the balcony shouts: 'Maestro! You forgot the cadenza!'"

Ben never forgot the cadenza. He sparkled like a Hungarian chandelier, and wherever he was, the room seemed to light up around him. He was especially fond of me, and always predicted that when I grew up I'd be rich enough to build Cecelia and Milton a swimming pool.

One bright Saturday morning we heard drums approaching, then a brass band, and rushed to the window. A fife and drum corps came tootling down the street followed by several marching bands. Both curbs were crowded six-deep with people cheering and waving flags; other people waved and shouted from windows across the way. 57th Street shook with happy noise. More bands and silk-hatted dignitaries paraded smartly past. At last the open touring car came into view, and the cheers surged to a roar. President Roosevelt, running for his second term, smiled and waved from the backseat, turning from side to side to acknowledge the deafening applause. All the bands in turn thumped out Roosevelt's jubilant theme song, "Happy Days Are Here Again," Milton's biggest hit. I had no notion that the President couldn't walk, that he was a victim of the same dread polio which had kept us away from other children in Central Park. Nor did I know that "Happy Days Are Here Again" was not just Mr. Roosevelt's song, and the rip-roaring anthem of the Democratic Party. It had just become the theme song of the nation's most popular radio program, *Your Lucky Strike Hit Parade*.

I didn't recall my father writing "Happy Days" back in 1929, when I was not yet four. But its success had been so phenomenal that Milton thereafter was forever trying to repeat it by coming up with a variation. All songwriters do this. A hit is such a bonanza, and the secret of its success so mysterious, that self-plagiarism is almost inevitable. Ever since I could remember, my father had been pounding away intermittently on something called "Get That Happy Habit," trying to get it right. "GET that Happy Habit! HAPpy, happy habit! GET that Happy Habit today!" I'd hear him singing and playing in the afternoon when I got home from school. Often I heard him singing it on the telephone to potential, or perhaps recalcitrant, collaborators. "GET yourself a honey! LIFE can be so sunny! BUT you gotta make it that way. . . ." Sometimes he worked on it late at night and I could hear it pounding through the walls. "GET that Happy Habit!" began to haunt my dreams.

I already suspected that our family was unlike anybody else's, and every new thing that happened seemed to confirm my doubts and fears. It was autumn 1935, and fervent political partisanship was sweeping through Lincoln. Children of Democrats flaunted their majority status by sticking Landon buttons onto the soles of their saddle shoes and skating on Alf up and down the terrazzo corridors. As soon as we fifth graders saw older children doing this, we couldn't wait to join in. I figured my parents were Democrats, but that evening, just to be sure, I asked Cecelia, "Which one are you voting for, Roosevelt or Landon?"

"Norman Thomas," she said.

Another astonishment was discovering the work of Anzia Yezierska in a Lincoln textbook. Until then, I'd had the impression she was washed up and had probably never been much good in the first place. Yet here she was in our fourth-grade reader. *Hidden Treasures in Literature* was the latest thing in textbooks, and its two examples of autobiography were by Anzia Yezierska and Mark Twain.

Laurel and I suffered frequent earaches and tonsillitis, and at the least sign of illness Dr. Jules Auerbach appeared at our bedside. This ear, nose, and throat specialist was a kindly German Jewish cyclops whom I never once saw without his round magnifying mirror strapped to his bald forehead. By now he had removed my tonsils and adenoids twice.

On days we had to stay home from school, Laurel and I delighted in answering the phone and writing down messages. Milton's calls came from men trying to arrange golf and bridge games, and occasionally from Ager, Yellen & Bornstein. Cecelia's calls were from press agents, or from Gerry or another of the female pals who accompanied her to the movies. No one left messages for Cecelia *and* Milton.

By now Laurel and I were spending summers in the Adirondacks at Camp Whippoorwill. Camp's uncomfortable all-girl ambience, so different from Lincoln's, drove me continually to compare myself with the other girls, and always to come up lacking. At the beginning of our second Whippoorwill summer, Cecelia and Gerry had set off for Europe newly outfitted by Mr. John, Gerry in a dashing red Three Musketeers hat with a long quill, and Cecelia in a tiny fez made from finely pleated, Roman-striped necktie silk. They returned bearing many wonderful presents, and full of jolly stories about their adventures. Rashly, I said I envied the wonderful times they described in Paris, Vienna, Prague, Budapest.

"Don't you remember?" said Cecelia. "We *begged* you to come with us. But you said no, you'd rather go back to camp." For the life of me I couldn't recall saying such a dumb thing. I disliked camp and would have given anything to travel with Cecelia instead. It was years before it occurred to me that I hadn't said it, that Cecelia had just made it up.

I do retain a kaleidoscope of bright images from that long-ago period. One afternoon Cecelia took me uptown to a Paul Robeson musicale at the mansion off Fifth Avenue owned by the parents of her good friend John Hammond. Tall, handsome, and toothy, with the first crew cut I'd ever seen, John was a renegade Vanderbilt who had fallen in love with Cecelia's writing in *Variety* while still a Yale undergraduate. John was now drama critic of *The New Masses*, a dedicated Communist, and, in his role as jazz expert, impresario, and record producer nonpareil, the man who discovered Billie Holiday, Benny Goodman, Count Basie, Lionel Hampton, and later Bob Dylan, Aretha Franklin, Bruce Springsteen, and many more. Laurel and I knew John as first and foremost among the many charming men who were nuts about our mother. Bill Morris and Jed Harris were others, Jed being a brilliant, charismatic but widely loathed Broadway producer and director — of *Our Town*, *The Crucible*, and a half dozen other theater landmarks — who gave the term *treachery* new dimensions. Laurence Olivier later modeled his Richard III on Jed.

In the music room of the Hammonds' mansion we sat on gold chairs in a chamber draped in gray silk. Many of Robeson's songs were well known to me, but only from my *Sandbag*, one-finger version. Hearing "Mary Wore Three Links of Chain" and "Ezekiel Saw the Wheel" rumbling out in full-throated glory made the occasion the most thrilling moment of my life.

Twist the kaleidoscope and up comes another astonishing memory: I'm sitting on the floor by Cecelia's knee listening to the Duke of Windsor on the radio resigning his throne because he can't go it alone, "without the support and strength of the woman I love." We are both sobbing, albeit for different reasons. For years I have felt close kinship to a famous pair of sisters exactly the ages of Laurel and me — Margaret and the older one, "Lillibet."

Twist again. Our tender-hearted, stumpy-looking Uncle Harry, the Communist math teacher, has come all the way from Brooklyn on the BMT to take us to see *The Three Little Pigs*. Although Cecelia is a movie critic, or perhaps *because* she is, we have never been in a New York movie theater before.

Another twist. After the horrors of a shopping trip with Cecelia for school clothes, we sometimes stop at her favorite tearoom, Mary Eliza-beth's. Waitresses in gray silk with white aprons serve French pastries, after which a woman sits down and reads our tea leaves. How seriously Cecelia seemed to take this mumbo jumbo! Discrimination, fierce and fine-tuned, was the hallmark of her work, of her very nature. Yet all her life she patronized clairvoyants, palmists, and horoscope-casters of the lowest order.

Big twist. Alistair Cooke, not long out of Cambridge, has published *Garbo and the Night Watchmen*, an anthology of the finest film criticism in Britain and the United States, and sent my mother a copy. Among the nine contributors are Graham Greene, Meyer Levin, and Alistair himself. Cecelia is the only female. Here she is on *Modern Times*:

> There used to be a time in pictures, a long time ago, when waifs were running wild. A waif was an unfortunate creature, simple and virtuous and pretty, in rags and with a sunny dispo-sition. Then waifs went out and [so] . . . it's mighty soothing to meet up with Paulette Goddard, a good, old-fashioned waif in *Modern Times*.
>
> It's no cinch to be "a waif" in a Chaplin picture. Chaplin's no skimpy waif himself, but Miss Goddard, peeling off even the black cotton stockings that used to be a waif requisite and skipping about barefoot, submitting to photography in the harsh and revealing sunlight of her many outdoor sequences, whisking around in makeup of no special tenderness, her dark hair realistically lank and unkempt, is nevertheless so cheerful, her beauty and vitality so genuine, her good humor so honest, even though she must realize deep down in her feminine heart that she'd knock 'em dead with her looks in any other kind of pic — she's such a good sport about the whole thing, that she finishes a waif stand-out on her own against the best waif com-petish in the world.

When Cooke arrived back in the U.S. he made a point of inviting each of the American critics to lunch. He was surprised, he told me, to find Cecelia a gentle, reserved woman not given to small talk. What stayed in my memory was the striking contrast between her quiet, almost melancholy manner and the wonderfully cynical brashness of her writing. I had expected a variation on Anita Loos, Dorothy Parker or, at least, Clare Boothe Brokaw (later Luce). They were the female literary gadabouts of the day. By contrast, Cecelia Ager might have been a Mother Superior on her day off.

Early in 1937 things began going wrong. First Milton got sick. A carbuncle appeared high on the side of his face, in front of his ear, dangerous because it put the poison so near his brain. At the same time I was subject to a plague of boils, which were treated in those pre-sulfa days by pouring peroxide into the crater and then swabbing everything with purple stuff. These twice-daily attentions were supervised by a faceless nanny in the hotel bathroom, accompanied by much screaming. I recall one crater on my knee so angry and deep that at the bottom I could see white bone glisten.

We were not just afraid for Milton, who lay all day in bed, his door firmly closed save for doctors and room service waiters tiptoeing in and out. Milton's absence from our daily lives put Cecelia in sole charge of us, and we missed his mitigating, softening presence. Cecelia had no *tenderness*. It was hard to be her daughter. Her texture was cold marble and sandpaper. So on the few times I did touch her — taking her arm in traffic, shaking hands, a cheek-to-cheek greeting after a prolonged separation — it always came as a shock to find her skin so unusually soft and warm.

In the early summer of 1937, our lives in the Salisbury, and in New York, ended with a bang, or, rather, two of them. First, my sore throats not having abated, Dr. Auerbach decided he would have to take out my tonsils a third time. I was recovering in Lenox Hill Hospital when we were told my room was needed for an emergency. Out in the corridor we saw bandaged, blackened people lying on cots — survivors of the *Hindenburg*, which had just exploded in New Jersey.

A few weeks later George Gershwin died "suddenly" in Los Angeles during surgery for a brain tumor. I heard about it when Cecelia brought me for my post-op visit to Dr. Auerbach, and their conversation soon segued into a prolonged discussion of Gershwin's death. They seemingly forgot that I was present, and I watched Cecelia gradually losing her cool as she and Dr. Auerbach discussed the likelihood that, if discovered earlier, the tumor might have been treatable. Gershwin had complained for some time of increasingly severe headaches, she said, and in recent months he had also been horribly depressed, couldn't work, and spent days lying alone in a darkened room. Lee had reprimanded him for drooling at dinner.

For the past few years George had been undergoing psychoanalysis with Dr. Gregory Zilboorg, who had already psychoanalyzed several of Cecelia's friends, including Moss Hart, Lillian Hellman, and Beatrice Kaufman, George Kaufman's elegant, highly literary wife. Dr. Zilboorg was the sole physician who had seen Gershwin during this period, and had always insisted that George's headaches and entire pattern of complaints were imaginary, a result of the neuroses that Zilboorg was treating. He had not considered an organic cause, nor bothered to check for one. The result remains one of the most notorious misdiagnoses of modern times.

By the time I learned he'd died, I had nearly forgotten George Gershwin and his feet under the piano. We had not seen him since the magic apartment went into storage, Milton had stopped talking about him, and I had stopped noticing the hideous portrait in our living room. But I listened to this conversation with growing alarm because even an eleven-year-old recognizes a real-life horror story when she hears one, and also because I had never before seen my ultra-cool mother in such manifest emotional distress.

CHAPTER FOUR

SIMON SAYS, MILTON DOES

How had Cecelia and Milton come to this strange pattern of living: their possessions in storage, their marriage on hold, their family life led only in restaurants? Why the carefully choreographed, bandbox picture of themselves that was all they permitted the world to see? Why insist on maintaining so difficult a juxtaposition — always together yet always apart? It is time to look back and try to trace the different roads that had led each of them to the Hotel Salisbury.

Let us start with Milton, born in Chicago in 1893. His family background is less complicated than Cecelia's. He was the most interesting figure — almost the only interesting figure — to emerge from his large family of otherwise stock characters in the American immigrant saga. The other interesting one was the rascally Simon Ager, who made his son's emergence so difficult. Unlike our Hollywood grandparents, Milton's parents were near strangers to Laurel and me. We never saw Fanny and Simon Ager for more than a day at a time, and sometimes for just a few hours. But you could not get back and forth to California without changing trains in Chicago, and Milton used the occasion to visit his parents. Cecelia often went straight on through, pleading some urgency, but it was clear that the Ager clan bored her, and she did not trouble to hide it.

One of Milton's brothers or sisters met our train, dropped our bags at a fancy, lakefront hotel, and drove us out to our grandparents' modest bungalow on the Near North Side. There the routine never varied. Fanny Ager would be found standing at her kitchen table chopping herring or chicken livers and singing to her canary in a clear, pure soprano. She was small and narrow-shouldered, wore spectacles, and smelled of talcum powder — or was that *me?* Her much older husband, Simon, wore sleeve garters and smelled of strong whiskey, tobacco, and bay rum. He sat stiff and silent in a corner of the little parlor until, one by one, all seven of our aunts and uncles and their spouses and children arrived, and Fanny emerged from the kitchen wiping her hands on her apron.

After a ritual exchange of gifts, and lots of oohing and ahing about how much Laurel and I had grown, the real business of the evening began as Milton's brothers and sisters started retelling the old stories about Pa. How good Pa always was with horses. How he could ride like an Indian. How handsome, swarthy, lean, and vigorous he had been. How shrewd his business sense, how prodigious his physical strength, his courage, sense of humor, and love of whiskey.

Simon must have been near ninety by then, and the round-faced man in spectacles was my Uncle Sam, a fifty-year-old grocer. I couldn't relate these people to the scalawags in the stories. Sam, Sol, and Phil, now sad-eyed and middle-aged, were the three strapping older sons who used to accompany Pa on his road trips. They bragged about how cleverly Pa used to cheat the dumb downstate farmers who bought his horses and mules. All his sons, Milton included, knew Simon's horse-trading tricks: how to temporarily fatten up a skinny old nag by feeding her salt and ginger, how to expand sagging withers with an air pump.

"But it wasn't flesh, it was air! Phony. Like all salesmanship," Milton would tell us afterwards. A born moralist, he had always been revolted by these flimflams. But Pa and his sons were still savoring them a quarter century later, by which time several members of the family were in the used-car business on Chicago's South Side, carrying on the family tradition by selling the gullible good-looking but undependable transportation.

I was content to admire Pa's drooping mustaches, his white hair against his dark skin, and the several charms on his watch chain: an ivory horse head, a Civil War memento of some kind, and three interlocked gold rings that attested to his fifty-year membership in the Odd Fellows Association. When I checked the Odd Fellows records many years later, I found that Simon had been initiated into the James A. Garfield branch in 1885, and could not have been a fifty-year member until some time after his death. But if you are nobody and have to invent yourself, if you arrive in a foreign country as an orphan boy with nothing to your name *but* your name, and you cannot even read or write, you create the persona you don't have. Simon Ager had done a great job of it, and his children all loved to pay him homage.

All of them but Milton, that is. Milton's homage was grudging. Central to Milton's opinion of Simon was that—unlike his adoring mother—his father had never understood him, had not believed in his talents, and had mocked his dreams. Music is no fit career for a *man*, he would sneer at the son he called "Suun."

"Music is for the *frohenszimmer*, for *fegelehs!*"—for women and fairies. The hurt inflicted on the son by the father's brutish ignorance would take a lifetime to heal.

Simon Ager had debarked in Manhattan at age fifteen or thereabouts, shortly before or during the Civil War, by then a professional orphan, and perhaps a real one as well. Simon was perforce a self-invention; it would be uncharitable to call him a phony. Doubtless he half-believed the stories about himself that he became famous for telling with such gusto in Chicago saloons in his middle age. Of medium height but strong and sinewy, with high cheekbones, leathery skin, and long gray mustaches, Simon was the neighborhood's self-appointed defender of Jews against the Irish, who liked to pull the old Jews' beards. His favorite hangout was Ike Novashelsky's barroom, where he offered to wrestle all comers, any weight. Fanny used to send her eldest son down to bring him home before he got too drunk. When that happened, Simon would climb atop two horses and ride them Roman-style through Chicago's Irish wards, holding both sets of reins in one hand, and with the other firing his pistol into the air while shouting, "I'm Simon Ager, King of the Jews! Come out and fight, you Irish bastards!"

To buy or sell a horse, which is what Simon mostly did for a living, a minimum of three drinks was necessary, he used to complain. "A little three-star Hennessy ain't bad once a day. Gives a fellow a little appetite. But you have to drink with a man when you think he needs a horse. And have another drink if he says he'll buy the horse. And then again when he pays for the horse. Always in the saloons. Is it a wonder Ike Novashelsky is getting rich?"

Simon sometimes wore one gold earring and said he was a gypsy. Sometimes he wore a Stetson and said he was a cowboy. Sometimes he said he'd fought in the Civil War. When he was about ninety years old, one of his duties was to take his great-grandchildren to the park. His favorite resting place was a bench reserved for Civil War veterans where he swapped war stories with the other old men.

One day five-year-old Gertrude Ager piped up from under the bench, "But Grandpa, you were never in the Civil War."

"*Niggerel!*" the old man snapped, "I'll never take you to the Park again!"

Simon's stories helped conceal the dearth of information he had about his own identity. He had been born about 1840 somewhere in the mists of Russia. Sometimes he spoke of a town called Volkovysk, on the route of Napoleon's retreat from Moscow, and of a cholera epidemic that had wiped out his parents. With the Czar's henchmen out beating the steppes for cannon fodder for the Crimean War, not even a twelve-year-old could feel safe. Another ever-present danger was the terrifying

Cossack horsemen who swooped down on Jewish settlements during po-
groms. One day, Simon said, he had simply walked away, heading west.

Alone, speaking only Russian and Yiddish, he made his way on foot
across Germany, sleeping in granaries and living on potatoes, until he
reached Bremen, or perhaps Hamburg. From there he caught a ship to
Sheffield, or perhaps Manchester. Safely in England, he found his way
to the home of distant cousins who had something to do with silver man-
ufacturing. He was by then thirteen or fourteen. He remained with them
a couple of years before he was told: If you had a trade, or any sort of
skills, we would send you on to other cousins, skilled people who handle
diamonds and precious metals in Johannesburg. But since you have no
skills, and can barely speak English, here is fifteen pounds and a steerage
ticket to America.

Simon later said that he had lost the money in a shipboard card
game and had landed in Manhattan with nothing to his name *but* his
name, and that this name was, in full, Simon Ager. He had no middle
names, and no immigration inspector had tampered with the spelling.
Simon Ager it was, and that was the all of it. Finally, Simon maintained
that the name Ager had no meaning beyond itself. It did not denote a
place, like Ginsberg, or a race, like Levy, or an occupation, like Schnei-
der or Magidson, or a biblical figure, like Abrahams or Isaacson. Ager is
just Ager, and there are not many around. All his life Simon searched
for other Agers, Jewish or non-Jewish. All my life I have done the same.

No one who knew him would ever suggest that my grandfather's
middle name was veracity. That he was so dead certain about his own
name was another aspect of his somewhat ad lib identity. He spoke a
peculiar patois of his own invention, part English, part Yiddish, liberally
sprinkled with German, Russian, and Polish words, and others of his
own coinage. The loaded sidearm that he always carried was his "smitty
westrun." His term for jam or jelly was "smully." Nobody knew why.

As his ship approached Manhattan, Simon told his children, he saw
a group of bearded men in wide black hats waiting on the docks. They
wore long, black, fur-collared coats, and each had a yellow tape measure
hanging around his neck. As Simon came down the gangplank, one of

the black-clad men questioned him in Yiddish. Having confirmed that the youth was alone, he ordered Simon to turn around, and measured his back with the tape measure. He strapped on a twenty-pound pack filled with needles, pins, tobacco, thread, and other sundries.

"Go sell these things. Bring the money back to me." He gave Simon a little push, and told him to walk south.

The roads were crowded with demobbed soldiers returning home and newly freed slaves making their way north. Using only sign language at first, Simon managed to sell his wares to the rabble along the roads. By the time he returned to the docks a few months later with his empty pack, he had increased his smattering of English, and his skinny frame had begun to fill out. A black-hatted figure measured his shoulders again, and this time gave him a twenty-five-pound pack. The men with the tape measures, Simon eventually learned, were prosperous German Jewish merchants with names like Hecht, Saks, Gimbel, and Horner, the founders of America's first department stores. As pious Hebrew elders, they were now discharging their charitable obligations by giving work to penniless arrivals from Russia and Eastern Europe, and staking them to modest amounts of wholesale dry goods they could not otherwise have afforded to buy.

By Simon's third trek, his shoulders had broadened sufficiently to enable him to carry thirty-five pounds, and he had devised several sly tricks to cheat his wretched clientele. He sold thread by the yard, instead of by the spool, measuring it off in time-honored fashion from the tip of his nose to the tips of his outstretched fingers. He sold needles and pins individually when he could. His most lucrative self-invented product was the cayenne pepper in small packets which he sold to sparsely bearded black men. They could have mustaches as luxuriant as his own, he assured them, by dabbing the cayenne on their upper lips at bedtime. The hair would become so thirsty during the night it would have to come out for a drink.

Simon walked when he had to, and traveled on the rivers when possible. He went back and forth several times to Georgia and Alabama, and once got as far as New Orleans. Wherever he went, he searched for other Agers. He found only one family, in Pine Bluff, Arkansas, and when they roasted a suckling pig to celebrate their newly discovered kinship, he ate it.

In Vincennes, Indiana, Adam Gimbel's father hired Simon and he tried to settle down. He decided there was easier money in burying people than in selling them things, and set up as a mortician. But it was depressing to hustle bereaved families, and he didn't know embalming techniques. Soon he was dealing in horses, which seemed to come naturally to him. But the community was too small, and Simon went on to Chicago. Here he worked for Henry Horner until it occurred to him: *Why give fifty percent to Horner?* He would go into business for himself.

To build up a stake to buy a livery stable, Simon bought a horse and wagon on credit, loaded it with cheap merchandise, and drove it south. He learned to arrive at the cotton plantations at dusk, just as the workers were coming in from the fields. The first thing he did at each stop was hire the four biggest men in the crowd and station them at the four corners of his wagon with flaming torches so heavy it took two hands to hold them aloft.

"So people could see the goods?" little Milton had once asked his father.

"No, stupid. So they couldn't *steal* them! They were all *gonovum*." *Gonovum* is the plural of *gonif*—thief.

If a sheriff came by and demanded to see his peddling license, Simon always handed over a bill of lading or other scrap of paper. Simon couldn't read it, but he knew that most likely the southern sheriff couldn't read it either.

At some point he acquired a wife who kept a boardinghouse, either in Vincennes or perhaps, by then, Chicago. He was definitely in Chicago by 1871, the year of the Great Chicago Fire. Although his livery stable burned down, Simon had a very good year renting horses to the Fire Department.

Itinerant peddlers ranged throughout the midwestern and southern states, and not every wandering Jew could get home on Friday night in time for the Sabbath. Whoever was next heading north carried messages for the others: Tell my wife I'll be home in two more Fridays, or three. Once Simon arrived home unexpectedly and discovered his wife in bed with a boarder. That ended his first marriage.

In 1876, by which time he was close to forty and the coproprietor of a livery stable on Halstead Street with an Irish partner, Harry McNair, Simon Ager married seventeen-year-old Fanny Nathan, my grandmother. Fanny had been born in Poland, and acquired some education at the University in Königsberg, East Prussia. She could speak and read English, German, Yiddish, and even Hebrew, which she learned from her father, a professional wise man variously known as Nissen Magidson, Nissen the Bookbinder, and Nathan Nathan. When the family arrived in Chicago, sixteen-year-old Fanny was put to work at a sweatshop sewing machine.

Nathan Nathan and his wife, Shana Gittel, were Orthodox Jews, and the parents of five children. But when the aging patriarch proclaimed himself so devout that he intended to die in Israel, Shana Gittel refused to accompany him. "I love my children more than God," she said, and moved in with her daughter Fanny, the only one of her children who would have her, bringing along her featherbed, her two sets of kosher dishes, and the wig that covered her pious shaven head.

"Was your grandfather educated?" I once asked Milton.

"He knew Karl Marx backwards — personally," was his contemptuous reply. Milton did not so much disapprove of the old man's socialist politics as he despised him for abandoning his wife and children in the name of God.

Fanny Ager had a sweet, fluting voice and always sang as she worked. She prepared different favorite foods for each of the eleven people in the household. She sewed so well that she not only made everybody's clothes, she made the curtains, the carpets, the upholstery. She knitted the socks and gloves, and even brewed the Passover wine.

It was easy to see why Simon married her. "But why did you marry *him?*" little Milton asked Fanny over and over, unable to understand what his sweet and refined little mother was doing with the coarse and brutal, much older man who was his father. At home, Simon carried a loaded revolver, and when he came home drunk and began shouting at Fanny, the children grouped around their mother for protection. "He didn't endear himself to me by that," Milton once dryly observed.

Each time Simon left to go back on the road, Milton asked his beloved mother the question again: How could she have married such a person?

"He brought me *Imberlach*," she always replied.

Imberlach is candied apricots.

Fanny bore Simon eleven children, of whom eight survived infancy. Little Moses, the fifth, was small and sickly, and his father and brothers called him the runt of the litter. Croup and diphtheria kept him at home with his mother until the age of seven. When he was finally well enough to go to school, his older sister Ann, who spoke the best English, took him to the famed kindergarten at Hull House, the Chicago settlement house founded by Jane Addams.

He looked about four. "Chase the sunbeam!" said a teacher, flashing a hand mirror around the classroom.

"Whaddya mean, *chase the sunbeam?*" he cried. "I'm seven years old! I can *read.*" Astonished, the teacher asked him his name. Heretofore he had been Moishke, more formally Moses.

"Milton Lionel Ager," he was amazed to hear his proud sister, who had just made the name up, reply.

Milton's mother and sisters adored him. Their favorite family stories were all about sweet-natured, talented little Moishke. When a doctor finished lancing his boils while the women held him down on the kitchen table, he sat up, stopped crying, and said, "Thank you, doctor."

Fanny would do anything to please her son. When he read about yachting in *Scientific American* and asked his mother to make him a yacht, she built one from three two-by-fours, a pair of skates, and a piece of canvas. The little boy was amazed that it never moved.

As small boys, Milton and his brothers worked in summer for a *gonif* uncle hawking peanuts on the Lake Michigan excursion boats. "Eat all you want," said the uncle. "But remember to put the shells back in the bags."

When Milton was nine or ten, Ann, a department store clerk, was promoted to store detective and immediately put down some money on a secondhand piano. "She wanted to bring some culture into the household." Ann hired a teacher for ten cents a lesson, and soon Milton was playing better than his sister. "I learned to play by listening."

Pa came home from the road, saw his son at a piano, and became enraged. Music was not a fit career for a man, he stormed. "*Shtay avek!* Be a lawyer, a doctor. Music is for *fegelehs*."

When these tirades began, Fanny quickly ducked behind her husband and winked her left eye, signaling, "Don't argue with your father."

It was a household where everybody worked. The girls started out at eleven or twelve wrapping purchases after school for Mr. Netcher, owner of the Boston Store. The big boys helped Simon on the road or in the stable. Pa sometimes took Milton's younger sisters to one of the Jewish music halls, left them inside, and went to a bar. "Simon didn't understand English too well. Going home one night, a fellow asked him what time it was, and Pa socked him in the jaw and knocked him down. He thought he was gonna bother the children."

Whenever Simon left, Milton again pestered Fanny. Did she really marry this man just because he brought her candy?

"I don't know if I can explain," she'd say. "I was lonesome. He was good-looking. A tall man, piercing eyes, big mustaches. . . . So he would *court* me and . . . well . . . well. . . . It's a woman's nature to want to get married!"

"But Pa was a natural wit, and they all adored him," Milton used to tell me. "I wasn't too impressed. I was going to other homes, where they had more culture. Ours was pretty low-down. I didn't really understand him until I had two children and began to know what a man's life was like. The job was to protect the females. Once they were married off, the trouble was over."

By the end of Milton's first year in high school, he had found a night job playing piano in silent movies for $15 a week, which he turned over to his mother. "I couldn't stand seeing everybody working and contributing nothing myself." Though he couldn't read music, "I knew the popular songs, so I would fake it. If I saw Indians, I'd play Indian music. If it was a love scene, 'Hearts and Flowers.'"

That summer Fanny found her son an $18 a week job at White City, a small amusement park with a little outdoor theater and a pitchman out front. Milton played the pitch, went inside and played the performance, ate the lunch Fanny had packed, and played a second show. On Saturday night, payday, "the ghost walks" as the expression went, and Milton asked for his money.

"Sorry, son, I'll have to pay you Monday."

"No. My mother won't understand."

"Tell your mother I had to pay the soubrette."

"No. I have to bring the money home. She's given me lunch and carfare. She won't understand."

"Tell her the soubrette's *pregnant*. She'll understand that!"

Milton loved to reminisce. But life as one of eight children living over a livery stable with an Orthodox granny, a gun-waving father, and a constant stream of uncles and cousins and half-brothers wandering in and out was unimaginable to me.

"What did Pa eat for breakfast?" I once asked my father in an attempt to fill out my mental picture of his boyhood.

"A potato from the barrel, a herring out of the brine, and a shot of bourbon," he replied, looking at me as if I must have come from another planet.

At fifteen Milton met red-haired Rayna Simons, a passionate, brilliant girl a couple of years older than he who came from a wealthy and cultivated family on the other side of town. Milton told her he wanted to become a songwriter, and Rayna brought him home to her parents' library, gave him some books on musical notation, and offered him the use of the family music room and grand piano. By the time Rayna graduated, Milton had taught himself to read and write music, and the kindly

Simonses, who had no sons of their own, had grown very fond of the uncommonly quick and eager youth.

Throughout his high school years Milton spent far more time with the Simonses than with the Agers, studying music and gradually reading his way through their library. Each weekend they brought him out to their country farm, always with a load of books under his arm, and he caught the electric train back to town barely in time for his first class. Slowly he taught himself to read Latin and Greek, and worked his way through the major philosophers, as well as the writings of the great composers, scientists, and political theorists. In retrospect, Milton appears to have preinvented Mortimer Adler's famed University of Chicago course on the one hundred Great Books of Western Civilization, and self-administered it from the Simonses' library. By the time his studies ended, he had formulated his own answers to the great ethical questions that have preoccupied mankind, and would stubbornly stick by them for life.

Milton was also writing songs. Though he later disparaged these early efforts as "juvenilia," not worth talking about, he knew enough to copyright them. His first two copyrights, "Say, Kid, Let's Become a Pair" and "When Two Lovin' Arms Are around You," were registered in 1910, his junior year at McKinley High School.

Rayna was by now a student leader and political firebrand at the University of Illinois, and Milton was very much in love with her. She must have loved him too, because I have a clear memory of the fine gold signet ring she gave him that he kept in his stud box but never wore.

Their romance was doomed from the start, however; Milton had no money and scant prospects. One day nice Mr. Simons tried to ease the pain in his heart by telling Milton that what he felt for Rayna was "only puppy love," and assuring him he would soon get over it. Milton felt mocked and deeply aggrieved. His revered patron seemed to be rubbing salt into his wounds.

High school graduation was still several months off, and he was due to receive a valuable financial prize for the humor column he wrote for the school paper. But after his talk with Mr. Simons, Milton completed his classwork in a rush, left town, and spent the next nine months traveling the Orpheum circuit as a vaudeville pianist and accompanist for Gene Greene, the early scat singer who popularized "Melancholy Baby." He didn't even come back to Chicago for graduation. And he never saw Rayna again.

Did he, I have often wondered, see the lengthy and unusual obituary of Rayna that was printed in *The New York Times* of November 22, 1927? Surely he must have; it filled a quarter page. Datelined Moscow, it began:

> Newspaper reporters become cynical — professionally. One sees too much of politics and of human nature spurred by ambition and greed. But occasionally there is an exception — reckless, self-sacrificing, whole-heartedly devoted to some cause, like the American, John Reed, whose body lies in Moscow under the Kremlin wall.
>
> An American, Rayna Prohme, who died here this morning [of encephalitis, at thirty-four] belonged to that small, rare group. . . .
>
> Five years she has devoted herself to the cause of the Chinese revolution . . . [but] that is only a bare part of the truth. Rayna Prohme, although not a member of the Communist Party, had given her whole being to the Chinese revolution. When the revolution failed, she accompanied Mme. Sun Yat-sen to Moscow. . . .

In fact, Rayna had done much more than "accompany" Mme. Sun. She had smuggled her out of Hangchow in the middle of a civil war, and escorted her on a dangerous two-thousand-mile journey across Asia. She also smuggled out Mme. Borodin, wife of the Bolshevik adviser and foreign minister to the Chinese government. Rayna by then was working for the Soviets as a paid secret agent. Her lover at the time was the world-famous foreign correspondent Vincent Sheean, who described her as

> slight, not very tall, with short red-gold hair and a frivolous turned-up nose. Her eyes . . . could actually change colour

with the changes of light, or even with changes of mood. Her voice, fresh, cool and very American, sounded as if it had secret rivulets of laughter running underneath it all the time, ready to come to the surface without warning. [Her laughter] was the gayest, most unselfconscious sound in the world. You might have thought that it did not come from a person at all, but from some impulse of gaiety in the air. . . . Her sincerity floated over her like a banner.

Like Rayna's first husband, the playwright Samson Raphaelson, Sheean was from Chicago, and Milton knew both men. How well? Again, I'm not sure. But when I was a girl, my father spoke to me of Rayna so often and so tenderly that I began to wonder if her name might not have been a little bit in his mind when he and Cecelia chose to name me Shana.

When Milton returned to Chicago in 1911 from his stint in vaudeville, he took a job playing piano in the State Street display window of Waterson, Berlin, and Snyder, music publishers. All the big publishers maintained a Chicago branch office laid out like the main office in New York. Out front was a demonstrator/pianist and a counter with salesmen. Wall racks displayed sheet music for sale to the public at ten cents a copy. Popular hits were reprinted and might stay in the racks for months, even years. Songs that didn't catch on were swiftly replaced by new ones picked by the publishers' "professional managers" from the offerings of dozens of hungry would-be songwriters clamoring and scheming to get their work heard. Established writers were put under exclusive contract. Each major publisher maintained a stable of ten or twelve of these, and a sufficiency of tireless, sight-reading pianists to demonstrate their work.

In the back of the store was a row of cubicles containing pianos where demonstrators and song pluggers played the firm's new tunes for professionals — live performers in vaudeville and burlesque out trolling for new material. If a new tune pleased them, they received a free "professional copy," one without the expensive, colorful artwork on the cover. If a bigtime artist walked in, staff arrangers were on hand to tailor the tune to the performer's special needs, or limitations.

Publishers paid themselves five cents on every copy sold, awarded the writers a one-cent royalty, often split among several writers, and used the rest to run the business. A single song that "hit" with the public reaped enough profit to underwrite the whole circus and make the publishers rich.

Tin Pan Alley had always been controlled by the publishers, inclined to be rapacious types even in the days of Stephen Foster. (Foster was one of many nineteenth-century songwriters who died broke.) In the first decade of the twentieth century, the Alley had begun moving uptown from 28th Street to the Forties near Broadway, and Henry Waterson, who had struck it rich in the jewelry business, began moving in on the music business. Eventually he would put together the Alley's first conglomerate of writer-publishers, sheet music stores, and a record company. He began by hooking up with Ted Snyder, a young composer who, like Milton, was facile at setting someone else's tune down on paper, or cranking out a serviceable new tune to fit another man's lyrics. Snyder then approached a singing waiter at Nigger Mike's Bowery café who had begun making a name for himself by writing his own material, mainly parodies and risqué lyrics. This was Irving Berlin, who came to work for Waterson and Snyder, Inc., in 1909 as a $25 a week contract lyricist. In the next couple of years, working mostly with Snyder, but also alone and with others, the slender, dynamic genius of American music had written nearly all the firm's big moneymakers, including both words and music for the Alley's greatest worldwide hit, "Alexander's Ragtime Band." By December 1911, Waterson felt forced to make Berlin a partner or lose him, and only weeks later, Milton Ager walked into the firm's Chicago office looking for work.

Talented, hardworking, and ambitious, Milton soon was made a staff arranger. Experienced writers passing through Chicago told him New York was the place a songwriter needed to be to break in, and as soon as he'd saved up three hundred dollars from his nocturnal piano playing, he asked for a transfer. Before he left town, the illiterate Simon Ager gave Milton a parting word of advice: "Remember, Suun, don't sign anything!"

The timing of Milton's move was propitious. In 1912 the music business already was changing fast. Within a decade it would explode in ways yet unforeseen. Mass-manufacturing of pianos in the United States had begun shortly after the Civil War. By 1910, an astonishing number of U.S. homes had a piano in the parlor. "The mothers forced the daughters to learn how to play," as Milton put it, "because music was a sign of culture. Most were taught to play the piano, because a violin had to be put under the chin, and you had to have a big dress on to play the cello."

In the cities, vaudeville and burlesque, dance halls and cabarets were the sole forms of mass entertainment, and catchy new songs and parodies were in constant demand. A single big hit could earn thousands of dollars for its writers, hundreds of thousands for its publishers. Most publishers were sharp businessmen who had jumped into the burgeoning new business looking for a fast buck; very few knew anything about music. Milton's boss, Henry Waterson, a former Pennsylvania diamond dealer, was almost totally deaf. His next boss, Leo Feist, had been a corset salesman. The third biggest publisher, and George Gershwin's first boss, was Jerome H. Remick, a former Detroit dairy owner. A rare exception among publishers was courtly Max Dreyfus at T. B. Harms. A onetime pianist and arranger, Dreyfus knew the business, had taste, and eventually would have nearly all the top-flight writers under exclusive contract, particularly writers of light opera and musical comedy. Dreyfus had early seen the wisdom of backing their shows in return for the exclusive right to publish their scores. Starting with Romberg, Friml, and Victor Herbert, he soon signed Kern and Gershwin and Vincent Youmans, and eventually the young Cole Porter and Richard Rodgers. Kern signed on because he saw a silk hat in the office and figured Harms must be a classy outfit. Later he learned that Dreyfus wore the hat to play for Jewish weddings.

* * *

"The Plugger is one of the darlings of Tin Pan Alley," writes Isaac Goldberg in his pioneering 1930 work, *Tin Pan Alley*.

> He it is who, by all the arts of persuasion, intrigue, bribery, mayhem, malfeasance, cajolery, entreaty, threat, insinuation, persistence and whatever else he has, sees to it that his employer's music shall be heard. . . . Scorn not the humble plugger, for in his modest quarters once labored a Max Dreyfus, a Jerome Kern, a George Gershwin, a Dick Rodgers, a Vincent Youmans.

And a Milton Ager. In 1912 the diminutive eighteen-year-old pianist and would-be composer moved into a $6 a week boardinghouse room on West 91st Street, and rented himself a small upright. His salary at WBS was $35 a week, and by 1914 his modest savings were gone, despite occasional one-night nightclub gigs filling in for the regular pianist. One day his boss said, "Milton, you're so pale! What do you do — take dope?"

"No. I *starve*."

Then Milton ran into Wolfie Gilbert, a kindly lyricist he knew from Chicago who had just scored his own first hit with "Waiting for the Robert E. Lee."

Milton confessed he was "literally starving" and Wolfie said, "Well, can you *write*?" meaning write *words*.

"Certainly I can write!"

"Then write some parodies and take 'em over to Jean Bedini."

Bedini, a former vaudevillian, had recently become a burlesque producer, and since burlesque comics could not survive without a constant fresh fodder of topical material, Bedini sold it to them as a sideline.

Milton swiftly scribbled a parody of the sentimental smash hit "M-O-T-H-E-R" and brought it over to Bedini's burlesque.

> *F is for the fist with which he hit me.*
> *A is for the anger with each sock.*

T is for the teeth with which he bit me.
H is for the heart as hard as rock.
E is for the egg upon his mustache.
R's for right, and right he's never been.
Put them all together, they spell FATHER,
A man who smells of beer and gin.

The three dollars Milton received for writing this marked the beginning of his career as a professional songwriter. He remained four more years at WBS pounding out other people's new songs in a tiny cubicle, and doing more of the same at night in honky-tonks and cabarets. He was writing tunes on the side, and learning his way around the fast-buck, hokeypokey world of Tin Pan Alley. Old Man Waterson was willing to publish a few of Milton's tunes, but refused to pay him a cent. Essential to success was finding the right experienced lyricist, and then persuading him to collaborate with an unknown, untested kid. Meanwhile he continued working all day and most of the night for thirty-five dollars a week. The morning he came in at ten A.M., after getting home at two A.M. from a plugging assignment in Coney Island, Mr. Waterson reprimanded him and installed Tin Pan Alley's first time clock.

The same year that Milton earned his first $3, Victor Herbert happened to walk into Shanley's Restaurant and hear the orchestra playing selections from his current hit, "Blossom Time." The Dublin-born Herbert, a larger-than-life figure, composed two grand operas and forty-five comic operas in a mere thirty years, at one point writing four operettas simultaneously at four different desks. Milton was scarcely in his class, musically or financially, but they shared certain moral attitudes, among them a strong distaste for being taken advantage of. At the time, songwriters and publishers earned royalties on their copyrights only from sheet music sales. Shanley's was an extremely popular place, and that evening it occurred to the composer and his companion, the brilliant attorney Nathan Burkan, that Shanley's was making a lot of money out of Herbert's unpaid contribution to the success of the establishment, and that he was probably entitled to a share of it.

Herbert and Burkan founded an organization called ASCAP—
American Society of Composers Authors and Publishers—for the purpose of bringing a series of lawsuits to legitimate their premise. They lost
in the lower courts, but finally won a unanimous decision in the U.S.
Supreme Court which established the epochal legal principle that the
public performance of music for profit—whether in theaters, cabarets,
vaudeville, or dance halls, and later in radio, records, and movies—
entitled the music's creators to a share of that profit. ASCAP became
the nonprofit, performing rights society which collected the monies,
called "the melon," and divided them among writers and publishers
according to a complex series of point systems, changed over the years
as ASCAP attempted to balance the value of a member's current
performances against the value of his hardy perennials, known as
"standards."

Many more legal battles had to be fought over a period of years to
make the Supreme Court's decision workable. In time, however, hotels,
roller rinks and even supermarkets signed up for a license to use music
by ASCAP members, paying an annual fee based on the number of seats
or paying customers. In 1921 ASCAP had 163 members and earned
$80,000; the next year, the figure had passed the $200,000 mark. Movies
became licensees in 1924, radio in 1930. By 1962 ASCAP was grossing
over $35 million from 40,000 licensees, and represented 7,000 compos-
ers and lyricists as well as more than 2,000 publishers. Today 65,000
writer/publisher members divide close to $100 million according to
complex, arcane, near-indecipherable rules. Milton joined ASCAP
in 1919, the year after he wrote his first hit, and soon was ranked an
AA composer, the highest rating available. In the 1920s and 1930s,
AA was probably worth somewhere between $50,000 and $75,000 a
year.

Like the early publishers, many early songwriters were musical
Flintstones. As Milton saw it, "They were fakes! They couldn't *read* mu-

sic, they could just write it!" Irving Berlin, a born genius with no training whatsoever who played on the black keys only, saw the matter somewhat differently. "The black keys are right there under your fingers," he once remarked, adding with some derision, "the key of C is for people who study music."

Milton was assuredly one of these, having mastered the principles of theory and composition, arranging and orchestration back in the Simonses' library. "It was simple," he used to tell me. "Put the harmony in the first chorus. Don't get the horns too low, or they'll sound like four pregnant cows."

Milton considered Berlin the greatest American songwriter who ever lived, and often tried to teach him the craft of arranging. But Berlin always refused. "Because if I learn *this*," he told Milton, "it's apt to take my mind off putting words and music together."

"He was right," Milton always added. "But because he couldn't read, he couldn't put it down. So he had to get another fellow to make a lead sheet. And *another* fellow would have to make the piano copy. And still *another* had to make the orchestration."

Melody came naturally to Milton, and making orchestrations was what he loved doing most. He could also read and play anything at sight and readily transpose into whatever key best suited a singer's range, qualities that made him ideally suited for his chosen profession. On the other hand, he was unusually idealistic, dangerously puritanical, inept at negotiation and compromise, and repelled from the start by the lowdown business practices of the mushrooming popular music industry. Tin Pan Alley, he was slowly discovering, was the secondhand horse business writ large.

Another of Milton's assets was an excellent sense of rhythm. Many years later the composer Charles Strouse characterized Ager's music as having "a very strong feeling for the two-beat, for the floor. The equivalent today is when somebody writes a real rock song."

Ian Whitcomb, the young British bandleader, writer, and Tin Pan Alley authority, has termed Milton "the Compleat Songwriter," meaning that he was "fully rounded . . . a real journeyman who, like Berlin, could turn his experienced hand to all the song-types of the Alley — ragtime, comedy, sob-ballad, Dixie celebration, novelty, blues — and write for the market."

Whitcomb also makes the important point, with which I believe Milton would agree, that "it is difficult to divorce music from words. These songs are little gems, and you can't really take them apart without losing their value — which is largely emotional."

Third, Milton had persistence, taste, and the ability to recognize talent. The first man he persuaded to collaborate with him, in 1913, was a composer-pianist and Pullman porter, Spencer Williams. Two years later, Williams's career took off with "I Ain't Got Nobody," followed by such jazz classics as "Basin Street Blues," "Everybody Loves My Baby," and "I Found a New Baby." Milton and Williams remained friends until Williams left the country in 1925 to accompany Josephine Baker to Paris, write all Baker's Follies Bergère numbers for a decade, and become the pianist at Bricktop's. Williams evolved into a kind of black Pied Piper, introducing American jazz and blues all over Europe and the French colonies of Africa. His work in Morocco inspired the Dooley Wilson character in *Casablanca*.

Finally, Milton was an innovator. The standard popular song was 32 measures: two 8-bar phrases, an 8-bar middle, and a final 8 bars plus a verse. "It stretched over the piano like a tapeworm," Milton used to say, and he wrote numerous variations on the formula. "I never count measures when I'm writing. It's what sounds natural to your ear. 'Happy Days Are Here Again' has fifty-six measures. 'Stormy Weather' has ten-measure phrases. 'I'll Get By' has six. There was a French song, 'Speak to Me of Love,' written in five-measure phrases. Don't ask me why. It's hard enough to speak of love in eight-measure phrases. Maybe it was French love."

From earliest childhood I remember Milton trying to explain the fundamentals of music to me. It was always hopeless. "All music is divided into duple time, which is 2/4, or 4/8, or you could have split time in the bass, for example," he would say. I had no idea what he was talking about, but I loved him, so I would listen attentively, faking comprehension. "Then there's triple time: 3/8, 6/8, 9/8, and 12/8. Of course, 6/8 is also 3/4." I would feel my eyelids closing. "One, two, three . . . one, two, three . . . one, two . . ."

He would usually mention Zez Confrey, a highly skilled Chicago pianist and bandleader who wrote "Stumbling," "Kitten on the Keys," and many other pianistically tricky works. He'd mention Gershwin's "Fascinatin' Rhythm," and his own tune for Sophie Tucker, "He's a Good Man to Have Around."

"All these were new rhythmic concepts," he would explain. "The most fully underappreciated group in the music business is the arrangers. Every arranger is a potential composer, because the arranger has to take a melody and make configurations. Distribute the harmony. Make it fall under the fingers. These things don't come from the heads of composers, you know. At least, not in this country. Tchaikovsky used 5/4 time in his Sixth Symphony. Delius used cross-rhythms in *Brigg Fair*. César Franck in his D Minor Symphony, last movement, used syncopation in 4/4 time." By this time, I was always fast asleep.

Milton was a born teacher, and the next day he would start trying to explain music to me again. It drove me wild that I loved my father more than anyone in the world, and yet whenever he talked about music and harmonics and all the other things *he* loved, I could never follow what he was saying, never *hear it*. So I lied. I pretended I could hear all the overtones he heard when he struck middle C. I pretended I liked the compulsory Saturday morning Young People's Concerts Laurel and I attended at Carnegie Hall. I pretended I understood duple time. Such deception seemed to come naturally to me. Perhaps it was in my blood.

Milton knew it was time to leave WBS and try freelancing, but he was crazy about one of the contract lyricists, Grant Clarke, and had been following the older man around for years trying without success to get his attention. A lanky, blue-eyed Christian Scientist from the Midwest, Clarke's attention was focused much of the time on alcohol, and occasionally opium, substances in which Milton lacked both interest and experience. What he wanted from Clarke was a *title*, but it took two years of trailing Clarke from saloon to saloon before he got one.

Trailing Clarke, Milton got to know his pal Wilson Mizener, and the gambler and bon vivant was so taken by Milton's air of innocence that for a time he used him as a shill in his gambling parlor, staking him to play all night if he cared to, at house expense. Despite Milton's repugnance for high-stakes gambling, probably acquired at his father's knee, he continued to hang around Mizener's casino because it was a good place to rub shoulders with the top showbiz lowlifes, the high Broadway demimonde, the people Milton needed to know if he was going to make it big on Tin Pan Alley.

Milton was after Clarkie because "ideas, song titles, and singable words came to him so easily. Example: "He's a high-falutin', tootin', shootin' son-of-a-gun from Arizona, Ragtime Cowboy Joe," which swept the country in 1912. Milton was also captivated by what he referred to as "Clarkie's clippity meter."

When he at last succeeded in attracting the lyricist's attention, he cried out in frustration, "Grant! Why do you *drink* so much?"

"To make my friends interesting," Clarke coolly replied.

One evening while Milton was stalking Clarke, Mizener showed up at his casino with a stunning women on each arm, one of them black and the other seemingly a gypsy. "Milton, I'd like you to meet my wives," Mizener said. "This is Grace Washington, she cooks my food. And this is Guinea Grace. She cooks my opium."

All the while, Milton was continuing to study harmony, counterpoint, orchestration, and so on. But his "real" teachers were his heroes Frank Sadler, Maurice B. DePackh, Arthur Lang, and Frank Skinner — the orchestrators who made the dance and show arrangements.

"They all particularly liked to score for Berlin. The melodies were simple, so they could use the classical devices of orchestration. But a fellow like George Gershwin, who was basically a pianist, had so many notes, they couldn't use their devices on his stuff."

Me: What devices?

"The flute configuration over the melody. The clarinet doing the same thing underneath. The bassoon under that. It goes back to Mozart. But it's very monotonous to write vertical harmony. So they were doing horizontal harmony."

While working as an arranger, Milton in his spare time was composing his own tunes and searching for a lyricist to work with until he was able to attract Clarke's attention. One early effort, with Howard Johnson, was "China (Way Out in Asia Minor)," changed to "China (We Owe a Lot to You)" after Johnson developed a surer sense of geography, as well as rhyme.

Milton often contributed title ideas himself. Another member of the WBS stable was William K. Jerome, a seventy-year-old Irish lyricist, writer of "Chinatown, My Chinatown," with whom Milton had recently written "Erin Is Calling." At their next meeting at Shanley's, a songwriters' hangout, Milton threw out his latest idea: "Why be afraid of a maid who's made of a shade of brown?"

"Where'd you get that?" said the old Irishman, instantly suspicious.

"Gauguin," said Milton.

"Don't read Gauguin," said George M. Cohan, who was seated farther down the bar. "Read Irving Berlin."

Unlike most established songwriters, Cohan was generous to younger men; Milton was one of many whom he tried to help. But Milton refused help. He was fixed like a truffle hound on Clarke. Buried treasure lay there, he knew; the problem was unearthing it. He was still living in his $6 room and spending many nights in Harlem jazz joints admiring the musicianship and inventiveness of the players. But he rarely joined in the fun. "I was a very straitlaced little fellow. I didn't drink or smoke until I was twenty-five. Grant put me off both."

Regardless of distractions, Milton kept writing. Tunes bubbled out of him without effort, and every few weeks he augmented his eating money by making a few freelance arrangements. His friend George Gershwin suggested Milton pick up an extra twenty-five dollars by making a piano roll, and brought him along to the Aeolian Piano Company in New Jersey. But Milton hated the work. "It took about a minute and a half to play a verse and two choruses, then *four hours* to make the corrections!" The rolls were cut electrically, and each wrong note made a tiny hole in the paper that the pianist had to glue up afterwards.

"George, this isn't for me," Milton said. "In the first place, I can't stand my own mistakes. And second, there's not enough money in it." Gershwin was still primarily a pianist at the time, studying seriously with Charles Hambitzer, whereas Milton burned to write songs.

Song subjects run in cycles. People were moving from the farms to the big cities, and many of Milton's early songs were about longing to go back home to Alabama, Indiana, Tennessee, Arkansas, Maryland, and "Carolina." In others, he pined for his Irish mother, his Jewish mother, his Italian mother, his darkie mother. Timeliness was everything on Tin Pan Alley, and every twist in national life was instantly reflected in the popular music of the day. Milton's World War I songs include "France, We Have Not Forgotten You" and "Tom, Dick, Harry, and Jack, Hurry Back."

"Who's Jack?" I once asked him.

Milton threw me one of his bleak looks. "The lyricist couldn't find a rhyme for Harry."

The advent of Prohibition inspired "(After the Country Goes Dry) Goodbye, Wild Women, Goodbye," "In the Sweet Dry and Dry," and the best of them, "It's the Smart Little Feller Who Stocked Up His Cellar That's Getting the Beautiful Girls" with a lyric by Grant Clarke.

Clarke moved from WBS to an even bigger publisher, Leo Feist, Inc., and Milton followed him. He kept pressuring Clarke for a title, and finally the older man said: "All right, kid. Take this title home and see what you can do with it: 'Everything Is Peaches down in Georgia.'"

Milton wrote a tune and played it for Clarke, who said, "Pretty good, kid! I'll finish it one of these days."

It was 1917, and pressure was building on President Wilson to commit the United States to join Britain and France in World War I. Grant Clarke immediately responded with "There'll Be a Hot Time for the Old Men When the Young Men Go to War," a homage to the 1896 minstrel show classic "There'll Be a Hot Time in the Old Town To-night."

Events were moving fast: war was declared in April, and by June we had 1,390,000 men in France. In this frenzied atmosphere, someone in Washington decided Clarke's song might encourage young men to dodge the draft, conceivably even to desert. The song was banned and copies removed from the stores. (U.S. authorities lacked the insouciance of censors in Britain, where a popular song parody of the period was "If You Were the Only Bosche in the Trench, and I Had the Only Bomb.")

At some point between April and June, the lyricist Irving Caesar walked into the offices of Leo Feist and placed a lead sheet on Milton's piano. Its title was "Won't There Be a Hot Time for the Old Men When the Young Men Go to War?"

"Irving," said Milton, "are you aware that our firm has already published a song called 'There'll *Be* a Hot Time for the Old Men When the Young Men Go to War'?"

"Yes," said Caesar. "But what of it?"

Songwriters talk a lot about stealing. But "stealing" is natural to music, especially popular music. An octave, after all, has only eight white notes and five black ones. The variations are in the combinations. Duplications are inevitable, and sometimes deliberate. The first four notes of "I'm Nobody's Baby" are identical to Tchaikovsky's main theme in *Swan Lake*. "Who's Afraid of the Big Bad Wolf?" is based in part on the "Champagne Song" in Strauss's *Die Fledermaus*. "Cheek to Cheek" is based on a Chopin Polonaise, Beethoven's Sixth provided the theme for "Oh Where, Oh Where Has My Little Dog Gone?," and "Water Boy" is based in part on Tchaikovsky's "March Slav." My favorite example is "Yes, We Have No Bananas," which merges Handel's *Messiah* note for note with Scottish folk tunes and may readily be sung as "Hallelujah, Bananas! Oh, bring back my Bonnie to me." Ager and Gershwin's boast "We steal. But we only steal from the best" arises from this context.

In the spring of 1918, the great Al Jolson, then starring at the Winter Garden in the hit show *Sinbad*, dropped into Feist looking for new material for his celebrated Sunday evening concerts at the Winter Garden. Jolson was the most dynamic and popular performer in show business history, so comfortable before an audience that watching him come on stage was like "watching a duck hitting water," as Samson Raphaelson once said.

That day Milton played his way through the entire Feist catalog, but Jolson liked none of it. "They're not for me," he said, reaching for his hat.

"Maybe the kid has something," someone suggested. Milton belted out the catchy tune he'd written for Grant Clarke's title "Everything Is Peaches down in Georgia."

Jolson was crazy about it. "Finish it, and I'll do it!" Clarke took about fifteen minutes to write a complete lyric, Milton knocked out a verse, and within a week Jolson was singing "Peaches" at the Winter Garden. Soon Bert Williams was also singing it in the Ziegfeld Follies, and Milton Ager had his first smash hit, right up there with 1918's other top favorites, "After You've Gone," "Caissons Go Rolling Along," "A Good Man Is Hard to Find," "Ja-Da," "K-K-K-Katy," "My Mammy," "Oh, How I Hate to Get Up in the Morning," "Rock-a-Bye Your Baby with a Dixie Melody," "Rose Room," and "Tiger Rag."

When the U.S. entered WW I, Simon and Milton Ager did their parts in characteristically different ways. Simon went down to the Chicago stockyards and sold horse meat to the Belgians. Milton was drafted into the U.S. Army Morale Corps, made a sergeant, and sent to the big military hospital at Fort Oglethorpe, Georgia. His duty was to entertain wounded doughboys just back from France by singing at the top of his lungs while playing a small upright on wheels that was pushed through the wards.

Fortunately for the wounded, the Armistice was soon signed, and Milton got back to Manhattan on New Year's Eve. After dining at the Automat he walked up to his old boardinghouse on 91st Street and discovered that his doting landlady had held his room vacant while he was away. He was so touched that when she died, Milton paid for the funeral and sent a wreath signed "Mother."

Having learned in the army how to make band arrangements, he briefly tried becoming a freelance arranger. He got $3 a page for arranging, and $10 apiece for making piano copies. This didn't even bring in enough to pay his rent, and soon he was back with Feist. He tried teaming up with a juvenile, Jack McGowan, who was playing in the hit show *Love Nest*, but burned to write lyrics. When they played their songs for John Murray Anderson, who was producing the artistic revue *Greenwich Village Follies of 1919*, he liked the tunes but not the words. "Thank God *one* of us made it!" said the generous McGowan.

Among the twenty-three songs Milton would write and publish with Leo Feist, Inc., after "Peaches," five were with Clarke, and several with a clever new partner, Jack Yellen. The first Ager-Yellen collaboration, in 1919, was a comedy number about the new federal income tax, "Don't Put a Tax on the Beautiful Girls (How Can I Live without Love?)." Yellen had been recommended to Milton by his kindly mentor George M. Cohan after Clarke once again vanished on a toot. Once more Cohan's instincts had been right on the money. A nimble-witted lyricist with an unerring ear for the vernacular, Yellen had written the 1915 hit "Are You from Dixie?" and several numbers for Sophie Tucker.

Yellen and Ager were a great match professionally, a "perfect marriage" in Tin Pan Alley lingo, though personally they had little in common. Yellen was a Poland-born graduate of the University of Michigan, a former sportswriter, and one of six brothers raised together in Buffalo, New York. All were strict Orthodox Jews. Milton called himself "a professional atheist." It didn't matter. Together, the two men had just the right mysterious mix of complementary talents that all songwriters dream of finding.

By 1919, John Murray Anderson, a stage director of extravaganzas, was on his way to becoming Broadway's most innovative producer of big, spectacular musicals and elegant little revues. A charming Scotsman, "Murray" was an unusual amalgam of showman and aesthete who soon became Milton Ager's patron and chief enthusiast. In time, Milton would write three of Anderson's twenty-nine major musical shows.

In 1920 Anderson was approached by a new and enthusiastic backer, the flamboyant banker Otto Kahn, and together they cooked up an idea for a new variety of high-priced, high-style revue-extravaganza to be titled *What's in a Name?* Anderson intended to write the book and lyrics himself, and invited Milton to compose the score. It would be his first Broadway showcase. When the producer couldn't find time to do the lyrics, Milton suggested Yellen, who later told an interviewer:

> There has never been a more aesthetically perfect production
> on Broadway than *What's in a Name?* — nor a more dismal
> flop. What the show lacked was comedy, an ingredient woe-
> fully lacking in all of Anderson's productions. A leading agent
> offered him a dynamic young *Follies* comedian for a tryout. An-
> derson turned down Eddie Cantor.

Instead, *What's in a Name?* starred the former heavyweight boxing champion of the world, Gentleman Jim Corbett. But the show's most noteworthy elements were James Reynolds's breathtaking scenic designs and costumes. Anderson describes Reynolds's work in his memoir, *Out without My Rubbers:*

> For the first time in a musical show drapes and draw curtains,
> of exquisite material and design, replaced cumbersome
> painted scenery, wings, and drops. The "treadmill," or moving
> stage platform, was introduced for the first time in America,
> and, perhaps most significant of all, "projected scenery." . . .
> There were great screens, thirty feet in height, on the panels of
> which scenes were projected by light. Many years later similar
> screens (also with the projection) were utilized in a musical
> play called *Allegro.* The critics acclaimed them to be "fresh
> and new." They were not; they had been used in *What's in a
> Name?* almost thirty years previously.

The morning after the show opened in the beautiful Maxine Elliott Theater, *The New York Times* reported, "*What's in a Name?* marks the most beautiful staging of musical comedy New York has ever known," and *The Christian Science Monitor* said, "Here is something that Mr. Ziegfeld's *Follies* have always missed."

Nonetheless, the show ran only eighty-seven performances, and Milton with a wry smile used to refer to his Broadway debut as "a *succès d'estime*." Fortunately, Milton's score contained one tremendous hit, "In the Spring a Young Man's Fancy Lightly Turns to Love," in which a pair of "mechanical" figures dressed as a Dresden china shepherd and shepherdess stepped down from a revolving music box and danced.

"A Young Man's Fancy" sold a staggering two million copies of sheet music, largely on the strength of the tinkling, Haydn-like "music box" piano arrangement Milton had written to be played as an instrumental second chorus. He'd made it so winning, yet kept it relatively easy to play, that the tune became known and advertised as "The Music Box Song." Soon dance bands coast to coast were playing the peppy, irresistible fox-trot, Gershwin made a piano roll of it, and Irving Berlin later told Milton he'd got the idea of naming his new theater the Music Box from Milton's song.

Another spectacular number began with a simple, charming ballad in which a young bride-to-be dreams of her wedding. Although "My Bridal Veil" was only moderately successful, Milton always said it was his favorite among everything he ever wrote. In Jimmy Reynolds's staging, the song gradually developed into an eye-popping showstopper: dozens of showgirls wearing authentic-style wedding gowns from every era from the Middle Ages onward descended a stage-wide staircase singing "What are the secrets you hold / Within each delicate fold . . ." while bearing aloft a gigantic golden veil big enough to roof in Madison Square Garden.

Soon after coming to Manhattan, Milton had met and grown to worship a small, rounded, elegant man then working as a rehearsal pianist, Jerome Kern. Of all the composers, Milton admired Kern and Gershwin most, though he also agreed with Kern's celebrated remark "Irving Berlin has no place in American music. He *is* American music."

Though the best of friends, Kern and Milton were never linked professionally, only mechanically, when Kern's minor effort "Our Little Love Nest" was put on the flip side of Milton's tremendous hit "A Young

Man's Fancy." The record, like the sheet music, sold phenomenally well.

Three months later, Milton scored another smash hit with "I'm Nobody's Baby," and Florenz Ziegfeld interpolated it into his Ziegfeld Follies of 1921. The song sold more than a million copies of sheet music, but Leo Feist, Inc., was notoriously slow to pay. At one point, the publisher owed Milton more than $90,000 in royalties. In addition, Feist refused outright to pay him for 350,000 copies of the sheet music delivered to a jobber who went bankrupt, and Milton was eager to break off relations with the firm.

By then Kern, Gershwin, and Vincent Youmans were under contract to Max Dreyfus at T. B. Harms. One day Gershwin said to Milton, "Why do you want to go back to that crummy place, Leo Feist?" and brought Milton over to see the crusty Dreyfus. The publisher was well aware of the music box song, and George asked Milton to play "Harp of My Heart," in which he had put a harp effect, and "Tick Tock," which had a clock effect.

"Did you study?" Dreyfus asked in some amazement.

"Yes, sir," was Milton's not untrue reply. "A great deal."

Dreyfus gave Ager a one-year contract at $100 a week to compose exclusively for Harms. He was still living in the $6 room and, "Well, 1921 was the worst year Broadway had ever had. Harding had just become President. Kern, Gershwin, Youmans — *nobody* could get a show on. There were no decent book writers." Times soon got so bad that Dreyfus asked all his contract writers to take a voluntary fifty percent pay cut. Milton was the only one who refused, telling his boss he couldn't live on $50 a week. Out of earshot, he added, "And if he wants me to tear up the contract, okay!"

Word of this defiance got back to Dreyfus, who summoned Milton to his office. "Every other person in the place took a cut. *You* wouldn't." Dreyfus called the young composer prideful and ungrateful, and vowed he would never back one of Milton's shows. "And I don't care if Caruso's in it!"

Dreyfus was known as a man of his word. Milton was soon offered the score of *The Gingham Girl*, but Dreyfus refused to publish an Ager score, and the producer had to turn to another composer. He picked Albert Von Tilzer ("Take Me Out to the Ball Game," "Roll along Prairie Moon") and the show ran a hefty 322 performances. Dreyfus never spoke to Milton again.

Milton was twenty-seven. "What the hell am I gonna do?" he said to Jack Yellen.

"We'll write a couple of songs," said Jack, "and go into business for ourselves."

Broadway's setback had turned out to be only temporary. The burgeoning record business was reaching incredible new heights; by 1922, 110 million records a year were being sold. The best setup for a songwriter was to own his own music company and publish his own work, as Irving Berlin did. Start-up costs were extremely modest, and writers who owned their firm would not have to share profits fifty-fifty with a publisher. Young Simon Ager had once reasoned exactly the same way about Henry Horner.

Jack and he were artists, not businessmen, Milton pointed out, but Jack said he knew just where to get the experienced professional manager they would need. He would recruit Ben Bornstein from the Harry Von Tilzer Music Publishing Company, Inc. (The music business had several very successful Von Tilzer brothers. Harry, the eldest, had composed "Wait 'Til the Sun Shines Nellie," "A Bird in a Gilded Cage," and "When My Baby Smiles at Me.")

Bornstein readily agreed to jump ship. He borrowed a few thousand dollars and rented some upright pianos, furniture, and a suite of offices in a dilapidated building just off Broadway. He had a sign painter gold-leaf the firm's new name on all the frosted-glass doors: AGER, YELLEN & BORNSTEIN, INC. In songwriters' billing, the composer's name always comes first — Kern and Hammerstein, Rodgers and Hart, George and Ira Gershwin, "because you don't whistle lyrics," as the saying goes.

Bornstein put an announcement in *Variety*, and had a printer print up copies of two new Ager and Yellen songs that looked like surefire hits, one a comedy tune, "Lovin' Sam (The Sheik of Alabam')," and a big, tearful ballad, "Who Cares?"*

Each of the three partners in the fledgling publishing firm had agreed to ante up $200 cash for start-up costs, and they met to seal the deal in their new offices on the night before they were to open for business. Proving that he was indeed experienced in the ways of the music business, Bornstein showed up at the meeting empty-handed, promising to contribute his $200 out of his share of the enterprise's future earnings.*

On this precarious financial footing, the new publishing company was launched. But Ager and Yellen were hot. Al Jolson was so captivated by the lachrymose "Who Cares?" that he not only interpolated it into his current smash hit, *Bombo,* about to begin a record-breaking sixteen-week run at Chicago's Apollo Theater; he recorded the song for Columbia Graphophone. Soon he had grown so enamored of the tune's guaranteed dissolving power on an audience that, after Milton brought him home for a home-cooked meal, Jolson began proclaiming nightly from the stage that Fanny Ager made the best *gefilteh* fish in town.

Yellen had provided the new team's second song, "Lovin' Sam (The Sheik of Alabam')," with a suggestive lyric that capitalized not only on the current passion for things Oriental — expressed in songs about Mandalay, the Shalimar, a Persian market, and of course "The Sheik of Araby" — but also on the rage for salty celebrations of black studs. Sam was a racetrack groom and "cullud Romeo" who, "Though he's just a valet for horses, [was] the cause of many divorces."

---

* Nine years later, the Gershwins wrote a different "Who Cares?" for William Gaxton in *Of Thee I Sing.* Theirs is the jazzy song that asks, "Who cares if banks fail in Yonkers, long as you've got a kiss that conquers?" The Ager-Yellen song sobbed, "Who cares — if my heart is ach-ing? At times when it's break-ing — who ca-ares?" The Gershwins were careful to title their song "Who Cares (So Long as You Care for Me)?" to distinguish it from Ager and Yellen's work. Nonetheless, Ira over the years often asked Milton, "Why didn't you ever sue us about that?"

"Well, for two reasons, Ira," Milton always replied. "First, I would never sue George for anything, would I? He had befriended me, and been so nice to me. And second, I don't think that 'Who Cares?' was an original title. I think there've been several other 'Who Cares?' But the public cared about this 'Who Cares?' That's the only difference."

* The Bornstein brothers were nothing if not adventurous. Ben's brother Saul had been professional manager of Irving Berlin Music until Berlin was obliged to purge him for various financial irregularities, whereupon Saul changed his name to S. Hamilton Bourne and opened up his own publishing company.

Jack and Milton's firm made big money from the start, publishing at least ten new songs of their own a year, as well as the work of other writers. Throughout the Roaring Twenties the team wrote and published an astounding 130 songs. Among the most popular was the tear-stained 1924 waltz "I Wonder What's Become of Sally?," deliberately written as a "counter seller," Yellen told David Ewen,

> a "counter seller" being a ballad not plugged professionally, but which the girls behind the music counters plugged at their pianos through friendship for favored song salesmen. I had friends among such girls in various cities. . . . It was strictly an ear of corn, but when I left Ager's apartment I had a feeling we had written something more than a "counter seller." My test of a song was the reaction I got after singing it to a performer. I was in our office early the next morning . . . [when] "Black Face" Eddie Nelson came in. I hustled him into a piano room, sang him the chorus, noticed his reaction . . . then rushed to the Pennsylvania Station for a train to Philadelphia, where Gus Van and Joe Schenck were appearing as vaudeville head-liners. Schenck was in my opinion the greatest ballad singer in show business. His peculiar half-tenor, half-soprano voice sold millions and millions of copies of sheet music.

Van and Schenck headlined the bill at the Palace the following Monday, and made "Sally" an instant hit. "Within a week our . . . offices were jammed with vaudevillians waiting to rehearse" the song, Yellen recalled, and even Jolson sang and recorded it.

Twenty-two years later, in the Cole Porter screen biography *Night and Day*, and early scene shows the ambitious young Cole walking into a five-and-ten-cent store, hearing a counter girl weepily plugging "Sally," and turning away in despair. "Too bad, Cole," says his friend. "You just don't have the common touch."

Milton chuckled when he told this story. "It was the only non-Porter song in the picture, and that year it made us more money than all of our other songs put together."

"Hard-Hearted Hannah (The Vamp of Savannah)," written the same year as "Sally," had a Milton Ager tune and an inspired set of lyrics by Jack Yellen, Bob Bigelow, and Charles Bates. A quarter century later Peggy Lee revived "Hannah" very successfully for Capitol, and the Ray Charles singers made a hit version for Decca.

Throughout the twenties, Ager and Yellen made money as publishers, and were among the best-paid songwriters in the nation. In 1927, a particularly good year, they had three major hits: the sentimental ballad "Forgive Me," the novelty ukelele smash "Crazy Words, Crazy Tune (Vo-do-de-o)," and "Ain't She Sweet?," the team's second biggest hit of all time. The song was popularized in vaudeville by Eddie Cantor *and* Sophie Tucker *and* Lilian Roth, and sold more than a million copies of sheet music. The shy little blonde who walked across the stage during Cantor's rendition was the still unknown Sally Rand. This song too had "legs." Twenty-one years later it was sung by Dan Dailey and chorus in the movie *You Were Meant for Me*, and eight years after that it was a choral episode in the non-movie musical *Picnic*, starring Kim Novak and William Holden.

Glad Rag Doll, Ager and Yellen's first movie theme song, was written for a Dolores Costello picture, and "Hungry Women" was written for Eddie Cantor, then starring in Ziegfeld's *Whoopee!* The Sophie Tucker picture *Honky Tonk* contained five Ager-Yellen hits: "I'm Doing What I'm Doing for Love," "I Don't Want to Get Thin," "He's a Good Man to Have Around," "I'm Feathering a Nest for a Little Bluebird," and "I'm the Last of the Red Hot Mammas."

Milton and Jack turned out stage shows as well as songs for movie and vaudeville performers. In 1922, their first year in business together, they wrote the score for *Zig Zag*, which closed out of town, but the following year they turned out a successful revue, *The Ted Lewis Frolics*. In 1928 came *Rain or Shine*, starring Joe Cook, and in 1929, the last and most prolific year of their collaboration, Ager and Yellen wrote a second *Almanac* extravaganza for John Murray Anderson, as well as the scores for the three aforementioned movie musicals and a dozen pop tunes.

*   *   *

Milton's answer to the old saw "Which do you write first, words or music?" was always "Neither!" To him, the title was supreme. He didn't want to have an entire lyric before starting to write. "Because the *idea* is what's important. The versifying can get in the way." He also disliked writing "to meter, like *Trees:* 'I *think* that I shall *ne*-ver *see.* . . .' That's like store teeth. Too symmetrical."

If Milton liked a title, the right chords and rhythm came to him instinctually, and after writing the title phrase, he "knew how the rest of the tune should lay out."

Johnny Mercer expressed the same idea when he said, "Writing music takes more talent, but writing lyrics takes more courage. The lyricist's job is to find the words already buried in the music, listening over and over to the melody until certain vowel sounds, images, rhyme patterns suggest themselves."

But Milton did not insist on working from a title. Many years later, when Sinatra recorded "Ain't She Sweet?" for Reprise Records' *Sinatra and Swingin' Brass*, Lawrence D. Stewart was asked to write the album's liner notes. After interviewing Milton, Stewart wrote:

> "Ain't She Sweet?," which, with *that* title, might seem to have
> no claim to intelligence, is a remarkable instance of thought—
> not instinct—producing a melody. . . . By 1927 . . . [Ager and
> Yellen's] pattern of work was set: Yellen would come up with a
> song title which would in turn suggest to Ager the beginning
> of a tune. Words and music then developed together. One day
> in 1927 Ager became interested in adapting a Wagnerian chro-
> matic device to the popular song. He took the first and sixth
> notes of the scale and then moved them chromatically toward
> each other in three steps—creating three chords which com-
> bined into a new, or "passing" chord. He liked the sliding har-
> monic effect, doubled it—by changing quarter-notes to eighth-
> notes—added an off-beat syncopated rhythm in the left hand,
> and he had a tune. . . . For the first time Yellen was asked to set
> a lyric to a completed tune. His first attempt was "pretty good,"
> according to Ager, "but I thought it could be improved." Yel-

len then took a different approach and [suggested "Ain't She Sweet?"].

They were working on "Ain't She Sweet?," as Milton told me the story, "when Jack came up with this absolutely *wonderful* polysyllabic word!"

Me: "What word?"

Milton: "Confidentially!"

The second eight bars — "Ain't she *nice* . . ." — virtually wrote themselves. Then suddenly they were stuck. "Oh, just vamp something," said Milton. "Some dummy lyric. Voh-do-di-o-do."

Jack's ears pricked up. "What is 'voh-do-di-o-do'?"

"That is a Negroism I heard in Harlem."

"It's great!" said Jack. "To hell with 'Ain't She Sweet?' Let's write 'Voh-do-di-o-do'!"

They did, and the catchy song, also known as "Crazy Words, Crazy Tune," capitalized on the ukelele craze and sold by the millions. When Leonard Bernstein was a boy, he told Milton, the song was his favorite pop tune.

Ager and Yellen finished up "Ain't She Sweet?" later that year. It sold even better and, like several of Milton's tunes, became a jazz standard as well as a pop hit. (Carrying on in the great tradition of stealing only from the best, two years later, in 1929, the team wrote "That's Her Now," which, as Michael Feinstein points out, "is 'Ain't She Sweet?' sideways.")

Ager and Yellen were making money as both writers and publishers, and were among the best-paid pop songwriters in the nation. The partners' relationship was sometimes stormy, but the storms were all on the business side. Their creative collaboration was smooth and rich. Tin Pan Alley historians refer to "the ubiquitous Yellen and Ager," and describe Milton's music as "explosions of happiness," "cheerful," and "bouncy," as was his essential nature.

Each month Milton sent money back to his mother in Chicago. When necessary, he bailed out floundering brothers and sisters. He was the sole success in the entire family. The need for money never ceased. When the little business of one brother looked ready to go under, because he had loaned too much money to another brother, and it seemed as if Fanny and Simon might lose their house, Milton sent $20,000 to help them buy it. The price was $27,000. The gesture aroused resentment as well as gratitude. Fanny was effusive, Simon uncharacteristically silent. Only when Simon had to sign the deed for the house did Milton realize his father's shame at being illiterate.

In 1928, the year of my best Hollywood train ride, Milton and Jack began writing the scores for four early talkies, two of them moneymakers and two stinkers. After Sophie Tucker's smash hit *Honky Tonk* came *The King of Jazz*, in which Universal Pictures intended to star the nation's best-known orchestra leader, forty-year-old Paul Whiteman. The studio had brought Whiteman and his big band to Hollywood on a train painted entirely in gold — sponsored by Old Gold cigarettes — and everybody then sat around for several months on full salary while writers tried to concoct a romantic story about a hero as fat as Whiteman. Then somebody suggested: instead of a story, why not make it a supercolossal revue? Whiteman recommended John Murray Anderson to direct it, and two years and several million dollars later, *The King of Jazz* was ready for release.

The picture was Hollywood's first all-Technicolor feature and, appropriately enough, production problems too were supercolossal. After Universal allegedly spent $30,000 for the rights to *Rhapsody in Blue*, and another half-million or so experimenting with set designs, it was discovered that the Technicolor printing of the time was limited to shades of red and green; blue would not become available for several more years.*

---

* Anderson in his memoirs reports that he and his designer "made tests of various fabrics and pigments, and by using an all gray and silver background finally arrived at a shade of green which gave the illusion of peacock blue."

Other innovations included Hollywood's first employment of a camera boom and its first usage of dubbed soundtracks for stars who cannot sing — in this instance, John Boles and Laura La Plante. The picture combined such improbable elements as Jimmy Reynolds's nuptial extravaganza, "My Bridal Veil," some corny burlesque blackout sketches, two animated cartoons in color, Bing Crosby singing "Mississippi Mud," cameos by Walter Brennan and Slim Somerville, and a grandiose piano fantasy in which "A Young Man's Fancy" is played simultaneously by seventy-five pianists at seventy-five white pianos. The score also contained several new Ager and Yellen songs: the endearing ballad "A Bench in the Park," and the movies' first massive tap dance number, "Happy Feet," choreographed by Russell Markert two years before he invented Radio City Music Hall's Rockettes and three years before the release of Hollywood's next tap dance extravaganza, *Forty-Second Street*. The biggest showstopper of all was a dancer who performed atop a revolving snare drum entirely naked but lacquered shiny black and brilliantly lit by powerful white sidelights. Colored gelatins placed in front of the lights turned his gigantic dancing shadow alternately red and green, and caused audiences all over the country to burst into wild applause.

When *The King of Jazz* first opened, in 1930 at the Roxy, *The New York Times* termed it "a marvel of camera wizardry, joyous color schemes, charming costumes, and seductive lighting effects . . . one of the very few pictures in which there is no catering to the unsophisticated mentality."

Ager and Yellen's two stinkers, released the previous year, were the odd baseball-vaudeville mélange *They Learned about Women* and *Road Show*, a formula backstage yarn that was a naked steal from *The Broadway Melody*. It even used the same stars, Bessie Love and Charles King, plus an untested young vaudeville comic, Jack Benny. When Milton played and sang the score for Irving Thalberg and L. B. Mayer at MGM, Thalberg pronounced it "quite ordinary."

"Now that you mention it, it is," said Milton.

By now he and his partner were not getting along well; Milton thought Jack was paying insufficient attention to their publishing business, spending too much time in Buffalo speculating in real estate and writing specialty nightclub material for his pal Sophie Tucker.

Milton in his thin-lipped mode telephoned Jack to report Thalberg's reaction.

"I'll have to find a new title," said the lyricist.

"When you do, call me."

A couple of days later Milton's phone rang. "I'm coming over. I think I have something."

Milton opened the door and silently led his partner to the living room.

"'Happy Days Are Here Again,'" Jack said. "What do you think?"

"I think it's great."

The partners sat together in stony silence. It was late on a Friday afternoon, and at sundown Yellen would have to stop working and go to shul.

Fifteen minutes passed. Then Milton said, "Here's the song," and went to the piano. He played a rousing march that would be used at the start of the picture to accompany the doughboys' return from France. The tune was in fact one of his "quite ordinary" ballad melodies, now played up-tempo, and strongly syncopated.

"What do you think?"

"Great!" said Jack. "But we need a verse." The sun was dropping ominously lower. "Just gimme the notes."

"I sat there," Milton told me later. "And *as* I played it, *he* wrote it!"

Yellen now grabbed his hat and coat and rushed out, leaving Milton at the piano to figure out the arrangement. "The only two things I did," he told me, "were to say to pronounce the 'The' before the word 'skies' like 'thuh,' not 'thee,' as some singers might. I also wanted a little melisma, what's called 'ornamentation' in classical music. A little leg, a little glissando. So I put in a riff for the trumpet, using a half-valve. If he's been trained, the trumpet player can also do something with his mouth, as the old horns used to, by changing his embouchure."

In syncopated march tempo, the tune was dynamite, but by now the studio had soured on the picture and decided it was not worth releasing.

The Yellens moved back to Buffalo, and the Agers returned to New York. Ager, Yellen & Bornstein, Inc., published the song, and the firm's ace song plugger went to work. It took six months, but a few smart bandleaders like George Olsen and Ben Bernie were quick to recognize the tune's unusual drive and include it in their nightly radio broadcasts, which in turn helped to build the song nationwide. MGM learned what was going on, took *Road Show* off the shelf, recut and reshot it so as to feature "Happy Days Are Here Again" no less than five times, retitled the picture *Chasing Rainbows*, and booked it into Broadway's Capitol Theater.

By now Ager, Yellen & Bornstein knew it had a full-fledged hit, with multimillion sheet music and record sales guaranteed. But just to hype things a bit more, MGM was persuaded to install powerful loudspeakers above the Capitol's marquee; each time the crowds moved in and out of the theater between shows, they heard the peppy tune blasting all over Times Square.

Milton never bothered to see the movie. More than thirty years later he was flabbergasted to hear Barbra Streisand, still relatively unknown, singing her famous version of "Happy Days," in which she turns the rousing march into a subdued and ironic cry of rue. Streisand's musical instincts were so acute, Milton recognized, that she "must have heard the original ballad inside the march."

By then, the song had become our family's musical oil well. President Roosevelt had made it his campaign song, and Presidents Truman, Kennedy, and Johnson had all entered the White House to its stirring strains.* In 1964, ASCAP's fiftieth anniversary, the society selected "Happy Days Are Here Again" as one of sixteen songs on its all-time Hit Parade of most performed standards. In 1988, the last year ASCAP published its annual all-time hit list, the song was still on it.

But the happy days at Ager, Yellen & Bornstein, Inc., had self-

* In 1972 Democratic Party officials jettisoned "Happy Days" and commissioned someone to write something "more modern," with predictable results that are, alas, still with us.

destructed for good in the wake of the stock market crash of 1929. Raking through the financial rubble that followed, Milton discovered that one or more of Jack's brothers had been speculating with assets belonging to the firm. Their investments included some obscure railroad bonds, and a Biloxi, Mississippi, fourth-mortgage business owned by another brother. Whether Jack or Ben was aware of the dipping never became clear. But it was obvious that the machinations had been carefully concealed from Milton, and he became near-incoherent with fury.

Was the deception merely a lapse of ethics, or a clear case of fraud? Might one or more persons be liable for prosecution? Distraught, Milton consulted the firm's legal counsel, Gilbert & Gilbert. "What should I do! Should I have this man disbarred? Should I make him jump out of a window? Tell me!"

Turn matters over to the district attorney, the lawyers advised. But this Milton could not bring himself to do, even though the losses totaled more than $100,000 in stocks, plus $50,000 still owed to the firm.

But neither could he bear to remain in business with such persons. Yellen tried diligently and repeatedly to make amends. He offered to give Milton his own stock in the firm, for nothing, and to pay back anything his brothers had misappropriated at a rate of $25 a week.

"Twenty-five dollars a week for two hundred thousand dollars is how many weeks?" Milton shot back. His puritanical nature made him unable to accept Jack's apology in any form. He saw an immediate professional divorce as the only acceptable solution.

Once the acrimonious negotiations with Yellen had been concluded, Milton went to the office and was surprised to find Bornstein still on the premises.

"What are *you* doing here!"

Ben said he still had a $40,000 stake in the firm.

"I'll give you $80,000 to get out!" snapped Milton, and he did. Bornstein used the money to open his own music publishing company.

Though stung by the firm's financial losses, my father had been utterly broken by the loss of trust. That his personal losses in the market had been perhaps ten times the amount in question is a fact I learned only fifty years later, from Milton's lawyer, long after both my parents had died.

One of the most bountiful partnerships in songwriting history had lasted exactly ten years. In the following decade Milton would struggle alone to keep the firm afloat. He and Jack never spoke to one another again. My father was an old man before he was able to speak even to me about these ancient and terrible injuries. In his last years he also managed a few cordial telephone conversations with Jack's second wife.

Yet Milton had never deceived himself about the unique and irreplaceable nature of the shattered Ager-Yellen "marriage." "I realized I had been the beneficiary of meeting Jack," he told me forty-five years later. "They were very successful songs."

But he waited several more years, until he sensed death was near, before confessing to me that his very first song after the bitter breakup, words and music both by Milton Ager, "What Good Am I without You?," had been written as a private message to Jack.

I looked it up. "Happy together, you and I," the verse began:

> We made our lives a song —
> Letting bad weather pass right by
> The world just rolled along.
> But things are diff'rent now that you have gone
> All by myself I simply can't go on!

Astonished, I looked up Yellen's first song after the split and found "I Still Call You Sweetheart (Sweetheart, As I Used to Do)." Jack's song too must have been a solo effort. Although the music is credited to the eponymous "Arnold New," no such person is listed in the rolls of ASCAP or in any other musical source.

In January 1933, Fanny Ager called to say that Simon was failing, and not expected to live much longer. Milton got back to his father's bedside in time to spend a couple of days with the old man and reconcile a lifetime's misunderstanding and mistrust. In those last conversations, Milton forgave his father's harshness. He understood that Simon had been intently focused on finding ways to earn money to support his family, and on protecting his women. There had been no room for any other considerations. Drinking and crude clowning were his ways of relieving the pressures that built up.

Milton could now attribute his own success to both of his parents: "My mother gave me encouragement. My father gave me enough *resistance*."

On his deathbed, the failed father at last acknowledged his successful son's accomplishments, the error of his own lack of faith in him, and the extreme slimness of his patrimony. He even managed a last witticism about it.

"Suun," Simon said.

"He always called me Suun," Milton would interrupt himself to explain whenever he recounted his father's dying words. "I called him Pa."

"'Suun,' Pa told me. 'I leave you de voild.'"

More than fifty years later, I read in our local newspaper that our town librarian was something of a Jewish historian, and was planning to write a book about "the famous walking Jews of Long Island," itinerant nineteenth-century peddlers who hiked with packs from New York City to the tip of Montauk Point, a 135-mile journey, selling their wares to villagers and farmers along the way. I called the librarian and told her that I was researching a book about my family, and had only the sketchiest information about my paternal grandfather, who had started out as just such a walking peddler.

I mentioned Milton, and, as it happened, the librarian's husband was a retired dance band clarinetist who knew all of Milton's tunes. Both of them were eager to be of assistance.

"Tell me every single thing you know about your grandfather," she said. "Don't leave anything out."

This took only about fifteen minutes, and when I finished, there was a brief silence.

Then she said quietly, "Your grandfather was a man considerably ahead of his time."

"What do you mean by that?"

"I mean that the Czar didn't start persecuting the Jews until about twenty years after your grandfather left."

CHAPTER FIVE

CECELIA IS

Although Cecelia was from birth the most important person in her family of five — parents and two younger brothers — I have never seen a photograph nor painting nor indeed any image nor memento of her as a child. I believe that Cecelia, as soon as she was able, insisted that all childhood representations of herself be destroyed. My earliest mental picture of her comes from a description by an elderly cousin of eight-year-old Cecelia arriving with Fanny in midsummer in New York City. Travelers from California had to endure a five-day train ride, sitting up all the way. Yet the immaculate child who stepped off the train with her mother wore a crisp, perfectly pressed white dress with pleated skirt, long sleeves, and a sailor collar, long white stockings, high-buttoned black patent leather shoes, and a black velvet band around her perfectly combed long blonde hair. In the earliest actual photograph I ever saw of Cecelia, made when she was fifteen and about to go off to college, she was dressed the same way, a replica of the

Tenniel drawings of Alice in Wonderland. I was in college myself when I found it, stuffed at the back of a high closet shelf, just after Cecelia had removed some things from storage to furnish a new apartment at 350 Park Avenue. When I returned from college the next time and searched for it, the picture had disappeared, never to be seen again.

The next youngest photograph I ever saw of her was a studio head shot, probably taken around the time of her marriage, since there is a matching portrait of young Milton. Cecelia's hair is bobbed, waved, and no longer blonde. But I didn't see these pictures until after our parents were dead, and Laurel had begun unearthing and sending me ancient cartons of Ager memorabilia, unopened since the Visigoths. During her lifetime, Cecelia had kept these twenties pictures hidden from view.

Not counting the Gershwin portrait, painted in 1931 or 1932, the first image of herself Cecelia allowed to be presented to the world appeared on our piano in the mid-thirties after one of her trips abroad with Gerry. A Hungarian photographer, captivated by her boylike chic, had produced a diagonal, waist-up portrait of a soignée woman in a loden jacket, her shining hair confined in a peaked net cap. She looks aloof, inscrutable, and coolly alluring, like a figure of Mercury poised in his rounds, or Thomas Mann's beautiful Polish boy Tadzio in *Death in Venice*. The photograph remained on our piano for some years, and when it too vanished into the maw wherein all Ager possessions and personal items ultimately were consigned, no other image of Cecelia replaced it.

Fanny Rubenstein as a mother was Cecelia's opposite: a warm, demonstrative, affectionate, indulgent parent who doted on children and was ever eager to give them whatever their little hearts might desire. Laurel and I as young children in California were often left in Fanny's care. She took us to the movies. She bought us ice cream. She plied us with goodies. She let us listen to radio soap operas in the afternoon. Indeed, she listened with us, all three of us cuddled up on her couch nibbling sweets and staring at the big radio cabinet draped with an embroidered

Russian shawl and standing near the gas fireplace in her stucco living room.

My favorite soap began with a big organ glissando followed by a plummy voice saying, "OUR . . . GAL . . . SUNDAY! The program that asks the question: Can This Girl from a Mining Town in the West Find Happiness as . . . Find Happiness as. . . ."

I can't recall any more of it because the moment the familiar voice said "girl from a mining town in the west," I began wondering whether *Our Gal Sunday* was really the secret story of Cecelia's life, the life she would never talk about. Milton reminisced endlessly about his childhood; Cecelia said not one word. I knew she had been born in just such a little mining town, Grass Valley, California. I knew that the California gold rush was somehow involved in the story, and that her mother, Fanny, had crossed the continent by train as a mail-order bride, and that the sour-tempered storekeeper who had sent back east to get her was Zalkin. I knew that Fanny was one of three poor but strikingly beautiful sisters, and that somehow or other Zalkin was their first cousin. Their father was a respected wise man and Hebrew scholar, and I knew that when he put his frightened young daughter on the train in New York City, he had made her a solemn promise: "If you don't like him, you don't have to stay."

Zalkin turned out to be a harsh, humorless, overbearing, whey-faced little man. Fanny did not like him at all, and wrote her father begging to come home. Well versed in the ways of Talmudic argument, he wrote back, "Yes, daughter, I did indeed make you that promise. But were you to come back *now*, the neighbors would say that he rejected you, and not that you rejected him." So Fanny had to remain; family honor compelled it.

"The neighbors," my mother would bitterly observe each time she told me this story, were the other immigrant slum dwellers crowded into Manhattan's Lower East Side.

Cecelia had first told it to me at an extremely early age. Later I heard it from Anzia. But beyond these meager facts I knew nothing of Cecelia's family history, and she flatly refused to satisfy my intense curiosity. I remember as a very small child, not more than four or five, begging her to tell me what happened next. What was her life like as a little girl my age? The idea that my sophisticated parents had once been children themselves fascinated me, and I reveled in Milton's endless stories about his boyhood. But Cecelia always answered my entreaties exactly the same way.

"If you were *really* interested, you would have asked" was her baffling, maddening reply.

The squelch worked, and by age six I had stopped asking. Years would pass, nearly fifty, before I understood the true meaning of her Delphic utterance: "If you were really interested *in me*, which you are not . . . ," the remainder of the sentence left unspoken. "You are only interested in your father. You only love your father."

While this was certainly true, it might seem odd that this woman noted for saying precisely what she meant, who never tinted or softened or mitigated her words, could never bring herself to speak what she so deeply felt. To say that her children didn't love her, and that furthermore this *mattered* to her, would have broken her inviolable rule against expressions of self-pity, even of self-concern. The rule also meant that she could never permit herself to *ask for* anything—anything she truly wanted, that is. Cecelia Ager asked for small things all the time. Indeed, in small matters, and some matters not so small, Laurel and I soon came to recognize our mother to be one of the most selfish and self-centered people we would ever know. Yet when it came to the truly important things, people had to *divine* what it was she wanted. If they couldn't, or simply didn't care to, they were deemed unworthy, and discarded.

As an adult I was still unclear about my mother's antecedents and had no idea how it was that her parents were first cousins. I remained in the dark until I started to write this book and, with the help of Cecelia's brother Victor, always the family historian, began to chart our complex genealogy. Like Cecelia, nine-years-younger Victor Rubenstein was born smart; in kindergarten he was chosen one of the exceptionally bright children on whom the Stanford-Binet IQ tests were worked out. He grew up to become a physician of orderly mind and tender heart, and he alone among the worldwide sprawl of relatives managed to stay in touch with all branches of our tangled family.

As far back as I have been able to trace it, the family came from an area of northeastern Poland then part of the Russian empire. Cecelia and Victor's great-grandfather was a certain Moshe Labe, or Leib, Jezierski, a renowned rabbi who headed the yeshiva in the province of Lomza. Reb Jezierski had five children, only three of whom concern us here: Cima, Bernhard, and Hannah.

Cima, the eldest, was a woman of fabled beauty, born about 1850, who married a rabbi in the neighboring province of Suwalki, and bore seven children. Three of the seven — two sons and a daughter — studied medicine in St. Petersburg and became physicians, a remarkable achievement in a Jewish family at that time, when the restrictions on education, occupation, and travel for Jews were at their most severe. Cima's youngest child was Zalkin, my grandfather.

Cima's younger brother Bernhard, a Hebrew scholar like his father, but not an ordained rabbi, lived in the nearby town of Plock. Bernhard Jezierski, always a poor man, married Shana Perl, whose ancestors had come to Polish Russia from Cordoba, Spain, and they had ten children. The seventh of Shana and Bernhard's children was Fanny, Cecelia's mother. That is how my mother came to be the daughter of first cousins. Such marriages were not unusual among Russian Jewish families of the period; the imperatives of religion were thought to override the risks of inbreeding.

Cima's younger sister was Hannah, the first of our ancestors to reach America. Hannah somehow got to San Francisco and married a prosperous barrel maker, Simon Levitt. When Simon's younger brother Harry needed a wife, Hannah sent back to Poland for her sister Cima's eldest daughter, Cecelia, and in due course Harry and Cecelia Levitt opened a San Francisco emporium called the Wonder Store.

Cima died young, in her mid-forties, while her youngest child, Zalkin, was still living at home. Only fourteen years old, he was as vulnerable to the czar's recruiters as young Simon Ager had once appeared to be. Zalkin's older sister Cecelia Levitt sent him passage money to America, and when he arrived in San Francisco, in 1895, she and her husband put the lad to work sweeping out their store.

Bernhard Jezierski, his wife Shana Perl, and seven of their ten children came through the Manhattan immigration center at Castle Gardens in July 1893. My grandmother Fanny was then about twelve years old. The sequence of the children's births is important: first four boys, then four girls, all born in Poland, followed by two more boys born in New York City.

The eldest Jezierski son, Max, had arrived in America in 1887, a few years before the rest of his family. He was nineteen years old and already married to a rich wife. An immigration inspector changed his name from Jezierski to Mayer, which was easier to spell, and six years later Max Mayer, by now a proud, English-speaking graduate of the Columbia University School of Pharmacy, was standing on the dock when his parents and brothers and sisters arrived. At the stroke of a pen, nine more Jezierskis became Mayers.

The problem, it will readily be grasped, was to marry off the daughters. What else could be done with them? As the wise Bernhard often said, "All vocations but one are for men only." The family moved into a wretched tenement in lower Manhattan, and the sons found menial day jobs and attended pharmacy school at night. Their mother and sisters toiled in sweatshops to help support them. Everyone agreed that Bernhard was too busy studying the Talmud to waste time grubbing for pennies. Better he should spend his days poring over his holy books. Such wise men, highly educated though not ordained as rabbis, were familiar village figures in Jewish life inside the Russian Pale, where both sides of my family originated. Another one of the breed was Milton's super-pious, Orthodox grandfather, Nathan Nathan or Nissen Magidson—Nathan the Wise. As young men, they were called *yeshiva bochers*. As they grew older and acquired families, such wise men, perpetual students, were regarded with a curious blend of respect and derision: respect for their learning mingled with a smiling, or smirking, acknowledgment that, unlike the baker or the fish peddler, they were incapable of earning a living and needed to be supported by their hardworking, more mundane, yet usually deeply respectful wives and children.

Soon after the Jezierski/Mayers arrived, the eldest daughter died of pneumonia. The remaining three girls made a striking trio. Helena, the eldest, had blonde hair and sapphire eyes and was so lovely that men followed her down the street. The middle daughter, Fanya, my grand-mother, had black hair and violet eyes. The youngest daughter, Anya, had red hair, blue eyes, and freckles, and was the family rebel.

Bernhard immediately applied for U.S. citizenship. The demand that he renounce allegiance to the czar of all the Russias must have caused a smile behind his curly red beard. Three years later he had his citizenship papers, and his loving daughters in a burst of patriotism Americanized their Polish names — Helena, Fanya, and Anya — into Annie, Fanny, and Hattie Mayer. Later, after Anya/Hattie became a writer, she decided to change her name back to its Polish original, which she spelled Anzia Yezierska. One by one, the four Mayer boys finished school and set up as neighborhood pharmacists, and their poor mother, worn out with childbirth, died soon after the birth of her tenth child.

Let us now back up in time a bit, and return to San Francisco. Zalkin Rubenstein has spent six or seven years sweeping the Levitts' dry goods store, acquiring a smattering of English, and saving every penny he can lay hands on. By 1900, his sister and her husband agree it is time to lend the young man money to set up a store of his own, and decide that Grass Valley, a thriving little gold mining town in the foothills of the Sierra Nevada range, is a promising location. But while Zalkin waits on cus-tomers, someone will be needed to sweep out and clean up the store. It is time for Zalkin to seek a wife.

Plenty of suitable Jewish women were available in San Francisco, but Zalkin decided instead to write to his wise uncle Bernhard in New York City and ask him to send out one of his daughters. Whether he was motivated by frugality, nostalgia, or pride of blood is unknown. Possibly he had seen Bernhard's bevy of daughters back in Russia. Family legend has it that Zalkin's first choice was Helena, the ravishing eldest daughter, but that she declined his proposal.

So Bernhard gathered up his next oldest daughter, seventeen-year-old Fanny, and put her on the train. Fanny had no say in the matter. Daughters in her world obeyed their fathers just as wives obeyed their husbands. As the wise Bernhard often said, "A woman alone — not a wife, not a mother — has no existence."

Fanny and Zalkin were married in San Francisco in 1900. On August 10, 1901, an advertisement appeared in *The Grass Valley Union*:

ZALKIN IS BACK AT THE WONDER

Having purchased the business of H. Levitt, I am ready to see all my friends, old and new. I have just put in a strictly first-class and up-to-date stock of

CLOTHING, FURNISHING GOODS, BOOTS AND SHOES, HATS, ETC.

I guarantee to please every customer and to treat all alike. Purchasers who are dissatisfied can return goods and secure others. I want your patronage, and promise to treat you right, both with goods and prices.

ZALKIN RUBENSTEIN "THE WONDER"

Their first child, born in Grass Valley in 1902, was my mother. Lonely Fanny took the child on frequent trips back east to visit the sisters she missed so much, only too happy to leave her hardworking husband behind. The beauteous Helena/Annie had married Abraham Katz, a diamond cutter, and each time Fanny came east, her older sister seemed to have a new baby. There were ten children in all, and somewhere along the way, "Katz" became "Kates." One of these ten is today Viola Kates

Stimson, an enchanting octogenarian actress who specializes in playing cute bag ladies and character parts. You would probably recognize her from her commercials for Kellogg's and Jack-in-the-Box, and she is the oldest regularly working member of the Screen Actors Guild.

Viola's memory is excellent, and it was she who described her rich aunt Fanny arriving in New York with her pampered little daughter. "We were poor relations," Viola told me. "In our eyes, Cecelia was extremely glamorous. Her clothes were exquisite. She had a great flair for style. Every year Fanny used to send us Cecelia's last year's clothes, beautifully packed in tissue paper and expensive dress boxes from I. Magnin's. *They* had money. It was never flaunted — but it was certainly used."

The family did not seem particularly Polish or Russian, Viola says, "though of course we were. But there was also a very strong German culture in the family. People were extremely ethical, and had a powerful sense of morality. The man dominated the home. My father believed in the Kaiser. The only revolutionary in the family was Anzia."

Fanny once invited her sister Annie and all ten of her children to a grand lunch at the Hotel Brevoort. For dessert, a cart of luscious French pastries was wheeled to the table. "No, thank you," Cecelia said. Ten-year-old Viola was "awestruck that someone could refuse! She was not dieting. She was bored, satiated, indifferent." Viola sensed that her older cousin was stifling in the climate of total adoration that oozed from unloved, unhappy Fanny. Cecelia seemed cocooned in her rich clothes of satin and velvet, a girl longing for plain fresh air. Red-haired, rebellious Anzia would provide the air.

Although not yet a published author at the time of the Brevoort lunch, Anzia was already a relatively prosperous and wildly independent young woman. The last Jezierski child born in Russia, she was eight or ten years old when the family arrived in New York, and already dreaming of one day becoming a writer. She would be the voice of her wretched, ignorant people torn out of one world and struggling to fit themselves into another. It was a preposterous dream for a greenhorn girl still striving to learn English, but as soon as possible, probably in her mid-teens,

Anzia had run away from her pious parents, scrubbed clothes in a laundry, and eventually become a protégée of a group of New York society women concerned with the plight of promising immigrants. Although notoriously uninterested, and ungifted, in any of the household arts, Anzia nonetheless convinced these ladies that her heart's desire was to become a teacher of domestic science to other immigrants; as a result, she was sent through Columbia University on full scholarship. In 1904, only eleven years after arriving in the U.S., she graduated, and her sister Fanny was so proud that, though eight months pregnant with her second child, Laurence, she came east for the ceremony.

Much as they loved one another, Fanny and Anzia were temperamental opposites, Anzia overwrought, demanding, egomaniacal in her needs, Fanny gentle, romantic, and self-sacrificing in the extreme. The emotional sisters spent much of their lives rushing toward and away from one another on cross-country trains, perpetually fighting and perpetually making up. The ongoing friction between the passionate sisters engendered intense heat periodically dashed by the ice of Zalkin. In this crucible Cecelia's recondite character was forged.

By the time of Fanny's Brevoort lunch, Anzia had married and divorced twice and, still bankrolled by the good-hearted ladies, was studying acting at the American Academy of Dramatic Arts by day and struggling alone at night to teach herself to write in English. Her five-year-old daughter Louise, whom she called Tinkerbelle, lived with her father and grandmother in a pleasant part of the Bronx, and was brought down to visit her mother in Greenwich Village on weekends. Anzia in short was free at last.

In his introduction to Anzia Yezierska's 1950 autobiography, *Red Ribbon on a White Horse*, W. H. Auden says about her childhood:

> She began life in a Polish ghetto, i.e., in the bottom layer of
> the stratified European heap. In the more advanced countries
> of Europe, like England, it had become possible for a talented
> individual to rise a class, a generation, but in Russia, above all
> for a Jew, it was still quite impossible; if once one had been

born in the ghetto, then in the ghetto one would die. For its in-habitants extreme poverty and constant fear of a pogrom were normal, and even so humble a desire as the wish to eat white bread was fantastic.

Auden's comments apply to all four of my grandparents. What a vast gulf there must have been between them and their own children! Cece-lia's childhood in particular must have been very odd. Being extremely pretty and far brighter than her parents — a "biological sport," other rela-tives called her — and having none of the limitations of an immigrant, Cecelia was the most important person in her family from the day she was born.

Her brother Laurence was born in Manhattan when Cecelia was two. When she was nine, her brother Victor arrived, by which time the family lived in Long Beach, and Zalkin took a two-hour streetcar ride each day to his wholesale clothing business in downtown Los Angeles. Soon the family had moved to Hollywood. Of Cecelia's early schooling, I know nothing; of her years at Hollywood High School, only that she once cheered so violently at a basketball game that she tumbled out of the balcony and broke her arm; of her four years at Berkeley, only that she breezed through with top grades. I know all this — the streetcar, the broken arm, the top college grades — from Victor. Cecelia simply never spoke of it. As a widow talking to a class of journalism students, she men-tioned that she had been "teacher's pet" in her English class. The one other thing I know about her college years is that she was fond of her good-looking roommate, Helena Zuckerman, and they remained friends for a long time. I don't remember Helena, but her father, Mau-rice Zuckerman, a genial, wealthy, roughneck farmer from Stockton, California, used to take Laurel and me for drives in the thirties in his flashy, cream-colored Packard convertible. Zook, as we called him, had early seen Stockton's agricultural potential and planted thousands of acres of vegetables, much of it asparagus. Known as "the Asparagus King," Zook was also known for having served time in San Quentin after shooting a man in a barroom for calling him a dirty Jew. On our drives with Zook, all three of us got a kick out of knowing about the loaded revolver he kept in the leather pocket of the passenger door.

By 1917, when fifteen-year-old Cecelia graduated from high school and went off to college "in bobby socks" — a teeny fact I recall her once inadvertently permitting herself to disclose — she must already have decided she would never return to the stifling atmosphere of her parents' home. From Berkeley she moved directly to the Columbia University School of Journalism. More important to her than journalism was a wish to put maximal distance between herself and her parents. Within months, Cecelia had moved out of her Columbia dormitory to live in Greenwich Village with Anzia. Or so their story went. More likely, this was a fiction concocted to appease the Rubensteins, the truth being that Cecelia lived somewhere near Anzia, and probably saw a good deal of her flamboyant aunt, who was by now a genuine literary celebrity.

After years of struggle and scores of rejection slips, Anzia in 1919 had found success as the impassioned voice of immigrant Jews crowded into New York's Lower East Side, especially the women among them. That year her first published short story, "The Fat of the Land," had appeared in *Century*, and was later republished in the *Best Short Stories* series. The editor considered it the finest piece in the book and dedicated the entire volume to its then unknown author.

In 1920, Anzia published *Hungry Hearts*, a book of short stories, and doubled her fame when Sam Goldwyn paid $10,000 for the movie rights and brought the author to Hollywood to help with the screenplay. He installed Anzia in a suite at the smart Miramar Beach Hotel, and gave her a personal bungalow and secretary at the studio. He saw to it that she met other writers whom she admired: Alice Duer Miller, Rupert Hughes, and her favorite, Will Rogers, a fellow peasant, she thought, who called her "gal" and invited her to stay at his Santa Monica ranch.

The studio publicity machine pumped out headlines: SWEATSHOP CINDERELLA WINS FORTUNE IN MOVIES. Interviewers lined up to talk to her. But Anzia the former scullion was so uncomfortable being waited on by platoons of maids and bellhops and doormen, and so resentful of having to tip all their outstretched hands, that after two days at the Miramar she moved in with Fanny and Zalkin and found a way to bank Goldwyn's $200 a week expense money. Such luxury couldn't last, she was certain; the whole place was immoral. "Babylon" was her pious father's name for it, and Anzia for once agreed. Hollywood's wealth and ease upset and disgusted her. When Goldwyn invited her to lunch to inquire about the plot of her next book, Anzia said she didn't know; she hadn't written it yet. Rambling almost incoherently, she tried to explain her state of mind. "I had to break away from my mother's cursing and my father's preaching to live my life. But without them, I had no life. When you deny your parents, you deny the ground under your feet."

Goldwyn beat a hasty exit. Then the incredible happened. Another studio attempted to steal Anzia from Goldwyn by offering her a contract for $100,000 over three years, enough money to take care of her for life. Bewildered, struck dumb, Anzia made the only choice she considered possible. She returned the contract unsigned and fled back to New York.

Possibly nineteen-year-old Cecelia took over Anzia's one-room apartment during the few months in 1921 that her aunt was away in Hollywood. Prohibition was then eighteen months old, speakeasies were everywhere; the Jazz Age had begun. Frigidaire was selling the first homemade ice cubes. Socialists like Cecelia marched in Union Square to protest the death sentences a Massachusetts court had just passed on Sacco and Vanzetti. Chaplin was starring in *The Kid* with Jackie Coogan, and Rudolph Valentino in *The Sheik*. But Cecelia in California had belonged to a group of slightly older, intellectual types who were snooty about the movies and didn't attend them. That year the new medium, radio, broadcast the first World Series, first stock reports, first band concert, and — from Detroit — the first newscast. Vincent Lopez, radio's first bandleader, did his first remote broadcast from the Hotel Taft — "Lopez speaking . . ." — and played the year's top hits, among them "Second-hand Rose," another great Grant Clarke lyric that Fanny Brice was sing-ing in the Ziegfeld Follies, and a strictly pop song: Milton Ager's "I'm Nobody's Baby."

The booming radio and record business stirred great new interest in classical music. Cecelia would have enjoyed the fashionable nights at the Metropolitan Opera, where Jeritza sang *Tosca,* and Chaliapin *Boris Godunov.* She may have seen the first one-man show of the painter Stu-art Davis, who later became her friend and the subject of one of her *Vogue* articles. She probably read Freud on dreams, Strachey's *Queen Victoria,* Sinclair Lewis's *Main Street,* and certainly Millay's "Renas-cence." At the theater, Cecelia saw Molnar's *Liliom,* with Eva Le Gal-lienne and Joseph Schildkraut; Synge's *The Playboy of the Western World,* with Thomas Mitchell; O'Neill's *Anna Christie;* Sissle and Blake's *Shuffle Along,* the first Broadway musical written and performed by blacks, with the teenage Josephine Baker. In Romberg's *Bombo,* she heard Jolson sing Ager's "Who Cares?"

"It was great to be twenty in the twenties," Aaron Copland once said. When Cecelia escaped her Columbia University dormitory and moved to the Village she was nineteen, and one of the most winning new girls in town. She was bright, good-looking, and vivacious, smoked a lot, stud-ied hard, bobbed her hair, and loved going to parties and dancing the Charleston. Her friends included intellectuals like Edmund Wilson, thespians like the Barrymores, and showbiz figures like bald, paunchy Bert Savoy, acknowledged to be the era's funniest, most brilliant female impersonator. She spoke of the unusual gentleness of "Margie," Savoy's female character, who was never bitchy or malicious, "merely marvel-ous." To all these people, Cecelia was known as "the Coed." None of them had ever seen a coed before, and she was just as fascinating to them as they to her.

How do I know all this? Because on June 13, 1975, Cecelia went to have lunch with her friend Lawrence Stewart, and he later wrote up the lunch in his journal:

Maybe I'm a bit low today because Arthur Kober died — not
that I was a part of his life, or he of mine. But when Celia told
me the news [she had come for lunch on the verandah here:
oeufs en gelee, white asparagus, hot croissants — the signifi-
cance of the menu will soon be revealed!], I was surprised how
many anecdotes came to mind. . . . Cecelia is one who can tell
amusing stories about the past, because the stories are of
people I know only as Names. Thus she mentioned James
Pope-Hennessey . . . Bert Savoy . . . Edmund Wilson . . . the
Barrymores. . . . Apparently no one had seen a Coed before,
and Cecelia was it. She said she soon met and married Milton,
for she decided that she needed to tie herself permanently to
someone she could introduce to her mother!

Stewart had not fully understood this comment, I thought. In Jazz
Age Manhattan, the gently raised California coed had probably gone a
bit wild; what she really meant was "someone I could introduce to my
mother." And the supremely correct, charming, and well-fixed little
songwriter she chose was, indeed, any mother-in-law's dream. But marrying him was also an act of willful self-censorship for which the
bohemian, free-spirit side of Cecelia's nature would scourge herself
ever after.

> . . . The white asparagus today [Stewart continues]
> reminded Cecelia of a George Gershwin anecdote. Once
> George came to visit Milton and Cecelia, ("this was before he
> was such a celebrity) and he asked me how to eat asparagus.
> I said, you cut off the tip and then you can eat the stalk with
> your fingers if you want. (I was improvising," she remarked.)
> George had just learned the technique and was terribly
> impressed that Cecelia did indeed have it down flat. [George
> was evidently unaware of Zook. — S.A.]
> When I remarked that George was occasionally gauche
> about his food requirements or manners (or so Lee had said)
> Cecelia said that was utter nonsense. "George wasn't
> gauche — EVER. He had instinctive grace."

Two of Cecelia's favorite twenties party-givers were the artist Howard Chandler Christie and Emily and Lou Paley. The Christie revels attracted painters and models and socialites, and the regular Saturday night parties at the Paleys' were an informal gathering place for the more literate and intellectual figures in show business and the arts. Oscar Levant, Vincent Youmans, Howard Dietz, Edward G. Robinson, Sam Jaffe, Fanny Brice, and the young John Huston could be found sitting on the floor sipping tea and listening for hours to Gershwin playing nonstop piano.

Emily's kid sister Leonore Strunsky was one of many young women in the crowd said to be madly in love with George. Milton Ager too was a habitué of the Paleys' parties, but I don't believe that is where my parents met.

Ager, Yellen & Bornstein, Inc., opened its doors shortly after Labor Day 1922. A few weeks later a vaudeville singer named Ethel King dropped in looking for new material. Ethel did a one-woman act on the Fox circuit inspired by Fanny Brice. It opened demurely, with the orchestra playing "By the Beautiful Sea" and Ethel coming onstage in a short bathing dress, carrying a pail and shovel. But all hell soon broke loose, and Ethel wound up belting out raucous songs and pounding a hot piano.

Ethel's real name was Ethel Mayer, and she was the youngest daughter of Max Mayer, the first Jezierski to arrive in the U.S. Ethel was the younger sister of Dr. Hannah Mayer Stone and one of Cecelia's cousins. She looked like Beatrice Lillie, never married, and died young, of pneumonia. This is the sum total of what I know about her. I wish I knew more, because our cousin Viola tells me that twenty-year-old Cecelia happened to be tagging along with her twenty-six-year-old cousin Ethel the day Ethel stopped by Milton's offices, and that is how my parents met.

Neither Milton nor Cecelia ever mentioned Ethel. The first I heard of her was after their deaths, from Viola, who in 1922 was in high school. Viola remembers Cecelia as "not round, but plump and curvaceous, with a delicate build — really darling looking. She was also very sensitive — much more than the other cousins — extremely self-centered, and terribly spoiled by Fanny. She had some small part on Broadway, just a walk-on, in *Rain*, but she also understudied Jeanne Eagles."

I was astounded. Cecelia had never mentioned being onstage, nor *Rain*, though she did talk about what a superb actor Walter Huston was, and I knew she was an old pal of his son John, the director. But the chronology seems right: *Rain* opened in November 1922, and Cecelia married Milton on February 1, 1923, after knowing him only four months.

The fact is, Cecelia and Milton told their children not one thing about how they met, and, with one exception, nothing about the early days of their marriage. Cecelia told me only two family stories ever, told them both when I was very young, and told them repeatedly. The first was about how Fanny had been bamboozled into marriage by her crafty father, and the second was how Cecelia herself was trapped into matrimony. When she accepted Milton's proposal, she telegraphed the news to her parents, and then changed her mind. But by that time Fanny, overjoyed, was on her way to New York.

"What could I do?" Cecelia used to say to six-year-old me. "Fanny was already on the train!"

The wedding took place in City Hall ten days after Cecelia's twenty-first birthday. Milton, now twenty-nine and a well-established songwriter, knew just about everybody in show business. One of his songwriting, nightclubbing pals was a dashing Irish politician, James J. Walker, author of "Will You Love Me in December As You Do in May?" who would soon be elected mayor of New York City. Walker arranged for the present mayor to perform the wedding in his office, and the only other person there save for the mayor's secretary, who served as a witness, was Fanny.

Cecelia never hesitated telling the story in Milton's presence about having changed her mind, nor did he seem to mind hearing it. Any time Fanny was mentioned, Milton interrupted to say what a darling she was, and how they had adored one another from the instant they met.

Cecelia's story is a prime example of her lifetime need to make someone else responsible for everything that went wrong. It also suggests that she, like her own mother — and like Milton's mother — had married a man she did not love. But there the similarity ends. My grandmothers longed for romance. Cecelia seemed to regard marriage, not just to Milton but to anyone, as some kind of less than completely honorable compromise, some fundamental sellout of self; I think she heard this idea first from Anzia.

Milton several times told me a story about Cecelia asking him what he wanted for breakfast the first morning of their marriage. He mentioned the same breakfast he ate at Lindy's, scrambled eggs and potato pancakes. Cecelia knew not one thing about cooking, and tried to make potato pancakes from a cookbook. Milton got hiccups which continued nonstop for three terrible days and nights. Every folk remedy was tried, to no avail. They were about to take him to a hospital when someone finally suggested the cure that worked. Hard-boil three eggs. Shell them carefully and save the thin membrane between the egg white and the shell. Discard eggs and shells, roll the membrane up into tiny pellets, and swallow them. There is nothing warm and fuzzy about this anecdote. Cecelia's covert hostility and fear and Milton's conflicted longing seem quite apparent. Until recently, I might have used the same words to describe my parents' entire marriage, as Laurel and I observed it. But few children see their parents clearly, and ours were harder to read than most.

The newlyweds moved to a small apartment on West 55th Street behind Carnegie Hall, a neighborhood that traditionally houses musicians and show people. On the afternoon of February 12, 1924, a blizzard was raging when Cecelia and Milton made their way to Aeolian Hall to hear the first performance of George Gershwin's *Rhapsody in Blue.* The place was sold out, and packed with standees. I don't know where Milton sat, but Cecelia sat next to Ira Gershwin in the front row, and before the night was over, she had won his heart forever.

Paul Whiteman, a former symphonic player who now led a big dance orchestra and billed himself as "the King of Jazz," had gathered the elite of the musical world to hear a ragbag, hastily thrown together concert intended to answer the grandiose question "What Is American Music?" As judges, Whiteman had recruited Serge Rachmaninoff, Jascha Heifetz, Efrem Zimbalist, and Alma Gluck, and invited every leading composer of the day to contribute. It was an interminable evening that included a jazz version of "Yes, We Have No Bananas," some "semisymphonic arrangements" of Irving Berlin songs, Edwin Mac-Dowell's "To a Wild Rose" played in dance tempo, and so on.

Gershwin's new composition was twenty-second of the twenty-three entries listed on the program. The perspiring audience had begun slinking out, blizzard or no, by the time the elegant composer came onstage, sat down at the piano, and Whiteman's clarinettist let loose with the electrifying jazz glissando with which the *Rhapsody* begins. Hearing it, Cecelia grabbed Ira's arm so tightly, and held on to it so long, that for the next several weeks the arm was black and blue. Ira told the story for the rest of his life, always adding that he'd never minded the painful consequences of Cecelia's fervor because it told him that here was a woman who would never, ever pull her punches.

Without question the twenties roared for Milton. He was at the top of his form, and Ager, Yellen & Bornstein, Inc., had got off to a very fast start. Enough money was available before my birth to enable my parents to rent a summer house in Great Neck, and move in the fall to a bigger apartment at 157 West 57th.

Viola remembers Cecelia being dazzled by Milton's fast-moving Broadway life, and my mother confessed as much in a seminar she gave in the mid-seventies for screenwriting students at the American Film Institute. She said it again to the group of journalism students she lectured to only three weeks after Milton's death. She relished the late nights, colorful showbiz characters, nightclubs, jazz joints, gin mills — scenes the Coed had never before encountered. She appreciated the contrast between Milton's civilized, gentlemanly demeanor and that of his flashy, low-down friends. However, Anzia was almost certainly critical of her favorite niece's sharply dressed, nine-years-older husband and his free-spending way of life. Anzia was fundamentally antimarriage, if not antimen, and her burning intensity and wild independence had guaranteed her a position of lifelong influence on her prosperous sister's only daughter. Anzia took full advantage of the situation, alternately seducing Cecelia with feminist dreams of freedom, and lashing her with guilts about her wealth and Anzia's poverty.

As for Anzia's own career, mounting guilt about becoming rich by writing about the poor was slowly beginning to stifle her ability to write about anything. She managed a novel, *Salome of the Tenements*, and another collection of short pieces, *Children of Loneliness*, but she felt alone in the midst of plenty, and inner anxiety consumed her. A quick trip to London was arranged, but meetings with Galsworthy, Conrad, G. B. Shaw and H. G. Wells only made her feel more like someone who had joined the community of writers under false pretenses, a fake and a liar. How could these people write so smoothly and elegantly, with no seams showing?

"Why worry?" wise Gertrude Stein told her in Paris. "Nobody knows how writing is written, the writers least of all."

Nor could Anzia overcome her extreme frugality. Long after her work had begun selling as fast as she could write it, she still lived in a bare furnished room. It was late 1923, some months after Cecelia's marriage, before she could bring herself to try enjoying the fruits of her success by moving to a luxury hotel on lower Fifth Avenue that offered liveried doormen, room service, and a grand dining salon. Even here Anzia chose a one-room apartment, and had it repainted and stripped of its overstuffed furnishings until it resembled, in her own words, "a nun's cell." When eleven-year-old Louise came to spend the night with her mother, she had to sleep on a "floor pad," she writes, and "supper or breakfast consisted of food kept illegally on the bathroom windowsill, cooked on a forbidden hot plate, and served from the pot on the only two . . . plates."

By the time I first knew Anzia, ten years had passed since *Hungry Hearts*, fashions in popular literature had changed, and my great-aunt had become a burnt-out case. Her lumpy outfits, passionate speech, and extravagant gesticulations made her so conspicuous even in her humble Greenwich Village neighborhood that as a seven-year-old I felt embarrassed walking on the street with her, or even sitting alone with her on Morton Street observing her perpetual *geshrei* and emotional disarray.

She had moved from the posh hotel and lived now in a cheap one-room walk-up, toiled for $23.86 a week on the WPA Writers' Project, had lost whatever savings she had in the stock market, and was virtually broke. One reviewer, less dazzled than most, had by then suggested that "her gift is not creative; she is a reporter and an autobiographical rather than a fiction writer." There was some truth to this, and by 1932 she appeared to have used up her material and lost her audience. After twelve productive years, six books, and scores of magazine stories, Anzia Yezierska for the next eighteen years would publish nothing at all. Cecelia during those years would move from being a star reporter on *Variety* to a well-paid stint as a Hollywood screenwriter to the position of movie editor and critic on the most prestigious and innovative experiment in American journalism in our century. How did she feel about her rather stunning ascendance as a career woman: naive Coed to savvy mugg in seven years; screenwriter to respected film critic, possibly the best of her generation, in another decade or less? She never spoke of it except to trivialize it, not to her daughters or, so far as I know, to anyone else; even Lawrence Stewart's journals are bare of any reflections by Cecelia upon her life and work. She talked wittily, sometimes winningly, and always with great insight about others, but never a word about herself or her work, except to dismiss its importance, to deem it minor, small-time. In some ways it was: nothing of her work exists between hard covers, with the exception of a few cracks in dictionaries of quotations — "Miss Hepburn's voice was lilting along as before: She is oblivious of her impact. Or inured to it. Or stuck with it" — and the twenty-three movie reviews reprinted in *Garbo and the Night Watchmen*. Even though her daughter too became a writer, even after she and her daughter finally managed to become friends, we never talked about what a writer's life was like, nor discussed one another's work.

*　　*　　*

Two or three weeks after Milton's death, Laurel invited Cecelia and her brother Victor and her favorite niece, Louise, and their spouses to dinner. I was traveling and couldn't be there, but Louise wrote me a letter about it afterwards. The others were worried about Cecelia's abrupt widowhood. She was not just stricken by Milton's death; she seemed suddenly without resources of any kind. Cecelia appreciated their concern, and had tried to make a speech thanking Laurel and Wray for their kindness. But even under these circumstances she revealed not one thing about her own feelings.

> . . . I think she had innate gallantry [Louise wrote]. She didn't complain. She seemed to think she was getting her just desserts, and she accepted it. She said, "The hell with me!"
>   That alone makes me love her.

CHAPTER SIX

HOLLYWOOD

In the summer of 1937 the Ager family again headed for California. This time Cecelia's career, not Milton's, compelled the move. Samuel Goldwyn, the same man who had brought Anzia to Hollywood, had now hired my mother. That a woman who had never written a play or novel, or even a short story, who had never written anything except her weekly *Variety* copy, and a couple of pieces in *Vogue*, should suddenly become a $250-a-week screenwriter, at ten times her *Variety* salary, was itself improbable, though no more so than the project she was being brought west to work on — *Graustark*.

Not even Goldwyn's closest associates could understand his obsession with this creaky 1901 mittel-Europa romance. The mogul for years had instructed his story editor Sam Marx, "Never *ever* buy anything about a mythical kingdom!" But Sam happened to be away when his boss bought the moth-eaten property. At the next studio production conference, Goldwyn bragged about his new acquisition, and sneered at Marx for missing it.

"But didn't you always tell me — no mythical kingdoms?" said Sam.

"Sure I did, God damn it. But I didn't mean *classics!*"

Goldwyn's classic begins in the Wild West, where a naive, Gary Cooper–type American falls in love with a mysterious woman on a train — the princess of Graustark, traveling incognito. What follows is three hundred pages of foul murders, mistaken identities, duels, disguises, frame-ups, impostors, spies, treacheries, and hairbreadth escapes. The scriptwriter's task was to transform the heavy narrative goulash into something which might appeal to American audiences.

Several writers, including Lillian Hellman, had already struck out when Beatrice Kaufman, Goldwyn's eastern story scout, suggested her friend Cecelia Ager. Bill Morris, acting as Cecelia's agent, shrewdly teamed her as cowriter with the highly experienced Donald Ogden Stewart, author of a solid string of hit books, plays, and movies, most recently *The Prisoner of Zenda.*

Fanny stood alone on the platform when Cecelia and Laurel and I pulled into Pasadena; though we had not been told about it, Zalkin had died the year before. A large part of Milton's world had died as well. He had lost his irreplaceable lyricist, lost his father, and lost his onetime close friend George Gershwin. In contrast to Cecelia's expanding, challenging new world, Milton's horizons were diminishing. The music business had been hard hit by the Depression, and a one-man publishing company was finding it difficult to attract new writers and was increasingly dependent upon sales of past hits.

We had boarded the train the moment school ended; Milton remained in New York for several months attending to difficult matters at the office. He was still writing, of course, trying out many new partners, on both coasts, and scoring a few big hits, most notably "Auf Wiedersehen, My Dear" in 1932 and "In a Little Red Barn" and "Trust in Me" in 1934. In 1935, the first year of *Your Hit Parade,* "Seein' Is Believin' " made the grade, and in 1936 "West Wind" and "You Can't Pull the Wool over My Eyes" also scored. But the singular "marriage" of Ager and Yellen would prove inimitable and, by the time we moved to Hollywood, our father's biggest days were in the past.

We children were completely unaware of the change in the parental balance of power. Cecelia rented a big Beverly Hills house on North Linden Drive, but when we rang the doorbell a butler said the other tenants had not quite moved out. A tanned and terrifically handsome man appeared and suggested we have a drink on the patio while he and his wife finished packing. "And, er, Coca-Cola for the little girls," he said, winning our hearts at once.

He was Alan Campbell, husband of Dorothy Parker, a small pouter pigeon of a woman with black bangs, demure demeanor, and extremely pretty feet and ankles. We had the drink, and another, and then someone scrambled the last of the eggs, and by the time lunch was over, everybody had become friends for life. We even got to keep the butler and maid while Dottie and Alan returned to New York, having completed their work on *A Star Is Born*.

Every day Cecelia drove off in her convertible to the Goldwyn Studios, a mysterious place I never saw. Milton mostly worked at home, at the same brisk tempo as before. His new lyricists were to me indistinguishable — men who arrived in golf clothes at odd hours, spent an hour or two with my father at the piano, and drove away, followed by lots more singing on the telephone. As an established composer, Milton was much sought after by young, new lyricists hoping to develop their ideas and by experienced old ones seeking to complete their false starts. Though Laurel and I detected no change in his work pattern, Milton later summed up his new situation with unsparing acuity. "When Jack left the firm," he said, "I became a song doctor."

Tall, owlish, and famously whimsical, Don Stewart had hit it off with Cecelia at once. She even liked his formidable girlfriend, soon to be his wife, Ella Winter, the former wife of Lincoln Steffens and as impassioned a revolutionary as Rayna Simons had been. Many other fine writers toiled for Goldwyn, and Cecelia joined them for lunch at the "writers' table" in the commissary, or one of the gin joints nearby. Dottie and Alan came back to work on *The Cowboy and the Lady*, and Lillian Hellman was adapting Sidney Kingsley's *Dead End*. Marc Connolly, Ben Hecht, Charles MacArthur, Jo Swerling, Rupert Hughes, I. A. R. Wylie, Charlie Lederer, Joe Bigelow, Garson Kanin, Sidney Howard, and Thomas Mann were also variously employed by Goldwyn in Cecelia's time there, providing a perpetual banquet of good, writerly company. One or another of Cecelia's new friends often came by for a drink after work, and then everybody went off to Chasen's or Romanoff's or Don the Beachcomber's for dinner.

Thanks to ASCAP, there was still plenty of money coming in, and thanks to Cecelia, we were spending it all. In time we would inhabit three North Linden Drive houses, increasingly grand, and all subleased, thrillingly furnished, from a woman named Gladys Belzer. Mrs. Belzer, whose exquisite taste nearly equaled Cecelia's, was Loretta Young's mother, and she earned a handsome income by leasing the empty, Spanish-style stucco houses which nobody could sell during the Depression, tricking them out from her own vast collection of antiques, augmented by rented studio furniture and movie props, and rerenting them at handsome profits to new arrivals in the lucrative Hollywood vineyards.

Our second house, at 629 North Linden, had just been vacated by Cecelia's friend Nunnally Johnson, a screenwriter who had moved around the corner to a house with a pool. Nunnally was a quiet-spoken, immensely witty man who loved children. His lanky, slightly awkward body bore the sweet face of some small Disney forest animal. He had never lost his Georgia drawl, and looked like a gawky country boy inside his well-tailored Saville Row suits. He smoked a lot of cigarettes, and drank a lot of whiskey, occupational diseases of writers then even more than today. Both my parents did the same, and as soon as possible, so did I.

Beverly Hills was the highest-income town in the nation, with fine public schools near enough to walk to. But they were not a patch on wonderful Lincoln, and classes left a scant impression on me. I felt more crazed than before by my need to be "popular," a longing that seemed more hopeless than ever among these tanned, happy, rich, tennis-playing children. Laurel and I were always invited to swim after school in Nunnally's backyard pool with his daughters, Nora and Marjorie, watched over by a swimming teacher. Beverly Hills children had teachers for everything. Laurel took tennis lessons from a Mr. Oiseaux at the Hillcrest Country Club. I was outfitted in jodhpurs several times a week and driven out to the Riviera Country Club for horseback riding lessons with the legendary English riding master "Snowy" Baker. Nunnally had even provided a dog for his children, much to the envy of Laurel and me, and it too had a teacher. Then the dog was sent away for advanced training at dog boarding school. One day the butler brought the phone to the pool. It was the dog school calling to say the dog was ready to come home.

"Do you offer any postgraduate courses?" Nunnally inquired.

Fanny was now a more important figure than ever in Laurel's and my lives. We spent weekends shopping and going to triple features like *Dracula, The Bride of Dracula,* and *Frankenstein.* She drove us down to see the La Brea tar pits, out to Eagle Rock, and even one hundred miles to Riverside to lunch amid the tropical gardens of the Mission Inn.

Victor's kindness too was overwhelming. When Fanny gave him a Ford convertible for graduation from Stanford, he volunteered to drive "a couple of little twerps" — Cecelia's mockingly affectionate term for her eight- and eleven-year-olds — on a tour of the Grand Canyon and Bryce and Zion National Parks. Victor had the same unusually gentle, sweet, and sentimental nature as Fanny's younger brothers, Uncle Bill and Uncle Harry. Cecelia loathed sentimentality, yet loved them all.

We were now living year-round on Cecelia's home turf, amid the places and people she had grown up with, yet she never permitted herself one word of reminiscence. Each time she drove us down Sunset Boulevard to visit Fanny, we had to pass Hollywood High School, the place where she had cheered the home team so hard that she tumbled out of the balcony. But it was Victor who told me this; Cecelia would never speak of her childhood. I can only conclude that it must have been stifling.

In a letter Anzia wrote to her husband, Louise's father, she describes a visit to Fanny when Cecelia was ten years old:

> . . . At my sister's I have all the love and tenderness, all the luxurious comforts a person can wish for — sunshine, flowers, automobiling, the finest food, and the most loving service of my sister who treats me like a mother her one child. I appreciate it — but — there isn't one *live* person here to talk to. No possibility of any mental or intellectual intercourse with anyone. My brother-in-law while he has a good heart and means well is unfortunately a coarse, vulgar boor whose mentality has been reduced to money-making and lustful physical enjoyment. The people he surrounds himself with are those of his own calibre, whose idea of sociability is time-wasting . . . meaningless, purposeless conversation [about] women or card-playing.

Another letter says:

> . . . I could not do my writing in such an atmosphere. . . . All I could do is watch my brother-in-law play pinochle. . . . My sister is ill and worn out most of the time from the harmful preventives of conception which she is so often forced to use as she does not want more children and her husband is most inconsiderate in his desire. . . .

Cecelia was looking more beautiful than ever; at thirty-five, she was coming into her best days. She was always suntanned, and she dressed in clear, light shades of melon, gold, cream, and beige. Her knot of hair moved from her nape to the top of her head, and the Mr. John hats yielded to flights of velvet bows in many colors, attached to combs. She wore two or three at a time, as if exotic butterflies had alit temporarily on her shiny, perfect coiffeur. She began to wear earrings, chaste, perfect teardrops of beaten gold or random assemblages of semiprecious stones, artfully set so that no gold showed. She acquired two strands of large, baroque, freshwater pearls, chosen for their irregularity. She took up high-style knitting and produced a series of boxy, waist-length jackets in an intricate ribbed stitch which exactly matched the colors of her velvet bows. Of immense chic, they had wide bands of crochet down the front, crocheted buttons and buttonholes, and looked as if they'd been bought in Paris at Chanel. She had also begun wearing a thick gold wedding ring, so chunky it might have been made by a blacksmith. She had several of these, and wore them for the rest of her life.

She bloomed in the presence of her expanding court of admirers, unusually witty and brainy men. Garson Kanin had worked for the Broadway producer George Abbott until Bea Kaufman sent him out to be Goldwyn's assistant, and the Morris office arranged a seven-year contract. Gar was twenty-four, and one of several men during that period who sort of fell in love with Cecelia. "I was sweet on her," Kanin later put it. "She was such good company! Smart, sharp, savvy, exciting to be with, fun to talk to, yet entirely female and adorable." And unlike most of the other gorgeous women in town, "you didn't have to talk down to her."

Many years later Pauline Kael expressed a similar idea when she described Cecelia's approach to movie criticism as "lighthearted and sneakily feminine. She was such fun to read!" — a compliment my mother would have appreciated.

Another great admirer was Nunnally, who was writing the screenplay of *The Grapes of Wrath* for Darryl F. Zanuck. That he was in mid-divorce, heartbroken and guilt-ridden about his children, who normally lived with their mothers, his two ex-wives, was not yet clear to me. One evening when he rang our doorbell, the prettiest woman I'd ever seen was on his arm. He introduced Dorris Bowden, just discovered by a Twentieth Century-Fox talent scout, and newly arrived in Hollywood from Arkabutla, Mississippi. Dorris had been cast to play Rose of Sharon, and Nunnally was falling in love with her. Cecelia soon became the naive twenty-year-old starlet's mentor, friend, and sure guide to Hollywood's strange folkways.

"Cecelia was the brightest woman I ever knew," Dorris told me more than a decade after my mother and Nunnally had died. "Marjorie [Marjorie Fowler, Nunnally's eldest daughter, a screen editor] and I still talk about her every time we get together. But she didn't ever parade it, or press it. And she was such a great — *great* — audience. I remember most her eyes, always so alert, and a gentle, expectant half-smile as she listened intently to whatever was being said. Of course, when she wanted, she could project the greatest *disdain* I have ever seen in my entire life!"

Dorris saw Cecelia as a woman "imbued with the culture of the Jazz Age, which she carried into the thirties and forties. This is why she was so free-thinking. She had stayed in the Roaring Twenties, while the world moved on. She had great taste, and a surgical eye that saw below and beyond the surface, into reality."

Dorris "worshiped Cecelia! To me, she represented independence and freedom from custom, just as — to Nunnally — I represented the high school girl he could never get a date with."

Another reality which Dorris saw quite clearly was that Cecelia was in love with Nunnally, and had sublimated her feelings by becoming a good friend and adviser to his young, socially insecure girlfriend. When Nunnally was finally divorced and free to marry, Cecelia took Dorris shopping for her wedding dress and trousseau.

Cecelia and Milton were now thirty-five and forty-four, and I was eleven, old enough to see that not only were my parents different from other parents, they had a seemingly miserable marriage. Why else would they spend so much time a continent apart? Milton returned to Manhattan several times a year to look after his business. The trips upset him, and his digestion worsened. Though he had no illusions about the music business, he was impatient, moralistic, quick to anger, and had become increasingly disgusted with Tin Pan Alley practices. He had "wanted to be Haydn," but found himself in a world where rip-offs and sleaze were becoming the norm, payola and chiseling rampant, and very few people meant what they said. Milton's ASCAP and publishing income allowed him to maintain a certain distance from the fray, and to hone his golf and bridge skills on a daily basis. Nor did he stop composing. Since he could hear everything in his head, he didn't always need to be at a piano. He could work on the fairways and on the street, as well as in his bedroom, and did, all his life.

One would not have suspected from his demeanor that Milton's ranking as a Tin Pan Alley all-star was sinking a bit with every passing year. He was cheerful by nature, always charming, often witty. Despite rare outbursts of fury, he seemed brimful of equanimity most of the time. But surely silent Cecelia knew.

When Milton was back in New York, she either dined out with friends or went to bed and closed the door as soon as she came home from the studio. Insomnia, overwork, hay fever, and headaches were blamed, but in retrospect it is apparent that my mother was an increasingly unhappy woman. When my father was home, they must have fought a lot. I don't remember the fights, but the following scene is very clear in my memory. One evening after hearing a loud door-slam indicating that Milton had stormed out, I got an idea. I knocked on the door of Cecelia's bedroom. She was seated at her dressing table, Kleenex all around her on the floor, wiping off her makeup, and I addressed her reflection in the mirror. "If you and Milton don't like each other," I said, "why don't you get a divorce?"

Several of their friends were in mid-divorce, and the term was a familiar one. Cecelia swiveled her chair around to face me. "Don't you remember? When you were eight, I *asked you* if I should get a divorce?" She waited a beat, her blue eyes fixed upon me. I could remember nothing.

"Well, you said no!"

I was ashamed to have forgotten something so important. For many years I tried without success to resurrect in memory the scene she had

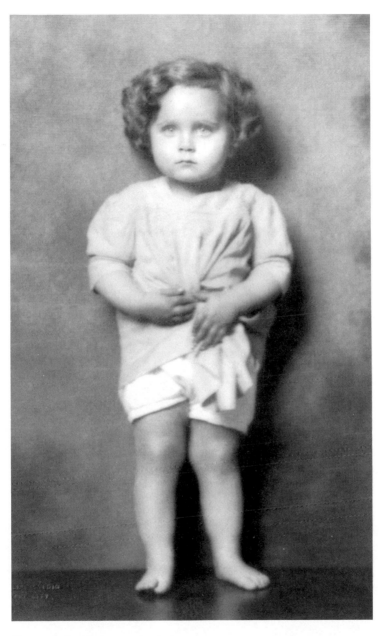

Shana at about nineteen months.

BELOW Cecelia's parents, Fannie and Zalkin
Rubenstein.

ABOVE Strunsky/Gershwin family house party, Belmar, New Jersey, 1926. To the left of the left-hand pillar, top row: Milton and Cecelia; second row: Marjorie Paley, Morris Strunsky, Elsie Payson. In the arch, top row: Lou Paley, Bela Blau, S. N. Behrman, Mrs. Arthur Caesar, English Strunsky, Harold Keyserling. Second row: Mrs. Bela Blau, Mischa Levitzky, Henrietta Poynter, Jim Englander. Bottom row: Howard Dietz, Cecelia Hays, Arthur Caesar, Emily Paley, Phil Charig, Leonore Gershwin, Ira Gershwin, George Backer, Harold Goldman. Front, center: George Gershwin. Behind George Backer are Anita Keen and Barney Paley. On the porch is Albert Strunsky, father of Leonore, Emily, and English.
Courtesy of Ira and Leonore Gershwin Trusts. Used by Permission.

LEFT Milton's parents, Simon and Fanny Ager (front row, second and fourth) and their eight children, Chicago, about 1920. Milton Ager is at extreme right.

RIGHT The advertisement for my father's music publishing company, which appeared on the back of all his sheet music.

BELOW LEFT George Gershwin's portrait of Cecelia, about 1932.

BELOW RIGHT Cecelia in about 1938.

ABOVE Anzia Yezierska, New York City, 1950. *Photo by Morris Engel.*

LEFT Laurel and Shana learning to sweep on Anzia's porch in Vermont, summer 1932.

BELOW Shana, Laurel, and Anzia in Vermont.

RIGHT Shana, lower left, at her high school graduation party.

BELOW At Shana's wedding, 1951. Left to right: Laurel, Cecelia, hostess Maria Martel, Milton, Patrick O'Higgins, Shana, host Marshall Mundheim, Mr. John. *Photo by Leonard McCabe.*

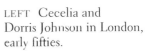

LEFT Cecelia and
Dorris Johnson in London,
early fifties.

BELOW Milton in the Agers'
apartment, 1947.

Cecelia at a Charlie Chaplin press conference, New York City, 1946.

just described. That it had never happened, that she considered her life or her marriage such a failure and needed so badly to blame it on some-one else that even an eight-year-old would do, took a long time for me to understand.

Ever since I could remember, my mother had engendered in me a pervasive sense of having done something wrong, I wasn't sure what. To figure it out, I was continually making up crimes, slights, oversights, sins of selfishness, insensitivity, or neglect, and wondering if I'd committed them. The idea that I had not done anything, and was reacting to false accusations, did not occur to me for many years. When it did, I tried to analyze where her need to do it came from. Why could nothing ever be her fault, a consequence of her mistake or neglect? Why did blame *have* to be displaced? I never found out. But I recognized her as a master gardener of guilt. She raked up the soil, and nourished and encouraged the tender shoots, and watched with satisfaction when it burst into bloom. Where did she acquire this skill? It couldn't have been Fanny; I doubt it was Zalkin. But she had the gift, a real green thumb.

The arch crime was *ducking*. It meant avoiding, flinching, shirking, failing to take responsibility, running away. An honorable person does not duck; he takes the grapefruit straight in the face. The second-worst crime was self-centeredness, failure to "think of the other person."

"Don't you *ever* think of the other person?" she asked her daughters repeatedly, with maximal scorn. The adult result of this conditioning was two anxious and hyper-considerate women who almost always thought of the other person first, put personal considerations last, and wound up holding the short end of the stick and wondering why they were so unlucky.

Dottie and Alan returned to Hollywood to work on *Sweethearts* for Jean-ette MacDonald and Nelson Eddy. Whenever they came to dinner, Lau-rel and I were permitted to join the adults, and on one such occasion Dottie sang us a plaintive, haunting song, "Stand to Your Glasses,

Steady," with noble and ironic words composed during the siege of Crimea. Milton went to the piano and played it, in Dottie's key, and played it a few more times, until we all had it memorized.

> *Cut off by the land that bore us,*
> *Betrayed by the land we find.*
> *All the brightest have gone before us,*
> *And only the dull left behind.*
> *So stand to your glasses, steady;*
> *This world is a world of lies.*
> *Here's a sip to the dead already.*
> *And a cup to the next man that dies.*

Every time Dottie and Alan showed up, we did the song again. "Stand to your glasses, steady," we would all sing out gallantly, four quavering sopranos and two clear baritones, lifting whatever beverage was at hand, none of us quite certain of the order of the words. Sometimes we sang, "This world is a world of lies," other times, "And drink to your comrades' eyes," still other times, "And drink to your sweetheart's eyes."

Another verse went:

> *We meet 'neath the sounding rafters.*
> *The walls all around are bare.*
> *The dead echo back our laughter.*
> *They know that we'll soon be there.*

At first our family used it mainly as a drinking song, to be sung at social gatherings. Slowly over the years we came to regard it as our official family song, sung at the drop of a downbeat, and always sung standing up, on every important occasion, festive or sad. Laurel and I still sing it today.

Surefire tearjerker that it is, Dottie's song turned out to be not quite what it seemed. It was easy to imagine the song being sung round the barracks at Balaklava by doomed young officers about to meet the Russians in the Charge of the Light Brigade. But when Laurel and I grew up and did some research, we found that the tune is an old Irish air, and the words are those of a long poem, "The Revel," by a nineteenth-century Irish poet, Bartholomew Dowling. Furthermore, what the men feared was not death in battle but death from cholera, the same cholera epidemic that had wiped out the parents of Simon Ager.

A low point in my life was going with Cecelia to get my first brassieres. She felt she had destroyed her breasts by binding down her bosom to look like a flapper, and was determined not to let her mistake be repeated in me. She must have lain in wait for the first sign of mammary development in me, and as I was a chubby child, it probably came early. Well before I myself had noticed anything, I found myself whisked into a Beverly Hills brassiere shop, and stood up half-naked and ashamed on a circular dais in the back room, where the special custom work was done. Under Cecelia's stern supervision, one of her kindly, ugly European refugee ladies was fitting me with a child's brassiere of plain white broadcloth. I had never yet felt as mortified.

The brassiere makers were good examples of a new group of people who played important roles in Cecelia's life from the early thirties right on through World War II. Cut-rate European experts could suddenly be found for every unusual task and skill. It was more than a matter of being able to find people who could fit corsetry on children and crochet yarmulkes. Quite suddenly there were first-class tailors and boot-makers and bead-stringers, and schnitzel-bakers and marzipan-makers and horoscope-casters. You could find trained professionals at cutting and sewing custom-made gloves, removing blackheads, giving enemas. A few years later, highly trained doctors were available for performing electrolysis on hairy teenagers, or fitting pessaries. Who did all these things, I used to wonder, before Hitler started forcing Jews to flee Europe?

Worse, from my point of view, all of these people spoke Yiddish, and every damned one of them, it seemed to me, asked me the same embarrassing question: "Do you know what your name means?" I knew, all right.

Shaineh in Yiddish, like *schön* in German, means "pretty," and is a common Jewish nickname. To me my foreign-sounding name, Shana Ager, not only emphasized how *different* I was from other children, it mocked the truth. I knew I wasn't pretty, and couldn't bear to discuss the matter.

Although Cecelia and Milton did not in any way reject or hide their origins — no ridiculous changes from Horowitz to Hewitt, Weinstein to Wallace for them — I was less secure. As a young child, this insecurity had become somehow all bound up with my awful name. The name was not merely Shana Ager but, I confess here for the first time, Shana Gittel Ager, Shana Gittel having been the name of Milton's Orthodox, wig-wearing grandmother. In the world of Lincoln School chums I had grown up with, kids from what I thought of as normal families, people like Cordelia Ware, Diana Marks, and even Bob Smith, being Shana Gittel Ager had somehow been just too much. I shrank from the shame of my weirdo name. Everything about me was freaky, I decided, not just my parents and the way we lived. It did not help when the Andrews Sisters released their incomprehensible hit record *"Bei Mir Bist Du Schön,"* and the old question "Do you know what your name means?" started up again with a vengeance. I became so unhappy about my real name that later, when I needed a pen name, I invented Rage Hasan, a Muslim-sounding anagram for the hated syllables which neatly blended a certain latent anti-Semitism with my self-loathing state of mind.

Our third Mrs. Belzer house on Linden Drive was the fanciest yet. It had a white grand piano in the living room, and above it hung an enormous, harp-shaped Venetian mirror with pink glass rosettes. Yet another of my mother's European refugees was a manicurist from Spain who came to the house weekly to do Cecelia's nails in the spartan manner she preferred. Liquid polish was vulgar; nails should be buffed only, with dry polish and chamois. After the manicurist had set up her little table and its array of instruments, she and I would practice the tango while waiting for Cecelia to come downstairs. Humming and gliding and counting aloud, we swooped and swirled across the tiled patio amid the potted palms. The manicurist brought her collection of tango records from home, and I became a tangoing fool, even though my only partner was the manicurist, except on those rare, thrilling occasions when Cecelia had time to practice it with me. She really was as good as Yolanda or Sally De Marco, and held her head absolutely level. I caught glimpses of it in the Venetian mirror as we glided and twirled. At other times she and I played jacks on the marble hearth with one of Milton's golf balls. She was good at jacks, too, and at pick-up sticks. Laurel was furious that Cecelia wouldn't play with her. But to Cecelia, there was nothing to discuss. Laurel at eight was simply too young to be any good.

Our parents had separate suites on either side of a sewing room that was the province of the French maid who came with the house. We also had a Chinese cook, and on my birthday he made the one childhood birthday cake I remember, with Milton's and my names and the cook's good wishes, he assured us, spelled out in Chinese characters of pink and green icing. After school, the French maid instructed a deliriously happy me in the intricacies of fine embroidery, lingerie folding, leather glove washing, and other ladies' maid arts which I have practiced enthusiastically ever since.

Laurel has very different memories of the servants. The Chinese cook was fired for enticing Laurel into his room with comic books, and a black chauffeur was fired for the crime of being driven into while Laurel was in the car.

Each year as Cecelia's birthday approached, the grim rules which governed maternal gift-giving drove me to ever wilder exertions in hope of finally winning Cecelia's approval, and at last I had found someone to help me. The French maid did an elaborate form of embroidery called trapunto: garlands of roses and other flowers were embroidered in tiny stitches on white silk. The space between the surface silk and the lining silk was then padded with vivid red and green wool yarn, which showed through the white as delicate pink and celadon. Encouraged by the maid, I decided to make for my mother's next birthday a set of trapunto lingerie cases to hold her monogrammed handkerchiefs and Paris nightgowns. Each case bore her name in elaborate script, traced by the maid, as well as a decoration of roses. I slaved in secret for months, and had to throw away several false starts stained by tiny drops of blood. Soon the maid put aside her own work to help me with mine, and we barely got it finished in time. For a twelve-year-old, it really was a masterpiece, even though the maid had helped a lot.

"Very nice," said Cecelia, and put it in her chest of drawers. I could not believe her disinterest. I still cannot. In ensuing years, as my skills grew, I would produce more and more elaborate needlework for her: hand-embroidered pillowcase sets, colonial-style samplers in fine cross-stitch, cloudlike crocheted afghans for the foot of her chaise longue, needlepointed pillows for its back. Each time Cecelia put one of my gifts aside, I was utterly crushed. "My mother doesn't love me," I sobbed to Milton.

"She loves you. She just doesn't know how to show it," he always replied.

The Gershwins had moved to Hollywood permanently in 1936, and Leonore made their big house on North Roxbury the social center for a revolving carousel of musicians, writers, entertainers, tennis players, and artistic refugees from Europe, a kind of permanent salon. Oscar Levant, Yip and Edie Harburg, Harold Arlen, several of the Marx Brothers, Dottie and Alan, S. J. Perelman, Aaron Copland, George's last girlfriend, Paulette Goddard, and Fanny Brice were all part of the core group. George had died shortly before we arrived, but Lee kept the merry-go-round turning until Ira's death in 1983, and her own death eight years later. The Agers were frequent guests at the beginning, less so as time passed. Ira after George's death grew gradually more reclusive and Buddha-like. "The Chinese gentleman," as Fanny Brice called him, often preferred remaining alone in his bedroom to joining the gentle merriment below.

During our years on Linden Drive, Cecelia developed intense, Gerry-like friendships with two California women, Millie Lewin and Mary Stothart. Mary was the wife of the composer Herbert Stothart, the music director of MGM. Millie was the elegant blonde wife of the

MGM producer and resident intellectual Albert Lewin (*The Good Earth, Mutiny on the Bounty, Captains Courageous*). Allie, a former English professor at NYU, would never have bought *Graustark*. His great value to the studio, in addition to his taste, was that he seemingly had read every novel ever published in English. An extremely witty elf, pushing five feet tall, he wore two hearing aids and was crazy about women. Many women adored him, though many others were taken aback by his ardor, and still others, I fear, merely taken.

The Lewins and the Stotharts were using their movie money to build beautiful modern houses. The Lewins had commissioned Richard Neutra, just arrived from Germany, to design a Bauhaus modern beach house on the sands of Santa Monica. They had no children, but they collected modern and primitive art, and lived amid a constant stream of artists and intellectuals, among them the writers Anita Loos and Salka Viertel, the filmmaker Robert Flaherty, the mime Angna Enters, the composer Virgil Thomson, the photographer Man Ray, the writer who was Garbo's lover, Mercedes de Acosta, Oscar Levant, and Marcel Duchamp. My favorite was the immense and jolly Danish explorer Peter Freuchen, who told me he needed fat little girls to sit on his lap to test the strength of his wooden leg. He himself had hacked off the real one in the Arctic because of frostbite.

One afternoon as we were leaving the Lewins' with Cecelia, Ellin Berlin, Irving's wife, drove up with three little daughters about our ages. They *all* wore patent leather shoes, pretty party dresses, even little white gloves, and as each one was introduced to Cecelia and shook her hand, she curtsied! I felt mortified, an eleven-year-old slob, rigid yet faint with envy and shame.

Mary Stothart, a decade younger than Cecelia, was a vibrantly beautiful painter very much in love with her husband. They had three children about our age, and had just acquired a spectacular building site at the other end of Santa Monica from the Lewins, on the rim of a plateau overlooking the golf links and bridle paths of the Riviera Country Club. Plans for another modern house were drawn, and the night before it was time to break ground, they decided to camp out on their new property, and invited Laurel and me to join them. Herb cut wood and built a grill and we all sipped champagne and cooked hot dogs and toasted marshmallows before crawling into our sleeping bags. Snuggling down, I thought to myself: *this* is a real family.

For our first California Christmas, our parents gave us the first bikes Laurel or I had ever laid hand or foot on, expensive Belgian machines with new-fangled hand brakes. Cecelia hired a war refugee Belgian bicycle teacher in ascot and beret who stationed himself at the bottom of our driveway and ordered me to get on my bike first and ride it down to him. Halfway down I hit an oil spot, braked, skidded, and broke my leg. Within moments Uncle Victor showed up, and he and Cecelia drove me to a doctor who put on a thigh-high cast which he said he would remove in twelve weeks. Laurel, a born cyclist, was soon zooming around the neighborhood, her pigtails flying straight out behind her. I never rode a bike again.

Six weeks later the doctor cut off the top part of my thigh-high cast, and I could bend my leg and bathe for the first time, if I hung my knee over the side of the tub. I crutched to my bathroom, turned on the tub, sank down in, then saw blood in the bathwater. Our French maid showed me what to do and provided Kotex.

The absence of proper sex education in so modern a family is surprising. Cecelia *had* once prepared me for menstruation, but I was only six or seven years old and misunderstood, remembering only that she said blood would flow. We were standing beneath the Gauguin when she'd explained it, and I'd been waiting ever since for blood to flow from my breasts. When the maid said I'd got it all wrong, I felt quite relieved.

Laurel and I lacked the sexual curiosity and awareness of most children. This may have been due to the vigilance of the frauleins, or the fact that we knew no other children, were bathed individually, never together, and each night tucked tightly in bed, hands outside the covers to discourage self-exploration. So far as I was aware, we might as well have been mermaids; between navel and knees, nothing existed — in my case at least, a state of numb, dumb, willed unawareness that lasted well past high school. In those days sex was not taught in schools, even progressive schools; it was the parents' responsibility. Probably Milton considered it a mother's job to enlighten the daughters, and probably Cecelia assured him she had done so. Otherwise I think his need to instruct would have compelled him to find a way to talk to us, and I am certain neither parent did. Their intellectual belief in sexual naturalness and their fundamental prudery were always in conflict. At the same time they were walking around naked, they were hiding *Life*'s thensensational picture story "The Birth of a Baby," moving the magazine around from drawer to cupboard to shelf to be sure the children did not come upon it. I always eventually found it, reread it, and returned it to its hiding place unsure of what I had seen.

At El Rodeo School, the last term was under way, and the seniors had been told to buy white clothes for our eighth-grade graduation; the following year we would start Beverly Hills High School. My dress was pleated sharkskin, making me look even more barrel-shaped than I was, especially on my crutches. Somewhere during this period I was told to prepare a graduation speech; I had been selected class valedictorian. I had never heard the word, and panicked. Milton took pity on me and wrote something that began, "Gaul was divided into three parts," a notion he had probably come upon in 1911 at McKinley High School. But it didn't matter. My attention was focused entirely on how I would look, not on what I would say.

I was hell-bent on getting the doctor to remove the plaster cast so I would not look like a cripple when I gave my speech. The day before the ceremony he cut it off. A lot of horrible dead skin came off with it, and my leg was so weak I could not stand, let alone walk, without the hated crutches. The next afternoon, with Cecelia, Milton, and Laurel in the audience, I crutched expertly to center stage and delivered my remarks. Once again, as at *Thumbelina*, people cheered. Afterwards, Cecelia told me she had heard other parents whispering, "They only chose that child because she's lame." Hearing this from my mother was excruciating. Why didn't she keep it to herself? I think because she herself had never been self-conscious, and really didn't understand children. I think she thought it was merely funny.

My interest in appearance was growing. When Cecelia went out, I experimented with her large assortment of cosmetics. She was expert, subtle, and conscientious about applying makeup, of which she had a vast array, much of it brought back from Paris in wholesale quantities. When somebody brought out Endocreme, the first $100-a-jar face cream, Cecelia was one of the first buyers, and for years a loyal customer.

Surprisingly, Cecelia was not angry the day she caught me trying out her makeup and silk stockings. Instead she bought me a lipstick brush and carefully showed me how to paint my mouth on, instead of smearing it on with the lipstick. She bought me a garter belt, and my own silk stockings in a padded green silk box. I think Cecelia was glad I was growing up. Little girls bored her, but she looked forward to having someone to giggle with about female things, someone whose company she could enjoy, no longer a mere child who needed looking after. So why didn't she say so? Instead, she began saying that, unlike herself, *I* was pretty, then never failing to add, "but you *destroy* yourself by . . ." The sentence had several endings: (1) plucking your eyebrows; (2) straightening your hair. As I grew older, she added (3) the terrible people you choose for friends; (4) the hideous clothes you buy. Like her, I never saw myself as pretty until I was past forty, and I was fifty before I could see from photographs how pretty my mother herself had been.

As I entered adolescence my craving for religiosity intensified. I'd always wanted to go to Sunday school, like other children, and didn't care which one. Frantic to believe in *something*, I had by now memorized the words to most of the Protestant hymns in our summer camp songbooks. I think my search for (any old) God was so urgent because my one real God — my vision of a Happy Family — had died so abruptly at the hands of the Visigoths.

I confided my cravings to Fanny, who at once saw to it that Laurel and I were enrolled in the Sunday school classes at the Wilshire Boulevard Temple, of which she was a member. She bought us each a copy of the Jewish scriptures, something we hadn't known existed, with our names stamped on the covers in gold. The perfect thing to wear on Sunday mornings, she and Cecelia decided, were some braid-trimmed coats and hats Cecelia and Gerry had brought back from Budapest. The Sunday school experience ended badly. Laurel and I were treated with stand-offish deference verging on awe, our outfits having led everyone to assume that we were Hitler refugees newly arrived from Europe. I probably would have terminated my religious education forthwith, had not Fanny discovered that students my age were eligible to attend Young People's Summer Dances in the temple ballroom every other Saturday night.

So I finally got the patent leather dancing shoes, and Cecelia herself escorted me to Bullocks-Wilshire and I. Magnin's for the two required long dresses. Fanny and I might have chosen something fancy. Instead I got a plain turquoise taffeta, and a lavender taffeta with ruching lined in scarlet that was not quite as bad; at least it had two colors. Cecelia's astringent taste was perfect for her, but her children always looked, and felt, like residents of some incredibly exclusive orphan asylum.

One evening I saw a tall, nice-looking boy crossing the dance floor in my direction. "Good evening. My name is Harlan Hertzberg," he said in the approved manner. "May I have the next dance?" Cecelia had just taken me to a movie with her for the first time, a matinee of Laurence Olivier in *Wuthering Heights*, a hero so romantic in a story so sad that both of us were dabbing our eyes as we came out into the purple twilight. Like Heathcliff, Harlan Hertzberg had large, deep-set eyes; I was hooked. In a few weeks, he said as we fox-trotted in sedate circles, he would be starting Fairfax High School. This was the last dance of the season. There *had* to be a way to see him again.

Thus began my first Grand Plot. A Grand Plot is a clever and grandiose scheme embarked upon to accomplish an objective which must be approached obliquely. You do this by creating an even bigger problem, in order to enfold the smaller one — the need once again to see Harlan Hertzberg's irresistible eyes — inside the larger. That first Grand Plot later evolved into a lifetime strategy for coping with the impossible. I would make my way through life by stepping from one Grand Plot to the next as needed, like Eliza crossing the ice.

I enlisted the help of my only friend, Sherma, a girl I knew from both school and dancing class. We enrolled together in Beverly High, and in due course we presented to the authorities a written proposal that our school initiate a comprehensive, student-run survey of comparative high school education practices throughout the region. Though a normal Lincoln School–type notion, the idea was unusual in Southern California, and it appealed to our school's sense of innate superiority that Beverly High would be the school taking the initiative. Most of our freshman year had passed before it came about, but eventually the school board, and then the Los Angeles Board of Education, approved our plan, and Sherma and I were appointed to put it into practice. Target school Number One was of course Fairfax High, and one unbelievable day in late spring, Sherma and I actually found ourselves sitting in the rearmost row of a Fairfax classroom staring at the back of Harlan Hertzberg's neck. That was enough. More would have been too much.

Milton Ager was now forty-five years old and had composed more than seventy hit songs. Nonetheless, his movie career might have ended almost inaudibly had it not been for Judy Garland. The last song he wrote in Hollywood was a ballad especially commissioned by MGM to showcase the dazzling talents of its new teenage star. The picture was *Listen, Darling,* in which Judy played opposite Freddie Bartholomew, and to me the song's lyric was as ridiculous as its casting. "When the thunder starts to thunder, don't go home and cry. They're playing ten pins in the sky."

But Milton gave sixteen-year-old Judy a lovely melody to sing, and she was grateful. In *Andy Hardy Meets a Debutante,* her next picture after *The Wizard of Oz*, Judy found a spot for Milton's 1921 lament "I'm Nobody's Baby," and her three-handkerchief rendition helped catapult the old weeper into the number two spot on *Your Hit Parade* for a fat eleven weeks. It also sparked new recordings by the Tommy Dorsey orchestra with Connie Haines, the Benny Goodman orchestra with Helen Forrest, and — my favorite — Mildred Bailey singing with a small jazz band that included Roy Eldridge and Teddy Wilson.

Comedy and topical songs rarely last, but Milton's hit ballads were seemingly indestructible. "Forgive Me," for example, was first popularized by Ruth Etting in 1927, revived in 1940 by Gene Autry in one of his cowboy movies, and revived again ten years after that in Eddie Fisher's big record for RCA Victor.

I don't know whether Cecelia's contract at Goldwyn was for one year or two; those records were destroyed in a fire. But a fragmentary document in the studio's legal files indicates that over the years a total of twenty-two writers worked on *Graustark*, including S. N. Behrman and Samson Raphaelson as well as Hellman, turning in a total of 1,238 pages. Of this number, 28 pages were a "preliminary treatment" by "Ogden Stewart" and Cecelia Ager.

It was early summer 1939, our lease was up, and the Agers decided to return to New York. Don Stewart went on to write *The Women*, and *The Philadelphia Story*, and eventually, alas, to become one of the screenwriters who chose to exile themselves to Britain rather than respond to a subpoena which would have required them to name names of Communists or former Communists to the House Un-American Activities Committee. Although Cecelia was never a member of any political party, not even of any club for that matter, her sympathies were always on the left, and grew more so during the Spanish Civil War. Several of the Hollywood Ten were her close friends, and her contempt for those persons who did squeal to HUAC was lifelong and irredeemable. Milton's solidly Democratic politics stayed closer to the middle of the road.

July and August were no time to move to Manhattan, so for a couple of months the Agers moved in with the Lewins, and Laurel and I stayed with the Stotharts in their brand-new house a mile away. It had a tennis court and kidney-shaped swimming pool, and a two-room suite for each child. Herb's daughter Carol was at college, and Laurel and I shared her quarters.

Next to Andy Hardy's, I considered the Stotharts the first normal American family I had ever encountered. I had never seen parents so demonstratively in love, nor so devoted to their children. Mary was vibrant and outgoing, with high color and dark hair. Herb had been a star college fullback, and was tall and strikingly handsome. In that period, he was busy scoring and recording the music for *The Wizard of Oz*, and twice smuggled me into the big music stage to watch him at work. He stood on a podium following the score with one hand, directing an eighty-piece orchestra with the other, and keeping one eye on the film unreeling on a huge screen above their heads.

They were a family much given to pool parties, barbecues, and other hearty entertainments. The year I was twelve, Mary had organized a scavenger hunt for my birthday, with adults assigned to drive us all over Santa Monica and up to Malibu. Before we left California, Mary organized a farewell costume party with me and Carol as "guests of honor." That such a splendid way of life was hardly "normal" did not occur to me, not even after *Life* magazine decided to document the life of the American family at three levels — poor, middle class, and rich — and chose the Stotharts to illustrate the rich.

The Agers and Lewins came over before the party ended, and everybody gathered around Herb's piano to sing "Stand to Your Glasses, Steady," which by that time we had taught them all. In a way, our family song seemed to me to describe our family. It was all about loyalty and loss and staunchness and honor and, as we continued to sing our song over the years, *to stand* gradually took on a special meaning for me, and perhaps for all of us. It had been to stand with Cecelia, to *stand by* her when Laurel's birth was expected, that Milton had reneged on the trip with the Gershwins to Paris to pay homage to Ravel. Now Cecelia's fierce sense of loyalty compelled her to stand with him at a time when Milton's career had leveled off while her own was in ascendance. That may have been why divorce was not an option.

"Stand by your sex commitments" was something Milton began saying to us almost every night at dinner at about this time. He said it to the end of his life, along with "Children don't ask to be born." He never explained what he meant by the phrase, nor to whom he was directing it, his wife or his children. It never occurred to me that he might be admonishing himself. A man stands by the woman by whom he has fathered children, no matter what. Some things are best defined by their opposites. To *stand* is the opposite of to *duck*.

CHAPTER SEVEN

WAR ABROAD, WAR AT HOME

Graustark was never made. With war clouds gathering over Europe, the subject may have seemed out of step with the times. But at home, the Depression was ending and things were looking up. In the general fizz of optimism, one of the most idealistic concepts imaginable had been germinating in the brain of a charismatic magazine editor, Ralph Ingersoll, former managing editor of *The New Yorker* and *Time*, and most recently editor of *Fortune*. Ingersoll dreamed of launching a new metropolitan daily newspaper of such high editorial quality that it could survive on circulation alone, supported only by its readers. It would accept no advertising. This unprecedented arrangement would free it from the commercial pressures which compromised the integrity of New York's eight other dailies. The fledgling paper would need a financial angel at first, of course, until sufficient numbers of the public had been won over, and Ingersoll had persuaded the Chicago department store tycoon Marshall Field to put up the necessary millions.

The new paper printed its first dummy issue in April 1939. Called simply *Newspaper*, while Ingersoll searched for the right name, the dummy came out daily for more than a year, and featured the work of Erskine Caldwell, Margaret Bourke-White, Dashiell Hammett, Lillian Hellman, Heywood Broun, and, soon, Cecelia Ager. Joe Losey, a young director who had admired Cecelia's work in *Variety*, had recommended her to Ingersoll as movie critic. He'd written to her in California, and hired her as soon as we returned to Manhattan.

The first issue of *PM*, a five-cent afternoon tabloid, went on sale on June 18, 1940, coincident with the fall of France. Its front page carried a noble Statement of Purpose — "*PM* is against people who push other people around" — and had great visual distinction: a two-color logo in black and Roman red ink, newly designed type, heavy nonsmudge paper. The political cartoonist was an unknown New Englander who signed himself "Dr. Seuss," and the regular comics page featured Al Capp's *L'il Abner* and Crockett Johnson's *Barnaby*.

Newspaper salaries were not high, and with Field's money Ralph could afford the finest talents in contemporary journalism. He stole only from the best. The sportswriter Jimmy Cannon came over from the *Post*, and Louis Kronenberger, the drama critic, from his job at *Time*. Managing editor was George Lyon, formerly of Scripps-Howard, and labor news was handled by Leo Huberman, formerly of *The Nation*. I. F. Stone wrote the political column, the brilliant designer Elizabeth Hawes was fashion editor, and editor-in-chief was the tall, bespectacled Ingersoll himself.

Both our parents were far busier than they had been in California. ASCAP in the fall of 1939 had entered into the fight of its life with the broadcasting industry, and Milton was heavily involved in daily strategy sessions. He had also begun negotiations to sell Ager, Yellen & Bornstein to the music division of Warner Brothers. Sometimes Cecelia went to *PM*'s Brooklyn office, but most of her work took place in Midtown screening rooms, or in the restaurants and hotels where she met subjects for interviews. Afterwards she returned home, closed her bedroom door, and typed like hell until it was time to phone for a copy boy to pick up her day's work.

"Home," this time, was a suite in the Hotel Warwick on 54th Street and Sixth Avenue, and once again the two wardrobe trunks stood in the Agers' two bedrooms. A few months later we moved across the street to the Hotel Dorset, where we remained, trunks akimbo, until I had graduated from high school and World War II was half over. Both apartments were glumly furnished and gloomily lit, and the now well established floor plan prevailed: separate quarters for each parent, on opposite sides of what I had come to think of as the living room neutral zone, where the piano was; off somewhere to one side, a kitchenette and a twin-bedded children's room. Because one parent or the other was always desperately "trying to get some sleep" behind the ever-closed bedroom door, Laurel and I were careful always to walk on tiptoe in the early morning. Now women in our sixties, we still do it.

For some reason, Lincoln School had no room for us — perhaps the Ager decision to move back east had been too precipitate — so, after making our breakfasts, Laurel and I took the Fifth Avenue bus down to Friends Seminary, a Quaker school on Irving Place. We didn't know a soul. Gerry had sent her son Nicky there while we were in California, but by the time we enrolled, he was off in military school. After school, we stopped at the Sixth Avenue Delicatessen to see our friend Irving, the counterman, ordered our favorite sandwiches charged to the Ager account, and took them upstairs for dinner. In bad weather, we could telephone Irving and have our order delivered. In fine weather we could walk up to the Automat on 57th Street and dine on all the foods forbidden when we'd lived just across the street at the Salisbury. If adult supervision was required, one of Cecelia's poor relations was temporarily pressed into service.

The Warwick and Dorset, like the Salisbury, were operated in part as "apartment hotels," offering furnished apartments for rental by the month, as well as rooms by the day. Many showbiz folks chose to live this way; when husband and wife both worked, often at odd hours, it was easier to leave housekeeping matters to room service and maid service.

I remember dropping by with Milton to visit his friends Sam Harris, the Broadway producer, and his exquisite wife, China, who lived down the hall at the Dorset, and Ed Sullivan and his wife, who were a few blocks away at the Delmonico. But I don't recall any other hotel-dwelling couples with children.

It was an expensive life. Each month Milton paid the hotel a heavy rent, and paid a second bill to keep our own lovely things drying out and shrouded in the darkness of a rented tomb. I thought of our real furniture as a dusty mirror image of the drab, rented hotel stuff on which we lived out our daily, rented lives as a fake mother, a paper cutout father, and their two wind-up-toy children.

We had returned to New York in September, the month Hitler's armies marched into Poland. In June, Victor had married his high school sweetheart, Florence Fox, a pert, dark-eyed music teacher, and honeymooned through the Netherlands on a bicycle built for two. Then they took a train to Warsaw to visit Zalkin's sister and brother. Marusia, a teacher, would soon perish in the Warsaw ghetto. Jerzy, a doctor, joined the Polish Army Medical Corps and in 1940, during the period of the Stalin-Hitler pact, was one of 5,000 senior Polish army officers and 15,000 troops killed and thrown into mass graves in the Katyn Forest by the Red Army, which then blamed the massacre on the Nazis. Victor was the last family member from our side of the water to see Marusia and Jerzy alive.

Now that the Agers were back east, dark clothes reappeared on Cecelia, luscious tweeds in purple and plum, each outfit the result of hours of fittings, repositionings of bust darts and waist nips, realignments of shoulder pads, alterations of hemlines. All these adjustments were the result of close, knowing consultation between my mother and the craftsperson of the moment, some tailor or dressmaker who spoke with an accent, through a mouthful of pins. For Cecelia's hair, Mr. John had invented fishnet angora caps in every shade, really yarmulkes, crocheted in Paris, some with matching scarflets, even gloves. They were stretchy, like hairnets, and attached with invisible hairpins so as to contain yet reveal the perfectly twisted blonde topknot.

Laurel and I were avid to return to Moore's. Nothing there had changed, except us. On our first night back, the old man sat down, glanced sharply across the table at me, and rapped his knuckles hard on the tablecloth.

"Moran!" he bellowed. "Bring me a plate of oysters. Don't open 'em," he warned, banging the table again. He was a former fishmonger, and his rapping had great authority.

The perpetually poker-faced Moran disappeared into the cellar. The old waiter had once got a $500 tip for placing a $5,000 bet on the Dempsey-Firpo fight, and all surprises after that had been anticlimactic. He reappeared bearing six bivalves on a soup plate of crushed ice. Mr. Moore expertly opened one with the tiny gold penknife on his watch chain, rapped his beat-up knuckles again to rivet my attention, and held the thing right under my nose.

"Listen here, girlie! An oyster has everything *you* have."

I looked down at the cold, mucoid flesh six inches from my face. "So don't leave your mother when her hair turns gray!"

This I understood only later was Mr. Moore's summation of the facts of life, his sex lecture, one he presented at the appropriate time to all adolescent females. But I had no idea what he was talking about. Sex, like love and death, was still very far in my future.

Richard Wright's *Native Son* had been made into a play starring Canada Lee which opened at a theater a few doors from Moore's. Not long after, the Old Man sat down with us one evening for his brandy. "Didn't think *they'd* be back," he said, nodding toward the big table near the door. A half dozen black men had just sat down and ordered drinks. The last time they had come in, Mr. Moore said with a tiny smile, he had instructed Moran to dump salt on their food before serving it.

At this, Milton excused himself, went over to the men's table, and didn't return for some time. By the time he did, Mr. Moore had moved on and Milton reported what had happened. He'd told the men how much he'd enjoyed their show, and asked if he could buy them a drink.

Only if he would join them, they replied. When he tried to buy a second round, the man beside him muttered, "Will you kindly get the hell out of here! We're the NAACP, and we're trying to shut this place down."

Cecelia's position as *PM*'s movie editor entitled her to free passes to every first-run movie house in town, and she sometimes let us use these in the afternoons. Our favorite was Radio City Music Hall, only four blocks away. We knew our way through a discreet little door on the 50th Street side, up a back stair to the backstage offices and loge seats. Even better than the movies were the stage show extravaganzas with thirty-seven precision tap-dancing Rockettes, vaudeville acts, a corps de ballet, and a full symphony orchestra. Cecelia enjoyed these herself, and whenever she came along we stopped by to say hello to her friend Russell Markert, who staged all the shows, and to Milton's brilliant bridge-playing friend Erno Rapee, who conducted the big orchestra.

Cecelia often was too exhausted to stay up after dinner, and I got taken in her stead to see many Broadway musicals: *Panama Hattie, Too Many Girls, Star and Garter, Louisiana Purchase*. Laurel was less fortunate. Tickets traditionally came in pairs, and we had no trouble getting them at the very last minute; Milton knew every box office man and ticket broker on Broadway. So if Cecelia couldn't make it, I went, and Laurel went back to the hotel. It never occurred to anyone to buy *three* seats. Milton must have been busy on November 17, 1939, for I attended my first Broadway opening night — Jerome Kern's *Very Warm for May* — on Cecelia's arm. In my purple taffeta, with braces on my teeth, I looked like a chubbier, shorter Chelsea Clinton.

Although our parents very much enjoyed meeting new people, and were themselves the best of company — witty, bright, beautifully mannered and au courant — the Agers only rarely dined at other people's homes, or invited guests to the Dorset for cocktails. Their entire social life as a couple took place in the two hours in each twenty-four which they spent in the town's top-flight restaurants, always looking their best, always at the top of their form, and Milton always picking up the checks. As Ira Gershwin often told Lawrence Stewart, "Milton Ager was the only person who never once let me pay for a meal. He was famous for it."

Social debts were acquired, and paid, in restaurants; jokes and wagers and predictions were made; news of the rialto was exchanged and savored; Laurel's and my school lives and medical and dental problems were discussed. But our parents still breakfasted and lunched and slept — ever more fitfully — apart, and their social as well as business lives involved two different sets of people.

In fine weather, Anzia occasionally picked me up after school. It was a long hike to her little walk-up room on Morton Street, and I was embarrassed to be seen walking with this woman in her baggy denim suit and peasant sandals, shouting about writing. Although she always promised me a cup of tea and a raisin cracker when we arrived, I soon saw I was not being entertained but shanghaied. What Anzia really wanted was for me to correct her English — no great honor. She was shameless in her need, and would as readily ask the postman or grocery boy for help. Once, she told me, she had burst into the tenement flat of her sister Annie seeking help with her writing, and found a pot of oatmeal boiling on the stove.

"I was so hungry! I hadn't eaten for days. I grabbed the pot and started to wolf it down, burning my mouth . . ."

"Stop! Stop! It's for the children!" Annie yelled, trying to wrest the pot away.

"You don't understand!" Anzia shouted, holding on. "I'm a *writer!*"

Writing was torture not just for Anzia but for everyone around her. Yet she let nothing get in its way. Friends, family, fun, food, even fatigue had to be pushed aside or sacrificed to her maddening, elusive muse. Her intensity was like no one else's. *Ardor* means "fire"; Anzia burned. Her presence was so powerful, she seemed to use up all the oxygen in a room.

My great-aunt's titanic struggles with writing were lifelong. Here is a bit of a university lecture she gave when she was over eighty:

I envy the writers who can sit down at their desks . . . and begin their story at the beginning and work it up logically, step by

step. . . . With me, the end and the middle and the beginning
of my story whirl before me in a mad blur. . . . I'm too much
on fire to wait till I understand what I see and feel. . . . I jot
down any fragment of a thought that I can get hold of. And
then I gather these fragments, words, phrases, sentences, and I
paste them together with my . . . blood.

She was also a creature of impulse. While deeply in love with the
poet Arnold Levitas, she had suddenly married one of his good friends,
a lawyer with whom she had developed an intense intellectual friendship. "He was more my kind," she explained to her daughter many years
later. But the lawyer's suit for annulment, filed six months after their
marriage, revealed that Anzia had deserted him on their wedding night.
The court papers were scandalous enough to attract tabloid attention,
and Anzia became known as THE MENTAL BRIDE. Reporters who interviewed the rebellious young schoolteacher were told:

> I have always looked only upon the mental side of marriage.
> My thoughts on matrimony have always been confined to the
> platonic relations of men and women. I wanted a chum, a
> friend, a mental companion. Mr. Gordon [her one-day hus-
> band] wanted a mate.

Within the year she had married Arnold and become pregnant.
However, Anzia was a terrible housekeeper and a loving but eccentric
parent. Louise was three when Anzia turned her over to Arnold and his
mother to raise, so she would have enough time for her writing.

Anzia also had a dangerous side. At the beginning of her brother
Bill's regular army career, she wrote to the War Department denouncing
him for failing to contribute sufficiently to the upkeep of their widowed
father. All ten children sent monthly checks, and Bill had missed only
one payment, while on his honeymoon in China. But Anzia's letter became part of his permanent military record.

I couldn't understand how Cecelia had been able to bear living with this all-demanding creature back when Anzia was rich. Perhaps my mother had married so impulsively to get away from Anzia, not Fanny.

Amenities at Morton Street were few to nonexistent. As soon as the crackers and tea brewed on her hot plate were disposed of, we set to work. Sometimes Anzia read aloud to me. More often she handed me a yellow legal pad scrawled top to bottom in smudgy pencil and demanded I tell her how to express herself more clearly. This was a challenge, as her ideas whirled in perpetual tornados of slavic emotion. Her handwriting was oversized, like Cecelia's, but bigger, wobblier, and sightly teetering. Her enormous, rushing words sometimes ran off the pad and continued on the back of an envelope or a paper bag.

We sat side by side at her plain trestle writing table, or else on the cot where she slept, which also served as her couch. A tin army trunk was a combination workbench and coffee table. The sessions were torture for me, and the struggle could go on for hours. Her writing seemed overwrought, almost crazed. I felt no empathy for the shrieking fishmongers and washerwomen who were her characters. But I never objected. I was no match for this becrazed writer with the strength of ten.

Sometimes she would declare a break and read me bits of Emerson or Thoreau, or a few lines from her all-time favorite, Oscar Wilde's *The Ballad of Reading Gaol*. When I read the poem today, I hear the Irishman's words in Anzia's heavy Polish accent.

What Anzia was showing me after school was raw material, fifth draft, or tenth, for her magnum opus, *Red Ribbon on a White Horse*, the autobiography on which she had been at work ever since I could remember. Her book's lovely title came from an old Jewish saying that her father had often repeated to his children: "Poverty becomes the wise man like a red ribbon on a white horse" — unless Anzia herself had made it up. Its story in 1940 when I was dragooned to work on the manuscript was not the same as the one she published ten years later, when she was nearly seventy. In our version, the main character was Jeremiah, a moonstruck old writer loosely modeled on two Greenwich Village char-

acters whom she knew, Joe Gould, the eccentric Harvard-educated dere-
lict also known as Mr Seagull, and the poet Maxwell Bodenheim. Jeremiah wanders around with a battered, overstuffed briefcase that contains
the manuscript for his masterpiece, his life's work, a biography of Spi-
noza which he refuses to show to anyone. Anzia befriends the outcast
Jeremiah, with whom she seems to identify, then loses touch with him.
After he is found dead, friendless and alone, Anzia opens his briefcase
and finds that it contains only illegible tatters, incomprehensible
scrawls.

Cecelia and Milton not only had separate friends, tastes, lives. By early
middle age, thirty-eight and forty-seven, they had developed different,
even antithetical sets of ailments. Milton's weak spot was still his digestion, and he had periodic bouts of stomach ulcers. During these times
he gave up Black Label scotch and subsisted on tiny meals of soda crackers, tinned fish, and milk, swallowed various nostrums, belched often,
and suffered greatly. Sometimes he felt his throat closing and couldn't
swallow. At other times he had to rush from the table and throw up like
a fountain. As the years went along, he was variously diagnosed as having
a duodenal spasm, a hiatal hernia, and assorted related conditions. The
cause was some infernal combination of stress and diet probably complicated by alcohol. I venture this because, when he was drinking, I sometimes saw him empty a glassful of whiskey without pausing to swallow, a
trick I have otherwise observed only among practiced alcoholics.

Cecelia's stomach could handle anything. Her aches were in her
head. All my life I'd seen the annual assault of hay fever and its resultant
liquefactions. During the Dorset years she also began to suffer, or reveal
that she suffered, migraine headaches. She described explosions of pain,
as if a spike were being driven into her brain through her eyes. A super-
sensitivity to light was the first sign. Nothing could then be done but lie
quietly in a darkened room and let the waves of pain roll over her until

the storm had spent itself. It could last forty-eight hours. During this time, sleep, music, or reading was impossible. No painkillers worked. Stoic endurance was the only option. I don't know how often these attacks occurred. Cecelia disliked talking about them, out of a primitive fear that talk might bring one on.

In 1940 I added another important book to my seminal library of six. *The Bedside Book of Famous British Stories*, edited by Bennett A. Cerf. My copy is inscribed "To my favorite bowling companion, Shana Ager, from Bennett Cerf." Why had Bennett, a tall and handsome man-about-town, and already owner of the Modern Library as well as head of Random House, gotten into the habit of coming by the Dorset a couple of times a week to take Laurel and me bowling? I have no idea. But it went on all that winter. Possibly he was chasing Gerry, I thought. I was unaware of her entanglement with Ralph Ingersoll, a romance for which Cecelia was serving as a combination lovelorn adviser and beard. Gerry was by then divorced, more gorgeous than ever, and a daily visitor to our apartment.

I refused even to consider that Bennett might be after Cecelia. For one thing, Milton didn't seem to mind having him around. Indeed, my father became fascinated with bowling himself. I liked to squeeze his orange juice whenever I was at home, and carry it in on his eleven o'clock breakfast tray. Often I found him already awake, practicing bowling. He lay flat on his back in bed, carefully aiming imaginary strikes ceilingward, varying each trajectory slightly with tiny pronations of his wrist. I understood it as part of his lifetime fascination with golf balls, handballs, billiard balls, and his general study of the properties of spheres in motion.

Milton, normally the most predictable of beings, had developed a couple of other new behavior patterns. He had begun spouting statistics about schoolgirl virginity. One of the newspapers was running some sort of series, and my father often quoted its findings. A couple of times I found him standing in the kitchenette in his undershirt, a glass of seltzer in one hand and the evening's virginity report in the other, waiting to engage me in solemn conversation. He also had stepped up the repetition of his twin mantras, "Children don't ask to be born" and "Stand by your sex commitments," and was saying them even before dinner, usually in the living room, over his first scotch. I understood what was on his mind, but the idea that he was worried about *my* virginity was so ludicrous I paid no attention.

Once I was safely out of Friends Seminary and returned to Lincoln, I looked back on the tenth grade as a hotbed of boiling hormones, even though I myself had remained unaffected. I was not just shy and aloof but two or even three years younger than my classmates. At Lincoln, the kids were closer to my own age but sexually underdeveloped — unless that was just *me* again. For me, all four years of high school were a time of milky confusion and only the dimmest awakening.

My cousin Gloria Stone, by now a sophomore at Cornell, invited me up for a football weekend. I was in eleventh grade, and amazed when I received permission to go. Cecelia's okay must have been premised on her longtime, unshakable faith in Gloria's mother, Dr. Hannah, or possibly Milton was away in Florida with Ben Bernie and the gang. At any rate, it was my first blind date; indeed, the first real date of any kind. We went to a fraternity house party, and drank a lot of rum and Coca-Cola. But I was accustomed to drinking at home, and by now smoking as well, and we got back to Gloria's dorm uneventfully. Having been treated all my life as an adult was in some respects beginning to pay off. All I really got out of the weekend was a couple of bawdy fraternity songs, instantly committed to memory thanks to my earlier training with *The Sandbag*. Later, at Vassar, the songs would be a rare asset.

Eleventh and twelfth grades back at Lincoln School were thrilling. In class, ideas were pursued, and wrestled with. Socially, I was still drawn to the lowliest and "cheapest" of my fellow students. This at least was Cecelia's often expressed opinion. My low-class taste extended to clothing, food, the kitsch ladies' magazines, and all varieties of pop junk. I liked the corniest of pop music — "Amapola," "Waltzing Matilda," "Tangerine." My favorite movie stars were Dan Dailey and Rita Hayworth.

Although careful never to appear "boy-crazy," I was quite aware that I preferred the companionship of boys to girls. Two boys in our class,

Jimmy and Alex, were fond of me and crazy about baseball. During the spring of 1941, the three of us ritually cut school one afternoon a week and took the subway up to Yankee Stadium to study Joe DiMaggio. One week, we agreed to watch just Joe's knees, the next week his elbows, the next his wrists. I did whatever Jimmy suggested, but out of the corner of my eye I watched Alex. He was the drummer in Lincoln's jazz band, the Blue Knights, and he treated me with sweet politeness verging on awe. Totally preoccupied with Jimmy and Alex, I had no notion that we were witnessing the most phenomenal hitting streak in baseball history.

I was to be a junior counselor at Camp Whippoorwill that summer, and begged Milton to lend me his gold signet ring, the one Rayna had given him. Cecelia considered jewelry vulgar, and I owned none and wanted to wear the ring to camp to pretend some boy had given it to me. My first day out on our lake, the ring somehow slid off my finger. I felt it go, watched it sink down in green water, glint once or twice, and disappear. I dived in after it and raked the muddy bottom with a canoe paddle. The ring was gone. That night, in tears, I called my father.

"Don't upset yourself so," he said. "It really doesn't matter." I knew it did matter, and could not fathom his kindliness.

One day that fall I came home from school and heard Milton bashing away on a mutation of "Get That Happy Habit!," now called "Keep 'Em Smiling," targeted to the millions of new defense plant workers, the same people whose advent made such a hit out of "Rosie the Riveter." The new lyrics, by Billy Rose, went, "Keep 'em SMI-ling! HELP 'em put it over. O-ver here and over there!" Milton was trying to improve on this. A couple of years later the song was finally published, with a memorable second stanza, "FOR the Screaming Eagle! AND the Lion and the BEAR!," a reference to the Russians recently having joined in the Allied war effort against the Axis.

The army had recalled Uncle Bill to Washington, where he served
in military intelligence, and rose to become assistant chief of staff. Isabel
was working for the OSS analyzing aerial photographs of China, and
part-time at the Freer Gallery as its curator of Chinese bronzes. Victor
turned up, resplendent in the uniform of a major in the army medical
corps, and on leave from a Chicago hospital where he was being trained
in tropical medicine before being sent to the Pacific. But in Hollywood,
Fanny still came to the Rubensteins' house once a week to shampoo his
blond curls, insisting only she knew how to do it properly. Her sister
Anzia claimed to feel sorry for Florence, Victor's wife.

In the spring of my junior year, one of the seniors invited me to be his
date on graduation night. Cecelia must have been doing triple duty at
PM by then, because this time I shopped for my own long dress, and
paid for it out of my new "clothing allowance," a device we had agreed
upon to cut down on Cecelia's constant sniping at my taste, and my
tearful defiance of her criticism.

"She doesn't love me!" I sobbed to Milton.

His answer never varied. "She loves you. She just doesn't know how
to show it." But I never believed him. No one who loved me could be
so unfeeling, so critical of everything I said and did and thought. The
dress I chose came from a cheap bridal shop that adjoined an irresistible
penny arcade. A pitchman selling lanolin hair products had a female
cohort who sat on a high stool with her back to the audience, her long
hair rippling down to the floor. "Next time ya happen to be in proximity
to a sheep," the pitchman yelled, "run ya fingahs lightly troo da wool!"
I never had the nerve to buy any, but I did buy a $35 bridesmaid's outfit,
and went to the dance a vision in yellow cotton lace. Cecelia hated it,
but I thought it looked great.

Our school had few traditions, but one was that after the dance the
seniors and their dates stayed up all night and greeted the dawn from the

deck of the Staten Island Ferry. I announced these plans at home one evening a few days before graduation.

"You will be at home at eleven o'clock," said Milton. He spoke in an Old Testament voice I had never heard before.

"But . . ."

"You will be at home at eleven," said the voice. "*And* you will telephone home at ten-thirty to say you are on your way."

Like a dope, I called. Milton demanded to know where I was calling from. Central Park West, I told him, at the class party given by the parents of one of the graduates. He then demanded to speak to one of these parents. I refused. My humiliation would have been unendurable. This turned out to be another mistake. Milton demanded the address, and said that if I didn't leave at once, he would be right up there to get me.

Sobbing, and furious, I came home. Milton was lying on his bed reading.

"Next year," I said grimly, "I am staying out all night," and thereby, without realizing it, set up the defining event of my lifetime.

My defiance of my father was all mixed up with overwhelming feelings of pity for his hotel-bound existence, exiled to the golf course by day and the Friars Club by night. As our 1941 birthday approached — my sixteenth, his forty-eighth — I felt so sorry for Milton, or perhaps for myself, that I determined to assemble a truly grand present, something that would in part "make it up to him" for having to roost "temporarily" in the Dorset while all his worldly goods, including his music and books and records and midget opera scores, were still consigned to the bowels of the Manhattan Storage and Warehouse Company. I would atone for my mother's indifference to household and archival needs by finding a copy of every song Milton had ever written, "stinkers" included, and have them bound in leather for his birthday.

Collecting the stuff was not difficult. Broadway crawled with dealers in secondhand sheet music, and Milton's work was well known. Paying for the binding was another matter. Uncle Harry, the kindly Communist, slipped me $100, and the rest came from my clothing allowance. I arranged the songs in chronological order, and had MILTON AGER and the appropriate dates stamped in gold on the spine. It came to four volumes, and the green leather books remained on his piano until he died, his only tangible record of his life's work. I have them now, every minor printer's misprint and wrong note painstakingly corrected in pencil in his own hand.

Collecting the music, I made an astonishing discovery. Many of the people I met while gleaning this harvest of song had known Milton personally, and had always assumed that a man who put in as much time as he did at golf and cards did not have a family. My very existence surprised them. A few years later, after I had begun writing magazine articles and meeting other writers, I discovered that the same thing was true of my mother. By then everybody in New York seemed to know or know of Cecelia Ager, and she had many friends in the worlds of journalism, show business, and fashion. But her personal life was entirely unknown. "Cecelia's your *mother?* We never even knew she was married!"

Both my parents were exceedingly private. That nobody knew a thing about them beyond what their restaurant persona revealed — that they were an appealing little pair, fashionable, amusing, on the qui vive, and mannerly and gracious to all — was just the way the Agers wanted it. As my friend Maya Angelou described them some years later, "Cecelia had the impenetrable privacy of an Art Deco silhouette. Her beautiful outline told everything about her era, and nothing about herself. Milton was a small man of gargantuan courage who valued everyone's wit nearly as much as he valued his own."

In twelfth grade, some of us worked after school in the kindergarten of a black church nearby. We grew fond of Reverend James Robinson, and he'd invited us to attend Sunday services. One happy morning, after singing our heads off, my classmate Betty and I went back down to her Park Avenue apartment and were sitting on the floor playing jacks when her older sister burst in shouting that the Japanese had bombed Pearl Harbor.

I had dreamed of going to Stanford University, like Uncle Victor, both because I loved him madly, and because the school was as far away from Manhattan as you could get. But when it came time to fill out college applications, in early January 1942, the Japanese were believed about to storm the beaches of San Francisco, and it was recommended that I apply elsewhere. Betty was applying to Vassar, and another friend to Mt. Holyoke, so I applied to all three and sat back to wait.

·   Jimmy Dorsey's band was playing at the Hotel Pennsylvania, and the boys who could afford it took us dancing there on Saturday nights. We traveled in a group of four or six, but my regular date was Alex. Like many overweight men, he was a superb dancer. On the taxi rides home, we held hands.

In 1942 Milton finally got rid of Ager, Yellen & Bornstein by selling the whole thing to Advanced Music Corporation for just over $25,000. His nineteen years as an entrepreneur were over. Now he was free to function only as a creator and artist, a life to which his temperament was far better suited. But the volatile music market had changed again. Broadcasting had become the preeminent buyer. The networks had banded together to fight ASCAP by launching a rival organization, Broadcast Music, Inc., owned and controlled not by writers and publishers but by the networks themselves. ASCAP had refused to renew the networks' licenses and forbidden use of its songs, thus condemning the public to endless repetitions of "Jeannie with the Light Brown Hair" and other materials in the public domain. After the ASCAP strike was settled, the networks filed an antitrust suit accusing ASCAP of being a monopoly. This ended in a victory for ASCAP and a consent decree in which the broadcasters agreed to abide by the court's ruling. But during the two-year standoff, the popularity of BMI-controlled country music and "race records," later called rock-and-roll, soared. By the time it was over, ASCAP's membership was heavily weighted with old songwriters, their writing style now out of fashion, living on royalties from old songs and gathering at intervals to mourn the passing of the golden days of Tin

Pan Alley. ASCAP ultimately acknowledged as much, and adjusted its payment system to be more reflective of current usages of its songs. When this happened, Milton's income went down another notch.

Cecelia had become a very hardworking newspaperwoman. *PM* had moved from Brooklyn to a broken-down building on Duane Street in lower Manhattan, and Cecelia went down there daily and ran the movie department. Heywood Hale "Woody" Broun, a young sports reporter, remembers her as

> immensely chic, and a formidably precise talker. She spoke with the same accurate weight with which she used to crush unworthy movies, and so I was surprised, in our few meetings, to find her kind, well informed about my not very interesting life, and encouraging about my future. When one considers that the sports department of *PM* was regarded by the rest of the staff as a sop to bourgeois depravity, and its members some-where down with the ordure disposal caste in Calcutta, her be-havior was not just surprising but unique.
>
> I found in Cecelia the same quality that I found in the much maligned Dorothy Parker, a battle cruiser front behind whose protective guns lurked a person who, sensing vulnerabil ity, would unload the guns.

I remember Woody then as immensely engaging, but about as ap-proachable as a fawn. That Cecelia put in the time necessary to know this extremely shy young man amazes me. She was doing double war-time duty as movie critic and celebrity interviewer, and often had two bylines a day, occasionally three, yet the quality of her work remained remarkably high. Years later I met Spencer Tracy, and he singled out Cecelia's review from this period of his performance in *Dr. Jekyll and Mr. Hyde* as "the lousiest, funniest notice I ever had."

In the picture, Tracy overplays both parts, and Cecelia's review be-gins, "Yesterday Abbott and Costello opened at the Capitol Theater."

Each year she personally reviewed some 250 pictures, and wrote about 50 interviews. Between March 15 and April 8 of 1942, for example, she interviewed Senator Claude Pepper; Bernard M. Baruch; General B. Somervell, head of the army's Services of Supply; Madame Chiang Kai-shek; Harold L. Ickes, head of the War Production Board; and Paul Robeson. Between June 10 and July 7, she got around to Mrs. J. Paul Getty; Elmer Davis, head of the OWI; King George II of Greece; General Dwight D. Eisenhower; Mamie Eisenhower; and Price Administrator Leon Henderson. How she managed this despite her recurring migraine headaches, and her active evening and weekend social life, I cannot imagine. No wonder she came home complaining of exhaustion.

To help her out, she got the paper to hire Anzia's daughter, Louise Levitas, the onetime Tinkerbelle, as her assistant. Laurel and I had never before met this gentle, shy cousin. Unlike Laurel and me, endlessly told we were "equal" and "adult," but strictly ruled and isolated by servants, Louise on her weekends with Anzia completely lived her mother's life, kept her mother's hours, shared her friends and books. She accompanied Anzia on her round of Village cafeterias and libraries, and was soon dragooned into helping out with the scrawled yellow pads. But she bore her eccentric parent no resentment, and now that she was on *PM*, did not appear to mind being treated by Cecelia as a poor relation. She was grateful for all Cecelia's fine hand-me-down hats and bags and scarves and gloves, and seemed happy to perform such tasks as toting Cecelia's ratty old mink coat around to various thrift shops for comparative appraisals, or taking Shana and Laurel to doctors' appointments.

Louise, raised by her father, had been unaware of her rich cousin's existence until she went to the University of Wisconsin, and occasional *PM* paychecks made out to Cecelia Ager started turning up in her mail, with no accompanying letter. Anzia relentlessly badgered Cecelia for money, and from time to time Cecelia endorsed her modest salary over to Louise to get Anzia off her back.

Later Louise became a writer, and in 1964 she married Dr. Mel Henriksen, an internationally known mathematician. She looked after Anzia all her life, and after her mother's death produced a much-respected biography. Louise is one of those rare women who became good-looking in middle age, and beautiful in old age. Now in her eighties, she is a figure of remarkable grace. One of her favorite people in the world was my mother.

As the end of high school approached, I vowed anew to keep my year-old promise to stay out all night — vowed to myself, that is. At home, I had learned, some things were better left unsaid. On graduation night, Alex and Gerry's son Nicky were to be our class's two designated drivers. Nicky was still attending military school, but I'd recruited him for graduation night to escort one of the extra girls.

That evening the girls got their corsages pinned on, and the boys' hair was slicked down, and everybody gathered at the big apartment of our class president. His parents lived on Fifth Avenue across from the Metropolitan Museum of Art, and they had invited all forty-three of us to a formal dinner dance, with a live band. This must have broken up shortly after midnight.

Aware of our Staten Island Ferry tradition, Betsy's mother and father had invited us all to Beekman Place afterwards for a dawn breakfast of scrambled eggs. It would have been unseemly to arrive there before dawn, but a three-hour ride on a ferry boat now appeared to some of us to be an unnecessary ordeal. Nicky had keys to his mother's new apartment, and she was away. People too tired to ride the ferry could rest there, he said, and we'd all meet later for breakfast at Betsy's. He tossed me the keys and led the other half of the class toward Staten Island.

Gerry's new apartment, at 52nd Street and Park Avenue, turned out to be large and amply furnished with three living room couches, and another in the dining room. We decided the girls could have the couches, and the boys could curl up on the carpets. Somebody awakened us in time to get over to Betsy's, and her mother's eggs tasted very good.

It was about six-thirty A.M. when Alex escorted me to the Dorset's revolving door and bid me a chaste good morning. Upstairs, I rang our doorbell. Cecelia opened it in her nightgown, her hair down. Behind her Milton was raging, waving his arms and shouting that he was going to beat me to a pulp. My mother flung her body across me as a shield.

"Don't you touch this child!"

"Where have you been?" my father roared.

"I *told you* I was going to stay out all night!"

"Where *were* you?" He was turning purple.

"The Staten Island Ferry," I lied.

"Let the child get some sleep first," my mother commanded, shoving me toward our bedroom while carefully keeping herself interposed between me and my flailing father. At some times, ducking is exactly the right thing to do, and this was one of them.

It was some hours before I awoke. Milton was gone. Cecelia had been on the phone with Gerry, who had told her where my half of the class had slept. My mother chastised me for lying, but I could tell her heart wasn't in it. She was exhausted from having been up all night keeping Milton from calling the police, or carrying out other wild threats.

My punishment was indefinite confinement to our apartment. But Camp Whippoorwill was starting in a few weeks, and I was due at Vassar in the fall. Alex typed an abject letter of apology to my parents on his father's impressive stationery. It was at once so manly, sweet, and lovelorn that he was allowed to pay formal calls on me during my imprisonment. I sat sulkily on the hotel couch smoking and knitting khaki leg warmers for the troops, while he sipped a scotch and soda and stared in mostly mute adoration. Milton lurked in his bedroom, in his undershirt, pretending to read, the door slightly ajar. I don't know where Laurel and Cecelia were.

After a few nights of this, Milton must have decided it was safe to leave us unchaperoned, because I know that the night the building across the street caught fire, Alex and I went out to look. Since we were already out, we walked up to the delicatessen and bought a sandwich before returning. For this transgression, Milton demanded an explanatory letter from me.

Handwritten, on Dorset stationery, frostily addressed "Dear M.," it ended, "I think the above covers everything that I can remember, and is a pretty accurate account of my sinful evening."

What made all this a defining event was not the letters nor the punishment, which was trivial. It was losing Milton, my lifelong best friend. Just when I needed a friend most, the person I had always adored and counted on for warmth and understanding and forgiveness had flipped and declared himself my mortal enemy, and I had no clear idea why.

CHAPTER EIGHT

PARK AVENUE

In the fall of 1942, my first semester away at Vassar, the Agers left the Dorset to live in borrowed splendor in Gerry's uninhabited apartment at 350 Park Avenue, corner of 52nd Street, the site of my debauch on graduation night. Gerry was now traveling back and forth to London and the unoccupied parts of Europe in some job connected with international war relief, and had subleased to my parents her palatial, rent-controlled premises. The furnishings reflected Gerry's moderne taste: quilted ivory satin upholstery, tropical flower paintings, bleached blond wood. But Cecelia was gradually replacing this stuff with prize pieces of the beloved Ager furniture, retrieved from storage and expensively recovered in printed linens and subtle chintzes identical to the ones Jimmy Reynolds had chosen in 1928. The triangular cabinet with lemon leaves stood in the corner beside the big windows overlooking the Racquet Club. The Napoleonic map of Paris reappeared above the sofa. Milton's piano was in the dining room along with Gerry's vast blue-mirror-topped table, and the two wardrobe trunks were down in a basement storeroom.

In a corner of the stately living room was Gershwin's portrait of Cecelia lit by the lovely scallop shell lamp. The painting was now about fifteen years old, and I no longer had difficulty recognizing my mother in the strong-faced, morose-looking woman with exaggeratedly deep lines between nose and mouth. Not unlike the painter of Dorian Gray, Gershwin had foreshadowed reality; he had been able to look into the future and see the middle-aged woman inside the jazzy ex-Coed who was posing for him.

Life at 350 Park Avenue was a kind of last hurrah for the Agers. Cecelia was forty, Milton forty-eight, and both were handsome "little personages," another of Cecelia's terms, like "twerps," for people she was fond of. Despite their different worlds, my parents were managing a mutual, and mutually complementary, social life. Their apartment became a kind of salon, a congenial, comfortable, convenient gathering place for both sets of friends. Cecelia presided with verve, charm, and style. Milton was a genial, witty, hospitable, and only slightly remote presence — the composer at his piano. Together they made the apartment a place to be in wartime and postwar Manhattan, a gathering point for people in the arts and journalism and liberal politics. Sundays began with cocktails, after which everybody went off to lunch at the Palm, or Al Schacht's, across the street — restaurants sure to have beefsteaks on the menu, even in wartime. I. F. Stone might be up from Washington, or Ralph Ingersoll home on leave, along with John Hammond, Jed Harris, Donald Ogden Stewart and Ella Winter, and, almost always, Dorothy Parker.

Lt. Alan Campbell was in the air force, and lonely Dottie often came by for a drink with Cecelia and Milton and afterwards accompanied them to dinner. When they rose to leave, none of them stood taller than five feet three. "Milton, you're every other inch a gentleman," Dottie would say. By now I understood what she meant.

One evening Dottie arrived with a new poem, still untitled, which she'd written to Alan and just sold to *The New Yorker*:

> Soldier, in a curious land
>   All across a swaying sea,
> Take her smile and lift her hand —
>   Have no guilt of me.
> Soldier, when were soldiers true?
>   If she's kind and sweet and gay,
> Use the wish I send to you —
>   Lie not lone till day!
> Only, for the nights that were,
>   Soldier, and the dawns that came,
> When in sleep you turn to her
>   Call her by my name.

"But Dottie, this is a war song!" said Milton, and she, grateful for his apt title, instantly telephoned it to *The New Yorker*. The following week she brought the Agers a copy of a lovely little portrait of herself, commissioned by *Harper's Bazaar*, that stood on our piano ever after. Alan later said the poem embarrassed him. But Dottie always insisted that "War Song" was her one true "poem," and all the rest were "light verse."

Vassar was only a two-hour train ride away, and whenever I turned up at 350, I was accustomed to finding odd ducks, famous ones, sitting there being interviewed by Cecelia. Once it was Wendell Willkie. Rumpled and in shirtsleeves on that warm autumn afternoon, Willkie was ruggedly attractive, and a compelling talker. When I mentioned Vassar, he discoursed on Poughkeepsie politics in surprising detail, then returned his attentions to Cecelia. After another hour of fascinating political monologue, the foyer door that led to the bedrooms opened and Milton emerged, wearing only jockey shorts and bedroom slippers and carrying a putter. Without saying a word, he putted a cotton golf ball through the living room and on into the dining room and around toward the kitchen. Mr. Willkie went home.

Another day I came home to find Cecelia entertaining her dashing friend John Huston, in town to promote his army documentary, *The Bat-tle for San Pietro*. Once Gerry was sitting there with a disheveled but dazzling Sterling Hayden. He was on leave from Hollywood and work-ing under cover for the OSS in Yugoslavia, whence he had returned only the night before. A skilled sailor, Hayden had been smuggling supplies to the Yugoslav partisans from small boats in the Adriatic. Gerry had met him on the train up from Washington.

Cecelia needed Gerry. She couldn't manage the salon alone; she lacked the energy, she said, which was scarcely surprising. She was work-ing as hard as ever, and often bedded by migraines. She needed the extraordinary vitality, the synergy, the catalyst of her vibrant sidekick.

Gerry kept a suite across Park Avenue at the Park Lane Hotel, and often joined us for dinner when she was in town. But much of the time she was in Spain, Israel, or London, where she was still involved in a passionate affair with Ralph. She looked more beautiful than ever, though a bit bigger than ever, more like a diva now than an actress, especially in her unflattering war relief uniform. Men were mad about her, and she'd had several love affairs with people of importance, one of them a wartime head of state. But Ralph was different. For the first time in her life she had fallen deeply, truly in love.

The Agers had no cook, but "Joy," as the cookbook was referred to, lay perpetually open on the kitchen counter, and anyone was welcome to tie on an apron and go to work. Other people sat around and watched, making snooty comments in fractured French. The star chefs were Moe Hoffenson, who worked with a lit cigar in his mouth, and Gerry, who cooked with her hat on. Milton had found Moe at the Friars. Another of the Agers' beloved diamonds in the rough, he owned the Masters Mart on West 47th Street, an early discount appliance store. In the navy, he had served as chief cook on a submarine and could turn out an entire soup-to-nuts meal, including a just-baked apple pie, without leaving a single unwashed dish or a speck of ash on the countertop.

Gerry these days possessed a stunning collection of new Mr. John millinery and endless supplies of scarce silk stockings and French per-fume. She chalked menus on the kitchen blackboard in a mocking, high-tone garble of French and Yiddish: *poulet de liveroo au krepola* meant chicken livers with kreplach (dumplings). Swept up in the general culinary enthusiasm, Cecelia, who had never been seen to boil water, became an accomplished cook. Most of the foods she made for Milton's suffering stomach — pressure-cooker boiled chicken or beef — were not very interesting. For herself she learned to make certain special favorites: creamed spinach, *oeuf à la neige*, and, oddly, boiled tongue. The next day she made herself tiny tongue sandwiches, thin as tea sandwiches, that had to be made only on *thin*-sliced white bread with *Bahamian* mustard, always with watercress, never lettuce, and even sliced in her special way. To be asked to make one of these *for* Cecelia was like being asked to make the first cut on the Koh-i-noor diamond, an honor nearly outweighed by the peril of failure.

A regular visitor to the Agers' was Ingersoll's friend Creekmore Fath, a Washington lawyer from Texas who was married to Jock Whitney's sister Adele. Creek was now in the OSS, doing intelligence work out of an office in the White House. As part of his cover, he had to spend a few days a month in Manhattan, and Cecelia had taken him in hand.

"Between the two of them, Cecelia and Milton knew everybody, it seemed to me, in New York City in the theater, and in music," Creek told me in 1992. "Whenever you went out with them, you spent half the time with people table-hopping, coming by to say hello, and sitting down for a few minutes.

"I remember very well the first time I went to the apartment for Sunday brunch. I got there and Dottie Parker was seated in the chair facing the door, with that miserable little dog. I was on the sofa next to her. We were having our Bloody Marys, and Gerry and Cecelia left the room to get hors d'oeuvres or something. Dottie was very, very pleasant. Then she leaned over and looked at me in that very sweet way she had, and said, 'Shit.'

"I was astonished. Cecelia came back in, and Dottie said, 'Look at him. He's blushing. He's never heard a lady say shit before.'

"'Dottie, he still hasn't,' said Cecelia. 'Now look at him when I say it . . . see . . . he didn't blush at all.'"

Transport to Britain was at a premium just before D-Day, and Gerry was desperate to get back to Ralph. So Creek had a chat with Mrs. Roosevelt, who arranged for Gerry to be flown to England on an Air Transport plane. Later Creek's friend Charles Marsh, the Texas newspaper magnate, asked Creek, "Did it ever occur to you that Ralph might not want Gerry in England?"

"But they're desperately in love!" Creek said. Marsh, however, proved to be correct. The one man she really cared about didn't care that much about her, and when Ingersoll rather abruptly married someone else, Gerry was shattered. She decided to take a house in Nassau to recover, and Cecelia went along. Six weeks later they both came back with stunning tans which made their blonde good looks stand out even more.

When no guests were around, Milton led a well-developed masculine day-and-night club life. Since he made friends easily, and was always a generous host, he did not lack companionship during the long days out at Glen Oaks, and long nights at the Friars. After the home-cooking frenzy abated, he again took Cecelia out to an expensive restaurant every night, along with us and any other friends who were hanging around, and he still worked every day at the piano, composing new songs, revising old ones, and playing and studying the work of other writers he admired, especially Rodgers and Hammerstein, and always Kern. He played the scores of new Broadway shows, analyzing how the effects had been achieved. He never expressed the least jealousy for contemporaries who had outdistanced him, and was invariably courteous and helpful to younger aspirants.

By the time a maid arrived in the late morning to clean, Milton was usually waiting downstairs for a golf partner to come by. One day a woman with a dog walked past him. "What's the matter? Don't you speak to an old friend?"

It was Dottie, who lived with her poodle C'est Tout in the New Weston, an apartment hotel four blocks away.

Milton apologized, and said he was confused and still awakening from his sleeping pill. "Do you ever take them, Dottie?"

"Do I! With sugar and cream!"

Upstairs, Cecelia and the maid always had a brief chat before Cecelia went off to work. She was extremely solicitous to people who worked for her, invariably mingling her household instructions with detailed inquiries about the maid's children, or her infirmities, or her errant husband, and never failing to remember the names of important persons in the servant's life. Her Old World courtesy, so different from her behavior with her daughters, never failed to astound me. When no one else was around, Laurel and I were the servants, brusquely told to put things away and tidy up, not just in our own room but throughout the apartment. Her orders were painful, not because of the work but the constant criticism. Good daughters, proper and grateful daughters, would have done these things automatically, without having to be asked.

Cecelia was paying less and less attention to Milton, and he was drinking more. He never appeared drunk, nor did Cecelia, but he probably had a whiskey or two after his golf game, two or three more before dinner, and more during his all-night bridge games. His habit of repeating himself was likely a reflection of the alcohol, though I didn't recognize it at the time. Even at worst he was never a noisy or violent drunk; he was a neat one.

When he got seriously high and wound up, Cecelia sent for his friend Dr. Jules Gordon, a fellow Glen Oaks member who was the team physician for the New York Yankees. Jules always arrived holding a nurse by one hand and his black bag in the other. In it was a vial of paraldehyde or chloral hydrate, "knockout drops." By that time Milton would be lying in the bathtub wearing only his shower cap. He had some idea about dying without making any mess, by dissolving, and was now waiting for someone to turn on the water and let him swirl gently down the drain. Though I saw this happen only once, Cecelia told me it had occurred a couple of other times. She mentioned it not to complain or criticize. It was clear she was deeply concerned about him, and indeed seeking my advice. I felt offended, and a bit frightened, that she should be inviting me into so personal an area of their lives, and had no suggestions.

If the Agers wanted to divorce, this would have been a good time. Their daughters were grown, and they had no reason to maintain the facade of their marriage. But though they often argued, I have no evidence that either of them seriously considered breaking up. After a big fight, Milton sometimes spent a night or two, never more, at a hotel.

One evening after dinner when Nunnally and Dorris Johnson had come back upstairs with the Agers for a nightcap, thrice-married Nunnally turned to Milton and asked him outright why he and Cecelia had never divorced.

"In one word?" Milton said.

Nunnally nodded.

"Ennui."

Cecelia said nothing. Milton handled the tensions of their marriage with witticisms, Cecelia by clamming up. At clamming up, she had no peer.

Many years later Dorris told me she'd heard that Cecelia too had had an affair with Ralph. Impossible, I said. Ralph was too arrogant and magisterial, not at all Cecelia's type. She was merely the beard for Gerry. Indeed, Cecelia served as beard to lovers of all persuasions, including Mr. John, who was forsaking Mr. Fred for the handsome, much younger Peter Brandon. She was a natural beard: she had great discretion, a taste for intrigue, and could be trusted not to gossip. Most important, her loyalty was not to convention but to feeling, which often means not to marriage but to love.

To judge from their grand apartment and the nightly restaurant dinners, the Agers were well-to-do. But the cost of living had begun its inexorable postwar rise, and though 350 Park Avenue was a rent-controlled building, all other expenses were climbing while Milton's ASCAP income was proportionally less as the period of his songs' great popularity grew more and more distant. He and his wife did not argue in front of others, but much of their private warfare concerned Cecelia's extravagance. She was now spending far more than he was earning, he protested, but she didn't seem to hear him. She was earning money too, and probably felt entitled to spend it as she liked. But she never said so. She never said anything, except to moan that she was exhausted, or had a headache, and was going to her room to lie down, an obviously evasive tactic that my father nonetheless respected. Milton, on the other hand, never pointed out that he alone as a matter of principle was paying their entire household and family expenses. Milton was meticulous by nature, and probably his sense of financial loss of control, coupled with his wife's ever-cold shoulder, contributed to his drinking.

At about this time, perhaps sooner, perhaps a bit later, Milton began living more and more in the past. I am not sure because, in these same years, as assorted opportunities came along to put some space between myself and the Agers, I grabbed them. Our diverging orbits swung us ever farther apart, and in very short order I had found my first job, first lover, and left home for the first time — events which would be swiftly followed by my first marriage, first love affair, first divorce, and, inevitably in our circles, first shrink.

"My parents are bohemians," I told him. "They have no home." When the doctor repeated this to my father, he was astonished, then angry. "Bohemians! I am the most conventional, bourgeois man you will ever meet. I love my wife . . . I love my children. . . . She thinks we're *bohemians!* What the hell is she talking about!"

Early in 1943, Fanny Rubenstein, not yet sixty years old, was found to have terminal stomach cancer. Anzia rushed to California to be with her sister, but became so angered by the disdainful way she felt she was being treated by Fanny's children that she left Los Angeles abruptly, before Fanny's death, then suffered agonies of remorse. She was haunted, she wrote to her daughter, by "the tragedy of . . . Fanny's whole life — how she had tried to get hold of life through her children — through overfeeding people tried to appease the loneliness, the hunger. And I who should have known better, left her when she was dying, because I allowed my-self to be hurt by Victor's uniform and Cecelia's fine clothes and her snobbery."

One weekend I came home from Vassar to find a large package in the front hall. It was a homemade affair, mailed from Chicago, and turned out to be a recording of a song Milton's mother had written, and had rented a studio to record. Several of Milton's sisters and brothers and their spouses had begun writing songs, an activity which clearly could bring in a great deal more money than the used-car business.

When Milton came home that evening, he put the big acetate on the Capehart and hit the button. A high and quavery but utterly true voice, unaccompanied by any instrument, but with a tremendous Yid-dish accent, sang out, "Franklin D. Roosevelt, I Love You." At the end, she chirped, "By Fanny Ager. Denk you."

The following December, Fanny died. She was eighty-five. Milton must have gone to Chicago for her funeral, but again I was away at col-lege and unaware. One rainy Saturday morning about a year later, Lau-rel was in the kitchen making applesauce in our new-fangled pressure cooker when we heard a huge bang. We all rushed in to investigate. Laurel was fine. The radio said an army bomber had just struck the Em-pire State Building. But for the fog, we could have seen the flames from our kitchen window. I noticed something bright up near the ceiling. A cheap jelly glass containing a lighted candle was up on top of the refrig-erator.

"What's that?"

"A *yahrtzeit* candle," said Milton. Today was the anniversary of his mother's death, he explained, and this was the way Jews remembered their dead. It was the first, and last, incidence of anything religious I ever saw in our household, with the exception of Cecelia's chic gold Star of David that she continued to wear daily at her neck or wrist.

Another weekend I happened to be home when the Traveler's Aid Society telephoned saying a foreigner was lost and looking for Cecelia. A little woman dressed like Anzia in denim and sandals soon appeared, fell into Cecelia's arms, and they both burst into deep, Slavic sobs. She was Zalkin's sister from Morocco, Dr. Eugenia Delanoë, whom Cecelia feared might be dead or in prison; no one had heard from her since the fall of France. Genia had a noble head of flying white hair, sapphire eyes, and spoke no English. Cecelia brought tea, and they conversed in French. The war had disrupted Genia's life in some unspecified way, and she was en route from Morocco to San Francisco to find her brother Charles, now practicing medicine there.

Milton got home from the golf course and addressed our visitor in Yiddish. She responded in torrents, and the conversation continued in high spirits until it was time to take her to Grand Central and put her aboard the train west.

As the end of my second year at Vassar approached, I heard that *PM* was hiring copy girls. When I went downtown to apply, the editor of the Sunday magazine asked if I'd be interested in trying out as a cub reporter instead. My assignment was to interview Gypsy Rose Lee, who was pregnant. The prospect terrified me, and I boarded the subway still trying to memorize a list of questions tucked into my little white glove. A uniformed maid opened the door of her East Side townhouse and led me to an atrium full of tropical plants. I stared at my list, frozen with fear. A parrot cawed. Half an hour passed before an elegant, awesomely enormous creature appeared. She was nearly six feet tall, and wrapped in a diaphanous tent of multicolored chiffon deliberately designed to call attention to her condition. Curls piled atop her head exaggerated her height, and she carried a Japanese fan. With elephantine grace she moved to a chaise longue, sank down, and turned her large eyes toward me, waiting.

I peeked into my glove. "Miss Lee, after the birth of your child, do you intend to resume your career?"

Silence. The parrot croaked. The lady fanned herself. "Honey," she finally said, "I can't have everything going out and nothing coming in."

Her retort was equivalent to tossing a rope to a drowning girl. A writer herself, she knew that the one thing that could save a green and

frightened kid was a good quote, so she threw me one. I rushed back to
PM to write my story, joyfully daring to think I had stumbled upon my
true métier and would never have to return to Vassar again.

I recognized that Gypsy had been trying to help me. That Cecelia
had also tried, that she was responsible for my being offered the tryout
in the first place, never occurred to me. Nor did she ever in her lifetime
suggest that such might be the case.

When fall came, I refused to return to Vassar. Milton insisted I finish
my college education. Not having had one himself, he tended to over-
value the experience. Cecelia, who knew more about it, didn't seem to
care if I went back to school or not. Whenever we met, which was as
infrequently as I could manage, she criticized my vapid friends, tacky
clothes, and low-class taste. "You would be so beautiful, if only you'd
stop straightening your hair and plucking your eyebrows."

Cecelia's perfectionism made her seem a domestic terrorist to her
children. It was impossible to see her constant carping as a way of expressing love, or her determination to make of me something better than
she had made of herself. Nor had I yet noticed that the object of her
most scalding criticism was always herself. Her impossibly high standards condemned her to dwell in a permanent hell of silent self-scorn,
and probably contributed to the migraines that tormented her. Yet, although the specifics of her criticism of me had not varied in seven or
eight years — to me, forever — something *had* begun to change. The job
at *PM* was giving me my first experience of genuine self-esteem, and
with it came a change in attitude. All my life I had feared my mother;
now I was beginning merely to dislike her.

Only recently I discovered that, in exactly the same period, Cecelia
was becoming a surrogate mother to Betty Friedan, newly arrived in
Manhattan from Peoria, by way of Smith College, burning with left-
wing ardor and an inchoate wish to become a writer. The New York
Newspaper Guild wanted to publish a weekly newsletter of union news,
and had hired Betty and Cecelia Ager to write alternate issues. To Betty,
Cecelia was "the epitome of New York sophistication . . . and also the

New Woman! She was immensely kind and encouraging to me. I thought she was the *real* Rosalind Russell!"

"And what did you think of me? I was working in the Sunday department."

"Oh, you!" Betty sniffed. "You were an *awful* snob."

Milton had begun insisting that I "contribute to the household." As soon as he started out, as a little boy selling peanuts, he'd turned over every penny to his mother. Now that I was working, he thought I should do something similar. I was outraged. My salary was $24.50 a week, the Newspaper Guild minimum, out of which I proudly bought my own clothes, and to hell with what Cecelia thought. Besides, at our scale of living, my few dollars in the kitty would have been meaningless. I felt insulted and misunderstood; brimstone crackled in the domestic atmosphere. Whenever we got together, Milton kept repeating "Stand by your sex commitments" and talking about "the importance of the family unit." In fact, Laurel and I were now full-grown — five-foot-three-and-a-half and five-foot-three respectively — and a kind of family mitosis had been under way for some time. Laurel would soon be going off to Radcliffe. Instead of two or three Poles apart, we were becoming four.

Most of the younger men had gone to war. I spent many nights hanging out with older reporters in press watering holes like Costello's Irish bar on Third Avenue. For real dates, I divided my time between two swains as unlike one another as the prince and the pauper. "Shana, I know your type," a wise friend told me many years later. "You're the kind of girl who goes out the door every morning with an empty leash looking for underdogs."

He was right, and Barney, my first underdog, was a prize specimen — small and ugly, with a bad stammer, a broken nose, broken teeth, and smashed hands acquired while earning college tuition by boxing for $10 in men's smokers after running away from the orphanage where he'd been raised. My other swain, Robert Shulman, was a born overdog in every respect except financially. He had movie star looks, sterling academic gifts, and a chilly, laid-back manner. At Columbia University, from which he had just graduated with high honors, Bob had been the protégé of Lionel Trilling, who had long dreamed of finding a true Renaissance scholar, a poet-astronomer, say, or a man of letters who was equally at home in a physics lab. Lionel thought Shulman, a scholarship student who had excelled in the study of literature but majored in physical chemistry, filled the bill.

I'd met Bob a year earlier at a party to which an older girl had taken me. Soon she and Bob were sharing a Greenwich Village apartment. No one else I knew, no one else I had ever heard of, lived together with someone of the opposite sex. They had since quarreled, and he was back living with his widowed mother in Forest Hills while waiting to be called up by the navy.

By January, I gave in to my father's pleas to return to Vassar. But education had nothing to do with my decision. I was falling in love, or thought I was, with Bob Shulman. Primal female competition was a part of it, for I couldn't figure out how I had managed to secure the affections of a man who had once loved my older friend, someone I viewed as the epitome of sophisticated womanhood and wonderful bohemian free spiritism. That he could prefer me to her was unthinkable. But once that seemed to be the case, the next step became inevitable.

Bob had finally been sent to navy radar school at MIT in Cambridge, and what I wanted most was to be able to visit him there unchaperoned. For my purposes, it would be far easier to escape Vassar's vigilance than the Agers'. Going to bed with Bob was becoming the subject uppermost in my mind. This virginity business had gone on long enough, I had decided. I was nearly nineteen, and avid to find out what all the women in the books I read were talking about. One night, in a Cambridge hotel room, I did. The experience was a painful disappointment.

"What do we do now?" I said afterwards.

"Now we change the sheets."

Vassar had finally become interesting. I had yielded to my longtime fascination with anthropology, changed my major, and was studying hard with a brilliant professor, Dr. Dorothy Lee, who brought her newest baby to class and nursed it while we discussed comparative child-rearing customs in Samoa and Melanesia. Though I now felt far more worldly than my presumably still-virginal sisters, I never mentioned my Cambridge adventure to any of them. Discussing it would have been far more daunting than doing it had been. Although Bob and I were now intimate, we didn't talk about it either. I'm not sure why, except that I was embarrassed by my lack of responsiveness, and he was a very cool presence, a scientist, and someone whose refrigerated emotions seemed to match my own. When he came to Vassar to visit me, he assumed the right to spend the night in my room. Discovery would have meant instant dismissal, and these nights, of panic more than passion, were soon succeeded by days of dread. An older girl I'd met at *PM* had by then told me where to go to get fitted for a diaphragm, and yet another Hungarian doctor had obliged. But when my period failed to come on time, I was certain for a number of hideous weeks that I was pregnant.

Bob completed the course at MIT and was assigned to the aircraft carrier *Saratoga*, which was about to rejoin the Pacific fleet. His few days of liberty before sailing occurred during Vassar's ten-day spring break, and we spent them hiding out in a hotel on West End Avenue, and rarely got out of bed. We must have gone downstairs to eat, but I can't remember leaving our room. In those few days in April 1945, everything changed. He was going overseas, we didn't know when or even if we would see each other again, and we clung to each other every precious hour of the day and night. I felt snug and secret and grown up and wonderful.

Sometime that week he must have asked me to marry him, and I must have agreed to do so when he got out of the navy. By the weekend I could hardly walk, and my face was blotched from weeping. Vassar was still on Easter vacation, so I returned to 350 Park Avenue at about ten A.M. on a Saturday morning. Milton's bedroom door was still closed, and Cecelia, oddly enough, was still in bed. But she'd heard me come in, and there was nothing for it but to go in and greet her.

She was reading the papers, her hair down around her shoulders.

"Hi," I said.

"How was it?" she asked, then added gently, "Are you all right?"

I was stunned. I was certain my departure from Vassar, and Bob's and my tracks thereafter, had been covered with jungle cunning. Yet she knew. She seemed to know everything but our room number. My humiliation at having been found out was made worse by the shame of having been so clumsy at hiding the truth.

Somehow she knew it all! I was so blinded by this incredible fact that I wasn't listening to what she was saying. When I did, my blood froze. My mother was assuring me that she was not going to say anything to my dreadful, ridiculous father. She was declaring herself a willing coconspirator in my secret life, just as she was in Gerry's.

Too late for that! I wanted to scream. Hearing my lifelong scourge offering at this late date to become my friend — indeed my ally against my still-mourned lost friend and new enemy, Milton — generated feelings of deep revulsion, and an urgent need to get away from her, from them both. I *should have* screamed; I wish profoundly that I had. But I couldn't scream at Cecelia. I had never in my life told her the truth of my feelings about her; I never would.

Up to now, fear of my mother had ruled my life; up to now she had won every contest. On that April morning fear transmuted into hatred and, suddenly powerful, I slammed the door on Cecelia with all my newfound strength in fierce reprisal for what she had done to the child who had been me. When at last she held out her hand to me, I bit it. I struck instinctively as a cobra. As I did so, I felt the last still-open portcullis inside me slam shut. Whatever muddled love I had felt for Cecelia while she taught me to knit, while we listened to Paul Robeson, was entirely gone, as if flowed away in some invisible underground river. I had become successfully walled-up, a prisoner in a castle, myself both the princess and the tower.

WAR SONGS

CHAPTER NINE

LOST

I was nineteen when I slammed the door on the Agers. I spent the next twenty years obsessed. One single idea, one Grand Plot, controlled my life and peopled my dreams. I would marry and have many children. I would make up to them for what I had suffered as a child. I needed a lot of them to demonstrate across a broad range of circumstances how a good mother behaves.

In thrall to my obsession, I married two men — the first two who asked me. Number One was Bob, now out of the navy and back at Columbia getting his Ph.D. on the GI Bill. Both of my parents were dead set against him. The Trillings might be amazed at his Renaissance qualities of mind, but these attributes, like his good looks, were lost on Cecelia and Milton. All they could see was that he had no money nor any immediate prospects. Milton was furious that a man would suggest marriage to a woman before he was able to support her. Cecelia plain disliked him, finding him surly, charmless, and arrogant. He felt the same way about her.

If we married immediately, I'd have to work, which was fine with me. I enjoyed working, and had no model for any but a working wife. Milton, however, had a very different image in mind. His son-in-law would be "a man who can take care of you," not a *yeshiva bocher,* a perennial poor student. At the time, I was unfamiliar with the term and totally unaware that I myself was the descendant of *yeshiveh bochers.* I had never heard of Cecelia's great-grandfather, the rabbi of Lomza, nor of her grandfather Bernhard Jezierski, nor Milton's grandfather Nathan the Wise. Nor did I know that I, like my grandmothers, was filled near to bursting with self-sacrificing Polish blood.

While Bob was still overseas, Milton had invited his widowed mother to Gerry's pretentious apartment to talk matters over. I liked Frieda Shulman, and had smelled trouble when my father, normally the most courteous of men, didn't even invite her to take off her coat. "Do you know what a *yeshiveh bocher* is?" he'd sneered, making clear he considered her son not a man but a mere boy, and a girlish boy at that. To the proud and gentle widow, Bob Shulman was sun, moon, and stars. To mock her belief in him showed a streak of crudity in Milton that I hadn't dreamed existed. At that instant, I felt so sorry for Frieda that I vowed anew to defy my boorish father and get married at the earliest possible moment.

"At least be married by a rabbi!" Bob's grandmother began pleading when she understood we were indeed about to run off. So we found one, and tied the knot one Saturday afternoon at a reform school for delinquent Jewish boys, in a chapel with bars across its stained-glass windows.

Our marriage, based on little more than my need to escape and defy the Agers, would soon self-destruct. But while it lasted I played at being a perfect 1946 wife, Polly Benedict newly married to Andy Hardy. I knitted him argyle socks and grew a geranium on our windowsill. Though I was back at *PM,* I avoided seeing Cecelia at the office, or reading what she wrote. In sum, I rebelled against my mother, the family feminist, in traditional fashion—by going in exactly the opposite direction. To attempt to outdo Cecelia in feminist independence would have seemed to me a form of Uncle Tomming. Instead I became the family reactionary, a passionate conformist, and consecrated myself to marriage, motherhood, and home cooking. I dreamed of maple bedroom sets, new kinds of casseroles, monogrammed towels, and for the next couple of decades endured, and caused, some very mixed-up, exceedingly unhappy days.

We had been married nearly two years, and seen virtually nothing of my parents, when Gerry called with the bad news that Cecelia had broken her leg. She had done this the day before she was to leave for Stromboli, invited there by Roberto Rossellini and Ingrid Bergman. Having scandalized the world by running off together, they had selected Cecelia as the writer to tell their story with tact and understanding.

Cecelia's rotten luck touched my stony heart, and I promised Gerry I'd stop by. I had not been to 350 Park since leaving it to marry Bob. I found my mother in bed, one plaster-encased leg propped high on a stack of pillows, looking small and sad. We lit cigarettes and she had begun telling me how the accident happened when her bedside phone rang. She picked it up, and I recognized the voice.

"Hello, Cecelia. This is Bob. May I speak to Shana, please?"

My mother squashed out her cigarette in the ashtray and sat up a bit straighter. "Bob who?" she sniffed. The invalid may have been down, but she was far from out.

I betrayed my husband with the first man who made a pass at me, then left him before he could do the same to me. I don't remember any actual blowup. Bob Shulman had one of the stiffest upper lips I've ever encountered, and the day I assured him our marriage was over, he simply moved out. We were only separated, not divorced, but Milton, overjoyed that I had at last "come to my senses," immediately began urging me to "tidy up your life."

Every time Milton said "Tidy up your life," I said, "No money." Divorce in those days involved a six-week residency in Nevada.

Cecelia saluted my new status by finding a pair of Hungarian tailors and commissioning them to make me a ravishing fawn-colored suit of softest doeskin/mohair/angora/God knows, with silk lining, hand-made buttonholes, and every other refinement of the tailor's art. The artisans, more of her refugees, might have been brain surgeons in the old country. I found my own apartment and, now suitably dressed and full of renewed energy, worked as a freelancer for *Junior Bazaar* and *Mademoiselle*, magazines where Cecelia had editor friends.

No longer attached to Bob, I felt free to drop by 350, and one day heard the dread strains of "Get That Happy Habit" again thumping through the apartment. The year was 1948 and Yip Harburg had asked Milton if he had a good tune for the new Henry Wallace third party. Sure enough, at the party's convention in Philadelphia that summer, "WE want Henry Wallace! FRIENDLY Henry Wallace!" pounded out of the loudspeakers.

Laurel was now out of Radcliffe, where she had majored in paleontology. But she was not interested in earning an advanced degree, and was reluctant to choose what she saw as the only alternative — a lifetime of dusting fossils in museum basements. Neither parent could help her, as Cecelia had always silently helped me. Eventually Laurel took New York State–administered aptitude tests, discovered she was superbly equipped for technical writing, a skill then much in demand by military contractors, and soon found a job she greatly enjoyed.

Commercial television was just starting up, and I got a job as script girl and researcher on an early quiz show, *Celebrity Time*, presided over by Conrad Nagel. The questions were rebuses, stitched together out of film clips and bits of old newsreel which we spliced at a film rental library. I was also responsible for obtaining props. Note for the TV Trivia Hall of Fame: I am the script girl who found the 9th Avenue bakery that made the most throwable lemon meringue pies in Manhattan.

After a year of this, I decided to permit Milton to pay for my divorce. In the course of getting it, a strange accident occurred which led directly to my second marriage. One starlit night at my Nevada dude ranch, another guest and I were sitting out on a rock with a couple of beers discussing the meaning of life when someone shouted that he was wanted on the telephone. He returned to the rock shaking his head in wonder.

The caller was the wife in the happiest marriage he knew, and they too had just decided to divorce. Incredible! Underneath our rock, the foundations of our world were shaking; three divorces — events once unimaginable — were all happening at once. The sad story was that the wife had fallen in love with her husband's best friend, and had just told her husband she was expecting his friend's baby.

Though I didn't know the wife or boyfriend, I had met the husband — he ran the film library — and now my heart ached for the poor fellow. So when he invited me to dinner a few days after I got back to New York, I headed for the Hotel Algonquin with my face a mask of compassion, and the old, warm Florence Nightingale feeling aglow in my stomach. His name was Stephen Alexander, and over dinner I heard the whole story again, this time from the horse's mouth, so to speak. After dinner we walked around the block, by which time my long-empty leash had acquired a new occupant and I was practically oozing compassion onto 44th Street. I never heard any more details about his marital breakup because, once our own relationship began to ripen, Steve forbade me to utter his first wife's name. He found the subject too agonizingly painful.

Why else I became so determined to marry this man I'm not sure. He had asked me, and I wanted to "make it up to him" for what he had suffered. I felt invigorated by his energy and enthusiasm for life. Friends praised him as handsome, a quality important to a young woman who, since Vassar, had been comparing herself, unfavorably, to her lissome classmates. I'd been a miserable misfit at college. Most of my classmates were much older, soignée products of girls' boarding schools. I had never laid eyes on such people before. They seemed to me to have come from another planet, some hotbed of social rest which raised young women of immense self-assurance, long legs, straight hair, and perfect complexions.

Steve was also a world-class underdog with a Horatio Alger history that touched me. His father was a Greek waiter, and his sweet Irish peasant mother a kitchen worker. Despite having grown up truly poor, Steve had made it through NYU and worked in the entertainment department of *The New York Times* and at the Theater Guild before finding his present job as head of United World Films, a Manhattan film library owned by Universal Pictures.

Finally, my obsession with having children aside, a passionate conformist like myself needed very much to *be* married, and this assertive, self-centered man, sure of himself and hypercritical of others, seemed to have the very strengths I lacked. That these were precisely Cecelia's qualities would not occur to me for some time.

That year, 1950, Anzia at last published *Red Ribbon on a White Horse*. She had wrestled with her demons eighteen years to produce this slim volume. In the final version of the story, crazy old Jeremiah and his briefcase are still present, but the main character has become Anzia Yezierska. She tells of her years of struggle, her stunning, overnight success, and her sudden, ultimately disastrous transport from poverty to Hollywood's tinseled wonderland. The book also describes the great love of Anzia's life, an intense but brief affair with a powerful Wall Street lawyer of impeccable Anglo-Saxon lineage. The impassioned immigrant girl and the reserved New England Yankee swiftly fall in love. He is older and solidly married, frozen like an ice-bound ship in his staid, puritanical life. Hot-blooded Anzia feels a crazy intimacy with this utterly different kind of man, and a certainty she is closer to him than his wife or children could ever be. In turn, her ardor has made the graying lawyer feel alive again.

Soon they are dining in romantic little bistros and taking long walks, and the lawyer is writing her passionate love letters, even poetry. But at their first embrace, she stiffens in fear, pushes him away, runs home — and then changes her mind. The next morning she rushes to his office to throw herself at his feet. "But he had turned overnight into a polite stranger." Coldly, he asks her to return his letters. Anzia refuses, never sees him again, but compulsively reads and rereads the letters until she has memorized them.

Later she tried to write out what his love had meant to her, but "pages and pages piled up on my table, formless, inchoate." Desperate, she took to pacing the streets of her girlhood, talking to the old Jews, the fishmonger, the janitress, the pushcart peddler, then rushing back to her room and writing about these people, trying to wipe her lost love from her mind. For years she sent out stories and collected rejection slips. Then came her first check, from *Century Magazine*. Soon a dozen magazines were after her. Each time she published a story, she sent the lawyer a copy, which he never acknowledged. But she had become a success. Interviewers, publishers, and finally movie producers now begged for her time, her work. "I, the unwanted one, was wanted. If I could not have love, I would have fame."

Anzia's little book boasted an introduction by W. H. Auden and a long blurb from Reinhold Niebuhr: "I do not know of a more honest and searching self-revelation than this book."

In Auden's view, Anzia's overnight success, and the mighty writer's block that followed, were expectable.

> The sudden paralysis or drying up of the creative power occurs to artists everywhere but nowhere, perhaps, more frequently than in America; nowhere else are there so many writers who produced one or two good books in their youth and then nothing. I think the reason for this is the dominance of the competitive spirit in the American ethos [the drive to make more and better material goods, better mousetraps, better washing machines]. . . . But a work of art is not a [material] good . . . but a unique good so that, strictly speaking, no work of art is comparable to another. . . . The writer who allows himself to become infected by the competitive spirit [is doomed because] . . . instead of trying to write *his* book, he tries to write one which is better than somebody else's book. [He is therefore] in danger . . . of trying to write the absolute masterpiece which will eliminate all competition once and for all and, since this task is totally unreal, his creative powers cannot relate to it, and the result is sterility.

Auden's introduction was responsible for much of the small sale Anzia had before her book was remaindered. One of the few copies extant,
now mine, is inscribed in her large hand, "To Milton with love from
Anzia, Aug 17, '50." Like so many of Anzia's declarations, this one too
was a wild overstatement.

The first issue of *Flair*, a high-style cornucopia of fashion and the arts
appeared in February 1950, with articles by W. H. Auden and Jean Coc-
teau, fiction by Tennessee Williams, and paintings by Lucien Freud.
The second issue included portraits of the famous by Saul Steinberg,
and "The New Hollywood" by Cecelia Ager. The woman behind *Flair*
was Fleur Cowles, wife of Mike Cowles of the Cowles publishing and
broadcasting empire. But the real editor was George Davis, late of *Mademoiselle*, where both Cecelia and I had published pieces. A brilliant editor, George had replaced Clare Boothe at *Vanity Fair*, later served as
fiction editor of *Harper's Bazaar*, and had the nose of a truffle hound for
unearthing new talent. Privately he presided over a sort of communal
brownstone for artists which at various times housed Auden, Benjamin
Britten, Paul and Jane Bowles, Truman Capote, Carson McCullers,
Richard Wright, and Gypsy Rose Lee.

By April, I had joined *Flair* as entertainment editor. The first story I
assigned was on Katharine Hepburn. In her romantic comedies with
Tracy, she was playing the woman I aspired to become. It didn't occur
to me that Garson Kanin, the man who for years had been "sweet on
Cecelia," and who with his wife, Ruth Gordon, had just written the latest
Hepburn/Tracy romp, *Adam's Rib*, had based his feisty yet adorably feminine character on a blend of his wife and Cecelia.

One of the first Manhattan office buildings erected after the wartime
construction freeze was the new *Look* Building at 52nd Street and Madison Avenue. The Friday before the *Flair* and *Look* staffs were to move
in, floor plans were distributed. I was to share an office with the travel

editor, Patrick O'Higgins, whom I had not met, and the plan showed an office with two desks, one beside the window, the other by the door.

"I'll get you the desk by the window," said Steve that night.

We sneaked into the empty building on Saturday morning, and were surprised to find someone already at the window desk, his back to the room. Bright sunlight streaming into the bare white office made it difficult to distinguish more than silhouette: small head, heroic shoulders, impossibly long legs. The figure turned, and I made out a classically beautiful young man with close-cropped ginger hair and blue eyes who wore impeccably cut riding clothes. He had just arranged an onyx and ormolu French empire desk set on the utility metal desk. Equally surprised to see the small woman and her companion standing in the doorway, the figure bowed slightly and, without a word, swept up his princely belongings and moved them to the desk beside the door.

Patrick O'Higgins, I later learned, was half Irish and half French and had survived six years of World War II service in the Irish Guards, compiling a harrowing, heroic war record. His mute relinquishment of the better desk seemed to me a gesture equal in gallantry to Raleigh spreading his cloak in the mud for the Queen. From that instant, Patrick and I were *copain* and *copine*, buddies for life.

Flair, however, lasted only six more issues. On Monday morning a week before Christmas, every staff member found a pink rose tucked into his or her typewriter, along with a pink slip informing us that the magazine was suspending publication. Mike Cowles's patience had run out, if not his money, and he and Fleur were filing for divorce. I telephoned the only other entertainment editor I knew, Tom Prideaux at *Life*, and asked if he could find me a temporary job there. I didn't require a big salary, just enough money to pay a whopping bill at Saks Fifth Avenue. Unbeknownst to anybody, I was planning by fall to be married and retire from the workforce.

Tom was a lean, tall, bushy-browed man of immense wit and knowledge of the theater. He had attended Lincoln School and, after Yale, returned there to teach English, then joined the original staff of *Life*. I was too young to have been in his legendary classes, but the older sisters of my friends had all had crushes on him.

When *Life* offered me a lowly researcher's job at $65 a week, precisely half my *Flair* salary, I swallowed my pride, my politics, and my brains and accepted. Cecelia, who had always loathed the Luces, especially because of their support of the China lobby, stopped speaking to me for a few weeks. Nine years earlier, when Time, Inc. scouts had trolled the Vassar senior class looking for recruits, I still shared enough of my mother's left-wing politics to turn up my nose and refuse an interview. But my politics, never very serious, no longer mattered. I was secretly preparing to marry a movie producer–in–training, and soon intended to retire into comfort and full-time, multiple motherhood. The mighty sway of my latest Grand Plot, swelling now to full crescendo, deafened me to my parents, to all voices, inner and outer, save its own.

When Steve Alexander asked me to marry him, I didn't think twice. I had no interest in going on being a writer. If anything, I was an anti-writer (as in antimatter, a word I had learned from husband number one). *PM* and *Flair* had been fun, but neither job was something to be taken seriously. I was twenty-five years old, and what I wanted most was to be a mother. A good mother. If not of twelve, at least of many. With this new husband, not a humble student but practically a Hollywood producer, I could finally afford it, and intended to begin trying as soon as possible.

Cecelia had not been abroad since her broken leg canceled out Stromboli. Then, in the spring of 1951, came what should have been her all-time dream assignment. French couture had recovered from the ravages of war and Christian Dior had devised "the New Look," obliging fashionable women to empty their closets and start from scratch. *Vogue* asked Cecelia to write a first-person account of what it is like to shop at a Paris couturier. Everything was to be first class and paid for by the magazine, including the dress. Cecelia checked in to the Hotel Crillon, looked over Dior's collection, ordered a model called Carmelite to be executed in shades of purple silk and velvet, endured endless fittings, and in due course sailed home with the dress on the *Île de France*.

There followed months of writing and rewriting. But the piece seemed jinxed; nothing worked. By the time she finished it, the deadline was so far in the past that *Vogue* had an excuse to turn it down. It was so long — thirty-six pages — and so overwritten, so tortured in syntax due to endless revisions, that it was close to unpublishable. Her agent submitted it to *Harper's Bazaar*, *McCall's*, *Holiday*, *Cosmopolitan*, *Ladies' Home Journal*, *Today's Woman*, *The Saturday Evening Post*, *Collier's*, and *Good Housekeeping*. It's too long, some editors said; it's too good, said others. The honest ones said that few readers cared about this sort of stuff anymore. Wrote Margaret Cousins, the savvy editor of *McCall's*: "while it entertained me, I think it would just irritate our audience, none of whom could conceive of going to so much trouble or spending $400 for a dress. It's too high-style for us common people. More like the lately departed *Flair*."

Poor Cecelia. So much of her great taste and concern was invested in things like perfection of hemlines, nippings of waists, and all the nuances of fit, shoulder width, seam alignment, and furbelow deployment — things in which people were no longer interested. The Paris dress story was a pathetic fiasco, and Cecelia was stuck with her vast, near-Talmudic horde of dressmaking knowledge. She was far from burnt out, and would continue writing for another seventeen years. But the subject she knew *most* about, *cared* most about, had gone the way of the bustle and the whalebone corset.

Both my parents thought very little of Stephen Alexander. But when my intentions became apparent, Milton announced that this time he would remain above the fray. "I am no longer going to tell you what to do," he said. "You're twenty-five now, old enough to make your own decisions. I may not agree, but I won't object. And if you do marry him, I will always treat him like a member of the family." Milton would keep his word.

Cecelia's anti-Steve maneuvers during the following year were vigorous, but worse than useless, merely providing an appealing seal of guaranteed parental disapproval.

In September 1951, Steve and I were married at the home of friends of mine who knew the way my parents felt, and offered us their townhouse and garden. The Agers came, along with Laurel, Mr. John, Patrick O'Higgins, and my *Life* friends Tom Prideaux and Mary Leatherbee. Leonard McCombe, a *Life* photographer, recorded it all for posterity. People made charming toasts and, before things broke up, Cecelia and Milton and Laurel and I sang a few choruses of "Stand to Your Glasses, Steady." Patrick swept me into his arms for an impromptu waltz through the garden, and Steve and I drove off to Mexico.

I moved into the brownstone on 58th Street that he had shared with his never-to-be-mentioned first wife, and we continued our jobs as before. A demon seamstress since Lincoln School, I now made red damask draperies with swags and pelmets for the bay window. My lunch hours were spent patrolling the furniture showrooms at Lord & Taylor and occasionally buying something nice on sale. I didn't have Jimmy Reynolds's knowledge or flair, but I had the unstoppable nest-building drive of a field mouse.

In 1952 Cecelia again began working full-time, as movie critic for the new magazine *Park East*, a fashionable Manhattan monthly. Her pieces were longer and better than the *PM* reviews; she had more time to work on them. In addition to a major monthly article, she wrote capsule mini-reviews of movies playing around town, a practice later picked up by *The New Yorker* and other magazines.

SHANE. Director George Stevens' mastery of the form arranges the eternal verities of the Western into a cool, mellow, space-filled, right-looking, right-acting, right-thinking, right-moving movie. Small boy idolatry of the gentle-strong-silent-mysterious Western hero (Alan Ladd) is transferred direct to the screen in the small person of Brandon de Wilde, a miniature stalwart completely capable of shouldering this tremendous responsibility.

In 1953, with Milton's sixtieth birthday approaching, a special present seemed in order. I decided to make him a bathrobe, blue-striped seersucker with a shawl collar and the opening bars of "Happy Days Are Here Again" embroidered on the pocket flap in red silk. The gift was not a total success. Lincoln School had taught me how to pin and sew a paper pattern, but not how to notate music. I knew the notes, but not how to indicate the correct rhythm. I couldn't even figure out the proper time signature, and settled at length for embroidering the five-line staff, a fancy treble clef, and the seven notes of the title phrase. Musically it was illiterate, but Milton wore the robe to the end of his life.

I worked as a researcher for three happy years. Tom Prideaux and his beloved Mary Leatherbee, our drama critic and movie editor, made the entertainment department seem a giddy, perpetual house party. The researchers included Margaret and Bob Ginna, Clay Felker, and Phil Kunhardt, all of whom became lifelong friends. Nobody but Tom knew I had once been a writer and *Flair*'s entertainment editor, and we never mentioned it.

Researchers in those days were batmen or subalterns to *Life*'s elite staff photographers, the big stars of the biggest, richest, most successful magazine in the world. Perhaps a third of the researchers were female. But the rest of the magazine was a male hierarchy, and researcher was as high as any woman should expect to rise. The fashion, food, art, and movie editors were female, and we had a couple of women photographers. But the upper reaches of the masthead were exclusively white male. There were a few Catholics and Jews, and we must have had some gays, but I recall no evident Latin American, Asian American, Native American, or African American of either sex employed in any capacity, with the sole exception of the photographer Gordon Parks, a black man not yet forty who already had made himself one of the magazine's shining stars. As I intended staying only a few months, and quite enjoyed working amidst so many men, the lack of opportunities for promotion did not concern me.

Shortly after I signed on, Gordon invited me for a drink after work. The *Time* and *Life* offices then faced the skating rink in Rockefeller

Center, and no parking was permitted anywhere. Crossing the street with Gordon, I was surprised to see two parked cars, a dark green MG roadster with wire wheels, and a white Jaguar, and astonished to learn that Gordon owned both.

Parks was dashing and beautifully dressed in Paris and London clothes, pantherlike and graceful of manner, and he must have looked great behind the wheel. He must also have handsomely paid off the parking police. As our friendship grew, I continually marveled at how thoroughly Gordon prepared and papered his path past all the cops and doormen and maître d's of the first-class white world, making certain his race would cause no untoward incidents for himself or his companions. In those days, when no other black people were seen strolling in Rockefeller Center, nor at the Plaza Hotel, nor in London's Claridge's nor the Crillon in Paris — to mention a few of Gordon's watering holes — this must have taken a great deal of papering.

As we sipped our drinks that first day, Gordon said, "My philosophy of life is this, Shana. Every place I plant a seed, I want a flower to grow." I found this rather profound, and remember thinking to myself, "My God, I don't even *have* any philosophy."

My life did have an organizing principle, not all that different from Gordon's perhaps, but so secret that I would not have breathed it to a soul. The important moments in my life were the visits I was making every few months to another Hungarian, Dr. Raphael Kurzrok, a gynecologist. Nothing was the matter, he always said after examining me. The babies will come. Just relax, take it easy, and don't work too hard.

Another uneventful year passed. Perhaps I *was* working too hard, Dr. Kurzrok was now saying. Why not take some time off? Stay home and keep house, take life a little easier. Why not, I agreed. Why not try moving back to California, in fact? I had been happy there, and Steve would be closer to movie production. On New Year's Eve 1953, we made a resolution. Monday he would start lining up a replacement at United World Films, and I would ask my friend Loudon Wainwright, *Life*'s newly appointed Beverly Hills bureau chief, to keep me in mind.

"Do not get out of that chair!" said Loudon. He cantered down to the managing editor's office and came back beaming. I was the person he'd wanted to ask for, it turned out, but Mary Leatherbee had said, "Don't be ridiculous. Shana is married to Steve, who can't leave New York." If I could be in California in a week, he said now, *Life* would promote me to bureau correspondent, raise my salary, lend me the money to buy a car, move our worldly goods to the West Coast, and keep me in a hotel until Steve had time to wind up his business and join me.

The following Monday I was there. Each day I got a lift to work, and weekends I went to driving school. By the time Steve arrived eight weeks later, I had got my license, acquired a used Chevrolet, and Mary Stothart had found us a romantic, unbelievably cheap house clinging to the side of a cliff above Santa Monica Canyon. A Dutch front door opened directly into a large living room with a big bay window overlooking the beach and ocean far below.

Days after I left New York, my parents precipitately decided to move back to California too. *Park East* had folded the previous year, and its editor, A. C. Spectorsky, decamped to Chicago to help Hugh Hefner found *Playboy*. My move west suddenly offered the Agers an excuse to abandon a way of life they had long been unable to sustain. I don't doubt they let Lawrence Stewart conclude that they wanted "to be closer to Shana," and Milton surely did. But for Cecelia, it was mainly a convenient excuse to close up shop on Park Avenue. If any other alternatives had come along, another Ingersoll, another anything, she wouldn't have budged.

She urged Milton to fly out to California and stay with me while she dealt with the moving mess. It seemed to me a wonderful omen that my first guest in my first house was my beloved father. Soon a moving van arrived with the Alexander possessions, and Steve had somehow got *Life* to include Milton's Steinway. It fit perfectly into our bay window, and again hearing a piano going at all hours was lovely.

In New York, Cecelia dragooned Laurel to help her, and hired a crew of moving men to wrap and crate every single item. Worn mops, old shoes, piles of magazines, wire hangers, jars of spices, and cracked teacups were indiscriminately packed, trucked out to California, and stashed at the Bekins Van and Storage Company on South Beverly Drive. Cecelia ordered a snappy new Mercury convertible from Milton's brother-in-law, and a friend offered to drive her and it west. At the last possible moment, Laurel quit her job and came along. California was full of military contractors, and she took scant risk in pulling up stakes.

When they appeared at my half-open Dutch door, Cecelia's brother Victor was on hand with champagne. Laurel found an aerospace job and moved into a converted garage apartment near Venice. Cecelia rented a furnished house on the edge of Beverly Hills, on the cheaper side of the tracks this time. She hired a cook and Milton rented a piano. A year later they moved again, dispensed with the cook, and resumed their lifetime custom of restaurant dinners. But even that house was deemed too expensive and exhausting for Cecelia to run, and soon they had moved a third time, into a sunny but small and tackily furnished Wilshire Boulevard apartment, a rear walk-up in a motel-like, two-story stucco building between Beverly Hills and Westwood that would be their final abode. It had daily maid service, and the familiar two-bedroom, two-bath layout, with neutral zone between. There was no room for a piano because Victor and Florence had given the Agers a large TV set which occupied the only available corner of the living room. Cecelia, as always, took the better bedroom. For her birthday I covered a dime store picture frame with purple velvet, glued on a narrow band of brocade ribbon, added a matte of yellow velvet, and inserted a photograph of Fanny Rubenstein wearing one of her Mr. John hats. Cecelia hung it on the wall opposite her bed, above her open trunk, and it remained the room's only decoration, except for a car dealer's commercial Christmas calendar, until the end of her days.

Milton's bedroom was half as big, about eleven by thirteen feet, with just enough room for a narrow bed, a small bookcase alongside it, and a little rented upright piano. The bookcase contained a few volumes on golf, bridge, music, and mathematics, and his favorite Irish writers, O'Casey and Shaw. On top were family pictures and a grinning publicity photo of Ben Bernie, who had died during the war. Under the single window was a child-size desk with one of Cecelia's old portables stashed below, for typing lyrics. The skimpy "easy chair" looked as if it belonged at a woman's vanity table, and the small, dark bathroom had a stall shower, no tub. The room was so narrow that he could get in and out of bed only on the side opposite the piano, on top of which were piled the four green morocco-bound volumes of his songs I had given him in 1950, his only record of his life's work except for the files at ASCAP. His room lacked adequate storage space, and underwear, handkerchiefs, and important papers were stored in his half-open trunk. He liked to read in bed, and for his birthday I bought him a motorized hospital bed so that he could shift it to various positions and get some relief from the painful arthritis that had settled in his neck and shoulders. He still played golf daily, but it would have cost $10,000 to rejoin Hillcrest, so he golfed at Rancho Park, the public course next door, and played bridge at the Wild Whist Bridge Club, one flight up on Westwood Boulevard.

So at ages fifty-two and sixty-one, when most people begin thinking about retirement, the Agers were back leading the same barren, rootless existence they had adopted in 1934. They lived now on a more modest scale than they had at the Salisbury, but its pattern was the same. More than the drab, rented furnishings, more than the total lack of possessions, and their entirely separate social lives — Cecelia lunching daily with people whom Milton had never met; Milton spending hours golfing and card playing with people who had never laid eyes on Cecelia — what got me were those two damned trunks in their bedrooms. The trunks were like twin radio towers beaming out the same crisp and crackling message to the occupant of the other bedroom: *One more wrong move out of you and I can be out of here for good! See for yourself — I'm already half-packed.*

Cecelia had far fewer Hollywood friends. Nunnally and Dorris, like many successful movie figures, had moved to London, for tax reasons. Allie and Millie Lewin had moved east and sold their beach house to Mae West, who painted it pink. Herb Stothart had died during the war, and Mary was now married to Dr. Paul Wescher, a Swiss art historian and director of the Getty Museum. Gerry lived in Mexico City, where a favorable exchange rate enabled her to lead the life of a comfortably fixed American expatriate. She designed and manufactured expensive costume jewelry, vaguely Mayan- and Inca-looking, and sold it at high prices through stores like Bergdorf-Goodman and Neiman Marcus, and also peddled it wholesale to private customers in Texas, Palm Beach, and Palm Springs. She employed an entire village of cut-rate rock carvers and bead-stringers, and had taken to calling herself "the Bead Woman of Alcatraz."

Gerry invited Cecelia to fly down for a visit, then asked her to drive a car back to Los Angeles for Gerry to use on her visits north. At the border Cecelia learned she was piloting a hot car, and was detained overnight until things could be straightened out. The episode left a bad taste, but their growing estrangement had deeper roots. Cecelia was becoming convinced that Gerry was using *her* friends, people like Mary and Millie, to advance herself socially and improve her bead business. I thought this ridiculous. Millie and Mary had bought Gerry's wares to be kind to Cecelia's friend. The stuff was too ersatz and crude for their tastes, just as it was too vulgar for Cecelia's. Her complaints about Gerry sounded like simple jealousy, and it surprised me that she did not trouble to hide such childish resentments.

Her ruthlessness, however, had not abated. It never would. Cecelia gave no quarter; she judged everybody. In a *New York Times* piece on the reigning Hollywood hosts and hostesses, Cecelia reported, "The Gershwins know about food, but their knowledge of wines needs attention."

Leonore Gershwin was so shaken that every Christmas thereafter she paid a personal visit to her wine merchant to search for something "good enough for Cecelia. Money no object."

"Lee was terrified by your mother's taste," Stewart told me.

Nor did Cecelia hesitate to accuse Ira of "padding a lyric." The occasion was a birthday party for Ira at the Louis Calherns'. Lee was in Russia with *Porgy and Bess*, "and Cecelia came out, all guns blazing," Stewart noted. "The song was 'Oh, So Nice!' and the lines she objected to were 'Awake or sleeping, / It seems / That you keep creeping / In my dreams.'

"It was obvious, Cecelia said, that he'd needed to find a rhyme for 'sleeping,' but how in hell could one person 'creep' into another's dreams?"

Ira had simply smiled. He loved Cecelia too much to point out that he'd already established the pattern in "How Long Has This Been Going On?" and no one had ever complained about "Dear, when in your arms I creep — / That divine rendezvous . . ."

Ira loved Cecelia no matter what she said because he knew that, despite the circle of flatterers which surrounded the ménage, he could always count on Cecelia to level with him. "Social hypocrisy was not an art known to your mother," as Stewart once remarked.

Now that the Agers were back in California, Milton very much regretted not seeing more of Ira, and he thought the reason was Cecelia's sharp tongue. He'd been horrified to hear her criticize Ira's lyrics. The culprit was not Cecelia, however; Ira had totally adored her since the long-ago afternoon in Aeolian Hall. It was the Little Professor who sometimes got on Ira's nerves. As Ira told Stewart, "Milton's always explaining my lyrics to me."

In my mother's defense, I must say that she judged herself more harshly than she did anyone else. Her impossibly high standards of performance, of behavior, of dress, and of professional self-effacement must have been responsible for her chronic depressions and exhaustion, and ultimately the reason she stopped writing. Like Milton, she lived by her own rules, and ultimately would die by them.

Cecelia was far from ready to hang up her vagabond shoes, however, and one spring she took off on a yacht around the Aegean with the supremely elegant T. H. Robsjohn-Gibbings. Gibby and Aig, as he called her, had been dear friends for years. He was the world's premier designer of classically beautiful, extremely expensive modern furniture. A tall, slim, fair man, scion of lower-middle-class British shopkeepers, he had long ago made himself so refined in appearance and demeanor as to seem practically transparent. The phony hauteur impressed clients, but around the Agers he was generous and kind, a witty, knowing chronicler of fashions in taste among the rich. Cecelia had encouraged him to write, and by now he had published sardonic and hilarious books on the interior decoration game, the "antiques" racket, and the peddling of modern art. *Goodbye, Mr. Chippendale, Homes of the Brave,* and *Mona*

Lisa's Moustache all were illustrated by *The New Yorker*'s extravagantly prim Mary Petty, and a blurb by Cecelia conveys their flavor: "Beneath this demure title smolders a mighty inflammatory pamphlet. Nobody can be indifferent to it; it scorches the complacent hearth. Mission accomplished: home will never look the same."

As a student architect, Gibby had fallen in love with the couches and chairs he saw painted on Greek vases. Now rich, and underwritten by the Goulandris family, he had moved to Greece and spent several years re-creating the classical forms in rare woods and metals. Gibby's adaptations had great purity and beauty, and *Life* was sending a crack photographer, Loomis Dean, to Greece to photograph them displayed against historic archaeological sites and marble ruins normally closed to visitors. Cecelia joined them, but not before first spending a week cruising around Sardinia with Truman Capote and friends. Following the Greek adventure, she explored some digs in Asia Minor with Mr. John and Peter Brandon, the postcard-handsome friend who by now had replaced the austerely heartbroken Mr. Fred.

How well Cecelia always got on with talented gay men! All her life she had surrounded herself with the likes of Jimmy Reynolds, John and Fred, George Davis, Lawrence Stewart, and many more. All of them were crazy about Cecelia. At first I thought these friendships were so valued by my mother because homosexuals were the only male companions of whom Milton would not become impossibly jealous. Later I saw how much these men adored *her*, both for her taste and wit, and for her entire lack of coy feminine pretense.

Milton seemed a bit lost so far from Broadway, and liked to quote a couple of songwriter friends. "Southern California is a great place to live, if you're an orange," Harry Akst had once remarked, to which Solly Violinsky responded, "No matter how hot it gets in the daytime, there's nothing to do at night."

Harry, the sweet, twinkly eyed composer of "Dinah," "Baby Face,"

"Am I Blue?," and many other hits, had replaced Ben Bernie as Milton's regular golf partner. He owned an extra piano, a worn but sturdy Steinway upright, which he had dragged through North Africa and Sicily during World War II, and all around Asia during the Korean War, accompanying Al Jolson on USO tours. Milton bought it and shoved it into his tiny bedroom.

My father was again spending a lot of time singing into the telephone. He and Tom Prideaux, by now a close friend, were collaborating on a charming and witty love song, "What Are You Doing in My Dreams?"

> *Who do you think you are?*
> *Walkin' right in without an invitation,*
> *Don't you think you've gone too far?*

But it was "Lost In Los Angeles," a country song with a gentle pony trot tempo, that best reflected Milton's state of mind.

> *Why am I lost in Los Angeles?*
> *Lost like a wan-der-ing star?*
> *I made it big in my home town*
> *And they told me I'd go far.*
> *Well, where did I lose my way?*
> *What didn't I do right . . . ?*
> *Got no job, no gal to hold me.*
> *Can't help feelin' up tight . . .*
> *I can't stay lost in Los Angeles*
> *By tomorrow I'll be gone.*
> *I'll hitch a ride to Riverside . . .*
> *Or some friendly town further on . . .*
> *Like Santa Fe or San Anton'*
> *And if I find that I'm still unknown —*
> *Then I guess that I'll just wan-der home!*

When overpowered by longing for a potato pancake, and when his stomach would permit, he drove himself to Nate 'n' Al's Delicatessen in

Beverly Hills. It was a straight run down Wilshire Boulevard, but none-theless perilous to every person on the road. Surprising in a man of his exquisite motor skills, Milton was a terrible driver. Even at 25 mph in the slow lane, he could never get the hang of it. One day in utter exasper-ation he simply got out of his vehicle, abandoned it at the corner of Wilshire and Gretna Green, climbed onto a bus, and never drove again.

Cecelia, an excellent driver who knew every shortcut and backstreet in town, thereafter piloted them to dinner each evening, and when nec-essary took Milton to the doctor. He learned to find his way every place else by bus: south to Rancho Park, west to the Wild Whist, and east back to Nate 'n' Al's, and was soon a popular figure among other regular rid-ers. But even as a pedestrian he was a menace. When stopped for jay-walking, a serious offense in California, he asked, "How fast was I go-ing, Officer?"

Though I drove daily to the office past the Agers' apartment, Steve and I saw them as little as possible. In this regard, my second marriage was worse than the first, not just because it lasted so much longer, but be-cause my second husband actively hated my parents and did not hesitate to express his feelings. If we didn't see them, the diatribes gradually stopped; whenever we met, they started again. So we saw them less and less. It was easier on me that way, and evidently on Cecelia as well, as she made no attempts to heal the breach. Every so often, Milton found some excuse to ask us to join them somewhere for dinner, but inevitably the old tensions and contests started up. Steve shouted about my parents in the car all the way home, and I resolved never to yield again. At home, he belittled them continually. Cecelia, he said, was arrogant, snobbish, selfish, self-centered, and vain. Milton was bad-tempered, narrow-minded, preachy, and moralistic. I didn't argue; I just tuned him out. But with all of us in the same room, that luxury was not available and, though Milton kept his prenuptial vow and was unfailingly cordial to my second husband, Cecelia did not trouble to conceal her contempt.

Among other things, she found him arrogant, snobbish, selfish, self-centered, vain, bad-tempered, narrow-minded, preachy, and moralistic.

I could not endure this. I had developed a powerful emotional allergy to angry voices, domestic discord, and maternal criticism in particular. Cecelia's frankness set up conflicts I found unbearable. I know now that if I had so much as hinted to her that I was less than happy with Steve, her attitude would have changed. But that was a possibility I did not hint at even to myself. Ostrich time. It was easier to avoid her, and often we did not speak — twice for over a year, during which times I occasionally met Milton for lunch. Nothing in life is as important as "the family unit," he'd say, as he had all his life. "The family" — even our family — was the one temple at which he worshiped.

"How can this be a family unit if the mother doesn't love her children?"

"Cecelia loves you. She just doesn't know how to show it," he always replied.

For six years, 1954 to 1960, I was one of *Life*'s four West Coast correspondents, responsible for covering all the news from Mexico City to Vancouver. I didn't mind getting little better than half the salary of my male colleagues. They had wives and small children; I didn't. In those days feminism had yet to rear its aggrieved head; family normalcy meant Ozzie and Harriet. The Roaring Twenties had been a far freer time for women than the Smug Fifties. I knew no married women of my own generation who worked outside the home. Since I did, I maintained my standing as a passionate conformist by investing very little of myself in the job. I covered Disneyland, singing chipmunks, hula hoops, topless bathing suits. In 1957 I interviewed Lassie. I also interviewed Sammy Davis, Jr., Frank Sinatra, Bobby Darin, Jack Benny, and Red Skelton. None of it mattered, none of it meant anything to me. I was like a woman under a spell, playing a Donna Reed wife but focused like an insect on one thing only: reproduction. Slowly the longing to become pregnant, the obsessive necessity to have a baby, had become the engine that pulled all the rest of my life along behind it. Nothing else mattered as much; eventually nothing else would matter at all.

The first of the California fertility doctors was a friend of Victor's. I used to see Joe DiMaggio in his waiting room, and realized that Joe's wife Marilyn Monroe was the patient ahead of me. The doctor's therapy of choice was a new British technique — he showed me intravaginal color photographs from *The Lancet* — that involved long needles loaded with hormones and cortisone injected directly into the cervix. The pain was excruciating, but the only noticeable result was an increase in hairiness and a slight acne.

Like Dr. Kurzrok in New York, the Beverly Hills man found nothing wrong, but after a year or so of his horror injections, I moved on. My next temple of fertility was the Tyler Clinic, a group practice in Westwood connected to the UCLA hospital and medical school. I was a faithful supplicant here for the next six years. Ed Tyler was a mild, bespectacled infertility specialist who had helped pay for his medical education by moonlighting as a gag writer for Groucho Marx. His clinic had a long waiting list. When Tyler learned that I was related to the birth control pioneers Doctors Hannah and Abraham Stone, he insisted on treating us with "professional courtesy," which meant he billed us at fifty percent of his normal rates. I say "us" because Tyler, unlike the previous two physicians, insisted on treating husband and wife as a unit — standard practice today, a novelty then.

I kept my identity as a patient at the clinic a secret. Important as the subject was to me, I never wittingly discussed infertility with a living soul. There was something terribly shameful to me about not being able to do the prime thing women had been put on this earth to do — "infertile" translated as "unfemale" — and the idea of talking about this, while it doubtless would have helped alleviate my anxiety and sense of disgrace, seemed to promise more pain than I could readily handle.

Once Tyler had taken a full history, made a thorough examination, and found nothing wrong, and nothing wrong with Steve's sperm either, he began to prescribe different hormone regimens for me, meanwhile

ABOVE Stephen Alexander, Shana, and Kathy, Los Angeles, 1961.

LEFT Molly Ginna and Kathy Alexander, Ireland, 1964

BELOW: Cecelia, Milton, Shana, and Kathy in the backyard of the Alexanders' California home, 1964.

RIGHT Milton and
Shana in London, 1963

BELOW Shana and
Nunnally Johnson,
London, 1963.

LEFT Shana's niece
Hannah Bentley
with her aunt in
Long Island, 1992.

ABOVE Victor Rubenstein, M.D., Cecelia's
brother, and his son Steve, San Francisco,
1991.

ABOVE Cecelia's friend Gerry Morris at home
in Mexico.

RIGHT Milton with his granddaughters, Hannah and Kathy, Canyon View Drive, 1965.

BELOW Shana interviews James Cagney, 1974.

LEFT "The only picture of me I ever liked." Portrait of Dorothy Parker by George Platt Lynes that stood on the Agers' piano.

BELOW Laurel and Wray Bentley visiting Shana at Canyon View Drive, 1964.

RIGHT Harry Craig in
Los Angeles, 1969.

BELOW Shana and
Harry in London,
1971.
Photo by Jules Buck.

LEFT Our last picture of
Cecilia and Milton,
1978.

BELOW Last picture of
Shana and Kathy,
Thanksgiving 1986.
Photo by Eleanora Kennedy.

LEFT Shana at home in Long Island.
Photo by Kevin McCarthy.

BELOW Michael Feinstein and Shana.

instructing me to continue charting my daily temperatures so we would know precisely when I ovulated. As I had already been keeping such records for four years, it was no effort to keep them for six more. Nothing was wrong. Dr. Tyler couldn't understand it. Soon we were taking more sophisticated tests. We took tests to determine if one of us was allergic to the other's sexual secretions. Ours were harmonious. I several times endured having pressurized gas pumped through my fallopian tubes — another moment of tiny agony — to see if they were blocked or obstructed. They weren't.

All this tension, and medical attention, is not good for anybody's sex life, or married life. In my case it induced a deep sense of utter, profound worthlessness. I kept working at *Life*, but nothing that happened there was important to me. All that was important was procreation. It became so important that I would never risk having a fight, or even a quarrel, lest we thereby fail to connect on what the thermometer said was the optimal day and hour. As I truly hated to fight, or even confront, as they say these days, and as my husband was bullying and tyrannical by nature, these absolute no-fight, no-encounter, make-nice-nice rules worked out well for a long time. I was always home on time, always pleasant company, never flirted with other men, and always played the good and obedient and nonquestioning wife. This being the case, Steve's part of the bargain was not outstandingly difficult to uphold, and our bourgeois little life tinkled uneventfully onward.

Well, not precisely bourgeois. The truth was that for our first two years in California, Steve was unemployed. He earned nothing. Not that he was idle. Every weekday morning he breakfasted at the Beverly-Wilshire Hotel drugstore, a hangout for agents and unemployed writers and actors to exchange gossip and read the trade papers. Next he drove to the gym and worked out, just as he had done in New York. Daily workouts had always been part of his life. He'd been a college gymnast, and spoke with affectionate familiarity of glutei and deltoids. A fall from the parallel bars had given him the trick knee that kept him out of the army, and both kneecaps bore surgical scars. Without the workouts, and the steam room, he couldn't function, he said. Having no understanding of or affection for exercise or sports of any kind, I took him at his word.

In a company town like Hollywood, everyone relied on unemployment insurance between pictures. But Steve was too proud to apply for it, and too cocksure that at any moment one of the many irons he had in the fire would burst into flame. He had prospects everywhere, and seemed so certain of success that I never doubted him and didn't even think much about the matter; it could only be a question of time. Wherever we went, even if it was only out to dinner, Steve left a number where he could be reached. He behaved like a doctor on twenty-four-hour call, and when we drove to Guanajuato, Mexico, on a ten-day archaeological vacation, he left forwarding numbers at every tiny village and *posada* en route.

At home I was always waiting for the phone to ring, or imagining I'd heard it. For a long time, I didn't acknowledge the silence; when I did, I couldn't understand it. *Why* wouldn't anybody hire Steve? It was weird, unfathomable. Was he a Communist? I began to wonder. What does he *do* all day long? Why the gym every single day? Despite the lack of any evidence, I wondered if he was homosexual. It never occurred to me that he might be underqualified, or afflicted with a kind of *folie à grandeur.* Nor did it occur to me that what I saw as strength others might see as empty braggadocio. I found his certainty amusing and reassuring. He might not know diddly-squat, but he talked as if he knew everything — the finest wines, the best tailor, the best way to cut down a tree, practice Zen archery, rappel down an Alp, drive a race car, survive in the desert, hang venison, fire an elephant gun, drive a dogsled, fight a forest fire. Steve knew it all. To a girl who believed she knew practically nothing, this quality had a strong appeal.

He was capable of erupting in sudden, thunderous rage. The first time I saw it happen was at an office dinner party chez Wainwright. After dinner *Life*'s senior photographer, J. R. Eyerman, began describing a wartime circuit of midget stripteasers who performed at seamen's bars up and down the West Coast. Steve took exception; he challenged Eyerman to "prove it." He seemed to feel that honor was involved, though whether his own or the midgets' was unclear. Earlier, he had accused me of flirting with another guest, and his mood was ugly.

Eyerman smiled thinly. Not only did midget strippers exist, he said. A tattoo artist in Gardena made a specialty of tattooing G-strings on midget strippers. At this, Steve flew into a titanic tantrum of disbelief, as if he were personally being mocked in some way, and wound up leaping through a window and demolishing a screen door while everybody else watched in stunned silence. He kept up the bellowing on the trip home, and it would have been foolhardy to argue while he was driving. In the morning, it seemed folly to reopen such a sore subject, and I never did find out what had set him off.

At last Steve ran into a high school friend who was building tract houses in the desert, and he offered Steve a job nailing shingles. Steve didn't mind the hard physical work. He found it amusing that he was a roofer while awaiting his debut as a movie producer, and bought an English-made toolbox from Abercrombie & Fitch.

Many years later, long after our divorce, I ran into someone from United World Films who told me that Steve had never said a word to anyone about intending to leave his job and move to California. Nothing. He had just not shown up one Monday morning. No wonder nobody at Universal Pictures would talk to him. In fact, they had barred him from the lot.

In mid-1956, Howard Hughes sold RKO Pictures to the General Tire and Rubber Company, and William Dozier, a former CBS executive who had married Joan Fontaine and then Ann Rutherford, was put in charge of production. A friend of mine arranged a job interview for Steve with Dozier, who needed an executive assistant. Steve had been just that before I met him, when he and his first wife worked at the Theater Guild, and Dozier hired him. Steve had a keen sense of status and came home jubilant from his first day on the job. He had gotten the sign painter to gold-leaf his name on his office door in letters only half as big as those on the doors of the other executives, and all in lowercase. In the reverse snobbery that governs such matters, Steve calculated that the difference would make him appear twice as important as everyone else.

Dozier's regime at RKO toppled after a year, and Steve was again out of a job. Subsequently he had several midlevel TV production jobs and wound up as a small-time literary agent. Over the decade 1954–1964 he was employed about sixty percent of the time, and dithered the rest away on increasingly grandiose TV and movie projects that never got off the ground. I never complained, and to the rest of the world we colluded in projecting the image of a happy, Doris Day, all-American marriage.

In the important part of my life, my gradual ascent into the stratosphere of the great infertility unknown under the monthly guidance of the Tyler Clinic, we were passing increasingly esoteric tests, always with flying colors, and I was undergoing more and more "procedures." When nothing happened, save for numerous early miscarriages, and nothing was ever found "wrong," Tyler's recommendations escalated into increasingly bizarre suggestions on how to fornicate. The one bathtub in our cottage was an old-fashioned, claw-footed affair, not very big, and once we had to do it there, underwater, me upside down. Steve was always obliging, and I was always extremely grateful.

Cecelia was still writing occasional pieces, for *The New York Times Magazine*, or its Sunday drama section, where her *PM* protégé Seymour Peck was now editor. Si had started at *PM* as a copy boy, and in 1946 she had made him the youngest critic in her department, where he reviewed pictures for the next two years. Si Peck would take all the Cecelia Ager he could get, but it wasn't much. Writing was getting harder for her the less she did it. I thought her stuff wonderful, particularly a long interview with Marlon Brando commissioned to coincide with the release of *The Men*. A few years later I was interviewing Brando myself, and he mentioned his loathing for doing publicity. "The only good piece was some lady from the Sunday *Times*."

I couldn't resist it. "That was no lady," I said. "That was my mother."

Between writing assignments Cecelia had plenty of time for long trips abroad, of which she made several. After she returned from the Greek islands pilgrimage, I learned that all these years she had kept the big diamond ring I remembered from childhood safe in the vault, and then, having taken it out for the cruise, lost it overboard in the Mediterranean. I would not have known about this had not Milton let it slip in the course of an unusually frank domestic flare-up at which I happened to be present. On the same occasion he at last put his tiny foot down and refused any longer to pay the storage charges on their household goods, moldering away since 1954 in the Bekins warehouse.

"Then I'll pay them!" she snapped, and thereafter she did. Although Cecelia was now in her mid-fifties, I had at last come to understand that she was hanging onto the furniture, as she had the diamond, against the arrival of the day when she would finally find the strength and resolve to walk away from her marriage and get on with her life.

CHAPTER TEN

FOUND

Steve found a house in Brentwood on Canyon View Drive, the first house anyone in our family had ever owned. It had a bridge, a canyon, huge trees, three fireplaces, four bedrooms, and seventeen bearing avocados. The gardens germinated a deep passion in me for weeding and pruning. On weekends I drove miles to visit nurseries. Cecelia sometimes joined me on these day-long expeditions hunting down giant specimens of zigzag ferns (*asparagus densiflorus myriocledus*) — a very slow-growing, feathery plant of uncommon beauty — or bromeliads, dull, spiny forms from which a pink or purple plume occasionally shoots forth like a neon skyrocket. Her enthusiasm for the weird plants was joyous and extremely discriminating.

Cecelia and I had rarely been alone together since I was a child. I'd always seen to it that someone else was present, a buffer to protect me from her withering scorn. Where had it come *from* — Cecelia's coldness and my dread; her icy amalgam of unsparing criticism and brutal honesty? It rendered me so averse to judging others that I have never written a book review. She could not possibly have got it from Fanny. But in overreaction to Fanny, perhaps. Cecelia may have cringed from being pressed to that warm, stout, sweet-smelling breast as much as I craved it. And how account for the mean part? The cold, cruel, self-centeredness, the disregard for children's feelings, the denial that children *have* feelings — was that Zalkin's heritage? In her grimness, her hauteur, her ability to conjure up guilt, Cecelia was like a Spanish cardinal from whom no forgiveness, no pardon, no remission of sins was ever available.

Yet there was an entirely other Cecelia, the attentive, discriminating, fiercely honest, winning woman so adored by Ira and Dorris and Gibby and all the rest. More than merely bright, this other Cecelia was coruscant, funny, smart, unpredictable, and by common consent the very best of company. I'd met her a few times myself: once on a vacation in the Bahamas at Gerry's house after Cecelia broke her leg; again at Pyramid Lake, the dude ranch where I stayed for my divorce, and Cecelia and Mary Stothart drove up to visit me a couple of times. On both occasions, Cecelia had treated me as a friend, not a daughter. The difference was breathtaking. It was Jekyll and Hyde.

Muffled in scarves and dark glasses, this other Cecelia and I drove for hours in my top-down Buick convertible or her little white Thunderbird, all the way down to Encinitas to seek prize cacti and succulents, up to Goleta for the cymbidium orchids, east to the hills above Claremont for the water lily farms. By mutual agreement, we refrained from discussing intimate matters, and for these few hours my companion was the rarely glimpsed Cecelia of Nassau and Pyramid Lake, a creature as individual and rare as one of her plants.

My thralldom to the Tyler Clinic was another subject we didn't discuss, but one frightening night I was rushed to the hospital for emergency abdominal surgery. My parents arrived after midnight to find me on a gurney in the corridor, already half-sedated, waiting for the elevator to take me up to the operating room, and none of us confident I would come back down. Milton held one hand, Steve the other. Cecelia was behind my head where I couldn't see her. When the elevator opened, she bent over and kissed me on the mouth. "See you soon, darling," said her upside-down face. She had never done this before, nor ever called me "darling."

The surgeon found an ovarian cyst and removed it, along with my appendix. The next time I reported to the Tyler Clinic, they must have felt sorry for me. "Do you really want a baby?" said the doctor, peeling off his rubber glove and reaching into the pockets of his white coat. "Here, call one of these fellows." He held up two handfuls of business cards. The same group of doctors who had an infertility practice in Westwood operated a birth control center in downtown Los Angeles. Sometimes the birth control measures failed, in which cases unwanted infants were privately placed for adoption by lawyers who hung around the place handing out business cards.

California adoption laws were less rigid than those of New York, where foundlings were still handled strictly along religious lines. Catholic babies were distributed by Catholic charities, Jewish babies by Jewish charities, Protestants by Protestants. What happened to infants of Coptic and Mormon and Buddhist mothers, God(s) knows. I was aware of this because Dr. Kurzrok had once told me that if we ever did decide to adopt, we would have a far easier time of it in some other state. In New York, a couple like ourselves would have to wait for a foundling to turn up who was fifty percent Jewish, one quarter Roman Catholic, and one quarter Greek Orthodox. Not long after coming to California, we had applied to a couple of adoption agencies, even though we still expected to have our own baby. I lacked the pride of blood that makes adoption unthinkable to some, and had taken a firm stand on nature versus nurture in about the fifth grade. Not surprisingly, in view of my upbringing, I believed nurture meant everything and genetics didn't count for a damn.

Life went on, and in the evenings our social lives centered around people I worked with, primarily Philip and Katharine Kunhardt, who lived near us with three children under six years old. Phil was a fellow correspondent, and Katharine was raising their youngsters with a tender respect I had never witnessed. I was astonished to walk in one day and hear her saying to Peter in his high chair, "Now, how long would you like me to boil your egg, Peter? Three minutes? Four? Or five?"

"Fwee," he said, and she did.

Steve, an excellent cook, often stirred up a big iron pot of pasta or stew and brought it over to their house for us to eat after the children had been put to bed, and the four of us became very close. Phil and Katharine had interesting parents and brothers and sisters who often came west to visit, and sent carloads of presents at Christmas. Katharine's father was an Episcopal minister, and Phil's mother, Dorothy, was a Lincoln scholar who also wrote children's books, among them *Pat the Bunny*. When Phil was a toddler, his parents had sent him, and all their other children, to the same dread Dr. St. Lawrence who had been the scourge of Laurel's and my childhood. How could we have turned out so differently, Phil and Katharine the very model of a happy WASP family, Laurel and I squirming through life like polliwogs, barely holding our heads above water?

I must have confided to the Kunhardts some of the horrors of the Tyler Clinic, because in 1957 when their fourth child, Sandra, was born, they asked me to be her godmother. Soon her grandfather, Reverend George Trowbridge, a lean, white-haired man with sapphire blue eyes, invited me into his study for a glass of sherry. The godmother's duty is to look after the child's spiritual well-being, he said, and "we are particularly happy that *you* are her godmother because, as the first Jewish godparent in our family, you bring with you your profound knowledge of the Old Testament." I smiled weakly into his beautiful Yankee face.

About a year after the hospital scare, and yet another heartbreaking early miscarriage, my fifth or sixth, Steve and I went to see one of the adoption lawyers. We met the young woman in question—a secretary from New Jersey seven months pregnant—signed the papers, paid the fee, and I was at my desk by ten-fifteen. Too excited to speak, I said nothing to anyone. For nine years, my unreal married life and my obsessive, humiliating attempts to get pregnant had moved along on parallel tracks at glacial tempo. At last it was over. That evening I was zooming joyfully home through the summer night when I flipped on the radio and heard, "... black market baby ring! ... three lawyers charged. ..." I pulled off the road and burst into tears. At home, we talked it over and agreed it was now too risky to proceed, and finally, at that point, I gave up. I was thirty-four years old. Some women are not meant to be mothers, and plainly I was one of them. In the morning I called the lawyer, told him of our decision, and then firmly put all thoughts of babies forever out of my mind.

Ralph Graves, *Life's* articles editor, had been quietly encouraging me for years to try writing for the magazine, but I had always pretended not to hear him. Writing was too difficult, too demanding, and I wasn't good enough at it. But now, having abandoned hope for a child, I began paying attention to my work for the first time since taking my "temporary" job at *Life* nine years before. Patiently, tactfully, Ralph teased words out of me with endless repetitions of the cable Gertrude Lawrence had sent Noel Coward after reading the manuscript of *Private Lives*: NOTHING WRONG THAT CAN'T BE FIXED.

Every year or so I was brought back to New York for a few days of R&R, and on one such occasion Ralph told me that Judy Garland, whose career had nosedived, was about to attempt a comeback. If I would go along on her cross-country tour from Texas to Carnegie Hall, and write a piece about it, Ralph could probably promote me to staff writer. In those proud and plummy days, *Life's* big photo essays and signed articles came only from staff photographers and staff writers; no freelancers need apply.

In six weeks on the road with Judy, empathy reached new heights. It started with a mutual confession that the worst part about being a little fat girl is having to look down at three rolls of stomach each time they put you on the toilet. Then we both caught colds, and when she burst a blood vessel in her throat, blood ran out of my ear. By Atlanta we both had the giggles, by Greensboro I'd caught her insomnia, and at Carnegie Hall I watched her give the greatest show of her career.

Inside the jampacked theater, tension hangs like a net between the audience and the big orchestra on stage. The overture begins, and one by one all the familiar hoped for melodies come flooding back. Each time the musicians launch a new one across the footlights, fans send back salvos of applause, and with every volley the emotional pressure inside the hall rises a few more degrees. Finally the vast space above the audience shimmers with visions of clanging trolley cars, men that got away, and birds flying over the rainbow. . . .

The star is waiting edgily in the darkened wings, borrowing a drag on somebody's cigarette, nibbling a mint, taking a last sip of *Liebfraumilch*-on-the-rocks. . . . The overture cannonballs toward its climax and just a few feet away the bass drum pounds its portentous rhythm: ". . . the road gets *rougher*, it's lonelier and *tougher* . . ." Without warning, Judy Garland suddenly turns her back on the watchers in the wings, sets her shoulders, takes what seems like a ten-gallon deep breath, and then — astonishingly, as one looks out from the darkness directly into the footlights' glare — she appears to glide away onto the bright-lit stage like a child's pull-toy, powered by the rising wave of the applause itself.

My next assignment was Tony Curtis. Ten weeks later I knew more about him than his psychoanalyst. It was long past time to stop interviewing and start writing, but I was frozen, totally blocked, a common phenomenon among those who've hit a home run their first time at bat. I remained in a paralyzed funk for weeks, staring helplessly at the pile of full notebooks on one side of my desk, the stack of blank paper on the other, and the silent typewriter between. I retreated from my office to a card table set up in the quiet of our beautiful bedroom shaded by tangerine trees. I stopped going out and just sat there all day long in a dressing gown trying to think of an opening sentence.

Late one Friday afternoon I was watching the shifting slant of sunlight through the tangerine leaves when the telephone rang. The caller identified herself as a social worker at Vista Del Mar Child Care Service, formerly the Jewish Orphans' Home of Southern California, one of the places we had applied to some years before, and by now forgotten all about.

"Mrs. Alexander?" she said. "Your baby is here."

We saw her the next morning, an enchanting infant with eyes like bright blue marbles. She was six weeks old, and — if we liked her — they hoped we could arrange to take her home right away. "If we liked her" referred to a promise made in their orientation class we'd attended a few years earlier: prospective parents would be able to meet and hold a child before making their final decision. They put her in my arms. So — what did we think?

"Some question!" is what I thought; a question for a used-car dealer.

"Yes," we said together. "She's beautiful." Yes, we would be able to pick her up Monday morning, and yes, plenty of time to make the arrangements. We rushed away and forty-eight hours later we were back, having obtained crib, diapers, bottles, and the all-important services of Rose Lowald, a professional baby nurse who could teach us the ropes. I had also managed to send off a first draft of my Tony Curtis story, and write two important letters. One was to our daughter, for when she grew up, recounting everything we'd been told about her natural parents. Vista Del Mar, a leader in the movement for open adoption, had told us a great deal. Her mother was short, dark, Jewish, and intellectual; her father was tall, blue-eyed, Canadian, Protestant, good at sports, and very musical. They were a married couple, but for some reason felt incapable of raising her, and believed she would have a better future with someone else.

The second letter was to myself, an attempt to sort out my many conflicting, churning reactions. I suddenly wasn't sure I could handle a child, nor even sure I wanted to. It had come about so suddenly, and so long after I truly had given up. Did I really want to resurrect dreams I had managed to put away for good, and the pain that went with them? I needed time to think, but time was not part of the offer.

Another thing: Our marriage was growing shaky. And while it was true that a child might strengthen it, adopting a child for that reason was unthinkable, akin to a mortal sin.

Another: Being a working mother had never been part of my old-woman-who-lived-in-a-shoe fantasy. Quite the opposite, in fact. We had told Vista Del Mar that once the baby came I intended to quit my job and be at home full-time. I still wanted to do that, but by now the wish was unrealistic. I earned more than half our income. But if I kept working, could I be a good mother too? Certainly Cecelia had not managed it. But I was not like Cecelia. And wasn't her unsuitability for motherhood a consequence of her nature, not her job?

Steve drove over our bridge, and we saw big, smiling Mrs. Lowald waiting to open the car door and take the baby from my arms. She hugged it to her ample breast in a practiced, one-arm grip, and the infant wriggled. "Och. You will have an interesting time with this one!" The wriggle had told her something about our daughter's hair-trigger motor responses.

The first thing Steve had said when I told him about Vista Del Mar's phone call was, "I'll bet the baby is only half Jewish." He had been right, and I thought he might be right again when he now said we should ignore the two promises we had made in the orientation class: that we would raise our baby in the Jewish faith, and that we would tell her she was adopted. Funds to run the free child-care service were raised entirely from the Jewish community, and that accounted for the first promise. But Steve argued that a half-Jewish child with nonreligious parents was better off choosing her own faith when the time came, and I agreed. The second promise was based on the certainty that unless our child knew from us that she was adopted, she was likely to hear the truth first from someone else and be very upset. The way to handle it, we had been taught, was to use the word "adopted" freely, and long before your child knew its meaning. When she asked, you explained that whereas other children are merely born, your child had been "chosen." Steve was for ignoring that pledge too. He thought the tactic sounded cruel. I thought it sounded necessary.

A bigger problem was choosing a name. I had dreamed of baby names for so long, searching for something short and blunt to go with Alexander, and nothing like Shana. Adam Alexander pleased me. Abner. Max. Sam. I hadn't really planned on a girl. Now I had to go almost all the way through the baby name book, down to "X," to find it; Xenia — "welcome stranger" in Greek. Steve insisted on including Shana, so her legal name became Shana Katherine Xenia Alexander, the Katherine being for Katharine Kunhardt, whom we asked to be her godmother.

The week after Kathy arrived I was back at work. Gifts and good wishes poured in from all over. My favorite was a note from Gibby:

> Shana, dear, you look so glowing in the picture. I think I can guess how you feel. You have reached suddenly into the future. All the best of you is going to be carried into another age by that tiny messenger on your knee. . . .
> But Aig as a grandmother, preposterous. I won't have it. Aig as a stinker — yes! As a grandmother — *out!*"

Cecelia just said that if this was what I wanted, well and good. She drove Milton over every few days to gurgle at Kathy while she and Mrs. Lowald had a cigarette on the veranda and reminisced about the good old days in prewar Vienna. That my mother had scant interest in cuddling our baby didn't surprise or bother me, and after Kathy's arrival, the coolness between Cecelia and me began to thaw, or else I was so mesmerized by my new daughter that I stopped noticing. Holding and rocking her was delicious. I loved the way she felt and smelled. I loved to blow on her neck and her belly button. I bought an old secondhand rocker, painted it yellow, and sat there giving Kathy her bottles. I bought the prettiest, softest baby clothes I could find. I spent hours singing to

her, or just walking around the garden with her in my arms. I bathed
her each evening, and when she got a little older, we had our baths
together. When she was teething, or otherwise distressed, I took her into
our bed. I had as much physical contact with her as possible, not only
because I enjoyed it, and knew it was important, but because I was very
aware of having been deprived in this regard. Kathy's life was going to
be different.

Our daughter's sudden arrival would turn out to have consequences
no one could have foreseen. She brought us great gifts and wrought
enormous changes in both our lives, gifts and changes I became aware
of before she was a year old. Kathy's advent freed me to express myself
more in my life, and in my work as well. She made me come alive in
every sense. At last the invincible tower wherein I had walled myself
up, convinced of my unwomanhood because of my unmotherhood, was
crumbling. Unconsciously at first, then deliberately, I began to let down
the drawbridges — I could almost hear the clank of rusty chains — and
watch the dried-up moat slowly fill with swans and water lilies. In a rever-
sal of the Sleeping Beauty myth, Kathy broke the spell on her mother.
Her advent released me into a new sense of womanhood. At last, at the
age of thirty-five, I could stop regarding myself primarily as a broken
breeding machine that had to be fixed.

As a staff writer, I could choose my own subjects but was always unsure
which stories to embark on, which to avoid. The editors helped, of
course, and on one occasion, Milton's solid advice proved invaluable.
Frank Sinatra's lawyer, Mickey Rudin, had called me to say that Frank
had decided to tell his life story. Was I interested in writing it? I'd have
to take a leave of absence, of course, but I'd get a big book out of it, and
the money would be ten times my salary, perhaps much more.

This was worth stopping by the Agers' on my way home to talk over.
We all knew Sinatra and had followed his career from its earliest days.
Milton knew him from the music business, and I'd been one of the origi-

nal bobby-soxers. Whenever Tommy Dorsey's band played the Paramount Theater, Cecelia loaned me her pass so that a friend and I could cut school and go down to hear Frank; she considered it an educational experience. She had later interviewed Frank several times, and confessed herself "absolutely floored by the blueness of his eyes." She'd also found him "very bright, a very honorable person, very good about being loyal to his young/old friends." So it was not too surprising a couple of years later during Frank's humiliating romance with Ava Gardner that when he and Cecelia found themselves seated next to one another at a political rally in Madison Square Garden, he'd literally cried on my mother's shoulder.

So, now, what did the Agers think of my wonderful book offer? Grab it, Cecelia was saying, when Milton interrupted her. "I'm not going to tell you what to do, Shana." This was his stock opening. "But consider this. Frank is mostly in Las Vegas these days, and you'd have to spend at least a year hanging around the place, which you hate, waiting for him to find time to talk to you. You have a young daughter whom you love, and who needs you, and you wouldn't see much of her while this was going on." Compressing his lips, he continued, "Besides, Frank's such a fickle son-of-a-bitch that after you put in the year's work he's apt to change his mind and decide not to publish it!"

The last part did it. Milton's analysis was so clear-headed that I turned down the offer the next day.

I worked at a luxurious pace, turning out articles about movie stars, elephant breeding, a woman's suicide attempt, or any other subject that interested me. Each piece required months to research, write, and "close," which meant going to New York to help decide on pictures, layout, and headlines. Vista Del Mar would have been surprised to know how much traveling my job entailed, but Steve was a watchful, devoted father and I had no hesitation about leaving Kathy in his charge.

On one of those trips to New York I saw Anzia for the last time. Now past eighty and losing her sight, she had moved to an old apartment building off Riverside Drive owned by Columbia University and used as housing for elderly scholars. Her small room replicated her Morton

Street flat, down to the carton of milk on the windowsill. She was overjoyed to see me, praised my *Life* success, and within moments had
hauled out the yellow pads. She could write for only a few hours now,
she said, and began at dawn. At about eleven o'clock she walked to a
Broadway cafeteria for lunch. She went to bed at nightfall, but her afternoons had been empty and boring until she discovered the Home for
Aged and Infirm Hebrews on Broadway at 110th Street, and volunteered
her services as a part-time social worker.

She was working on a book of short stories about the elderly residents. All were exactly the same people they had always been, only older,
she said with a faint smile. The bumbling librarian at the *Jewish Daily
Forward* was now running the library at the Home, and doing it in the
same exasperating way. The terrible fiddle player who used to panhandle
in front of Carnegie Hall was now driving other residents crazy by practicing in his room and playing all the same wrong notes.

The story we worked on that afternoon described the birthday party
ritual for the Home's oldest resident. The festivities took place at the
noon meal; who knew what might happen by suppertime? Anzia pic-
tured the parade of elderly wrecks tottering into the dining room on
canes or crutches, several of them blind, some pushing others in wheel-
chairs. The birthday presents were humble — an apple or an orange
saved from last night's dinner. But the air was festive, and the toasts no
less hearty for being drunk in plain water.

It was traditional that the second oldest resident propose the first
toast. An old man stood up. "We are gathered here today to celebrate
the birthday of Sadie Solomon, who is one hundred and nine years old
today!" He raised his water glass high. Three dozen other glasses lifted
tremblingly skyward.

"Long life to you, Sadie Solomon!" they cried.

The Agers had never celebrated birthdays or any other holidays. So why
I should suddenly care that they had a fortieth wedding anniversary com-

ing up I can't say. But on February 1, 1963, Steve and I invited them to dinner at Beverly Hills' in-most restaurant, having arranged beforehand for Cecelia's favorite flowers and champagne. On our second bottle, we recommenced the old ragging of Milton: Why would he never go to Europe? Why must he always be so stubborn? The four of us could even make the trip together.

"All right," he suddenly said. "I'll go."

Steve now took over. He knew the great hotels of Europe, and would make all arrangements. One week only, Milton cautioned. I said I could get our housekeeper to move in for that long to look after eighteen-month-old Kathy, and the four of us agreed to spend seven days investigating London. If this works, I was already thinking, as Cecelia must have been as well, we can try Madrid next. Budapest! Bangkok!

Nonstop overnight air service from Los Angeles had just begun. Steve arranged the tickets and booked rooms at the Dorchester. He hired a limousine to pick us all up and drive us to the airport. In those days, one did not board a plane through an indoor chute. You had to walk out onto the tarmac and climb a set of rolling steps. The four of us had reached the platform at the top of the steps when Steve announced he wasn't coming. A big movie production deal was about to come through; he simply could not leave Los Angeles. He had arranged for a car and driver to be waiting at Heathrow. He would telephone the hotel to be sure we arrived safely. . . .

People in line behind us were pushing forward. The stewardesses were urging us to hurry along, please. Bewildered, nonplussed, Cecelia, Milton, and I allowed ourselves to be hustled aboard, three pairs of eyebrows lifted high in silent astonishment.

The flight was interminable, but we had sleeping pills. The car was waiting as promised, and we arrived at the Dorchester by seven A.M. and were greeted by apologetic, bowing figures in morning coats. Terribly sorry, rooms not quite ready . . . mind waiting just a bit in lovely Oliver Messel suite . . . ?

The suite had been the scene of a large banquet the previous night; rumpled napery and empty wine buckets were still there. But impatient

Milton had already had enough. He climbed on top of the table, curled up in the center, and closed his eyes.

"If anybody comes by, Cecelia, just have them put some parsley around me and an apple in my mouth."

Rooms were soon found, and I sank unconscious into cool linen sheets. About eleven-thirty A.M. my phone rang. It was an old friend, Ernie Anderson, now a movie publicity man living in London. Due to a favorable tax situation, London in the sixties had become a major hub of movie production, and Ernie Anderson was the class of the field. Mike Todd, John Huston, and Ingmar Bergman would let no one else handle their work. A former jazz impresario, Ernie was fully aware of both my parents' accomplishments. He was working on a picture in which Peter Sellers was playing James Bond, and would send a car to bring the four of us out to the studio for lunch and an on-set peek at a hilarious gag Peter O'Toole was about to play on Sellers which . . .

Wait! How did he even know we were here? A note in *Variety*, in the column listing showbiz Americans in town. Steve must have done that too.

Steve wasn't here and the Agers were asleep, I said. But Ernie was insistent. The car would be downstairs in twenty minutes, and he'd book a table for four. O'Toole would have a friend with him, an Irish playwright and "very ugly man who is catnip to women." This turned out to be H. A. L. Craig, a large, balding, smiling man who failed, I thought, to live up to either part of his billing. When he briefly left the table, Ernie whispered, "Not one screen credit to his name, yet suddenly he's the hottest screenwriter in the world. He wrote an Irish story Brando swears is the greatest screenplay he's ever read. Huston says flat out: 'I'll direct anything Harry Craig writes.'" Their current project was *Waterloo* with Burton and O'Toole as Napoleon and Wellington.

The day wound up with O'Toole insisting everybody join him and his wife for dinner, my parents included. I doubted they'd be able to make it, I said. But Craig insisted on accompanying me back to the hotel, and soon two spiffily dressed little people emerged from the elevator and we adjourned to the bar. In a strange land, with a charming stranger to entertain, the old Agers had reappeared, a little older, but essentially the same witty couple people used to enjoy dining with at Moore's. Harry and my parents took to each other at once, and the difficulty I'd anticipated in persuading them to come to dinner with a bunch of strangers failed to materialize.

Harry smoked the strongest of French cigarettes and that evening through a blue haze he told me about himself. He was the father of nine children, three with his wife, six born before he left Ireland at age twenty-seven. He now looked about fifty. His father had been a Church of Ireland parson whose tiny parish near Limerick had only nine parishioners, counting his wife and four children. All this, communicated sotto voce beneath the general revelry and olive oil/tomato sauce miasma, made clear that here was a man experienced with women, a somewhat worn Don Giovanni ever game for one more go. In his long life as an Irish litterateur and Lothario, however, I doubt he had ever before attempted to seduce simultaneously a virtuous wife and her worldly parents. But the challenge must have appealed to him.

We saw Harry daily thereafter. He arrived at the hotel each morning before lunch, parked a small car with a trunk full of diapers and other laundry, and was prepared to guide any of the three of us who was available around whatever part of London we chose. He had an awesome knowledge of history and literature, as well as of the most interesting restaurants and wines. All of us appreciated his sweet nature and appetite for life, and his unusual command of language. No voice I'd ever encountered was as compelling as Harry Craig's, especially when "speaking verse," as he called it. He did this professionally on the BBC, and privately many times a day.

One day the Agers went to lunch with Nunnally Johnson and some other friends, and Harry insisted on bringing me to his favorite restaurant, Wheeler's in Old Compton Street. The place was very like Moore's, down to the polished brass, old Irish waiters, and sawdust on the floor. Harry's rich conversation was laced with plenty of Yeats, Shakespeare, Byron, and Donne. Over a last brandy, he spoke a haunting Auden poem about a pair of doomed lovers standing on a bridge. Its last few lines:

. . . In its glory, in its power,
This is their hour.
Nothing your strength, your skill, could do
    Can alter their embrace
Or dispersuade the Furies who
    At the appointed place
With claw and dreadful brow
    Wait for them now.

Six days had passed, and Milton and I were packing up when Cecelia said she was having a fine time and would stay on in London an extra week. Milton's lips became tissue-paper thin, but he could not have been too surprised. Once Cecelia had been given her head, it was always difficult to rein her back in.

The morning Milton and I left, Harry appeared at the hotel bearing a Santa-size sack of Japanese-made toys for Kathy. We had reached the airport boarding lounge when I was paged on the telephone. "Safe journey home," said Harry's lovely voice.

Back on home turf, my relationship with the Agers returned to near-minimal. My major concern at home was making sure Kathy wore her football helmet while tricycling around the garden, lest she be beaned by a ripe avocado. When she was three and a half I began dropping her off at nursery school on my way to work. We had by then found Anita, a splendid young housekeeper from Holland with years of U.S. experience looking after young children. Anita picked up Kathy at noontime, and took care of her and the house until I got home.

Kathy was an uncommonly bright child. Every night I read her a story, and if the book was one of her favorites, *Good Night, Moon* or *Where the Wild Things Are*, she said the words along with me. She hadn't memorized them; she was actually reading. But when it came time to put her in bed and tell her a bedtime story, I was a flop. I couldn't make anything up. I'd once fantasized being the mother of twelve children, yet now that I had one, I couldn't fantasize a thing. I write exclusively nonfiction for the same reason. Steve on the other hand was a natural-born Scheherazade. He could invent endless stories, spin them out over months, adding new embellishments each night. One story, about a polka dot elephant, edged out the others, and the nightly saga of its adventures went on for years, the plot developing in maturity and complexity right along with Kathy.

But unwelcome changes were also taking place on Canyon View Drive. The Tyler Clinic had not made me a woman, it had kept me a mermaid. Now that we were freed from the doctors' command couplings, our cocooned life together had begun to fray. I resented it increasingly when Steve got to stay home while I went to the office. Even when he worked—as assistant producer on a TV western, *Mackenzie's Raiders*, for example, or as a midlevel executive at Screen Gems—he could usually get home by six, whereas I often had to be out of town on assignments.

There was something else. In between jobs, he claimed to spend all his time at the gym, or in the library, developing movie ideas. But this was not quite true. Several times I caught glimpses of his car in my rear-view mirror; he had taken to following me around. I didn't know why, and I never told him I knew about it. If he was turning paranoid, as I sometimes suspected, that was another matter I preferred not to face.

I was resentful of all the hours he got to spend with Kathy. Now that we finally had a child, I was the parent who had to go away on business, and he was the parent who most often got to play house. It wasn't fair. When I came home tired, we bickered. He wanted me to describe my days. I felt entitled to leave the office at the office. The squabbles developed into fights, and the fights escalated. Steve was by nature bullying, shouting, tyrannical, tireless, and, I grew to realize, covetous of my life. I hated fighting, feared confrontation, and usually refused to respond, which goaded him into further escalations of surly bellicosity. That Steve had been a genuine underdog, and that originally I had prized him for being such a plucky one, was something now entirely forgotten.

One night, unable to sleep, I crept to the kitchen to make some warm milk and switched on the radio. A convention of marriage counselors was in town, and a strongly German-accented voice was advocating "more fighting for happier marriages!" I slept for a few hours, turned the radio on again about six A.M., and heard him again. His bluebird message and Schickelgruber voice made a hilarious contrast, worth an interview perhaps.

Dr. George Bach turned out to be a hotshot Beverly Hills psychotherapist whose specialty was human aggression. He claimed to have professionally analyzed 23,000 marital fights, including at least 2,500 of his own. The sight of gifted marital gladiators in action thrilled him as the sunset does the poet, and he was certain his theories could cut the national divorce rate by up to ninety percent. Aggression is a basic, self-protective instinct, Bach argued, a relic of our caveman past. The drive to fight is as natural as sex, he said, and must not be repressed. The problem lies in learning to handle the "intimate enemy" — wives, husbands, children, parents, sweethearts, friends — the people one loves the most, and hence would sometimes like most to kill, but toward whom one nonetheless feels basic, underlying goodwill. Bach's answer: learn to *program* your aggressions. Fight, but fight fair; avoid low blows. Learn to fight elegantly and constructively, so as to deepen your knowledge of the other, and increase the areas of intimacy.

My article, "The Intimate Enemy — The Fine Art of Marital Fighting," imagined "a vast Stillman's gym of domestic discord," identified ten common styles of intimate fighting, and prescribed remedies.

> Over there, lolling about on the canvas, watching TV, walking out, sitting in a trancelike state, drinking beer, doing their nails, even falling asleep, are the "Withdrawal-Evaders," people who will not fight. These people, Bach says, are very sick. . . .
>
> And over *there*, viciously flailing, kicking, and throwing knives at one another, shouting obnoxious abuse, hitting below

the belt, deliberately provoking anger, exchanging meaningless insults (You stink! *You* doublestink!) — simply needling and battering one another for the hell of it — are people indulging in "open noxious attack." They are the "Professional Ego-Smashers," and they are almost as sick — but not quite — as the first bunch. . . .

The third group of people are all smiling blandly and saying, "Yes, dear." But each one drags after him a huge gunnysack. These people are the "Pseudo-Accommodators," the ones who pretend to go along with the partner's point of view for the sake of momentary peace, but who never really mean it. The gunnysacks are full of grievances, reservations, doubts, secret contempt. Eventually the overloaded sacks burst open, making an awful mess. . . .

The fourth group are "Carom Fighters," a sinister lot. They use noxious attack not directly against the partner, but against some person, idea, activity, value, or object which the partner loves or stands for. They are a whiz at spoiling a good mood or wrecking a party, and when they *really* get mad, they can be extremely dangerous.

I did not recognize these descriptions as fairly accurate portraits of Cecelia, Steve, me, and Milton, nor would I have then guessed that my own already well stuffed gunnysack could not keep on accumulating crud too much longer before it blew.

The piece brought bids from a dozen book publishers. George needed me as a collaborator because he "could only think in German." We signed with Doubleday, and began meeting in my patio two afternoons a week. George talked and I took notes on a yellow pad, and read a rough draft back to him at the next session.

Every couple goes through the same seven phases of intimacy, George believed. We had covered the first phase, Courtship, and were working on the second, The Honeymoon. Phase Two "is psychologically exhausting," he said, "because the danger of the whole house of cards collapsing is so great. The *Götterdämmerung*, which is inevitable, occurs on an average of five months and nine days after the wedding."

"No, George, wait," I interrupted. "You said last week it was nine months and five days . . ."

"Vot de hell difference? Sooner or later they have a big fight!"

Slowly I began putting George's wonderfully wacko theories not only into English, but into practice — fighting back, not evading; expressing grievances openly; getting out my aggressions by buying a dozen cheap wineglasses and flinging them one by one across the kitchen. But I waited to do this until Steve was out of the house; the pseudo-accommodator in me was very firmly entrenched.

A particularly bad moment occurred over Easter weekend. Steve was then working at a small literary agency. I was writing a cover story on Burt Lancaster, who had just made *Birdman of Alcatraz* and was plugging it on a cross-country train tour that would end in Washington, D.C., with Lancaster calling on President Kennedy to appeal for the real Birdman's release. I had to go along because the only times Lancaster was free for interviews were between stops.

A surly man at best, with a boastful vanity that reminded me of Steve, the actor grew nastier as we went east, and I decided to skip the White House and cut out early; I already had plenty of material. I got home two days ahead of schedule, and called Steve at his office.

"Oh, Mrs. Alexander, don't twist the knife!" cried Millie, the motherly phone operator.

Steve was no longer employed there. He'd been fired on Good Friday when the bosses found out he was maneuvering to steal a few hot clients, jump ship, and open up his own agency. I was thunderstruck. Once again he was out of work!

I simply could not confront Steve, nor "have it out" when something like this occurred. Fear of his rage was part of it, but bewilderment was part of it too. I didn't understand it when he did these things. He wasn't a crook, not truly dishonest, I was sure. It was more a sort of Walter Mitty problem.

* * *

In 1962, Laurel married Wray Bentley, an MIT-educated engineer, inventor, and onetime uranium prospector who seemed as eccentrically brilliant as she. They both worked in the aerospace industry, she as a technical writer and he as a computer programmer. A large and genial man of Welsh ancestry with piercing black eyes, Wray, like Laurel, had a beautiful singing voice, an offbeat sense of humor, and oddball tastes. They spent their free time at road rallies, Wray driving a silver Corvette and Laurel navigating with the help of his circular slide rule, a plastic snail of coiled calculations at least twelve inches across.

The wedding was held at Victor and Florence's house, and Cecelia provided the wedding feast. Since everyone in the family, especially the bride and groom and the three Rubenstein children and Kathy, was wacky about Baskin-Robbins 31 Flavors, the meal consisted of steaks and a choice of all thirty-one flavors in unlimited amounts, plus a wedding cake and excellent champagne.

Hannah Bentley was born April 30, 1963. Laurel, a word puzzle aficionado, chose her name because it was a palindrome, and in memory of Cecelia's cousin Dr. Hannah Stone. Milton thought she was named in honor of his hit "Hard-Hearted Hannah." It hadn't occurred to him that no young mother with brains intact would name a daughter for "the meanest gal in town. / I saw her at the seashore with a great big pan. / There was Hannah pouring water on a drowning man."

The moment Laurel married Wray, Steve Alexander ceased to be our family's bottom dog. Cecelia appeared to despise her second son-in-law even more. Nothing personal, I was finally able to recognize, when I noticed how offhandedly our mother was treating her second granddaughter compared with her first, and once again making no effort to hide her preference. Cecelia's dread birthday was again at hand, and that year the Bentleys brought her a studio portrait of her newest grandchild in a handsome frame. I could scarcely believe Cecelia's comment: "This doesn't look like Hannah. And it's an awful dress."

I felt very sorry for my sister, and she felt dreadfully aggrieved all over again. So why did she never show it? Why did the Bentleys staunchly, doggedly continue to invite the Agers down for dinner every holiday, despite all? Usually Laurel also invited Victor and his family, or Viola, the aged actress, or some other relatives as well, both because she has genuine family feeling and probably to relieve the tension of having to be alone with her mother. I always drove the Agers on these occasions, as Cecelia found night driving a blinding ordeal. While she was dressing and preparing to leave, she poured forth a long litany of complaint, moaning and groaning and saying things like "I *hate* going to that slum!" and "Laurel and Wray are just too damn *fat!*" Her criticism escalated until it became so unpleasant that Milton roared "*Shveig!*" and she shut up.

Once at the Bentleys', a pleasant, beautifully cared-for house and garden only a block from the beach, Milton charmed everybody by playing his songs on Laurel's electric organ, and the food was always surprising and delicious. The Bentleys produced spectacular dishes from their luxurious kitchen, things like crown roast of lamb followed by *mont blanc,* or roast goose with apple compote and *oeufs à la neige.* Cecelia was treated like the Dowager Empress, offered the plumpest pillows, choicest cuts, and so on, and accepted it all as her gracious due. No one would have guessed the shocking outburst at the Agers' apartment that preceded each visit.

At my house, the fights with Steve were becoming more frequent, and turning physical. But we had Kathy and I would not let myself even think about divorce. One set of parents had already given her away. I told no one about the fighting, not even the expert, George Bach. I was ashamed of it, much as I had been ashamed of my failures to get pregnant.

By midsummer of 1964, our longtime friends Bob and Margaret Ginna were in Dublin where Bob was producing *Young Cassidy,* a movie about Sean O'Casey for which Bob had written the script, persuaded MGM to finance it, and John Ford to direct. The Ginnas and their children had rented a Georgian house for the duration, and frequently urged us to visit. So when Steve and I had our next big fight, I called Margaret and said through my tears that I was leaving him, and Kathy and I would arrive the following morning. At Dublin airport, John Ford was carried out one door on a stretcher as I carried Kathy in the other. The director had collapsed on the set after only a week of shooting, and as soon as Bob deposited us with Margaret, he had to rush to London and find a substitute.

Three-year-old Kathy toddled around the gardens with Molly Ginna and her older brother Peter, and accompanied them on rides in their pony and trap. After a few days' R&R with Margaret and the children, I felt better and returned to Los Angeles determined to try again.

As a result of all the editing care and attention, *Life's* prose was creamily smooth, but it had a rather Olympian, impersonal sound, and in 1964 Loudon Wainwright talked the editors into letting him write a signed biweekly column of personal opinion. "The View From Here" was an immediate hit with readers, and managing editor George Hunt asked me to write a column to alternate with his, an idea I found terrifying. Although an experienced journalist, I had never written the word "I" in my life, save in private correspondence. On the printed page, "I think" or "I feel" would have to stand up naked as a stick in front of thirty-five million readers.

"Think of a name for your column that makes clear a woman is writing it," Hunt said. I proposed "The View From Her," but nobody laughed, and George Bach finally came up with "The Feminine Eye." To ballyhoo the new columnist, Phil Kunhardt wrote an "Editor's Note" about me that ended with a quote:

[In thirteen years at *Life*] "I've learned how to be a journalist and a girl, too. All my clothes are specially made to fold flat in a suitcase and they have pockets in them just the size of a small notebook. It's a marvelous life, this life in a man's world. I'd climb the walls if I had to live by the feminine mystique."

The truth was that, heretofore, I *was* living by the feminine mystique. The job had been my safety valve, but my values and attitudes, especially in regard to gender, were stuck in the 1950s. A surprise consequence of calling myself "The Feminine Eye" was that gradually, belatedly, I began to develop one. I slowly realized that, scared or not, I vastly enjoyed my work and probably had the greatest job and best expense account in American journalism. I could swoop around the world at will, a female Green Hornet. The entire planet was my beat. Nobody could change a word of my copy without my approval, and on every column I had the devoted attention of the best editors in the world.

One day the Time, Inc. publicity department called to say someone wanted to interview *me*. It was Pierre Berton, "the Johnny Carson of Canada," and they had set up a poolside interview at the Ambassador Hotel. I got my hair done and drove downtown. As I approached the pool, Pierre's TV camera, the first I had ever faced, started rolling and he began reading aloud from a Time, Inc. publicity handout. "Mrs. Alexander, it says here that you were *Life*'s first woman reporter, first woman staff writer, and now first woman columnist." He paused a beat. "Don't you feel a little like the house nigger?"

I told the Johnny Carson of Canada there was nothing wrong with being a token woman, providing you didn't stay in the job too long. I didn't tell him, or anyone, that the place I felt like the house nigger was not in the office but at home. Steve had finally gotten a commitment to produce a movie, based on one of my *Life* articles. Only then did I learn that ever since I'd been writing them, Steve had been making the rounds of movie studios, a copy of one of my forthcoming pieces in hand, telling the executives that this big story was about to come out in *Life*, and he could deliver exclusive rights if the studio would let him produce it. I didn't of course own my stories. *Life* owned them; I was on staff. But his scam had finally worked, and he had sold my story about the thwarted suicide attempt to Paramount Pictures for Anne Bancroft. The studio had agreed to pay him $70,000, and this news was so welcome that I swallowed my anger and joined him in pretend jubilation.

Our family life was a mess by then, and so was I. The fights with Steve had become frequent, and he was very strong. I was too much an expert on marital fighting to blame him for hitting me. I would have hit him too, if I could; if I'd had a gun, I might have shot him. But he stomach-punched me a few times, and when I tried to flee, he lay down in the driveway and defied me to run over him.

I had talked to a divorce lawyer, and started many times to drive to his office. Each time I got into my car I was overcome by nausea and had to lie down. I am a sturdy sort, and nothing like this had ever happened before. But I had always been deeply troubled by the fact that our daughter's real parents were married. To me this meant that she had already been given away once. Divorce would make me the second mother to do this to her. The conflict literally made me want to vomit.

Life would never have sent me to Vietnam. Too many male reporters were in line ahead of me. But I heard that a Tokyo road company of *Hello, Dolly!* starring Mary Martin was going to South Vietnam to entertain the troops. "Get there in time, and you can go in with them," said a tipster friend. I jumped on the next flight to Tokyo. The following morning, my fortieth birthday, I boarded a troop transport containing Mary Martin and forty singers and dancers. What followed was surreal. At Saigon's airport, the door was yanked open and out of a tropical downpour appeared a bevy of graceful singing and dancing girls in native dress carrying flower garlands which they entwined around the necks of the twenty-four chorus boys, all of whom wore full combat gear. In the next week we traveled all over South Vietnam, a musical comedy inside a live war, escorted by four jeeps with mounted machine guns, and helicopters flying cover, from air base to air base, through crowds of peasants, chickens, melons, children. Within this surreal world, I was living simultaneously in two other surreal worlds. One was Truman Capote's Kansas nightmare, *In Cold Blood*, which I'd brought along to read. The other was the personal nightmare of having to come to terms with the need to file for divorce. Ironically, it was Kathy's surprise arrival which had broken the spell under which I'd lived since marrying Steve. From this far place I looked back at the life I had made for us, and despised what I saw.

Ultimately I devised another Grand Plot, this one with a lady-or-the-tiger ending; he, not me, would make the final decision. I had to be in New York on June 13 to attend *Life*'s Hunt Ball, the annual company bash for our managing editor. The date was also Steve's forty-fifth birthday, so I arranged a surprise party for him a day ahead of time in the wine cellar of Scandia, his favorite restaurant. I ordered his favorite food and wine and invited the five other couples we knew best. My Plot was this: if Steve did not pick a fight after we got home that night, I would do nothing. But if he attacked me one more time, I had arranged with a lawyer to serve him with papers while I was in New York. This would force him to leave our house, something he had been refusing to do. And if receiving the papers made him really explode, as I feared it might, I would have protection by the time I returned to Los Angeles.

Eleven of us were assembled around the wine cellar table when the appointed decoy arrived with Steve.

"Surprise!" everybody yelled. "Happy Birthday!"

"I want a divorce," Steve blurted, perhaps to be funny, or to cover his embarrassment, and in the hubbub the others didn't hear. But I did, and was dumfounded. The party went fine, but when we got home and he again became abusive, I resolved to file. In the morning I phoned the lawyer from the airport and told him to put the plan into action.

"Oh, Shana, *please* don't do this!" Steve cried out on the phone a couple of days later. But the distance between us enabled me to be cold and firm.

Everybody we knew was floored by the news, especially the guests who had been with us in Scandia. Milton said he hoped I knew what I was doing. Laurel said she hoped I'd be happy and pointed out the obvious: that it was going to be very hard on Kathy. Cecelia's astonishing response was to buy me a pair of lovely wrought-gold earrings from Tiffany with detachable bangles like Balinese temple bells. Only months later, she, the woman who hated jewelry, presented me with a massive bracelet made from a knotted hawser of Tiffany gold. Perhaps Milton was right about something he had told me all my life. Perhaps Cecelia did love me, but for some reason could not allow herself to express it in a normal manner. Maybe that was why she was showing it now in the manner of a tired businessman with a young mistress.

At Thanksgiving I brought Kathy on a sentimental journey east by train to spend the holiday with the Kunhardts, and to let her enjoy the same transcontinental ride I used to love. Alas, it meant nothing to her, and my old bones on their old tracks felt sorely shaken. On my last night in New York, I ran into Bennett Cerf, still head of Random House and now a star performer on *What's My Line?* "Remember me?" I said. "I was Shana Ager, and you used to take Laurel and me bowling."

Bennett was overjoyed, and insisted that I visit his office in the morning. Not possible, I said. We were on the noon plane. Bennett was adamant. He would send his limo to pick us up at the hotel, have it wait downstairs while I dashed up to see the sumptuous new Random House quarters in the Vuillard Houses, then drive us to the airport. It would have been rude to refuse.

The next morning we loped through the offices, Bennett tugging me by the hand. In his paneled inner sanctum, he said, "I want to autograph a book for you to show Cecelia. But hand it to her personally; don't give it to Milton." He scribbled something on the flyleaf and I rushed back down to the limousine.

The book was A. E. Hotchner's memoir of Hemingway, and in it Bennett had written, "For Cecelia's lovely daughter who, if memory serves, may possibly be my own."

In Los Angeles I stopped by the Agers' en route home from the airport, gave Cecelia the book, and said I'd be back to join them for dinner. The moment we left, Cecelia marched into Milton's room with the

book, and by the time I returned, Milton was holding a music manuscript, the ink still not quite dry. "The next time you see Bennett," he
said, "give him this."

He had written out a lead sheet for "Trust in Me" and inscribed
it, "For the father of Christopher Cerf, who I am absolutely positive is
not mine."

The time had come to work out the details of our divorce, and the only
clear thing in my mind was guilt about Kathy. It seemed monstrously
unfair to deprive a child of her father just because I could no longer
stand to live with him. I felt this so strongly that I made a serious custody
mistake, one with consequences that would contaminate all our futures
in ways I did not foresee. A wise lawyer or child psychologist, or possibly
even a natural mother, would have known better, but none of these was
around. I arranged that Kathy would live with me, but spend all her
weekends and holidays with Steve, who would keep our house, so that
Kathy would be on familiar ground. I would take the furniture, save for
what was in Steve's and Kathy's bedrooms, and move with Kathy and
Anita to a rented house nearby.

By June, I had described our incompatibility to a Santa Monica
judge and received the interlocutory decree granting me a divorce, custody of our daughter, and a final year together on Canyon View before
we would have to find another home. Kathy by now was finishing second
grade at the Mirman School for Gifted Children. Like Lincoln, it had
superb teachers and tiny classes, and she was thriving.

When school ended, Steve took Kathy east to visit the Kunhardts at
their vacation home in Maine. Anita went back to Holland on vacation.
Summer in Brentwood was hot, dry, and empty. The Green Hornet was
free to buzz anywhere in the world, wasn't she? All it took was a call to
my editor, and the promise that material for a good "Feminine Eye"
could be found at the end of the rainbow.

I called Ernie Anderson. "Any good stories in Europe?" I asked. Peter O'Toole was about to do O'Casey's *Juno and the Paycock* in Dublin, he replied, and there were certain to be riots. Theatergoers would never accept the Liverpool-raised O'Toole's attempt to fake an authentic Dublin slum accent. I figured I could get twelve hundred words out of that, and booked a flight.

The plane landed in a thrashing rainstorm. A strapping young Aer Lingus steward told me to grab his arm and we struggled together down the steps and across the wind-lashed tarmac huddled in the lee of a black umbrella that he held out before us like a knight's shield. We reached shelter, he collapsed the umbrella, and there shaking off raindrops stood Harry Craig.

CHAPTER ELEVEN

PERSEPHONE RETURNED

"The Feminine Eye" had just trashed Ian Fleming's pop icon, British secret agent 007, and suggested an alternative:

> My own hero, in contrast to Fleming's, would be rumpled not slick; warm, not cold; flawed, not perfect; tarnished, not toiletried; . . . in short, man, not superman.

And then, in Harry Craig, I'd found him. The next years — the decade with Harry — would be the richest of my life. Neither of us had believed possible a full-blown romantic love affair in middle age, me forty-one and he forty-five or forty-six when we began. "Middle age," however, denoted something very different to him and to me. Harry, a veteran of countless adventures with women, and two really grand passions, had thought that part of his life over. He had not dreamed himself capable of being overwhelmed by his feelings a third time. Yet I'd brought him what he called "a new running of the blood." For me, a woman whose heart had been so long asleep, it was a first running of the blood, and I was shocked by the changes in myself. The portcullis was finally all the way up, and all my drawbridges down. Instead of being secretly closed, guarded, controlled, ever watchful, I was secretly open, free, unfurled, alive. Two writers in love, we were soon writing to each other daily, sometimes more often, and were always together in our minds, me ever aware of what time it was in Rome, where he now lived, he tracking the fast-changing geography of my Green Hornet life and punctuating it at all hours with surprise flowers and transatlantic phone calls.

When we'd met in London with my parents, Harry was a drama and poetry critic and a writer of radio verse plays on historical subjects for the BBC's Third Programme. By the time we met again, three years later, he had become a full-time screenwriter for Dino De Laurentiis, moved to Rome, and his earnings had increased a thousandfold. Dino had just acquired his own film studios, Cinecittà, had access to billions of lire, and was making grandiose movie production deals all around the world. He adored Harry, and almost always insisted that Harry accompany him, or go in his stead. Dino's English was poor, and he appreciated Harry's outstanding skill at negotiation, a talent honed during his early years cycling around Ireland unionizing turf workers.

In those same three years, I had become a high-flying journalist on a world pass. Our new situations allowed for frequent rendezvous in better hotels worldwide. We met most often in London and Rome and Manhattan, but also in Paris and Stockholm and Mexico City, Washington and Vienna and Jamaica, Cork, Salzburg, Nice, Durango, Cairo, Venice, Chicago, the Dordogne. A pattern evolved; when Kathy was with Steve, I was free to rush to Harry. When she was with me, Harry found reasons to come to Hollywood or, later, New York.

If Harry and I had spent longer periods of time together, instead of mostly just a week or two grabbed here or there, we might not have lasted so long. In many ways our love affair was more like a protracted, impossibly romantic courtship, eight or ten years of flowers and letters and secret, sudden meetings and wrenching partings, followed by more flowers and letters and desperate phone calls until we could manage the next time.

But Harry was no mere romantic. He was a true man of letters with a classical education acquired during seven years' study at Trinity College, Dublin. He knew more about words and their uses than anyone I have met. His original screenplay for *Waterloo* was the finest film script I have ever read. He had limitless patience, kindness, and generosity. He was full of life, always smiling, and his newly ample pocket money never lasted long. He gave it away to impecunious friends, of whom he had many, and spent a great deal on me. He never turned up without gifts stuffed into his old raincoat. Often it was jewelry: jade earrings, a gossamer chain, a crucifix made by Coptic monks, a blue opal ring that flashed like a trout. But once a pocket held an Etruscan stone horse head a farmer had turned up in his field. Another time he arrived with the coat over his arm, one sleeve tied in a knot. When he opened it, a load of white truffles tumbled out.

Rumpled, warm, life-embracing, and rarely judgmental, this unusual man was everything I liked, and like no one I had known. He always included, never excluded—unlike Cecelia, Bob Shulman, Steve. Each time we met, he threw open wide the half-shut door of life's possibilities and held out his hand. Come, he said, let's go in. In one way or another, he did this for everyone; he was a kind of Aeneas, one of the reasons that made him so universally loved.

As caught up as he by suddenly flooding feelings, I saw but four problems ahead, which I thought of as the Big Four. One: He smoked continuously, and the ash fall was like being in perpetual proximity to a small but nonstop volcano. All right, I would cover the floors of our future home in wall-to-wall gray industrial carpeting.

Two: He was never on time. I am punctual, and he could be as much as three or four hours late. This I would solve by giving him a watch, a gold pocket watch from Tiffany & Co. How to tempt a socialist and founder of the Dublin Labor Party with so bourgeois a bauble? Get Tiffany to engrave his party's slogan — NO FREEDOM WITHOUT THE FREE-

DOM OF THE WORKING CLASS — on the back, and make a fob from a snippet of my blue hair ribbon. Harry was enchanted. He named it Beautiful Watch, was never without it, slept with it always beside his bed, never lost it, and remained just as tardy as before.

Three: He snored. His big, broad chest rumbled and shook like a locomotive in a tunnel, and I was a semi-insomniac. So we would sleep in separate bedrooms. My parents lived the same way.

Four was Mrs. Harry. That was the one problem he was going to have to take care of; I could handle the rest.

We had begun in Dublin, and we met next in Rome, then Los Angeles, then San Francisco. In Sausalito Harry bought me a hand-wrought gold ring fashioned like a curl of feather — an appropriate symbol, we agreed, for the strong ties that had begun to bind us. Best of and beyond all was the windy afternoon climbing Telegraph Hill when Harry stopped and grasped me by the shoulders and said with great seriousness, "Shana, you have fifteen good years left! *Live* them!" It was clear he meant: have many lovers. Just don't let me know.

We had a few fights, of course, but the grievances were nearly all mine, and they never lasted very long. Harry was so loving, charming, and all-forgiving, and our time together so precious, that grudge-bearing seemed a monumental waste. Once, driven to distraction by some thoughtlessness or slight, I angrily returned the ring made like a gold feather and vowed never to see him again. The next time he turned up, he brought another, much lovelier ring, this one made like a gold rope.

The Agers were an important part of our lives, always visited when Harry was in town. Milton got a bit thin-lipped at times about our unconventional arrangements, but he never said anything outright, and both my parents vastly enjoyed Harry's company. Harry loved Cecelia and Milton doubly — because they were my mother and father and because of the unique people they were in their own right.

Four remained the big problem. Mrs. Harry would not give her husband a divorce. Furthermore, they had three children whom Harry could not bear to injure in their tender years. Five or six years later, by which time we had got it all straightened out, and Harry was eager to marry me — though not yet free — I refused. By then I had given some thought to what life might be like as Mrs. Craig. As lovers, we could probably have endured, especially if we kept sufficiently apart. But I still believed a nice girl married the man she loved and slept with, even if the "girl" was nearing fifty. The passionate conformist within me was far from dead. I still longed for marriage, despite all, and ultimately let this longing destroy the true love and entire happiness I had always yearned for and knew I had at last found.

When the interlocutory year of my divorce was nearly up, I rented a house in Santa Monica only a few blocks from Canyon View Drive. Cecelia, who took intense interest in everybody's living arrangements except her own, came along with Harry and me to approve my final choice. It was on a spacious corner lot, and I finally had the swimming pool Ben Bernie always predicted. Behind the pool was a little guest house for Harry to occupy when he was in town. Harry mockingly named it Slave Quarters, but my lawyer had insisted that his residence be technically separate from my own. This would protect us from Steve's threat to sue for Kathy's custody on grounds that I was an immoral, unfit mother.

I bought a king-size bed of sunny yellow bamboo to symbolize my new freedom, and Cecelia gave me a sumptuous blank book with creamy paper and marbleized endpapers. She said to use it as a diary of my new life, and for a few weeks I did.

That same year, 1966, Cecelia nearly gave up writing. First, *The New York Times* asked her to do a Sunday piece on the blossoming of Rodeo Drive as the far west outpost of expensive European shops like Gucci, Ferragamo, Vuitton, and Hermes. But when Cecelia discovered the elegant merchandise being bought in bulk by unwashed rock stars, she was so offended by the grossness of vendors she had once cherished that she refused to write about them.

Her Waterloo was a Sunday *Times* assignment on Jack Lemmon, commissioned to coincide with the release of *The Odd Couple*. For some reason, she couldn't get it right. Her old Royal portable was set up in her bedroom on its utility rolling stand, flanked by a pile of studio handouts, a box of Kleenex, a few number 3 pencils, a glass of water, a roll of Lifesavers, and her interview notes scrawled in pencil on a few sheets of copy paper folded in thirds, the way the muggs did it on *Variety*. Every day she staggered to her typewriter, rolled in a couple of sheets of copy paper with a carbon between, sighed, lit a cigarette, tried again. She sat there all day; the maids and Milton tiptoed around her. She wouldn't talk to anyone, wouldn't answer the phone. She nibbled snacks but had no time for regular meals. The deadline came, and went. Several increasingly tense conversations with Si Peck ensued. Milton was on standby to rush the finished copy to the post office by taxi at any hour. Cecelia was in her dressing gown, pacing, muttering, ripping half-typed pages from her typewriter and hurling them to the floor.

Milton finally lost his temper. "Cecelia! No more!" he roared. "We can't live this way!"

She was grateful to him for ending the terrible siege. She never spoke about what had (not) happened, and it would have been too cruel to ask. But now I think I understand. Years and years of the kind of continual writing on deadline that Cecelia did on *PM* can wear you out in a particular way. The composer Gioacchino Rossini, a fast man with a quill, wrote thirty-nine operas in nineteen years; wrote his masterpiece, *The Barber of Seville*, in thirteen days; and by age thirty-seven, feeling written out, gave up theater writing forever. Something similar may have happened to Cecelia after writing 250 signed movie reviews and 50 byline interviews per year for seven or eight years. She did two or three more pieces for *The New York Times* after the Lemmon fiasco, but all were on people she already had written about — Hepburn, the Fondas, Astaire — persons of whom she had long ago formulated an underlying opinion that merely needed updating to accommodate present circumstances.

In 1966, I began a marathon *Life* interview with Marlon Brando, then in Rome shooting *Reflections in a Golden Eye* for John Huston. A leonine presence with a noble head, small broken nose, eyes like bruises in a Mayan mask, Brando was a close friend of Harry's, and over the ensuing years he was often the beard for our meetings. Though Harry was only a year or two older than the actor, Marlon was one of many men who saw in Harry a model of the loving, forgiving father he'd never had. Marlon was so taken with Harry that he used to go up to other people on the movie set, or even on the street, seize them by the shoulders, and say, "I *love* Harry Craig!"

Marlon was a supple, sensual, lazy, charming trickster, and a riveting storyteller, but the *Life* assignment took me seven years to complete. Though Marlon loved to talk, and could hold forth for many hours on a dazzling variety of subjects — bioaquanautics, tropical sex practices, Indians, Eskimos, Buddhist philosophy, the ten deadliest animals in the world, Japanese erotica, the social life of apes, the Black Panther Party, poisons of the Amazon — he loathed talking for publication. He considered submitting to an interview "navel-picking," and had only agreed to see me in the first place, I came to realize, to help out his lovestruck friend Harry.

The day Marlon told me how each passing year made acting more difficult, because dredging up each new characterization forced him to dip deeper into the dark well of himself, I recognized that Cecelia had a similar problem with writing. It gets harder every time.

"It's like sustaining a twenty-five-year love affair," Marlon said. "There are no new tricks. You just have to keep finding new ways to do it, to keep it fresh." My mother required the same of herself, and finally the game grew too tough.

At about the same time she cut back sharply on her writing, Cecelia took up bonsai cultivation with the same fervor with which she had embraced ferns and bromeliads. Soon small but exceptionally fine specimens of the little trees began appearing around her apartment and along the sunny part of the stairway outside her door. Many long conversations took place with little old Japanese nurserymen. This group of expert though barely English-speaking miniaturists had replaced Mr. John and

Gibby as consultants in arcane decisions. The line of a brim and the line of a branch are not all that different; what counts is the stunning perfection of the line itself. Come to think of it, my mother was very Japanese. She had none of the round and jolly equanimity of the Chinese, nor any of their massive pragmatism. Rather, she had the tinge of lunacy, of hysterical purity and perfectionism that I associate with Nippon.

Seven-year-old Kathy was thriving in school, and had grown intensely attached to two cats I'd got her at Christmas. Sometimes she *became* a cat, crouching, purring, leaping, and lapping up milk from a saucer. Brando was now back home in his mountain aerie above Beverly Hills, and one afternoon Kathy came along with me to his house. He walked out to greet us, and noticed that the little girl curled in the backseat was pretending to be a cat. Instantly he became a lion, and the two of them spent the next hour in joyful play, springing onto tabletops, leaping across the backs of the sofas, hiding, sniffing, snoozing, eyeing, pouncing, and never uttering a sound.

Life marched on. The horrifying year of 1968 brought the assassinations of Dr. Martin Luther King, Jr., and Robert F. Kennedy, then the appalling sight during the Democratic Convention of maddened Chicago cops clubbing antiwar kids in Grant Park. After covering this, I found it next to impossible to refocus "The Feminine Eye" on the trivia of American life. I was also sick of traveling and hotels, and sick of the continual highs and lows of my life. I wanted to stay home, be with Kathy, and work in my garden; I wanted to live a "normal" life. I wanted to see Harry on my ground, and my terms, not his, even as I acknowledged that his advice to *live* had been correct.

Life with and more often without Harry would carry on in the same vein for a half dozen more years. None of the Big Four problems got solved except the separate bedrooms, which we always arranged on our travels. Our travels were not the problem. It was the time in between the travels that I found unsatisfactory. More than anything, I wanted a home life with Harry, and our homes were still entirely apart. He had by now asked his wife for a divorce and she had agreed, but begged him to wait a year while she entered psychoanalysis, and he had agreed to that.

The times when Harry left were like stripping off my skin; glorious freedom turned into stinging pain each time he returned to his family. His departures tended to coincide with Christmas and the other occasions Kathy left me to return to Steve. I tried taking Harry's advice and substituting another man, but it never worked. Waking up next to someone I hardly knew made me feel far lonelier than awakening alone. I knew that Harry too found the pain of parting unbearable, and eased it by arranging to see some other woman before returning to his wife. I didn't mind. He was free to do as he liked. But the pattern of our relationship was slowly beginning to throttle me.

Early in 1969, a person named Ed Fitzgerald called from New York and offered me the editorship of *McCall's*, then the world's largest women's magazine.

"I can't run a magazine," I said. "I work solo. I've never even had a secretary." He mentioned a whopping salary. "Of course, I *could* be your Number Two, and tell your editor how to make a women's magazine relevant to real women, which yours certainly isn't . . ."

"No, no, *you* must be the editor. But of course we'll get you a Number Two, someone to actually run the staff, the budget, and all that." His offer would more than triple my income, pay to move me and Kathy back east when the school year ended, and provide enough in stock options and other perks to pay for her education in the years to come.

The Agers were all for it, happy to see me moving up in the magazine world. It would be hard on Kathy, of course, but no harder than transplanting Laurel and me back and forth to California had been when we were children. We had always been an essentially bicoastal family, and Kathy could fly back and forth to spend holidays with her dad.

The announcement that dear old *McCall's* was to have its first woman editor generated a surprising amount of press attention, and feminism had nothing to do with it. Magazine publishing was entering a period of seismic upheaval, due chiefly to television. Advertisers were

finding they could reach more people more effectively with a TV commercial than a magazine ad, and rates were becoming competitive. The
publications affected most acutely were the large mass magazines,
which cost far more to produce than the revenue from newsstand and
subscription sales; the difference had to come from advertising. The
truth was that the big magazines were as doomed as dinosaurs. Within
four years, the three biggest—*Life, Look,* and *The Saturday Evening
Post*—would be kaput, and *McCall's* would be leaking money so badly
they couldn't even give it away.

After I'd signed on, Ed Thompson, *Life's* managing editor back
when I was first hired, asked me to lunch. Ed led up to his subject gradually, reminiscing about old *Life* stories and people I didn't remember,
and others long dead, before finally coming to the point. "Those days
are all gone, Shana. Finished. All the big magazines are finished." He
nailed me with his cold, blue-eyed stare.

"They just want you for a figurehead, lady. They need a totem pole
they can moor their sinking ship to." He stopped to relight his cigar. "So
sit there and look pretty. Smile and wave your balloon. Just don't for
God's sake try to *do anything!*"

The week before leaving California I cooked a farewell dinner for
the Agers and Bentleys. Nobody else was present but Harry and Kathy
and Anita and the cats, all of whom would be joining me in the fall, once
I'd found a suitable apartment. At seventy-five, Milton was still extremely
vigorous, and before dinner Harry had no difficulty persuading him to
play all his hits, in sequence, into a tape recorder. Before each song,
Harry interviewed Milton about how it had come to be written, placing
the familiar tune in its time and context. Their conversations added
up to a BBC-style documentary on Tin Pan Alley, and Harry intended
them to ease Milton and me into starting work on the book many
people had been urging us to write. Despite many attempts, a satisfac-
tory history of the glory days of the Alley had yet to be written. We
were the ideal team.

Milton's farewell gift to Harry was an Irish song composed in his
honor:

Rory, get the dory,
There's a herring in the bay.
Rory get the dory
E'er the herring swims away.
Oh Rory, oh, begorrah oh,
We're going to eat today!
Rory get the dory,
There's a herring i-i-i-in the bay!

Then we all belted out our family song, "Stand to your glasses, steady / This world is a world of lies," with even nonmusical Harry singing along. All this was committed to four tape cassettes, wrapped up in Harry's carefully written program notes, and put into a safe place for the move east.

The next twenty months were the worst of my life. I hated being editor of *McCall's*. The magazine was a mess and I couldn't fix it. I was the seventh new editor in nine years, and the staff had been variously demoralized, plundered, and shot up by my predecessors. The new management that had hired me was as ignorant about running magazines as I was. The situation was hopeless. I forgot all about Ed Thompson's sage advice and actually tried to *do something*, sometimes putting in eighteen-hour days, which meant seriously neglecting Kathy. Nobody could help me, not even all my magazine editor friends, and I couldn't help myself. In the end all I did was stub my toe and embarrass myself in a particularly painful fashion.

Kathy and Anita had arrived in New York after Labor Day and I took a limousine out to the airport to meet them. Kathy was holding tightly to Anita's hand.

"Where are the cats?" I asked.

"They didn't come," Kathy said.

"Why not?"

"Because they didn't want to."

*   *   *

McCall's was the *real* Graustark, a place of total unreality. The underlying reason for ladies' magazines, I learned, was never ladies' needs but advertisers' needs. Manufacturers of soap powder and diapers and Tampax were assured an all-female readership. But the average family income of our subscribers was $13,000; fewer than one in four had gone beyond high school. The magazine we were trying to sell them, more accurately, to *give* them — the price being only a fraction of what it actually cost to produce it — was aimed not at serving their needs but exciting their fantasies. The editorial pages showed readers an impossible, never-never land of furs and jewels and designer clothes. Our Christmas dinner menu featured roast suckling pig, fantasy food not even moderately rich readers could afford, and certainly could not find at the supermarket; even if they did, it would not fit into any known home oven. In seventh grade at Lincoln School, our class had made a field trip to West Virginia, and each child lived for a week with a sharecropper's family. One sharecropper's daughter had a Hormel ham ad tacked to the cabin wall beside her bed. "If ah gits hungry, ah licks it," she said. The relationship of our magazine to its readers was the same. *McCall's* was the lickable Hormel ham ad writ large.

The one good part of the experience was being reunited with Patrick O'Higgins. Before leaving California I'd hired him as my executive assistant, in charge of supervising the big, luscious fashion, food, and home furnishings spreads *McCall's* was noted for. Patrick's unflagging loyalty, taste, and good cheer pulled me through a terrible time. The twelve issues we put out before I removed my name from the masthead contained some worthwhile things: book excerpts from Germaine Greer's *The Female Eunuch*, a biography of Dorothy Parker, and *Dr. Seuss's Book of Wonderful Noises*. Betty Furness wrote a fine consumer column; Andy Warhol illustrated a shoe story with beguiling watercolors of cats; S. J. Perelman wrote "The Machismo Mystique." We published the first soul food recipes ever seen in a women's magazine, by Verta Mae Grosvenor; French food by Julia Child; and "Is Baby Food Safe?" by Ralph

Nader. Jean Stafford covered the Sharon Tate murders, Pablo Casals described "The Meaning of Love," Gloria Steinem wrote a critique of *Playboy*, and, during the Biafran civil war, the last foreign correspondent to hop onto the last plane out, by which time the rebels were shooting up the airstrip, was Kurt Vonnegut for *McCall's*.

But the pain was disproportionate to the product. Kathy was now eight, and the pliable small child I'd left behind in California was developing her own independence and personality. She attended Dalton, a private, coed school, and got good grades. But she never took part in class discussions, the teachers said, and her table manners were the worst in the school. Kathy was ill mannered at home as well, aggressively so, and I didn't know what to do about it. I felt guilty about the new drabness of her life. The cats and Steve and Laurel and Hannah and the Agers and the Mirman School all were gone, and Anita had been replaced by Rose, a serene Swiss woman.

Our vast new apartment could accommodate twenty-four dinner guests, with excellent food and service supplied by the kitchens of *McCall's*. Kathy's room had twin beds so a friend could sleep over. Harry and I had separate bedrooms, and Milton's big Steinway stood in front of a wall of bookcases. Harry appeared frequently, always laden with presents. Once it was a set of nested Russian dolls for Kathy, bought when he and Dino visited Moscow to rent the Red Army for a forthcoming epic on the fall of Byzantium. For me that trip produced amber beads and an ancient, Babylonian-looking hand mirror with a handle of incised bone. The bronze mirror, once highly polished, was now green-black and pitted. "To remind you of the vanity of women," said Harry with a smile.

Weekdays, Rose got Kathy up and dressed for school while I read the morning papers. We had breakfast together, and I dressed while Rose took Kathy down to the school bus. I didn't see her again until evening, often not until after her supper. I tried to be there in time to help her get ready for bed, brush her teeth, talk about the day, read her a story, sing the songs she liked, and tuck her into bed and kiss her goodnight before going out to dinner with Harry or, if he wasn't around, falling into bed myself. "*Guten abend. Schlafen Sie gut*," I said automatically before tiptoeing out, just as Milton had said to Laurel and me. I knew that Kathy was angry at me for torpedoing her life, but I believed she was even more angry at her "birth mother" for giving her away, and was taking that anger out on me. It made her new hostility easier for me to live with. Often while getting her ready for bed I used the word "adopted," as Vista Del Mar had instructed, until one night she shrieked, "Mother, please stop telling me I'm adopted! I *know* I'm adopted!"

I never spoke the word again. But I knew it was too late. Her words, even today, are a knife scar in my heart, though nothing like the knife I put in her heart. Every applicant for an adopted child should know the following story. My friend Dorothy had finished putting her adopted five-year-old daughter to bed and was about to turn out the light when the child interrupted their usual routine.

"Mother?"

"Yes, dear."

"Mother, you're the only person in the whole world I know is not my mother."

Cecelia came to New York en route to visit old friends in Europe. She took Kathy to the planetarium and Radio City Music Hall by day, and in the evenings I tried to take her to some of our old restaurants. But Cecelia's New York was gone, Al Schacht's and Voisin and Moore's torn down, along with her favorite specialty shops. Still she enjoyed prowling the city alone, often walking great distances, and her eye remained acute. One day she spotted three dusty plants in an upstairs window in the wholesale fur district and bought them for me. They were gigantic zigzag ferns that must have sat in the furrier's window untouched for thirty years. Repotted and placed in the three big, south-facing windows of my living room, they soon exploded into vigorous fountains of fresh acid green.

*   *   *

Forty years had passed since Cecelia Ager started out on *Variety*. The field in which she'd pioneered was now a serious subject taught in graduate schools. The kind of kids who once longed to write the Great American Novel now flocked to film schools to become directors. *Garbo and the Night Watchmen* was republished in Britain and the U.S., and outsold its thirty-three-year-old first edition by twenty to one. Alistair Cooke wrote a new introduction to his "casual chronicle of pleasure and pain in the movies, put together by eight youngish men and one gorgeous woman in the 1930s," and updated readers on his contributors' lives. The entry on Cecelia was so scant I figured she wrote it herself. "Cecelia Ager was an early feminist and later *aficionado* of popular songs, Democratic politics, women's fashions, and bonsai cultivation." "Women's fashions" must have been inserted by Alistair. The subject had become passé, as no one knew better than my mother.

Alistair almost broke my heart when he wrote to me a few years later, "Had your mother been picked up in the 1930s or 1940s by *The New Yorker*, she would without doubt have been a legendary figure. Maybe, like a marvelous Spanish cartoonist I know, she was — as he used to put it — 'born tired': that is to say, without enough drive or ambition to knock down *The New Yorker's* door."

Though I hated my impossible job, I hated the way it ended even more. After twenty months of struggle, I had finally persuaded a friend to join our staff as my long-promised, never supplied Number Two. Then, behind my back, management offered my friend the top job, providing she agreed to collude with them in concealing the truth from me, as well as from our advertisers, their real concern. In the present climate they dared not risk yet another change of editors. I didn't begin to smell a rat until the weekend before she was to report to work. By Monday lunch, now certain of the sellout, I left my big office over the clock in the Grand Central building and never set foot in the place again. My lawyer negotiated the remainder of my contract and worked out a generous settlement.

It was Christmas 1970, and I returned to California with Kathy for a quiet family holiday. I stayed with the Bentleys and at Laurel's insistence Steve brought Kathy to join us for Christmas. I saw a lot of the Agers, and Victor's family, and Anzia's daughter Louise and her husband, Mel. Everybody knew what had happened to me — it had been well publicized in the press — but they had the grace not to grill me if I didn't want to talk about it, which I didn't. I felt crushed by my first professional failure, and was astounded to find Cecelia absolutely rock-like in her support of me, and not at all interested in hearing the details. If she was worried about what I'd do next, she kept it to herself. My mother's lifelong reluctance to discuss or even acknowledge my success turned out to apply equally to my failure. I didn't understand it, but I was deeply grateful.

Kathy too had hated New York. She missed her dad, didn't see enough of me, and couldn't do what she'd enjoyed most in California — biking and swimming and climbing all day long, and sleeping in a hammock in a backyard tree at night. After two miserable years in Dalton, I enrolled her for seventh and eighth grade in a coed Adirondacks boarding school, run very much like a combination of Lincoln School and Camp Whippoorwill, where she again began to thrive. I also rented an isolated two-hundred-year-old farmhouse out in the potato fields of eastern Long Island, not far from our friends the Ginnas, so that we would have a country place to spend weekends and vacations, and Kathy could be with her friends Molly and Peter.

By 1972 I was a columnist again, this time for *Newsweek*, with the same generous arrangements I'd had at *Life*, including the opportunity to fly back and forth to California at will. Cecelia was seventy but looked much younger and, despite constant sighs of exhaustion, her vigor, like Milton's, seemed undiminished. Her meticulous attention to her personal appearance was in striking contrast to her disinterest in her domestic surroundings, save for her little trees and rare plants. The apartment's rented furniture had become exceedingly shabby, and when the Agers drove down to La Jolla for their annual medical checkups at the Scripps Clinic, the apartment house management sought to please them by replacing everything with clean, new stuff. Cecelia got home, didn't like it, and demanded the old things back. They already had been given away to charity, but Cecelia was firm, and eventually managed to repossess all her tattered and scarred old stuff from Goodwill.

In mid-January 1973, a note arrived from Milton. "We are having our golden, Thurs. Chantal back room with all the members of both families invited. Have already congratulated her. If you wish to, same address."

Fifty years! I could scarcely believe it. I called to say I'd be there too, and Milton read me the opening to his speech. "Some of you may wonder what has held us together all these years. It is one of the great forces of nature — the one called *inertia*."

At a party on my way to the airport I ran into S. J. Perelman, one of the rare people still around who not only knew both my parents, but knew they were married to each other. I told Sid I was en route to celebrate their fiftieth anniversary, and mentioned Milton's opening gag.

"Tell Milton I'll bet he can't think of a rhyme for inertia," said Sid, knowing just how to jab a songwriter in his soft underbelly.

My plane was late, and I made it to Chantal just in time. A surprise gift from Ernie Anderson was a rented piano, with pianist, so that Milton wouldn't have to provide the entertainment at his own party. I slid into my seat beside him, and sotto voce delivered Sid's challenge re *inertia*.

"How about 'better-or-worse ye'?" Milton whispered back, a terrible rhyme, but a good indication of what was on his mind.

We feasted and toasted and the good singers — Laurel and Wray, Victor and Florence — offered some nice close harmony on Milton's songs, and a few choruses of "Stand to Your Glasses, Steady." Cecelia, seated at the far end of the long table from Milton, was costumed as if she were about to make her entrance in *The King and I*. She wore an outrageously becoming pink-and-orange silk thing, had jabbed a couple of glittering, trembling Balinese hair ornaments through her topknot, and looked more like the creation of a Grecian goldsmith than a fifty-year American wife. She was coquettish and a bit tipsy, sang along charmingly off-key, and wound up doing a solo of her favorite song, "Oh, You Beautiful Doll," written in 1911 by two fellows nobody had ever heard of. Though we'd all seen this performance before, there was little doubt that tonight she was a very happy woman. Milton gazed down the table at her with adoration, looking like a most loving budgerigar.

As an anniversary surprise, I celebrated my parents' marriage in my next *Newsweek* column, described the party, and the tough, vivid, fiercely independent fifty years that had preceded it, and ended with a few (I thought) graceful sentences:

> In the end, I must admit that I cannot know what tides re-turned them always together, no matter what noons and moons pulled them apart. But I don't think we will see many more fifty-year marriages. They are a miracle, nearly extinct. My mother and father are the snow leopards of the social con-tract.

Milton called to say how much he liked it. Cecelia said nothing, but the day the issue came out she brought it over to show Lawrence Stewart at lunch. She was very proud, he says, and he was surprised when he saw she intended to leave the magazine behind.

"Here. Don't you want this?" he asked.

"No," she said. "I've read it."

A few years later the piece was republished in a collection of my work, *Talking Woman*, and Cecelia gave Lawrence a copy of the book inscribed, in an unmistakable comment on my views of the Ager mar-riage, "To Lawrence, with love from the author's parents, Ma & Pa Kettle."

Life made my Marlon Brando article its March 1 cover story, to coincide with the release of *The Godfather*, and a couple of weeks later Kathy came home from the Adirondacks for a long spring vacation in our per-fectly restored pre-Revolution house with Franklin stoves in every bed-room and a stone fireplace large enough to roast a Volkswagen. Harry too came back, his gift this time the just-published, thousand-page edition of *The New Oxford Book of English Verse*. On the flight over, he had dealt with the book's eccentric index, which lists its 884 entries by poem number, rather than page number, making it near to impossible to find anything, by writing out for me on the back flyleaves the page numbers, authors, and first lines of seventy-seven favorite poems he wanted to make it simple for me to find. It was a painstaking job, and had the effect of a note corked in a bottle. "Whatever happens to me, to us, I want to be certain you at least have these" was its clear message.

Reuniting our little simulacrum of a family was tonic for the three of us. Kathy loved scary places, and one afternoon Harry transformed our earthen cellar with sheets and guttering candles into the spooky Underground Railroad hideout for fugitive slaves that it had once been, and led Kathy through the place moaning hideously while she squealed with delight.

But after Kathy went back to school, the atmosphere of our lovely love nest slowly began going sour. At first I wasn't sure why. Harry and I had never before lived for long in unrelieved intimacy. In California, he'd had the refuge of Slave Quarters; in New York, I'd had the office; always, we'd had the leavening of many other people around. Now I felt sickened at times by the constant smell of strong French tobacco, and at night his snoring rattled our two-hundred-year-old walls. Long silences and bad vibes abounded. Too many of his promises had not quite come true. Things that I had formerly willed myself to ignore — his tardiness, the perpetual ash fall, a general untidiness — I now found irritating, sometimes infuriating. Frenziedly, I needlepointed myself into a coma of oblivion, dreading the moment he would again leave me, yet looking forward to it as well. The trouble was that I couldn't live day in, day out in his unconfined, high-octane way. I was finding it increasingly difficult to work with him on the scene. Unlike Harry, I hated writing; it was too hard. To force myself to do it, I required spartan conditions — deadlines, blank walls to look at, silence, order. Yet rumpled, warm, flawed, tarnished Harry was so entirely perfect for *me*. I knew I would never find another man like him. Emotionally, he was a rock; and always the mental tone was higher, the air clearer, the heart more alive with Harry around. *Live*, he had implored me, and I'd watched his benediction make me grow and flower and put out new shoots.

One day the owners of my house decided to move back. Impulsively, I bought a large house on a country lane only two potato fields from the ocean. It had stately proportions, wonderful light, and an immense upstairs bedroom-and-office suite running the entire length of the house, with windows on three sides. The front door opened directly into a vast, multiwindowed kitchen–and–dining room, and on the far side of the big living room was an attached but separate ground-floor suite with its own entrance. This could become a perfect teenage nest for Kathy, I thought, but she elected to transform the attic space above it into her private domain.

The year after I bought my house, Steve came east for good. Still unemployed but now afloat, having sold our Brentwood house for more than $600,000, he moved in temporarily with the Ginnas. On Mother's Day in our local pub he met Kelly Patton, a woman as fond of underdogs as I once had been. A Peter Pan–like child-of-nature type from Alabama with a cap of prematurely white hair and wide blue eyes, Kelly was primarily a regional theater director. She specialized in children's theater, and had held odd jobs as a clown and a veterinarian's assistant. But her true vocation, it appeared to me, was finding fathers with motherless children and then raising the children as the most wonderful fairy godmother–cum–stepmother a lonely child could imagine. She had done it before. Soon she and Steve were living together, along with assorted disabled cats, crippled dogs, sick birds, and other transient fauna, in a little A-frame house nearby, and Kathy and Kelly adored one another.

"She just kind of liked to be around me, and I liked having her there," Kelly told me many years later. "We could be together for hours doing our own things and never say a word. She didn't invade my space, and I didn't invade hers."

Kelly reminded me at the time of a cuckoo bird, that is to say, a bird which lays its eggs in other bird's nests. But she may in truth have been the luckiest thing that ever happened to Kathy. One smart thing Kelly did right away was to treat Steve's impossible nature as a ridiculous joke, something she and Kathy could share and laugh at together. This took a lot of the bile out of Steve, and bonded Kathy and Kelly more tightly together. I wished I had thought of it.

One day Kathy and Molly and three or four other eleven-year-olds spent a morning making pancakes under Margaret Ginna's supervision. I'd had to leave my typewriter when it was time to pick up my daughter, and when she wasn't quite ready, I snapped at her in front of the others: "I *told* you I'd be here at two o'clock! Why aren't you ready? You *know* I'm late!"

Hearing Cecelia's irritable, imperious voice issuing from my own mouth, I felt like a medium in a trance. After we got home, Kathy disappeared. In the past she had occasionally walked the seven miles to Steve and Kelly's house without telling me, but this time she wasn't there. We searched everywhere, and by nightfall I would have called the police had not Margaret urged me to give it a few more hours. I found her the next morning in a one-horse stable hidden in the brush behind a friend's house. She had spent the night pretending to be a horse. We threw our arms around each other, both of us crying and making promises; I would never be mean to her again, and she would never again run away.

Kathy's disappearance had been particularly upsetting because so entirely unexpected. I didn't understand how harshly I'd spoken to her. Cecelia talked that way to me all the time. During the hours of Kathy's absence, Margaret and I talked about having once been daughters, and what it was like now to be mothers ourselves. She advanced a theory of parenting entirely new to me. One must not expect to get love back from a child, she believed. Affection, respect, enjoyment, loyalty — you hoped for all of it. But the particular kind of love, and responsibility, that a parent feels flows only in one direction, like the Nile. The love you give to your children they give to their children, who in turn give it to theirs.

Cecelia had felt very differently. The awful scenes she made about her birthday presents, I could see now, were a part of her terrible need to get something back, coupled with her prideful refusal to ask for it. She wanted the same thing her children so longed for, the thing we got naturally from Milton — unconditional love, love with no strings attached. But this was something she didn't know how to ask for, and hadn't known how to give.

In Kathy's life it was becoming daily more apparent that I was the parent who made her brush her teeth, wear her glasses, and do her homework, while Steve and Kelly were the fun parents, the ones who were always at home, the ones who had not just dogs and cats but mice and gerbils, the ones who put on elaborate holiday celebrations with oodles of gifts and delicious, homemade feasting at Christmas, Thanksgiving, Easter, and whenever else possible. In short, it was no contest, and for a while I was extremely bitter.

Harry Craig loved speech, especially Irish speech. Once in a pub he had been delighted to overhear an enraged man working himself up to fight his neighbor. "Och!" he boasted. "They'll have to *dig* me out of him!"

Six years had passed since I'd given up keeping the diary of my new life, and very little in Harry's domestic arrangements had changed: no divorce, no showdown, no real resolution of any kind. Yet he was so charming, and made such magical things happen, that it was proving very hard to let go. I knew by now that Harry would simply have to be dug out of me, and that I would have to do the job myself.

My beloved was not an easy man to reject. He had to be p-u-u-s-h-e-d away, and he kept coming back. I had given up writing to him, but he still called and wrote me, and his letters, rubber-banded according to year, now filled the entire file drawer of my big desk. Between our birthdays in October, mine the sixth, his the twentieth, came a letter that shocked me. Harry wanted his letters back, ". . . a sort of sacrament . . . and a copy of myself I should like to have." He intended to write our love story, and needed them as a road map.

"Drop dead! The letters are the only thing I *have!*" I wailed — on paper, I'm afraid, as well as to myself. I was shamed by the contrast between the somber dignity of his request and the histrionics of my reply. But I kept the letters.

The following year, 1974, two critical things happened. In the spring Patty Hearst was kidnapped, snatched from the obscurity of her utterly ordinary life and deposited like a bone on the front pages of the world. I knew instantly that I had to write the book. Everything I'd written about for twenty-five years — the struggles between parents and children, rich and poor, black and white, the peculiar role of California as pop culture seedbed for the rest of the country, the awesome new power of the media, the student rebellion, civil rights, the women's movement — everything that most interested me about America was wrapped into this case. Patty was another rebellious daughter, as I had been, and as Kathy was becoming. So were the kidnappers. The so-called Symbionese Liberation Army was a bunch of college girls with empty leashes, all of them hanging onto one symbolic shared underdog, the black escaped convict Donald De Freeze. The story was a family tragedy at a time when the American family was beginning to fall apart, and pseudo families thrived. It was full of drugs, sex, terror, violence, and race war, and full of myth, too; it evoked not just memories of the Lindbergh baby, but much older, archetypal myths about evil dragons and captive maidens, about Sleeping Beauty and Persephone and Helen of Troy. The story was a metaphor for what America had become, and for the forces tearing her apart. I even had the book's title: *American Pie*.

A good idea, the Agers agreed, and more encouragement came from my old friend Tommy Thompson. A dashing Texan, Tommy too had been a *Life* staff writer before finding the courage to jump ship and begin writing his own books. Now Tommy urged me to do the same. "Jump!" he said one day at lunch, and held out his hand.

That afternoon I called the only literary agent I knew, Swifty Lazar. We all knew him. He used to book Ben Bernie's band. A day or two later,

Swifty had arranged lunch in New York with Tom Guinzburg, head of Viking Press.

"Tell him all that stuff about Patty, kid."

They didn't call him Swifty for nothing. That afternoon I got two calls. "Hey, kid, gotcha $115,000. Not bad, huh?"

"Congratulations!" said Guinzburg a few moments later. I was thrilled, I said, and rushed back to San Francisco for the newest break in the case. Patty, as Tania, had just stuck up a bank.

That fall, Kathy was "kidnapped," by Steve and Kelly. Or so I saw it at the time. The truth was, the war between her parents was pulling our thirteen-year-old daughter apart. She needed to have one home, not two, several child therapists told us, and the choice had to be hers. Soon she was happily living full-time with Steve and Kelly, and I was unhappily living alone. No Harry, no daughter, no entanglements of any kind combined to render me as Apart a Pole as anyone was likely to find.

Then the SLA burnt up on live TV during the firefight at their Los Angeles hideout, and nobody knew whether Patty was dead, or alive and underground. What's more, I couldn't discuss the problem with my editor. Elizabeth Sifton was greatly respected, and a very kind young woman, but she seemed reluctant to talk to me and, as time went on, I gradually convinced myself she loathed me. Twelve months after signing the contract I had nothing to show her but a thin folder of disorganized notes, false starts, and half-written paragraphs. The contents reminded me of crazy Jeremiah's tattered briefcase.

Over the past eleven years I had become without realizing it a professional miniaturist, an acclaimed writer of one-page essays. The longest article I had ever written was 10,000 words. Now I had contracted to produce a whole book—ten times that much—about someone who wasn't there, and whose family wouldn't talk to me, and whose story I didn't understand. I had accepted, and was spending, all the money my agent had got Viking to advance me, and Swifty had commenced sending me little blue notes of encouragement: Hurry up and finish that book, kid, so we can sell the paperback rights and get the really big dough.

Viking had scheduled me to talk about Patty at a convention of the American Booksellers Association. The two other luncheon speakers were Maya Angelou and Studs Terkel, each one an old friend and seasoned writer, hence entitled to utter the four words I hate hearing most: How's the book coming?

Not coming, I told them both. Stuck. Worse: can't talk to editor; can't get her to talk to me.

Their advice was identical: talk to Guinzburg.

I did, confided my unease, and complained that his editor was being too nice to me. As I put it, "She acts like Mother Cabrini. I need Adolf Hitler."

"Elizabeth Sifton is not only the best editor we have at Viking," said Tom. "She is quite possibly the finest editor in the book business."

Another year passed; it felt like two. To be closer to my publishers, I acquired a Midtown Manhattan roost, a ten-by-ten-foot onetime maid's room atop the old Hotel Delmonico, thirty-one floors above Park Avenue. Viking's offices were less than a block away, but Elizabeth still would not come to see me, although I knew she made overnight plane trips to remote hamlets to work with her other writers. In fairness, I should say that these writers had given her actual *manuscripts* to work on. I hadn't given her even Chapter One.

It was 1975, my fiftieth year, and suddenly I had three jobs and no life. In addition to the column and the book, I'd signed on as a commentator on *60 Minutes*, a small Sunday afternoon news show that filled in after the football. I was the liberal half of "Point/Counterpoint," opposite the conservative newspaper columnist James J. Kilpatrick. To handle all this, I needed to spend a couple of days a week in Manhattan. I moved down to two narrow rooms on the twenty-first floor and a couple of Patrick's friends glazed them a delicious eggplant–dark brown color known in the 1920s as *tête de nègre* — a term I remembered from Jimmy Reynolds — that wonderfully concealed the many cracks and bumps in the ancient walls. Nest-building again, I added matching carpet and lots of cheap mirror; it looked great.

The rundown but once elegant Delmonico was possibly the last remaining apartment hotel in Manhattan. Did I see a pattern here? Not at all. I was much too busy. Soon I gave up *Newsweek*. Most news seemed anticlimactic to me after Nixon's resignation in August 1974, and I left the magazine after writing a column on Warren Burger which pleased nobody. Management thought it too tough, and I thought it not tough enough.

In the fall of 1975, after seventeen months underground, Patty Hearst was finally apprehended in a seedy San Francisco apartment. When the FBI burst in, she wet her pants. I knew how she felt. Persephone's unexpected reappearance meant I had no more time to lose, and I raced back to San Francisco. The Hearsts had retained F. Lee Bailey and were letting him run the show. Even if Patty had not been in jail, I could not have got near her. Bailey guarded her more zealously than the FBI. Eventually I learned why: as soon as he was hired, Bailey had made a quiet deal with Putnam to write his own book about Patty.

Having struck out in San Francisco, I went home by way of Los Angeles to see the Agers, and hit a home run. It began with another maternal tirade about ducking. I told Cecelia about not being able to see Patty, because of Bailey, and she started up once more: "You're ducking again. You're always ducking." She'd said this all my life. Though her scorn and contempt were clear, I'd never understood precisely what she meant. This day, suddenly, it hit me: I couldn't have been *born* ducking; I must have *learned* to duck. Why? The reason I was always ducking was that she was always swinging! And with this brilliant deduction, a power shift occurred, unmistakable as one of the small earthquakes Californians get used to. Fifty years an underdog, and suddenly, without warning, I felt my power waxing and hers beginning to wane. I looked around at the faded, seedy premises and heard my own voice issuing my seventy-three-year-old mother an ultimatum. "Give it away, or throw it away, I don't care which. But *get that stuff out of there!*"

I could see she knew that I was talking about the things in storage, and kept going. "If . . . you . . . don't . . ." — and here I lowered my voice dramatically, just as she had taught me — "I . . . will . . . never . . . speak . . . to . . . you . . . again."

Cecelia acquiesced instantly, her only proviso being that she personally did not have to do anything beyond calling the warehouse to authorize my entry. Fine, I said, and with a huge sigh of exhaustion she picked up the telephone.

The scene at Beverly Hills Transfer and Storage the next morning looked like the last reel of *Great Expectations*. The Agers' possessions had been there longer than anyone else's, and the warehouse staff behaved as if the greatest disinterment since Pompeii was about to take place. The things filled three storerooms. I was after the furniture only, and had everything else — cartons of personal files and papers, some left over from the Rubensteins, fifteen or twenty Mr. John hatboxes, ridiculous household goods like dish mops and cracked cups — moved into one small, low-rent cubicle. I salvaged the items I liked most, some of which, such as the drums and our childhood table and chairs, had rested in rented darkness for forty-three years. The map of Paris was black and peeling; the fake Gauguin had disappeared. Laurel did not want or have room for much. She asked only for the triangular walnut cabinet that held lemon leaves. I chose the drums and tables and chairs, my father's desk, a lovely little early American chest of drawers that had been Cecelia's, and a couple of small *bergères* with the stuffing falling out, told them to ship it all to me in Long Island and give the rest to Goodwill. Somehow, in the same round robin furniture exchange, I also took possession of the Gershwin portrait of Cecelia, and hung it in the maid's room off my kitchen.

For years Laurel and I had mused about the portrait, the furniture, and why Cecelia had so long ago put their lives into storage, and wouldn't or couldn't make a move, and why Milton was willing to put up with it. Other family members had wondered too. "I never understood why Milton didn't leave Cecelia. She was so *neglectful* of him!"

Louise once said to me. Across the room, Mel looked up from his newspaper. A man doesn't leave a woman he's once made pregnant, he said. Male honor forbids it.

Liberating the furniture of the magic apartment, or what remained of it, had turned a magic key. I felt a new boldness, a surefootedness I had never known. It might not be too much to say that recovering the bright box of my childhood had given me my adulthood as well. Now that I had the portrait, I commenced to think anew about the man. Laurel couldn't really remember him; she'd been too young. But I knew that in the magic apartment George had been a part of our lives. After the Visigoths, he wasn't. As years passed, Milton had become increasingly reluctant to discuss him, and Cecelia increasingly willing, bearing out Harry's adage that every woman's failed love affair follows the same track from passion to regret to nostalgia.

If Cecelia and George did have a private relationship, how far had it gone? I was inclined to think my mother had followed Anzia's pattern; that the affair was unconsummated, Platonic; that Cecelia had enjoyed a flirtation with a man who was catnip to women, but that it had got no farther. Harry and I had often speculated about Cecelia's love life, our only point of agreement being the hope that it had in fact existed. That Cecelia's romance with Gershwin was unconsummated was an idea Harry found inconceivable. Though generally I deferred to his vastly greater experience in matters of the heart, I was sure I was right about Cecelia. I knew her better than he did, I said.

Today I am not so sure. I have doubts in several directions. I had heard hints for years that Gershwin was homosexual, his well-known liaisons with Kay Swift, Paulette Goddard, and others notwithstanding. Dr. Zilboorg had famously advised his patient that any man who hasn't married by the time he is thirty is at least a latent homosexual. Of those I'd talked to about the matter, Lawrence Stewart had been the most insightful. Despite persistent rumors, the only printed reference he'd ever seen was a single line in Glenway Westcott's journals, which Stewart had read in proof. In the published book, the line was gone. Its disappearance could be interpreted simply as evidence of the great power of the surviving Gershwins. But Stewart, himself gay, had suggested the most compelling evidence that Gershwin was not: no man ever, anywhere, had claimed to have slept with Gershwin. In the braggart-prone gay world, this fact alone could be accepted as sufficient proof that no man had.

On the other hand, my friend and first cousin David Wallenstein, a gay man of impeccable memory who knew my parents extremely well, recalls an extraordinary dinner conversation with them when Cecelia was over seventy, Milton over eighty, and David about twenty.

> *David*:   Wasn't George Gershwin gay?
> *Milton*:   Absolutely not!
> *David*:   Are you sure?
> *Milton*:   (defensively) Yes! I often loaned George the key to my apartment when he had dates with women.
> *David*:   Yes, but did you ever *see* the women?
> *Cecelia*:   (disparagingly) Milton, for God's sake! George was a fag.
> *Milton*:   I never knew that . . .
> *Cecelia*:   Maybe he didn't like you. . . .

ACT III

HAPPY
DAYS

CHAPTER TWELVE

HAPPY DAYS

Between my house and the white rail fence along the road I had planted a formal little apple orchard, twenty-one semidwarf trees neatly pruned and set in three precise rows like the orchards Harry and I had admired along the Loire. I'd been waiting two years to see the young trees come into full bloom. That May it had happened. The sight was so pretty that a couple of neighbors I'd never met wrote notes thanking me for beautifying the neighborhood. It seemed a wonderful omen for getting down to work on my book.

Apples were on the trees now, and still I had no book. I was seated at my desk in my double-size bedroom-office upstairs when I heard the wheezing croak of an eighteen-wheeler coming to a stop, an unusual sound on our country lane. I looked out, and parked beside my orchard was a cross-country moving van. The driver who stumbled out appeared to have been stoned since Kansas City, at least. In the back of the otherwise empty van was a pile of splintered wood, scraps, and shreds — the

Bekins shipment! More than forty years in storage had dried out and sundered some of the treasures beyond recognition to anyone save the seven-year-old child who evidently still lived inside me. A pair of little Italian chairs with delicately carved piecrust backs, the ones my parents ate dinner on while Laurel and I sat on the couch and watched them, had splintered almost into matchsticks. The gracefully carved, serpentine stretchers that braced the legs of Milton's desk were totally smashed. Tattered upholstery was now tacks and rags. With the help of some devoted local craftsmen, I actually paid, at enormous expense, to have all the stuff glued and sewn back together and trucked to the Delmonico. Afterwards, we didn't dare sit on the piecrust chairs, but they looked wonderful against the *tête de nègre* walls and mirror, and the drums at least had held up splendidly.

The Patty Hearst trial was set for late January 1976. Soon I would move to San Francisco for the duration, and would bring along all my old magazine pieces. In my free time, I would choose the material for *Talking Woman*, a second collection of magazine pieces I was publishing to fill the void while I struggled with Patty. The title was a vaudeville term I'd learned from George Burns. Most women in vaudeville were silent smilers — coat holders for magicians, targets for knife throwers, dancing partners. A "talking woman," like Gracie Allen, one who could actually open her mouth and say something, got paid double.

Over the summer Steve had persuaded Kelly to drive him to Hollywood in her little Volkswagen. There they would collaborate on film scripts and sell them to his many movie contacts. This new plan left Kathy once more temporarily homeless, and moving back with me and attending East Hampton High School wouldn't work; I still had two jobs in New York City. Kelly, an experienced teacher, thought a good boarding school was the best choice, and Kathy and I drove to look at several. Kelly said she thought Kathy might like Concord Academy best. So when the time came, I paid the tuition and they drove her up to Massachusetts.

The Hearst trial began January 26, 1976, and lasted eight weeks. By the end of Week One, I knew I had found my form at last. "No problem in the world is too big to solve if you can find a large enough plastic bag," Tom Stoppard once said. I would use the trial as my bag. A trial has the classic Aristotelian unities of time and space, and would allow me to stuff all my other observations about America, men and women, mothers and daughters, and all the rest, in around the edges and empty spots. These "other observations" were the filling of American Pie; the courtroom stuff was the crust.

I found an empty Nob Hill apartment, and rented enough furniture to suit my spartan needs. My spirits were high. Liberating the Ager furniture had strangely affected me. It had emptied my gunnysack, and in consequence I could see and enjoy Cecelia for what she was, instead of resenting her for what she couldn't be. Among other things, she was a connoisseur of hype, a lifelong anatomist of con, and the daily Hearst circus was turning into just the sort of media razzle-dazzle that might amuse her. Besides, she loved San Francisco. I suggested she come up and hang out for a few days, and she was on the next plane.

I installed her in a corner room in a suitably fashionable hotel near my own apartment. Clay Felker and Gail Sheehy, in town for the trial, took us out for a gala dinner. Clay and Gail knew Cecelia's work, and made a great to-do about finally getting to meet her. Afterwards, in the hotel lobby, we ran into F. Lee Bailey and joined him for a nightcap. As always, my mother bloomed in the presence of an approving male, especially a savvy mug type like Bailey, and it was around one o'clock when she went up to bed and I walked home.

I heard the phone ringing as I let myself in the door. It was Concord Academy. They had been calling me for six hours. Kathy had disappeared. A note on her pillow said "I've run away, I guess." I was not to worry that the temperature in Concord was only ten degrees, said the telephone voice. "Every trooper and highway patrolman in Massachusetts is out looking for your daughter."

They found her the next morning, eating pancakes in Howard Johnson's. She'd spent the night in her sleeping bag, had about thirty dollars, and had decided to walk to Los Angeles to visit Dad and Kelly. On the phone, Kathy sounded a little scared, but rather pleased with herself, and I was pleased with her too. I admired her gumption, I said, and told her I'd call her back after speaking to Steve. School cannot be jail; if she hated the place that much, we would have to make other arrangements.

Soon Kathy was in Los Angeles, living with Steve and Kelly and attending Fairfax High School, where I once had sat and stared with teenage lust at the back of Harlan Hertzberg's neck. When Kelly called a few months later to say she'd found a good, traditional private school that would be better for Kathy, she transferred again.

60 Minutes had moved to prime time, and the ratings were going up. Jack and I were the Punch and Judy show at the end, and for a while it was fun. Learning to argue the defense budget or health care or nuclear power in ninety seconds was meticulous discipline, equivalent to learning to en-grave the Lord's Prayer on a grain of rice. Doing it at all was the triumph.

Among the show's new fans were William Paley, head of CBS, and his beautiful wife, Babe, already suffering from the cancer which killed her in July of 1978. They were a touching couple, beautiful invalid and lovelorn tycoon perpetually enraged by his losing battle with her mortal enemy, the crab. Babe was one of many women who adored Patrick O'Higgins, and the Paleys sometimes invited Patrick and me to their elegant little dinner parties. We were always asked to come a few minutes before the other guests, and over a glass of champagne in the library, Babe would say, "We do so love your 'Point/Counterpoint'!"

"Yes, we watch it every Sunday," purred the Chairman, as he was known.

"Do tell us how it's done!" Babe would ask, and they listened like eager children each time. A great deal of preparation went into our spon-taneous-seeming debate. Jack lived in rural Virginia, and every Monday morning, by telephone, we talked over the week's news and agreed on a topic for the following Sunday. Point then had twenty-four hours to write out an argument and telephone it to Counterpoint, who taped it, and had another twenty-four or thirty-six hours to compose a rebuttal. Early Thursday morning Jack and I each drove more than two hours to our respective TV studios, in Washington and New York and, while the makeup was being applied, our carefully crafted scripts were typed onto TelePrompTers. Reading them on camera took about a half hour of studio time apiece, after which we went home. We worked on the show's slowest day, Thursday, and rarely saw anyone but the producer and crew. More than 100 million people watched the show, five times more than had read "The Feminine Eye," but I never felt the least stage fright. It was scarier to talk to the children in Kathy's class at school. So far as I was concerned, I wasn't even talking to Jack, only to Joe Schwartz, the big, kindly cameraman dimly visible behind the spotlights' glare.

Cecelia and I, by now two almost equally tough cookies, had finally begun warming up to one another. She was unmatched as a listener, and her ability to empathize was immense. Yet her failure to listen to her young daughters, failure to see us as people — and failure to curb her tongue — had hurt the most. I couldn't figure it out. But I could see how bored she was on Wilshire Boulevard. Milton got away daily to golf and bridge, but a woman like Cecelia needed more stimulation than TV and the little twenty-four-hour news radio, shaped like a cheese sandwich, which she had taken to sleeping with to dull her insomnia. She daily went out to lunch, to escape the maid, often with the lonely or troubled children of my friends.

"I don't know if you know: we had many, many lunches together," Patty Meyer, a young Hollywood writer and producer, later told me. Patty is a daughter of school friends of mine; I had not known at all. "What impressed me most was *her strength!* And she was so encouraging to me, when I was so discouraged, halfway through Harvard."

Herbie Stothart, who had become an art historian, lunched weekly with Cecelia while going through a painful divorce. "I couldn't have made it without her," he believes. My friends Tommy Thompson and Maya and C. K. McClatchey had lunch with her when they could, but also told me they'd seen her lunching alone with a magazine.

We'd had a good time together in San Francisco, and when the Long Island weather warmed up, it was not outstandingly difficult to persuade her to come and spend a few weeks with me. Milton, of course, would not budge. Putting the two of us alone together was taking a big risk. In the past, I'd seen to it that others were around, as a buffer. Otherwise her criticism of me might get too strong, and I'd have nowhere to turn . . . or if you prefer, to duck.

But this time it wasn't bad. It was downright pleasant, in fact, and there were a few real surprises. Smith College had invited me to be its commencement speaker. The easiest way to get there from my house was by air, and Cecelia and I flew up together in the little two-seater charter, skimming over the blossoming springtime of New England. She wore a standout raspberry Marimekko dress, and some sort of matching feather in her hair, and didn't look like anybody else's mother, and wowed the Smith girls.

I told the graduates I was insanely pleased to be among them, as it was my first college commencement ever, Vassar's diploma having arrived by mail, thanks to my extracurricular studies inspired by Gypsy Rose Lee. I looked out over the sea of smiling faces. Cecelia's bright plumage was easy to spot amid the black-robed girls, and she was smiling too.

"Fail early!" I told the students. "Fail while you're still young enough to stand the shock. When you don't expect anything more. Before you're too old and stuffed-shirt-rigid to bear it. Also try to have a disastrous love affair as soon as possible. Don't wait until you're my age. It hurts too much." This went over well, their hearts being still too tender to understand the truth in what I was saying. "Keep it short," Cecelia had wisely advised, so I told them to be joyous, to be themselves, to take charge of themselves, and to jump into life, and sat down to much applause, including my mother's.

A couple of weeks later we went in to New York because I had to debate Bill Buckley on the Merv Griffin program. Cecelia sat in the front row. I'd once termed Buckley a "closet liberal," and he'd been gunning for me since. Today's topic was civil rights, and when I mentioned the crucial 1954 Supreme Court *Brown vs. Board of Education* decision, Buckley said I had my facts all wrong. His magisterial manner withered me, and I shut up for the rest of the program. But I'd been right, Cecelia said later, and had just fallen for a cheap trick the snake Buckley had picked up on the Yale debating team. I felt much better.

Gail Sheehy and Clay Felker summered in a house across the street from mine, and one Sunday afternoon in the confusion of transporting children, houseguests, and maids back to the city in two cars, their dog was left behind. Gail called, and soon Cecelia and I found a beige Lhasa apso dripping green slime from the pond. I dumped her into one of the large steel kitchen sinks and began spraying off the stinking ooze. Cecelia brought a bunch of Turkish towels, and by the time we got the shivering beast cleaned off, dried, and fed, we had both begun to fall in love with it.

Thursday morning when it was time to tape *60 Minutes*, we drove Gail's dog to New York, went to the same pet shop, and bought one exactly like it, a clone. "I don't think four hundred dollars is too much for a dog, Cecelia, do you?"

"Not a first-class dog like Muffin!"

We didn't know what we were talking about. Muffin was the first dog ever, for either of us.

Irwin Shaw, a gentle, sexy bear of a man, had rented a summer house down the road. I told Cecelia about getting an A+ as a seventeen-year-old Vassar freshman for writing a terribly long, haughtily dismissive critique of Irwin's first book, *Sailor off the Bremen*. I dug out the paper and showed her my instructor's sardonic comment, "Probably the most definitive analysis of Shaw's work ever written!" The next afternoon, to my horror, she marched down the road and showed it to Irwin, who took it with great good nature. But the stunner was seeing my austere Cecelia, she who had been so contemptuous of "Sparkle, Shirley, sparkle," behaving just like a gushy, show-off stage mother herself.

One day we drove to Sal Iacono's chicken farm to buy truly fresh eggs. Sal raises his own poultry, and as I parked the car Cecelia pointed and said, "That one's a Rhode Island red." If she had been able to identify a MiG-21 Fishbed I would have been less surprised. How in the world could my chic little mother identify breeds of poultry?

"We had chickens in the yard in Long Beach," she said. It was the first time I'd ever heard her mention Long Beach. The bird triggered something, and on the drive home she finally told me a story about her childhood. It was the first and last time. A few years after the Russo-Japanese War, the Japanese fleet sailed to Long Beach, and the public was invited aboard to tour the mighty dreadnoughts. Cecelia, about seven years old, took the tour along with her beautiful, violet-eyed child-mother, and a Japanese officer fell in love with Fanny. He sailed back to Japan, and his wife, but every Christmas thereafter he sent Fanny a remembrance, always elegantly wrapped. Cecelia's job, a part of their mother-daughter conspiracy, was to intercept the gift before Zalkin saw it, and help keep it hidden.

I was floored. To me, Fanny was the stout little woman looking out her Sunset Boulevard window and saying, "Tell de Jap to turn de spreen-kles." That a mother and a daughter could be like girlfriends and gang up together on the father stunned me, though of course that's just what had happened to Kathy and Kelly and Steve.

By now Steve and Kelly were not getting along well, and this summer Kelly had brought Kathy back to Long Island with her, and she lived with us during Cecelia's visit. Kathy and her grandmother were good friends, and my mother's presence in the house meant I got to see more of my daughter. Cecelia was now the buffer which kept Kathy and me from grating on one another. Instead of remaining alone in her attic, Kathy joined us in the kitchen and gradually became the fine cook we relied on to help feed the three of us, and guests as well. Steve had taken pains teaching her to cook, and for years she'd been a dab hand in the kitchen and had an extremely discriminating palate. She thought nothing of spending an hour or two making a perfect cheese soufflé for one, or a single sublime crêpe suzette. It was like the old days on Park Avenue when we feasted on "poulet de liveroo au krepola," except the food was better.

Kathy wanted desperately to play her favorite game with us, Dungeons and Dragons, and brought all her books and other materials down from the attic. Cecelia tried, at least, and I thought showed great patience. I didn't want to play, couldn't and wouldn't. It was a fantasy game, and I couldn't fantasize.

The Democratic National Convention hadn't happened yet, but Jimmy Carter was clearly the candidate, which meant the party would have four days' airtime to fill, and a party bigwig next door got the idea of presenting a plaque to the writers of "Happy Days Are Here Again." It would be a nice, sentimental touch, he thought, to have the two adorable little old guys who wrote the party's famous theme song appear in the stands, totter down to the podium, spotlights tracking them, band booming out the song, to receive their award. Cecelia was in on the plot, but we kept it from Milton in case it didn't work. Ultimately, it didn't. The reason: four years earlier, at the Miami convention, back when Frank Sinatra was still a Democrat, he was annoyed by people in the stands taking bows and otherwise distracting attention from persons on the podium, and had got a party rule passed banning "impromptu" off-the-podium stunts. Sinatra was now a Republican, but the rule stood.

At least, that was the official explanation we got. Quite possibly Milton himself killed the idea. He turned out to have known about the plot all along—it had to have been Cecelia who told him—and had tried applying a little pressure of his own. He rewrote his first hit, "Everything Is Peaches down in Georgia," two ways—"Jimmy Carter's Peaches down in Georgia" and "Jimmy Carter's Peanuts down in Georgia"—and hired some ancient song plugger to try to peddle these variations to the party chieftains.

After the idea fell through, for whatever reason, Milton sent me a note: "Don't feel bad about H.D.A.H.A. You are not a natural-born song plugger, unlike Tubby Garen, the Big Ligoner."

On the telephone, he explained. It happened to be the closing night of the 1932 convention in Chicago, and Ager, Yellen & Bornstein's ace song plugger Tubby Garen, known as the "Big Ligoner" (big liar, in Yiddish) was attempting to get backstage at the Black Hawk Hotel to see the bandleader Vincent Lopez. As usual, Tubby's pockets were stuffed with orchestral parts for "Happy Days Are Here Again." Frozen out by Lopez, the plugger wound up at the stockyards. Pushing into Mr. Roosevelt's trailer, Tubby saw him sitting wrapped in his navy cape, a favorite garment ever since his days as assistant secretary of the navy.

"Mr. President, have I got a song for you!" said Tubby, waving some sheet music at the startled candidate. "It sounds *just like* 'Anchors Aweigh'!"

Talking Woman, my second collection of magazine pieces, was published in December 1976, and once again the reviews were wonderful, the sales minuscule. This may have had something to do with the book's timing. I am the only author I know of whose publisher booked her to appear with Johnny Carson on the *Tonight Show* on December 26.

I flew home and slogged back into my Laocoönian struggles with the saga of Patty Hearst. In my enthusiasm for the Tom Stoppard plastic bag theory of literary composition, I had by now created a book perhaps two thousand pages long, and was still finding new things to stuff in. More than three years had passed since my lunch with Tom Guinzburg, and about eighteen months since I had spoken to anyone at Viking. For four years, Milton had been waiting with wordless Japanese patience for me to finish up Patty so that we could begin collaborating full-time on a book we both cared much more about — the story of Tin Pan Alley's glory days as Milton Ager had known and lived them, the book Harry had made the BBC-style tapes for before we left California.

I was looking for a taxi on Park Avenue when I noticed a beautiful woman about a block away who looked exactly like the Gerry Morris of thirty years before. It couldn't be, of course. But it was. Repeated plastic surgery had kept her face from sagging on its perfect bones. "Remember that mole on the back of my neck, Shana?" She took my hand. "It's up on the top of my head now. Feel!"

When Gerry was in town from Mexico, she lived one block north of the Delmonico in a tiny duplex that had been left to her by one of her lovers, possibly Mike Todd. Others of her lovers had been painters; portraits by Rufino Tamayo and other important Mexican and French artists covered her walls. A Cuban hairdresser from Saks Fifth Avenue did Gerry's hair every morning that she was in town, in return for being allowed to live in her apartment while she was away.

One day out of the blue, Harry called from JFK Airport. He was changing planes, he said, and could arrange to take a later flight if I would meet him just for one drink. He needed a new piece of hair ribbon for Beautiful Watch, he said; the old one had worn out. That did it. I met him at the Regency, so steeled against falling for his old charms out of new loneliness that I became instantly drunk.

After the drink I took him up to Gerry's apartment. She was not impressed. It was ridiculous for me to be alone, she said when he left, and vowed to find me "a good man," implications obvious. She began introducing me one after another to all her old boyfriends — a department store president, a Columbia professor, an Israeli businessman, a dress manufacturer, somebody from Wall Street. Their fine qualities and tiny failings were adumbrated, as well as an estimate of their net worth. All were unmarried, Jewish, and "looking," at least sort of. Such individuals are extremely rare, and I couldn't imagine how she had collected so many specimens of what I regarded as a vanishing breed. None of it worked, of course; the planning sessions with Gerry were far more fun than the dinners with middle-aged men. They "weren't my type," I told her, without a clear idea of what my type might be. The truth was that I had learned to pretend to like being Apart.

Gerry always asked after the Agers, and may have given Cecelia a call for old time's sake. But they never got back together, not even after my parents started coming east to visit me. Eventually I realized that all three of them preferred to keep their good memories intact, rather than risk having to revise them by meeting again after so many years. Preferring one's own company is one of the hazards, and comforts, of growing old.

My social life picked up when James and Gloria Jones, after many years' residence in Paris, bought a large, Charles Addams–looking house in a Hamptons hamlet near my own. When Willie Morris saw the Joneses' collection of medieval French furniture transplanted to the Long Island potato fields, he nicknamed the place Château Spud. The Joneses for years had been the hub of a devoted circle of writers, editors, artists, and associated bacchantes who now began to whirl in and out of Château Spud. The former Gloria Mossolino of Pottsville, Pennsylvania, its chatelaine, is one of the shrewdest, wisest, and most loving women I have known. Like Gerry Morris, she is a beautiful woman who has gone through life pretending to be a dumb blonde. Soon Gloria and I were telephoning one another daily just as Cecelia and Gerry used to.

James Jones had had a bad heart for many years, and by spring several episodes of congestive heart failure made it apparent he could not live much longer. He was desperate to finish writing *Whistle*, the third novel in his trilogy that began with *From Here to Eternity* and *The Thin Red Line*. His Scribner's editor, Burroughs Mitchell, now retired, had moved to a nearby motel to work with Jim on his good days.

James Jones had fought death all his life, and fought his own with a manic energy and resolve, so that his dying took a long and terrible time, always a few good days interspersed with bad, with occasional trips to the cardiac intensive care unit of Southampton Hospital. His final hospital stay lasted more than a week, during which family friends sat day and night with Gloria in the small waiting room. When Jim was awake, she and their teenage children, Kaylie and Jamie, sat with him. When he dozed off, they returned to the waiting room. In Jim's last days he asked for "The Lake Isle of Innisfree," one of the Yeats poems I knew by heart from Harry. I went home and copied it out of a book to be sure I got the punctuation right, and when somebody lost it in the general hubbub,

went home and typed it out again, glad to have even a tiny part in helping Jim ease his way out of this world on his own terms.

During this period Maya Angelou came to spend a few days at
my house. Outside her room, on a table beside the fireplace, my now
elephantine manuscript lay swollen and helpless until I could bestir
myself to lug it upstairs to my desk. I had created a monster manuscript too big to move in one trip. Piled up, the pages stood nearly
two feet tall.

Maya, who is six feet tall, and seems to grow taller when she has
something important to say, put a big brown hand on top of the teetering
pile of paper and said slowly, "Shana, when are you going to finish this
fucking book?"

She spoke in a deeply righteous voice, and let her words reverberate
in the silent air.

I mumbled something about my difficult editor, but she cut me off.
"Four years of your *life*, girl! You don't *have* that much time to waste.
You have real *work* to do." She was talking about the book I intended to
write with Milton. "Why not call that fellow who's out here helping Jim
Jones? Get him to edit it. Get *somebody*, for God's sake. *This*," she turned
her back on the offending heap of pages, "is ridiculous."

Maya's scorn, like her tears and her laughter, flows out in a powerful
torrent. I called Burroughs Mitchell and explained my situation. He said
he needed to think it over, and talk to his wife. He'd never done a freelance editing job before, and didn't know what to charge.

The next day he called back. "Would eight dollars an hour be too
much?"

With help I hauled my mountain of manuscript to Burroughs's
Manhattan apartment. He put up a card table in his book-lined living
room and sat there with my manuscript and a little pile of yellow stickers,
the kind professional editors used before "Post-it" notes were invented.
Two weeks later, a twenty-inch-high manuscript had become two ten-
inch stacks, one of discards, the other full of little yellow signal flags
to indicate where splicing was necessary. I put the yellow-flagged stack
through my typewriter one more time to perform the necessary anneal-

ing and cleanup, a matter of five or six buoyant weeks' work, and brought it to Elizabeth Sifton's office at Viking.

She looked like a different woman: softer, prettier, more human. She thanked me warmly, and promised to get the whole thing read over the weekend. Monday morning she called to say how pleased she was with what she'd read, and asked me to come in to discuss a few minor fixes.

"Thank God it's finally over," I said, sinking into a chair. "Swifty will be thrilled. He's been nagging me for years to finish this, so he can make the big paperback sale."

Elizabeth looked at me strangely and excused herself. She returned carrying a letter I hadn't ever seen, from Lazar to Tom Guinzburg, written at the time of my book contract, affirming that Viking had put up only $15,000 of my $115,000 advance. All the rest had come from Bantam. The "big paperback sale" he'd been promising me had in fact already been made, by him, to Bantam, for $100,000 in 1974. Lazar had neglected to tell me of Bantam's involvement, and the book contract I'd signed didn't reflect it.

Her news, mind-boggling as it was, cleared up a minor mystery. Rollene Sahl, then head of Bantam, was a woman I scarcely knew. But we traveled in the same circles, attended the same parties, and drank at the same bars, and someone was always saying to me, "You know Rollene, of course," and I would fib and say, "Of course," and she would take my hand in both of hers and inquire searchingly, "How's the book coming?"

I continued to fly to California five or six times a year, and each trip reminded me that it is possible to age gracefully. Cecelia and Milton were living proof. They never became gross or idle, and their faculties remained sharp. They kept up with the arts and world affairs, continued taking good care of themselves, brushed their teeth twice a day, and saw their doctors frequently. Milton, an unusually tidy man, spent a half hour every day at his child-size desk doing what he called "getting my affairs in order" — promptly paying their bills, writing letters, dispatching checks to charities and relatives, occasionally retyping a new lyric or correcting old misprinted notes in one of the green books.

Their well-established pattern of independent living, despite the cramped quarters, continued just as before, and for a long time I did not notice that he was gradually taking over some of Cecelia's former duties in their still-divided lives: making more of the decisions about where to eat, and with whom, paying more and more of the bills, supervising the disposition of the tidal accumulation of newspapers, books, and magazines that threatened to swamp the place, doing more ordering, answering more phone calls, directing the maids. Every evening they still held the same inane discussion about which restaurant to choose. I had listened to them in nightly wonder for forty years as they spoke the same Beckett-like ritual lines: "I must go on. I can't go on. I'll go on."

Or, in their version:

> He: Where would you like to go tonight, Cecelia?
> She: (in tones of terminal ennui) I don't care where
> we go.

Although the dialogue hadn't changed, their dinner hour had crept inexorably forward, goaded by the demands of Milton's finicky stomach. By now, the better restaurants in their neighborhood were accustomed to the very early evening appearance of two small-scale people, both impeccably turned out in small hats, scarves, jackets, good shoes. They knew the owners and waiters and headwaiters by name. Milton even knew the busboys, and never failed to tip them individually.

My parents did not of course escape all the rigors of old age; Milton had a prostate operation, and two years after that Cecelia had a mastectomy. Both surgeries were successful, and earned them each a few more good years. Each time one of them needed an operation, I went out to California, and in the course of my visits made a few astonishing discoveries.

Before Milton's operation he went to have a chat with Victor, his doctor brother-in-law. In recent years Milton had occasionally asked Victor for a testosterone injection, and my uncle had discreetly obliged. But the evening after Milton's visit, Victor could hardly wait to call me about it.

"Guess *what?*" It had become clear to Victor that, both our presumptions to the contrary, the Agers still had an intimate life.

Although Milton did not of course mention this to me, he was remarkably open about his fear of cancer, and told me how much he dreaded "having to wear a diaper again." As matters turned out, he escaped both fates.

On my visits to California, a new warmth between my parents was apparent. Cecelia was manifesting a tender, indeed *motherly*, concern for Milton's well-being. She had taken to microwaving him little spinach soufflés, or boiling tiny new potatoes, to accompany her barely simmered small salmon filets in the flavorful but bland and salt-free stock made with fish heads that took an hour to prepare.

For his part, Milton told me, "I am just *elated* by Cecelia's great show of love and affection! She listens to my stories! She laughs at my *jokes!*" He shook his head in happy wonderment. "Whenever I say anything, she says, 'Oh, you're *wonderful!*'"

"She's right," I said. "You *are* wonderful."

"Shana, I'm a tough little guy. Like Irving Lazar. Except I'm honest." We both grinned.

When Laurel telephoned to tell me Cecelia had breast cancer, I called my mother, and she sounded completely calm and told me please not to bother coming out; I was much too busy, and Laurel could take care of everything. She had no sense whatsoever of the extra care Laurel was already taking, the errands she was running, and the sacrifices she was making by driving hours on the freeway after work several times a week bearing pots of boiled chicken or lobster salad.

By the time I arrived, it had been decided that Victor would escort Cecelia to the hospital and get her settled. She left the apartment carrying a chic overnight bag, her cheese-sandwich radio, and an armful of carnations Victor had brought along. She was smiling and serene, and I thought her equanimity genuine.

The prospect of Cecelia's surgery was more difficult for Milton to contemplate, as I saw when I joined him for dinner that night, and the next night, and picked him up the following morning to bring him to the hospital for his first post-op visit. Only one visitor was permitted, and I waited in the lobby. When Milton came downstairs he was almost ecstatic with relief.

"Oh, Shana, you should *see* her!" he exclaimed. "She looked so small, so beautiful! She's like . . . like a little Venus de Milo!"

It was not hard to know what he meant.

CHAPTER THIRTEEN

THE FURIES

*6*0 *Minutes* was becoming one of the nation's top-rated TV shows, and thanks to its huge success, increasing numbers of people wanted to interview me. One day I was brought up short by something I heard myself telling a reporter from *The Washington Post.* Was it correct, she asked, that my father had written "Ain't She Sweet?"

"Not only that. I was born on his birthday, his first child, and he actually wrote the song for me," I lied. "I'm the *She.*" I didn't know why I'd said this, any more than I knew why I'd put pins in the butter when I was five; it just seemed like a good idea. Later I learned that she had telephoned Milton to check it out.

"Absolutely!" he'd told her.

At about that time John Hammond published his life story, *On Record,* and muddied up pop music history a bit more by writing glowingly about Cecelia, "the wife of Milton Ager, the composer of such hits as 'Happy Days Are Here Again,' 'Five Foot Two, Eyes of Blue,' and 'Ain't She Sweet?' (which was written in honor of their daughter Shana, now journalist-writer-editor Shana Alexander)." Opposite this, in the margin of the tenderly autographed copy John had sent to Cecelia, Milton wrote: "Lie."

"If she had not been married and the mother of two small children," John continued, "I might well have tried to be more than a friend to Cecelia."

Opposite this, Milton wrote, *"What!"*

Like Milton, Cecelia recovered well from surgery, and by August she was ready to visit me again, and this time persuaded Milton to come with her. Except for their annual trips to the Scripps Clinic, it would be his first time out of Los Angeles since the three of us had flown to London fourteen years earlier. He was now eighty-three and Cecelia was seventy-five, and fourteen-year-old Hannah came along to lend a hand. During their visit Kathy was coming back to join Hannah in their old attic hideout, and I anticipated a cozy family summer.

The night they arrived, Milton insisted on taking the five of us out to dinner in a restaurant, like old times. As soon as we got home, Kathy and Hannah zoomed off to climb a tree in the moonlight, and I watched Cecelia and Milton walking ahead of me on the path to the kitchen door. Their appearance had changed remarkably little over the years. Both were still trim, stylish, and brisk. As they made their way through the garden, the saved fish from dinner fell out onto the lawn through the leaky bottom of its doggie bag, and Muffin bounded out to dispose of it. After a lifetime of carrying home half-eaten restaurant dinners in doggie bags, we had an actual *dog*.

My parents fit well into the guest suite, and seemed quite content to share a bathroom for the first time since 1934. With Cecelia and Milton guests in *my* house, another wonderful shift in the family balance of power took place. I was hostess as well as daughter, and they were at the top of their form. I was thoroughly familiar by then with the difficult ways of houseguests, and Milton and Cecelia were so thoughtful and considerate and delightful to have around one might have concluded that houseguesting was their real profession.

Little seemed to have changed. We were all older, but I scarcely noticed. Milton was still uttering his Delphic warnings, "Stand by your sex commitments" and "Children don't ask to be born," and talking about "the family unit." He had a great tolerance for repetition, whereas we had almost none, and had tuned him out years ago.

But I was wrong; one thing had changed. The moment Cecelia started treating Hannah the way she had treated Laurel and me, as a household servant, Hannah walked out. The provocation was an order one morning to tidy up Cecelia's bedroom and make her bed, followed by criticism for failure to pick up used Kleenex. Hannah immediately called Laurel, announced she wasn't going to be kicked around and was coming home that evening. I was upstairs working, and didn't hear about all this until Hannah came up to say goodbye.

"Soft-Hearted Hannah," I'd always called her, but my young niece had done something her mother and I had never dared. She had defied the tyrant to her face, and when she left, I gave her a silent cheer. The next day Laurel, become suddenly Cecelia-like, made Hannah write me a smarmy thank-you letter for the lovely visit.

I hired a daughter of the family next door to help out for a few hours each morning and, domestic problems settled, the adorable, witty little couple who were my houseguests became the toast of the Hamptons summer season. Restaurant dinners in the Hamptons in summertime are an ordeal, and we ate at home as much as possible. While Milton played his Steinway in my living room, Kathy and Cecelia and I cooked one dish apiece, and we dined in the kitchen, often with several guests. Afterwards Milton entertained for hours, playing everybody's requests, telling anecdotes, accompanying in the proper key anybody who felt like singing, and generally enchanting the crowd around the piano. Cecelia enthroned herself at the far end of the room and talked movies and show-biz. Kathy sat on the stairs and listened. The warm, rich family life I'd always longed for was finally happening now in my own living room, with my friends the guests, and my parents the stars.

Betty Comden and Adolph Green and Phyllis Newman, Gloria Jones, and the classical piano team of Gold and Fizdale and many others vied to have us as guests. Kathy disliked parties and preferred to stay at home, unless we were going to the Barretts' — Mary Ellin Berlin Barrett, eldest daughter of Irving, and her courtly writer husband Marvin. On those nights, Mary Ellin and Milton sat side by side on their little piano bench playing favorite, little-known Irving Berlin songs to each other, and the rest of us sang along as well as we could.

One evening around sunset Milton and I were strolling in my apple orchard and he said in his wonderfully direct way, "You know, Shana, I feel sorry for you. You're all alone."

I didn't feel alone, I replied. All writers are alone most of the time. I at least was surrounded by many good and interesting friends, especially during the Hamptons summers. I truly loved my house and garden, entertained frequently and well, had an enviable professional life, and — when necessary — a great, quiet, private place to work. I was past fifty, and finally felt more or less "grown up." At least I knew by then that character is fate, and had learned what my own was made of. Fear and shame had ruled my early life; Kathy had been the key that unlocked me at last. But fear and shame had always been tempered by laughter and crazy hope. Taken together, these four elements had been the cornerstones of my life. They were like Simon's four big black men holding up their torches to illuminate the wagonload of sundries that was me.

Anzia Yezierska had died in 1970 in the California nursing home where Louise had brought her for her last months; she must have been close to ninety. Eight years later, my great-aunt's reputation had begun a modest renaissance, if not quite a Hollywood comeback. Her work gradually was being reprinted, and scholars were uncovering the truths behind the self-created fiction of her life. Today virtually everything Anzia wrote is back in print, and critical studies of her work abound in both the U.S. and Britain. A novel has been written about her life, and Yezierska is ranked as a significant figure in American women's fiction, mentioned alongside Gertrude Stein and Toni Morrison. The most comprehensive study is Louise's biography, *Anzia Yezierska: A Writer's Life*, published in 1988 by Rutgers University Press.

The real excitement started in 1977 when a scholar at the Center for Dewey Studies at Southern Illinois University, Jo Ann Boydston, published a slim volume of John Dewey's poems. Dewey was a major intellectual mandarin of the early twentieth century, renowned as a philosopher, psychologist, and educator, but scarcely known for his poetry. Few even knew he wrote it, and no one knew he had written passionate love poems and letters to Anzia Yezierska.

John Dewey was the original of the Anglo-Saxon lover who reappears variously disguised in all of Anzia's work. All the love letters and poems she quotes were real ones written to her by Dewey during their brief affair in 1917. A decade later Dewey tossed his copies of the poems into a wastebasket, whence they were retrieved by a faithful secretary and preserved in the voluminous archives of the great man's work. Then a trove of Anzia's love letters to him was unearthed. The scholars toiled, matching paper watermarks and typewriter characteristics until slowly the great hidden secret of Anzia's life stood revealed in the light of day.

Anzia, a night-school teacher, had met Dewey at Columbia at the height of his reign. Soon he'd invited her to join his seminar on political and educational theory, along with Irwin Edman, chairman of Columbia's philosophy department, the writer Paul Blanchard, and Dr. Albert C. Barnes, the eccentric Argyrol king and millionaire art collector. Anzia was there to contribute the immigrant point of view, but found herself too timid to speak. When summer came, Barnes set up a sociological research project to study a Polish community in his Philadelphia neighborhood, and Anzia was hired as researcher and translator. Dewey came down to visit, and loaned her the first typewriter she'd ever had. Soon she was daring to show him her stories; he encouraged her, and their affair began.

Their story is told most fully in *All I Could Never Be*:

> Far behind them was the city with its noise and crowds. They seemed all alone, at the edge of the earth. . . . They leaned toward each other. . . . He kissed her fingers, one by one. . . .
>
> "Do you love me?" he whispered, drawing her closer to him, kissing her neck, her mouth. . . . "Dearest!" Suddenly his lips pressed her lips with fierce insistence . . . a wild alarm stiffened [her] with fear. The shattering impact of his lips . . . his hand fumbling her breast! . . .

She breaks away and runs home, then rushes to see him the next morning. When he demands his letters back, she shrieks, "No! All I have now is my letters! They are my light in the darkness," and so on.

Louise believes that Dewey was as shocked as Anzia by their first embrace, appalled that she tried to pull away the moment he put his arms around her. "From a passionate, alluring woman . . . she had changed without warming to a prim, incongruous adolescent," Louise writes. "The picture of himself as an aging fool, which he saw in her frightened face, repelled him."

To avoid Anzia, Dewey took jobs in Japan and China, remaining out of the United States for three years. All this is told most clearly by Louise. Her book is filled with revelations about Anzia's artifice and her self-mythologizing. Although her stories were written as if she were a greenhorn just off the boat, her command of English was greater than it appeared, and her knowledge of literature extensive. Nor was Anzia at the time of the affair the poor immigrant girl she pretends; she was about thirty-five and Dewey fifty-eight. Was the real affair consummated? Louise thinks not, and I tend to agree. More than likely, Anzia remained the "mental bride" of her first, one-day marriage.

Only after reading Louise's book did I understand what had really been inside fictional Jeremiah's battered briefcase all those years — the Dewey poems and letters. Anzia herself was Jeremiah, and the papers in the briefcase were both proof that she had been loved and evidence of the terrible rejection she had suffered. Magically, over time, Dewey's words became the talismans which released Anzia from her lack of confidence and fear of failure, and the engine that drove her at last to succeed as a writer, and to sell her work.

One wintry night Time, Inc. threw a big formal party at Radio City Music Hall for former *Life* staffers and all the celebrities who'd appeared on *Life*'s covers. It was a publicity stunt, but six of us from the Hamptons decided to show up anyhow, then beat a retreat to 21 to have our own old-timers' dinner, "separate checks." Gloria Jones, Adolph Green and Phyllis Newman, Betty Comden, Tom Prideaux, and I made up the party. Tom was one of Broadway's most beloved bachelors, and the others had seen him at opening nights and at their own dinner parties for half a century. But his private life was entirely unknown.

At 21, welcome alcohol flowed and soon beautiful Phyllis leaned across the table, batted her eyelashes, and said, "Tom, we've all known and loved you for so long. Tell us, *where* do you live?"

"In the past," he replied.

By March, 1978, I had completed Elizabeth's suggested revisions on my manuscript, now retitled *Anyone's Daughter*. Titles are usually hard to find, but sometimes they suddenly shout themselves out to you. This had happened a year earlier when I was rereading the so-called *Tania Interview*, Patty's twenty-seven-page autobiography written after she had switched sides and become "Tania," a gun-toting revolutionary. Who were her newfangled outlaw companions? "We could be anyone's daughter, son, wife, husband, lover, neighbor, friend," Tania had said.

To be sure, I typed it out on a blank page:

ANYONE'S DAUGHTER

It looked a bit like the title of one of Anzia's books, the story of an immigrant girl named Anyone (pronounced "Annie Ownie") who toils as a scrubwoman to raise her fatherless child. But I kept it, because I knew by now that Tania's message had been correct. Anyone's daughter, caught in the same terrifying circumstances as Patty, might have flipped out and joined her captors, as she had. The Stockholm syndrome, psychiatrists called it, named for a Swedish bank robbery in which female hostages locked in the vault with and totally at the mercy of their captors began falling in love with them.

Two weeks before Easter, I impulsively took off for Greece to celebrate my own deliverance. My companions were a psychiatrist and his teenage children. We would continue on to Israel after resting a while in a pleasant seaside hotel in Piraeus and exploring nearby ruins. Two days before we were to leave Greece, Israel invaded Lebanon, which threw a serious hook into our plans. It might now be unwise to bring the children to Israel, in case there was difficulty leaving, and I frankly didn't want to go now either. As an American Jew, I might be asked to comment on a sudden military strike which I knew nothing about except that I didn't like it.

The Greeks are excellent stonemasons, and our hotel bathrooms had floors, ceilings, walls, and countertops made of hand-hewn gray tesserae. I had just stepped out of the shower the next morning when I heard Harry's unmistakable voice reverberating out of the stonework, reciting the Yeats I had heard him speak so often, "An Irish Airman Foresees His Death":

> *I balanced all, brought all to mind,*
> *The years to come seemed waste of breath,*

A waste of breath the years behind
In balance with this life, this death.

I rushed downstairs to find my companions. "Harry's talking to me out of the bathroom wall!"

The psychiatrist, a friend of Harry's and a Jungian, believed in mystical experiences. "It's a sign!" he exclaimed. "It means you must find Harry, wherever he is, and have him meet you tomorrow in London. You know he'll always come at once to any place you are."

I found him deep in the Libyan desert, on location making *Lion of the Desert*, an Arab-financed movie starring Anthony Quinn as Omar Mukhtar, the veteran Bedouin guerrilla fighter who led the struggle to resist the Italian colonization of Libya in 1929–31. Through the crackle of static, Harry's voice was clear. Although it was Easter week, and airplane bookings impossible, I managed the next day to fly to Munich and on to London.

Harry was waiting for me behind the ropes at Heathrow, just as he had been so many times before. He was thin again, his raincoat flapped on his large frame, and both of us wore glasses now. He had found an Arab-owned hotel in Knightsbridge and booked adjoining suites. His next picture was *Saladin* and he had urgent scenes to write, so we forced ourselves to work each morning until lunchtime, he at one desk, Beautiful Watch on the table beside him, me next door at an identical desk in an identical picture window tinkering with my Patty manuscript. Harry was eager to read it, and when he pronounced it "fine, very fine," I felt a change in my breathing. It was a lovely week of fair spring weather, flowers blooming in every windowbox. We had long lunches in the same old restaurants, walked our old walks, went to the same theaters and museums, and saw no one but each other. It was a quiet, serene time in which we didn't need to say or do much. We knew one another so well we communicated in old codes and symbols. During those six days I entirely made up with Harry. The gunnysack of old resentments raveled away in the warmth of his presence. It was not a "new running of the blood," nor even a reconciliation. We did not intend to resume our old relationship. It was a peacemaking, a binding up of old wounds, a mostly mute acknowledgment of enduring love despite all.

When we came home in the evenings and stepped off the elevator to our side-by-side doors, we embraced tenderly and retired to our own rooms. That was my wish, and once I'd indicated how I felt, he did not protest. That was not Harry's nature. Always his stated wish had been to make *me* happy. That was what made him happy, he said, and I felt the same way. Again. So it didn't matter. It was a beautiful week which wiped away all the piss and bitterness of the past few years.

Last mornings before parting had always been unbearable. We'd tried to make them less so by devising a complex departure plan. Now the familiar old choreography began of packing up, retrieving laundry, checking for lost items, getting cash, finding plane tickets, making phone calls fueled by last-minute gin and tonics, leaving notes, and distributing tips. When all that was finally done, we planned a last lunch at Wheeler's in Old Compton Street before Harry had to go to his airplane, and I to mine.

I was standing at my closet removing my clothes from their hangers when he came in and embraced me. "You mustn't mind about our not sleeping together," he said. "I didn't want you to see my body, either. It has grown old." I flooded with gratitude and understanding. He had articulated my own feelings, feelings I had not understood or dared put words to until he spoke them. I wept and continued packing.

In the summer of 1978 the Agers again came to stay with me. Both of them were still trim and erect. Milton now carried a walking stick, but his fitness and inborn sense of timing were intact. When he'd teed off a couple of months earlier at Rancho Park, a bystander, amazed to see a tiny man in his eighties send the ball sailing out of sight, had inquired how tall he was.

"Five feet two," Milton had replied. "Formerly five feet three."

On their first morning, I came down to let Muffin out and found

Milton in the kitchen making his tea. He was still wearing the blue seersucker bathrobe I'd made for his birthday twenty-five years before, the one with the opening bars of his biggest hit embroidered — all wrong — on the pocket flap.

"I'm concerned about Cecelia, Shana, and I need your help." I glanced up sharply. He'd never before asked me to intervene in his dealings with his often difficult wife.

"She has become quite deaf. But she's too vain to wear a hearing aid. So she's lip reading," he said. "Will you speak to her?"

He padded back toward his bedroom, cup in hand, and moments later, having heard his door close, Cecelia appeared to brew her coffee in the little French porcelain pot she'd brought from Los Angeles, along with her special coffee beans and a supply of lump sugar.

We chatted while she went through her café au lait ritual, grinding fresh beans, warming her pots beforehand with hot water, putting her croissant in the microwave. At the opposite counter I made my own coffee, all the while keeping my eye on her in a mirror. We stood back to back and fifteen feet apart; she *couldn't* be lipreading.

When she turned around, I turned too. "Cecelia, Milton says you're deaf."

She put her hot milk and coffee and croissant on the little tray and picked it up. "Only to him!" she said cheerfully and sailed serenely out, her thin silk peignoir floating behind her.

Kathy was a whiz at mathematics, and that spring had won a National Merit Scholarship and been admitted to Harvard, MIT, and Swarthmore. But she was still only sixteen, had attended five schools in the past four years, and wanted to take her senior year over again at the George School in Pennsylvania, a fine Quaker boarding school where Kelly hoped to get a teaching job. I thought it was a good idea, and sent the tuition. After a couple weeks of rock climbing in Colorado with Outward Bound, Kathy had returned tanned and hard-muscled and was back with us for the duration of the Agers' visit.

One night the carpenter stopped in to repair the kitchen floor. Years ago, as a young carpenter, he had built most of the house, and in the decade since I bought it, we had become good friends. Grizzled now but still handsome, he was apparently a black man but always referred to himself as a Shinnecock Indian. I introduced him to the Agers, and he pulled out a picture of his newest grandchild.

"They're not married, of course," he said. "That's the way they do things today."

Cecelia and I were still talking to him when, in the living room, the music started. I'd heard Milton's piano as long as I'd heard my own heartbeat, and the sound always drew me like a pull toy. Soon I was back in my accustomed position, standing in the curve behind the rising notes where the strings grow short. Tonight he was playing "High Brown Blues," an early hit written in 1922, the year he met Cecelia. He rarely played it anymore, and I'd never heard him do it in this low-down, raunchy, honky-tonk style.

"I've ... got ... those ... doggone aggravatin', 'sassinatin', woman-hatin' High Brown Blues."

It was a small musical joke, I realized, a sly dig at our carpenter's roots. "You never played it *this* way before, Milton," I said.

"If I hadn't played it this way once, you'd never have been born!"

We had some friends in a few nights later, and everybody had gathered around the piano when Gloria Jones's playwright friend Ed Trezinski, author of *Stalag 17*, overcome by equal parts nostalgia and scotch whiskey, shouted, "As Jolson said, 'I could sit here and listen all night!'"

"That's not what he said." Cecelia, surrounded by her own admirers, sat enthroned in a high white wicker chair at the far end of the room. But her low-pitched voice was quite audible.

"'You ain't heard nothin' yet!' is what he said."

Milton spoke up quickly to cover Ed's embarrassment. "My partner and I went out to Chicago one time to ask Al Jolson if he'd sing a new song we'd written called 'Who Cares?'"

"Who cares," Gloria sang out, "if banks fail in Yonkers ..."

"No," I corrected her. "There were *two* 'Who Cares?'"

Now rescuing Gloria from embarrassment, Milton played a phrase of the Gershwins' "Who Cares?," written ten years after his own, and kept talking. "So, Jolson sez, 'Sure I'll sing it.'

"'Gee, that's great, Al!' sez Jack. 'We'll give you a cent a copy.'

"'What're you talking about!' sez Al. 'I wouldn't take a cent a copy from pals like you and Milton! If you wanna *do* something . . . I'm getting married again. I'll send my wife over to pick out something at Steinway's.' "

When the laughter died, Milton asked Gloria, "Do you know *my* song? It's the song that got me Cecelia, the song I broke her heart with." He played and sang his "Who Cares?," a torchy ballad I doubt any of them knew:

> *Who cares*
> *If my heart is aching?*
> *At times when it's breaking*
> *Who cares?*
> *Oh, gee! poor me!*
> *How often I get feeling sentimental*
> *But no one gives a continental . . .*
> *. . . I guess I'll phone*
> *The old maids' home*
> *Gee whiz! How tough it is*
> *When there's nobody who cares!*

"And *that* won you Cecelia!" said Ed.

"Well, that was the song that she liked," Milton said quietly. "*And* she liked 'High Brown Blues.' "

He played the verse and chorus gently this time, in what his directions on the sheet music call "toddle tempo":

> *I re — fuse —*
> *To let my heart grow fond*
> *Or re — spond —*
> *To the jelly roll-in' of a mid-night blonde . . .*

I thought I caught Cecelia throwing him a wink, though in the dim, smoky light one couldn't be sure.

Milton entertained our friends so long and hard one night, playing and singing past one in the morning, that the next day he didn't feel well. A local doctor did an EKG and diagnosed a mild episode of heart failure. Nothing to worry about, but best to have some follow-up tests done in New York Hospital, as a precaution. He was, after all, almost eighty-five.

While Milton was in the hospital, Cecelia could stay nearby in my apartment. Our neighbor and friend Leif Hope, an artist who has made a second career out of helping people, offered to drive the Agers to the city by car; no need to alarm anyone unduly by calling an ambulance. Kathy and I got Milton packed up, and he was sitting at the piano, walking stick and hat at hand, waiting for Cecelia to be ready, when I joined him on the piano bench.

"Do your doctors know everything you're taking?" I asked. Milton visited two or three doctors for different complaints, was on many drugs, and had mentioned adding a Valium to the mix the night before.

"Of course."

"*Everything?*"

"Everything but the Cracker Jacks."

"Was the Valium for the arthritis?"

"No. Nothing helps the arthritis. Look at my hands."

I took his small right hand in my larger ones, the hand with fingers broken by handball, the hand I'd hung on to in the hospital corridor at age three, and so many times since. His misshapen fingers, especially the index one, were swollen at the base and slightly blue. *How had he been able to play piano with these?* I wondered. Yet I'd heard him playing daily ever since he'd got here. I remembered discovering yesterday morning that my driver's license would soon lapse, and rushing off to renew it. EXPIRES ON BIRTHDAY, it warned. "*It* may," I'd thought to myself, "but he — that is, *we* — haven't yet."

"Pretty tough now to play the piano, huh?" I said.

He smiled. "Always was."

Muffin barked and we heard Leif at the kitchen door. "Come on in, please!" Milton called out. "Have a drink if you feel like it. I'd like to play you a new song, one I just wrote for you."

Leif stood in the curve of the piano. Milton grinned up at him, cocked his right eyebrow, and sang, "Don't Tell Me Your Troubles (And I Won't Tell You Mine)."

That winter he had the song copyrighted and published; it was his last.

"Point/Counterpoint" was now in its fourth year and, unbeknownst to me, had made me one of the country's favorite comic characters. *Saturday Night Live* did a parody of Jack and me in which I was always addressed as "Shana, you ignorant slut." Being unaware of it, I didn't mind, and many high-fee lecture requests — which I mistakenly ascribed to the popularity of *60 Minutes* — were rolling in.

It was late October, the height of the fall lecture season, and I had been on the road nearly three weeks. My last gig was New Orleans, where Jack and I had done one of our custom-made, extra-high-price "Point/Counterpoints" for the Wholesale Grocers Association of America.

October 23, 1978. I came home by taxi well after midnight, a three-hour drive from JFK Airport to a dark and empty house. Muffin was still at the kennel. I let myself into the kitchen. The red light on the answering machine on the counter was blinking on and off. I turned on the lights. The message tape was chock full and had turned itself off. Half-choked voices, in many accents, seemed to have come in from all over the world: "Oh, Shana . . . I'm so sorry . . ."

"Oh, Shana. I'm so sorry." At first I thought Milton had died. But it was Harry.

I screamed in the empty house. When I understood, a great vacuum opened inside me, and all of Harry, every memory, every word, every jot of love rushed back and hit me so hard in the chest it knocked the breath out of me. I got a bottle of Irish whiskey and sat down at the kitchen table and began calling around the world for confirmation and more information about the unbelievable, inconceivable event. He had died in Rome, that was all I knew. I called Ernie, the Kunhardts, Marlon, anyone I could think of. I called Rome and London and Ireland and Hollywood. Nobody knew much. Someone thought it was cancer. They would try to find out and call me back. I called Irwin down the road. No answer. I tried to stay off the phone so people could call me back. I was weeping inconsolably. I didn't know what to do. I drank as much whiskey as I could, hoping to pass out. I called my parents and, between sobs, told them the little I knew. I was incoherent, and said I'd sleep awhile and call them back. I put my head down on the kitchen table. Harry couldn't be dead. If he were ill, he would certainly have written and told me, or telephoned . . . where was Beautiful Watch? . . .

I woke a few hours later and called the Agers, bleak and desperate for a comforting word. They each picked up a bedside phone. I'd forgotten how early it was in California.

"I loved Harry Craig. He was a wonderful man," Milton said, and I had been so needful of hearing these words, from this man, that when they came I felt as if cool water had been splashed across my burning face. Then he said, "But Harry will have a lot to answer for."

"What do you mean?"

"His father was a clergyman, wasn't he?"

Surely Harry's father could have been no stricter a moralist than my own.

Cecelia cut in. "Shana, I've been thinking about Harry all night since you called. I haven't slept . . ."

"I'll let you talk to your mother now, darling," Milton said and hung up his phone.

"He was so . . . so *unusual*," Cecelia continued, her voice thick with grief. "I've been trying hard to sum him up, in a single sentence, and I think I've found it."

I knew she too had loved Harry, and was overcome by a desperate need for her mystic, healing insight. I pressed the phone to my ear so hard it hurt. My other hand was clamped as tightly to the edge of the kitchen counter as that of a drowning person clinging to a lifeboat.

"What's the sentence?"

"He never quite made it."

I felt my fingers begin to slip.

Harry had looked thinner in London, but I'd had no idea he was ill. I think now that he may already have known or suspected his cancer, but because of his lifelong avoidance of doctors, his "fear of catching hypochondria" as he put it, he was depending not on modern medicine but on Yeats and Catullus, using them as magic talismans to hold off the crab. I believed too that I had helped kill him by administering so massive a dose of rejection.

The position of a mistress — more accurately, a hysterically grieving ex-mistress — turned out to be extremely difficult. I found out when and where Harry was to be buried — in the family plot in Dublin's Mt. Jerome cemetery — and tried to send flowers.

"Oh, Mrs. Alexander, not *Ireland!*" wailed the clerk. The country was in the midst of another bank strike, and a telephone strike as well, making floral delivery impossible.

Eventually I learned that over the summer Harry complained he'd hurt his back in a taxi. By the time he got to the hospital, the cancer had already spread from his lungs to his back and brain. Nothing could be done but give morphine, and wait. It took six weeks. He played chess with his twin brother until the next to last day. "Dick, I'm going before the firing squad," he'd said, so Dick was certain Harry knew. He died three days after his fifty-seventh birthday.

I understood but couldn't believe. How could he have died without getting in touch with me! My mind kept returning to Beautiful Watch, which I knew must have been at his bedside. I went a bit crazy. Harry's death seemed to precipitate a sort of slow-burning nervous breakdown, like the slow-burning reaction in an atomic pile as they pull out the cadmium rods. I stayed drunk for a few weeks. To hear Harry's voice, I played again, for the first time in years, the tapes we'd made just before leaving California of Harry and Milton doing the BBC-style program of Milton's songs. Then, somehow, I lost the tapes. I tore the house apart; the tapes were gone. All I could ever find was Harry's careful, handwritten notes in which they had been wrapped.

Kathy and Muffin were in the house . . . she must have come home for Thanksgiving . . . and visitors wandered in and out . . . I don't remember much. My grief was consuming, oceanic, wildly out of proportion to what Harry Craig was by then in my life. I couldn't understand the enormity of it. Later, two shrinks offered the same explanation. They said that heretofore I had always been able to get Harry back when I wanted. But death was farther away than Rome, a place I couldn't call him back from. I didn't, and don't, agree. I think it was some terminal eruption of the kinds of volcanic emotions Harry used to arouse in me. I had never felt them before we met, and when he died I knew I would not feel them again.

Some months later Dick Craig came to visit me in Long Island. He brought me a bronze medallion he'd had an artist cast for those most dear to Harry, only six copies in all. On one side was Harry's portrait in bas relief with his dates. On the other was an architectural shape encompassing three towers: Trinity College, Dublin; the Campidoglio in Rome; and a classic muezzin's tower to represent Harry's deep knowledge of Islam. Engraved behind the towers was a small stanza of Yeats:

> For the good are always the merry,
> Save by an evil chance,
> And the merry love the fiddle,
> And the merry love to dance.

I keep the medal among the family pictures on my bureau, the same early American chest of drawers which once stood near Cecelia's bed in the magic apartment, its chaste flagon of New Mown Hay on top. The medal is propped against my remaining bit of blue hair ribbon, alongside the corroded mirror to remind me of the vanity of women.

What got me through the few months after Harry's death were the nightly phone calls to Milton. At first we talked mostly about Harry, and about the meaning of love and the ways it worked on people, and these long conversations began to sustain me. The calls were easy to make. It was three hours earlier in California, and my father was a night owl anyway, with few other demands on his time. After a while, to justify my nightly need to talk, the conversations also became interviews for our Tin Pan Alley book.

In all the five years I'd struggled with Patty, Milton had never once said, "Hurry up! Finish that thing and let's get started on *our* book. I'm getting old!" Nor had such a thought occurred to me. I'd never had his — and Harry's — acute sense of the inevitability of death, nor felt time's winged chariot at my back. I knew I was exactly like Cecelia in this regard.

Milton had stunned me one day that summer by saying, in response to some offhand comment about my misspent life, "What are you worrying about *that* for? Your life is three-quarters over already." It *was*?

But always our nighttime conversations circled back to love and its meaning. In them, we were just two people talking about love and loss. The conventional formalities of parent and child had burnt away in the fires of grief.

In the course of these talks, which I taped as interviews for our book, I learned some fundamental things about the music business, and about my father's own life.

>   Ma: Patrick O'Higgins called. He said he spent a couple
>   of hours with you. And then . . . he started to gossip. He
>   thought you were drinking too much.

Sa: Drinking! I was so drunk I could hardly see at that point.

Mu: Goddammit, what kind of a friend is that! Son of a bitch! You have reason to drink. You're not a drunkard.

Sa: Of course not . . . I was drinking as much as I could to try to get drunk, but it didn't work. But . . . as Patrick told me he was not drinking at the time, I must have seemed excessively drunk to him.

Ma: It's a mental reaction. You want to get yourself into a different mood, whether you take whiskey, or whether you take cocaine or marijuana. This is me talking. A guy who didn't study psychiatry. It's because you've become sorry for yourself. You're lonesome. You've got no one to talk to. You've got no one to listen to. You've got not too many people to do things for. You're a little higher cut than the people around you, and you lower yourself to their level. Why? Because you want to be a nice person, be known as a cute person. Everybody loves you, fer chrissakes! You have the nature of a politician.

Sa: (laughing) What a funny thing to say, Milton.

Ma: Somewhere, you've gotta toughen up . . .

Sa: I have toughened up, sweetheart.

Ma: . . . and you have to do it yourself. I'm your father. I wouldn't dare say to you, "Cut out the drinking, Shana." I couldn't be like that to you. A person who's done the great things you have done, and who's past fifty! How could I do that? You've gotta see it yourself. Could my parents do it for me? I said no, no, no to every goddamn thing they suggested!

Sa: (laughing) I love you, darling. I'll be there soon, you know. . . . Listen, darling, the only reason that I was drinking is that I've been grieving over Harry. And when you have a lot of pain you drink, you know.

Ma: You were grieving about it. But you can't make any sense out of it, don't you see? What did you let the guy go for?

Sa: I didn't have a — he always stayed married. I couldn't get him.

Ma: He didn't want to marry you?

Sa: No, it was more that his wife wouldn't let him go . . .

Ma: Oh well, the hell with it.

Sa: To hell with it. *I* let him go.

Ma: In the first place, you are now old enough to know what love is. Love has nothing to do with being married. The purpose of marriage is that you shall get the property that you're entitled to, and the children will get the property they're entitled to.

Sa: That's right, darling. And he didn't have any property, so it didn't make any difference. I didn't have any either . . .

Ma: You're not a sloppy girl. You're not a pushover where all they do is give you a drink, take you up to the house . . .

Sa: No. I loved Harry. You know that.

Ma: . . . But you must . . . spare yourself, so you'll live longer; so you'll write greater things. So you'll keep on writing more. Because you can't retire and run a garden . . . You haven't got any man working for you. I feel sorry for you.

Sa: I don't feel sorry for myself, because I . . .

Ma: Oh, yes you do.

Sa: No, I don't. Really, Milton. I used to, sweetheart . . .

Ma: You cry . . .

Sa: I do not!

Ma: You don't show it. You're like me. I've never seen you cry in public. You've never seen me cry in public. But I grieve over many things. . . . The point is to get the right philosophy. Get it from yourself. You don't need any headshrinker, unless you do have something that's blocking you that goes way back to your childhood, your first marriage. Or your second marriage.

Sa: I used to have it. But it's all gone. I don't have anything that's blocking me. I'm very strong, very clear. I have a right to grieve about Harry, and I have a right to have some drinks. And in the morning I work. And I've written a marvelous book. And it's finished now, you know. Almost finished, and . . .

Ma: This is far from your last book.

Sa: That's what Maya told me. She said: "You have fifty books in you."

Ma: The point is this — *you mustn't be like me.* I became

so goddamn sonofabitch mad at the whole world. I'd say,
These guys are goddamn crooks! They can't play anything but
in the key of C! They can't read at all! And *I* have to play a piano copy that I've worked at, the knack of which I've acquired.
I have to play for an idiot like Ben Bornstein! The sonofabitch
can't play it, so it shouldn't be published that way! So I had to
put out songs with simple little arrangements. Lacking the
proper syncopation. Because *he* couldn't play it!

In the midst of one such rambling, late-night conversation Milton
suddenly said, "Do you want to know, Shana, what the most important
thing is that ever happened to me in my whole life?"

"What?"

I expected some new revelation about his career. But it wasn't a
song, and it was nothing about his family either. It was something that
had happened a year after he'd married Cecelia and was at the height of
his success. One day Mr. Simons, Rayna's father, was in Manhattan and
dropped by Milton's office at Ager, Yellen & Bornstein.

"You were right, Milton," Mr. Simons had told my father that day.
"I'm so sorry Rayna didn't marry you."

Between Thanksgiving and Christmas Kathy called to say she would like
to invite a boy from George School to spend a couple of days with us
before she flew out to California to join Dad and Kelly for the holidays.
If he wasn't her first boyfriend, he was the first one I had met, a fine-
looking, long-haired, mannerly young man. That he adored her was obvious. Late one snowy afternoon the three of us were sitting on the floor
in front of the fireplace, and when Kathy stepped out of the room, he
exclaimed, "Isn't her hair beautiful? Look how it shines in the firelight!"
My heart turned over. I was so happy to be included, embraced in their
love, and not stiff-armed, slunk past, and lied to — which is the way I
would have treated my mother under similar circumstances. I was happy
that Kathy was at last using the downstairs suite I'd wanted her to have.

For long periods, they didn't come out. When they did, they looked dreamy-eyed, lost. The boy's great-grandfather was a famous American composer of the post–Civil War period, and that weekend the three of us sang all his songs, from the *Sandbag*. We cooked our own food and saw no one else and I felt honored and thrilled to be a part of their romantic few days.

I had now been on *60 Minutes* more than four years, and wanted out. "You *can't* quit the top show in television!" friends said. But each week's ninety seconds, now often cut to sixty, took me a full four days to prepare. For Jack, the most successful syndicated columnist of his day, it was easier. His opinions appeared three times a week in well over three hundred newspapers coast to coast. His brain and typewriter were well oiled and in peak working condition. For me, the scramble to research, think out, and write a weekly position on farm price supports, or U.S. foreign policy in the Middle East, was a staggering task. What's more, as I used to tell lecture audiences, Jack didn't have to do any research as he had made up his mind on all issues thirty years ago.

Finally, Kilpo was a professional conservative, and his TV role a natural fit. But I was not a liberal, not essentially political at all. I was a part-radical, part-conservative oddity, and my role as the CBS house liberal was increasingly uncomfortable. Being a trick dog ultimately grows tedious, unless the rewards are great. Ours remained constant at $600 a week apiece, without medical or any other benefits, right up until the day I quit, by which time our show had been number one for some time, and I calculated that an advertiser paid the network $245,000 for a three-minute spot like ours.

February 1, 1979, was the Agers' fifty-sixth wedding anniversary, and I sent flowers. This sort of sentimentality meant even less to my mother than to my father, but had come to mean a lot to me. I telephoned early that evening, and Cecelia said, "He's finally moved out!"

What had happened was this. For the past few years, Milton had been talking about a reworked deal he intended to sculpt with Warner Brothers Music, the company to which he had sold Ager, Yellen & Bornstein, Inc., some forty years before. Now he was going to sell the songs themselves. He thought he could sweeten the pot, as he put it, and thereby up the total price, if he added some new songs to the old list. Though he didn't say so, my father was making a last attempt to provide for Cecelia after his death.

Ten original songs, words and music by Milton Ager, no collaborators, was what he planned. He had been revising a few of these songs for a couple of decades or more, and the lyrics in all their infinite variations had become achingly familiar to Cecelia, Laurel, and me. But all ten tunes were gloriously vigorous and melodic. They did not in the least seem to be the work of a faltering artist, of an old man, and their titles might be taken as a window into what was on his mind: "Don't Tell Me Your Troubles (And I Won't Tell You Mine)," "(Life Is a) Winding Road," "All Ashore," "Happy Go Lucky Little Birds (Keep Quiet!)," "But What of It?," "Don't Fool around with the Moon," "It Was Raining, I Remember," "This I Love above All." There was also a children's song, "Willy, the Woolly Bear," and a rousing, muscular waltz, "Just . . . One . . . Girl at a Time."

All ten had yet to be fully set down on paper. Arranging and orchestration were still the aspects of composition that he most enjoyed, but it is work which takes time and space and intense concentration. For this undertaking he decided he needed a proper workplace, a haven from interruption by phones, by chambermaids, and—particularly—by his wife.

Most tenants in their building were elderly retired people. Occasionally an ambulance arrived, and a vacancy occurred. The last time that had happened, Milton had quietly snapped up the space, and arranged for piano movers to push a rented upright into the empty ground-floor apartment. Cecelia had been unaware of all this until that very morning when, after having shaved and dressed, Milton emerged from his room and told her it was now his intention to go downstairs and get some work done. Picking up his silver-topped stick, he had walked carefully down the single flight of paint-peeling steps and disappeared.

Although normally he was hungry by five-thirty, that evening he was still not back upstairs by Walter Cronkite time.

"He's still down there!" Cecelia chortled again. "In his 'studio'!"

Her glee surprised and somewhat disconcerted me. But she, confident he would be back upstairs in an hour or two, was exultant. The unexpected joy of once, just once, not having to go out to dinner at five-thirty P.M., an hour she regarded as late afternoon, merely in deference to the extremely finicky demands of another person's belly, had put her into high spirits.

"But tell me, darling, how are *you?*" she asked me now on the phone. "Is anything *happening?*"

"Happening," I had recently come to understand, was Cecelia's code word, or euphemism, for *men.* "Are there any interesting new men in your life, or are you still hung up on Harry?" is what she was asking. Only a couple of years back, she would never have indicated the least interest in how my life with men was going. But I was brought up short by another word she had used: *darling.* It was only the second time she had called me that, the first having been twenty years ago, just before I was taken upstairs to surgery. Hearing it this time made me feel that Cecelia might be going soft, and I didn't like the idea.

February in Long Island at the beach is bleak and drear. Before the month ended I was back in California treating myself to a little vacation. I stayed with Maya Angelou and her husband, Paul de Feu, in their house in Pacific Palisades. When it was time for me to head for the airport, with a stop at the Agers' en route, Paul insisted on driving me. I did not know I was seeing my father for the last time.

A maid was vacuuming the little living room, and Milton was with Cecelia in her room, for the first time in my memory. She looked tired and he seemed shrunken. He sat at her desk wrapped in the pink mohair Irish blanket Harry and I had bought Cecelia, looking chilly, cranky, and old. Recently he had had a pacemaker implanted in his chest, and ever since he'd complained he couldn't sleep and couldn't work. "They've put in a goddamn metronome!" he fumed.

Paul, an athlete, sized up the situation, went into Milton's room, found a putter, and came back into Cecelia's room acting goofy and pretending he didn't know how to hold it. Soon Milton felt compelled to show him the proper grip. Now Paul pretended he didn't know how to putt. Again Milton had to get up and show him. They moved back into the slightly roomier living room, and Cecelia and I followed, both of us teary-eyed and amazed. Paul was slowly bringing Milton back to life.

Now he started asking him how he had written each of his big hits. Milton answered patiently and, knowing these answers well, I stopped listening and began to chat with Cecelia.

Suddenly I heard my father, the Professor, explaining patiently, "All songwriters steal, Paul. But some of us only steal from the best."

Then he glanced over at me to be sure I was listening, and said, "For example, I stole 'Happy Days Are Here Again' from César Franck." Blue eyes twinkled right at me. "But they'll never find it!"

CHAPTER FOURTEEN

WORLD OF LIES

Milton's heart was failing, and Cecelia had several times driven him to a small nearby hospital. Early one morning she found him on the floor and called an ambulance. Laurel and Victor soon arrived at the hospital, and once the nurses had got Milton settled in, Cecelia went across the street with her brother and daughter for a bite of lunch. When they returned, the hospital would not let them into Milton's room.

Like the man himself, my father's departure was orderly but not ordinary. The unusual precision which characterized his speech, his golf swing, and his wide-ranging mind also marked the exquisite timing of his exit. He even managed to give it a final fillip, a little something extra which showbiz old-timers call the *Getavasia*, the getaway. James Cagney, who spoke Yiddish, had once explained the term to me during an interview, springing suddenly to his feet and executing a swift ruffle and flourish of intricate footwork on polished floor. Back when Cagney was a specialty dancer in vaudeville, he'd ended his act with this. "Just as you're going offstage, you give them something special to remember you by."

Milton's *Getavasia* was a stunner. He made his final exit on Sunday, May 6, 1979, which happened to be the exact publication date of *Anyone's Daughter*. He died at the very hour when friends and I were sitting under the wisteria in Gloria Jones's garden drinking wine and toasting my first book reviews. After this I told them some stories about my parents and, off-key but *con brio*, sang them a couple of Milton's songs.

I drove home carefully through the green-gold primavera landscape after that first glorious al fresco lunch of the new season, head reeling and mind sparking with wine and song and diffusions of love. Back in my sun-dappled kitchen, alone with Muffin, I telephoned the Agers, and then my sister. When I got no answer at either place, I called Victor's son Larry, a specialist in geriatric medicine who had been helping to advise on my parents' health problems. When Larry's telephone gave a busy signal I knew, knew absolutely, what that business must be. I stayed seated at the kitchen table watching the meadow of waving grasses below streamers of bright cloud and waiting for the telephone call I knew was coming.

By managing to die on this precise day, my father seemed to be offering me a last piece of advice: Do not take either of this day's events too hard. Find their balance and proportion. Let the one counterbalance the other. Once, years before, at dinner in some restaurant, conversation had flagged, and into the momentary silence Milton had flicked a characteristic dart. "Somebody say something," he'd prompted. "I'm a countertalker."

That he was, and one of the best, and he'd taught me to be one too. One of the few criticisms he ever offered me had occurred when I first appeared on *60 Minutes*. Milton telephoned afterwards and said he liked the content of my remarks, but not the delivery. "Why do you drop your voice that way at the end of a sentence? You sound like a lousy trumpet player."

"Huh?"

"Don't run out of breath like that!"

Now he had run out of breath, and the long adventure which had begun so auspiciously for both of us when I was born on his birthday, thereby becoming my own father's birthday present, was over. The special father-daughter balancing act which seemed in my egocentrism to have begun with my birth was now counterpointed by his death, and my book, *Anyone's Daughter*, only made me feel with an ache that I wasn't.

The events of the following week were surreal. Laurel and Cecelia called me as soon as they got home from the hospital. Milton had left written instructions for immediate cremation, and this was accomplished on the afternoon of his death. But he had not left any word regarding a service of any kind. This to us was quintessential Milton — his wishes very firm in one area, and in the other modest to the point of invisibility. *No service at all?* Could that really be what he wanted? A man who had been "getting my affairs in order" every day for twenty-five years?

I listened.

"If you wish to, go ahead."

"If you wish to, go ahead."

I could hear his firm baritone quite clearly — the pregnant pause after "wish to," the drop-off at the end of the phrase, instructing his family of females how to manage his death, as he had done in so many other matters. "You're an adult. I'm not going to tell you what to do." That's how he'd always begun his opinions, how he'd always framed and styled his advice. In the ear of my mind, I could hear his voice saying the words aloud. I can hear it now.

So that Sunday evening on the telephone, Cecelia and Laurel and I tried to decide what he would have wanted, and because we knew him so well, and because he was such a consistent man, this was not too terribly difficult, though the obstacles — chiefly my looming book tour — seemed alpine at the time.

Here is what we decided. As soon as we hung up, I would notify *The New York Times* and supply details for the obituary. We also decided that I should go ahead with the mammoth, seventeen-city, eight-week publicity tour my publishers had arranged. We were a showbiz family, we kept telling one another, and the tour was already booked, so I might as well try to do it. That's what Milton would have wanted.

A truly backbreaking schedule was set to begin at seven A.M. Tuesday with my appearance live on the *Today* show, followed later that same day by taped appearances on the Merv Griffin and William Buckley shows, plus three or four radio and press interviews. It went on at this pace every day, with stops in Chicago and Texas, leading up to a Los Angeles arrival the following Sunday, Mother's Day, which launched several more weeks of promotion up and down the West Coast from San Diego to Seattle. After that, Denver and Atlanta and God knows where else. The Viking people figured the world had forgotten all about Patty Hearst by now, five years after the event. Unless someone — namely, me — went around the country forcibly flogging the old story back to life, they were unlikely to sell many books.

As I contemplated running this mad marathon in the wake of my father's death, the critical matter to me was that I not break down and weep in public. Hearing even one bar of Milton's music, I knew, was certain to dissolve me into a Francis Bacon–like smear of tears and snot.

"Couldn't you get them to promise not to mention Milton, and not to play anything?" said Laurel.

"All *they* care about is the book," said Cecelia.

We were all too stunned by grief to realize the Faustian bargain we were setting up. If the TV hosts and book people would promise not to mention the only thing in the world I now cared about, I would promise to go all over America talking with hearty enthusiasm about something I suddenly didn't care about at all.

The reviews so far had been wonderful; the book was the biggest triumph of my life. But I would be unable to enjoy it. Furthermore, I had just promised my mother and sister — two women about whom I sometimes had ambivalent feelings — not to shed one public tear over the death of the person I had loved most in all the world. I needed to weep for him now, and I believe he needed me to weep, and that was the very thing I was arranging not to do. Not to weep for my father's death would be the biggest lie of my life.

Monday morning the *Times* published a lengthy obituary, complete with a handsome photograph taken in 1935 which none of us had ever seen. That afternoon friends drove me to Manhattan, and while we were on the road the people at Viking began rejiggering the tour dates so that I could get to Los Angeles by Thursday night or Friday morning.

By the time I reached the Delmonico Monday evening and again called California, Laurel reported that they had now decided they did want to have some sort of gathering, if not precisely a service, as soon as I could get there. But we had a problem: whom could we get to play the piano? Milton had always been the one who played the piano at every family gathering, at every drop of a hat, in fact, for as long as any of us had known him.

Well, surely somewhere in Southern California another piano player could be found, I said with impeccable logic. We were all three in a state of shock but talking quite rationally.

"Yes, but somebody else wouldn't know Milton's *style*," Cecelia said firmly.

"And where could we find him the *music?*" Laurel said. "And the *place?*"

There was a songbook in my piano bench back in Long Island, I said, something like *25 Popular Favorites through the Years*, which contained most of Milton's big hits. Perhaps we could send somebody out there to get it, and actually put the precious thing in my hands before I left New York tomorrow. "Yes, somebody on a motorcycle," said Laurel.

"That's it! A motorcycle!" I burbled. We were all half out of our minds, and I was exhausted from playing six shows a day, like a demented vaudevillian, and phoning California in between.

People were being very kind. Somebody actually found a motorcyclist. Laurel found and rented a chapel behind the Westwood Movie Theater in a cemetery that she referred to as "the Marilyn Monroe place." We knew where she meant. And somebody else found a piano player named Ben Oakland.

"Who the hell is Ben Oakland?" said Cecelia in the next call.

At some point after this I was packing for Chicago, and again talking to Cecelia and Laurel on the phone, when somebody dropped a manila envelope into my lap — the songbook! "Don't worry, at least we've got the music!" I shouted, and began leafing through the pages as we discussed the other details. Most of Milton's big hits were there: "Happy Days Are Here Again," "Ain't She Sweet?," "I Wonder What's Become of Sally?," "Hard-Hearted Hannah," "Trust in Me," and a half dozen more. Then the book fell open to someone else's song, "The Java Jive," and at the top of the page, under the title, I spotted the magic words "Ben Oakland."

"Hey! Here's Ben Oakland!" I exclaimed. "He's the guy who wrote 'The Java Jive.' You know," I sang off-key into the phone, "'I love coffee, I love tea. I love the Java Jive and it loves me.'"

There was a split-second silence. Then Cecelia sang back softly, almost gaily, "A cup-a-cup-a-cup-a-cup-a-cup," and we knew that everything was probably going to work out all right.

The long black car picked us all up at the Agers' apartment to drive to Milton's memorial service. It was three-thirty Friday afternoon, five days after his death. My mother was quiet and composed, smaller than I remembered. Laurel looked tired. Hannah had come from high school, and Kathy had flown from college and met me two days ago in Chicago. We had finally arrived in Los Angeles that morning.

The car stopped and the five of us, Cecelia and Laurel and Hannah and Kathy and I, walked through a rose garden to a modern chapel, lots of glass, lots of people, many familiar faces, many more flowers inside. Wray was already there, rigging something so we would have a tape of the service. I was astounded by all that Laurel had done. Up front, a pianist was playing softly. Ben Oakland. It was "Ain't She Sweet?," played at half tempo, in an old-fashioned, multi-arpeggio'd style, as people were finding their seats. Then the seven gong notes of "Happy Days Are Here Again" boomed out, like church music.

The taste and impromptu style of the whole thing seemed to me absolutely perfect. People showed up for Milton's memorial whom Cecelia had thought never to see again, like Jed Harris, and there were a few people Milton *hoped* never to see again, old Friars like George Jessel. It turned out that Ben Oakland had come out of a hospital bed to play for Milton, and that he had been found through the good offices of George Jessel, a man Milton had cordially loathed for sixty years, and that Jessel's price for Oakland was that he, Jessel, be allowed to give Milton's eulogy.

A young rabbi said a few words, read a passage from Ecclesiastes, and sat down.

Jessel got up to speak first, ancient military decorations dripping from his lapel, and Cecelia and Laurel and I smiled and squeezed hands, glad that Milton couldn't hear him. Maya and Tommy Thompson came next.

"I speak of Milton Ager as a chosen daughter," said Maya. "I chose him. He's been an uncle and father and friend to me. And an inspiration. . . ."

Steve Rubenstein, Victor's youngest son, sang "Willy, the Woolly Bear," a song about a caterpillar that turns into a butterfly which Milton had written long ago for all the children in the family.

Laurel, who was in charge of arrangements, had been saying all week that she wanted me to speak. I'd told her that I couldn't possibly handle it. I had my rights, too, and one of them was not to have to cry in public. She remained insistent. "I'm *bereaved!*" I'd shouted at her when we finally met in the Agers' apartment.

"You *have* to speak," she'd said, lowering her voice just like Cecelia. There was no appeal. So finally I just got up and did it ad lib.

I come here from a very surreal experience. I couldn't get here until this morning, because I had written a book called *Anyone's Daughter*, and had to make some public appearances. And wherever I went . . . I wanted to say, "I am *not* just anyone's daughter. My sister Laurel is *not* anyone's daughter. Cecelia is not *anyone's* wife. Hannah is not *anyone's* granddaughter. And Kathy, who made a tremendous effort to get here, and really got *us* here, is not anyone's granddaughter." . . . [And so] I didn't have time to prepare remarks, which would have taken me a whole lifetime anyhow.

But Milton had the most *surprising mind* of anyone I've ever known . . . something was *going on* in his mind all the time. And you never could tell what it was going to be. I remember one night last February at Maya's house, Maya was cooking dinner. There was no furniture to sit on. Your house was new, Maya. So Milton was sitting on a little carpeted step, waiting for dinner. And when dinner was ready, I said, "Milton, do you mind if I help you up?"

He said, "Why not? I helped you enough times."

. . . Milton loved the mind. And he loved ideas. He loved the family above all things. . . . He loved words, and therefore, he particularly loved . . . Ireland. I thought I was Irish for a long time, because we were raised in Dinty Moore's restaurant. And when I got to Ireland, I discovered that I was at least half right. [In the background on the tape, Cecelia's laughter is quite audible.]

His mind was so surprising, so alert, and so interesting, that I always took notes of what he said, especially in the last years, because I was writing a book about him . . . and I thought I would just tell you the last extraordinary conversation I had with him, the day before he died. I called, and he said, "Shana, I never followed the Jew part in me, the Oriental part. I always more followed the German line."

I said, "What do you mean by that?"

And he said, "Irving Berlin went with the Russians. And George Gershwin went with the Russians. But my mind" — and he was speaking of his philosophic mind, as well as his musical taste — "my mind is more Germanic than Russian. But the Russian has a little touch of the Oriental in it, like Rimsky-Korsakov. And I *liked him!*"

That was a musical conversation, which I couldn't fully understand. But then he said, "As far as I'm concerned, the line that I took in my life was the correct one. Always take the attitude that the way you have proceeded is the right one. I always did. I've been narrow. But I find that I proceed better if I go on the theory 'No, I don't want to change.'"

I said to him, "Milton, have you changed much?"

He said, "Fundamentally, no. I'm a basic nonbeliever."

But he meant that in a special way.

He said, "I've always been stubborn, and narrow."

He said, "I don't let them change me."

He said, "My authority is myself."

Cecelia was smiling approvingly as I returned to my front-row seat beside her, and I spotted Lee Gershwin already on her feet and making her way up the aisle toward us, dragging a young man by the hand. "Celia," she said, ignoring the rest of us, "you can't read music. So I'm lending you Michael. This is Michael. He knows how to catalogue Milton's manuscripts for the Library of Congress."

Michael was Michael Feinstein, Ira Gershwin's secretary, a slender, shy-looking youth who turned out to know something much more important: how to help Cecelia in her early grief. Michael came to see Cecelia that weekend, and came nearly every day after that at first, then two or three times a week. He not only catalogued the stacks of music he found in Milton's room, stuffed in the drawers of his child-size desk, and in the wardrobe trunk. He played Milton's songs for Cecelia by the hour, reading the ones he didn't know from the green books, and sat and talked to her, and asked her many questions about the music and about the man who had written it. She soon adored this engaging young man with lots of curly dark hair and large green-blue eyes. He might even have seemed to her some sort of reincarnation of the very young Milton, as in a way he did to me, or perhaps the son she'd never had.

The book tour continued relentlessly. Someone had arranged a limo to take me around to interviews and TV spots in Los Angeles during the weekend, and I brought Cecelia with me, to give her something to do. The young black driver understood the situation — Milton's death had been widely publicized — and told her that after I left he would be her private chauffeur and take her shopping or wherever she needed to go, no charge; he wouldn't tell his company.

Tuesday evening I had to go back on the road. Cecelia rode out to the airport with me, sitting in silence for a while. Then I felt her silk-soft hand reach out and take mine in the darkness.

"Oh, Shana. Don't ever be alone. It's so terrible," she said, sounding pathetic, sad, real, and very un-Cecelia-like.

"That's what I've been trying to tell you, ever since Harry died," I replied, sounding very Cecelia-like indeed.

A few weeks later her favorite nephew, Steve Rubenstein, a columnist on the *San Francisco Chronicle*, sought to distract Cecelia from her awful aloneness by inviting her up to address his journalism class at the University of California. He sent me a tape, and what I heard in her brief remarks, and in the long question period that followed, was my mother's rigid control, her absolute determination to avoid any reference to the fact that her husband had died less than a month before, though it was quite clear from the questions that Steve had already told the class.

What Laurel had referred to as "the Marilyn Monroe place" is a small Westwood cemetery off Wilshire Boulevard, entirely hidden by high-rise buildings. Most people are immured in crypts in marble walls, but it also has an informal garden where bronze markers are set flat on the ground amid grass and flowers. Laurel managed to secure a space near a bench underneath a flowering tree, and in due course Milton's bronze plaque appeared there. It has nothing on it but his name and dates, and a small music staff on which a few notes appear:

No words accompany the bronze notes. You have to stand there and look down and hum to get the message. But they're very easy notes, and most anybody recognizes that he has just hummed the opening strain of "Happy Days Are Here Again." What a nice touch! Laurel thought this up during the period Cecelia was visiting her nephew in San Francisco, and I was still staggering through my mindless book tour.

Eight long weeks later, I finally got home. I had told everybody not to play Milton's songs so I wouldn't cry in public, and now that I was home and free to cry, I couldn't. All the tears had dried up on the road. And so many tears had been shed for Harry, it was possible I had no more. "After the first death, there is no other," Dylan Thomas said.

Laurel was the executor of Milton's estate. Boxes began arriving from California, things she'd found while clearing out the last Bekins storeroom and thought might be useful for a book, if I ever got around to writing one. Most of the contents were unsurprising: some army band arrangements Milton had made during World War I; a few early tunes sketched in a penciled notebook; a 1932 check for $25 from George Gershwin to Milton for a box of cigars; a June 1976 slangy letter from lyricist and ASCAP board member Sammy Cahn saying that he was organizing the Songwriters Hall of Fame in Times Square. One wall was to be dedicated to THE SONGMAKERS! and Milton's name could be on the wall for a minimum donation (tax deductible) of $1000. Milton sent a check that day. "What a very elegant man you are!" Cahn wrote back, and requested "an 8×10 head shot of yourself and the five or six songs you want to be remembered for."

"He means to say *titles*," the Little Professor had scribbled on Cahn's letter, and on the envelope had scrawled, "Ev'rything Is Peaches down in Georgia (first hit), I'm Nobody's Baby, A Young Man's Fancy, I Wonder What's Become of Sally?, Ain't She Sweet?, Happy Days Are Here Again, Trust in Me."

Cecelia's boxes contained several well-aged gifts of my needlework, still in their original wrappings, and a few freelance magazine articles and scraps of correspondence. A 1948 note from John Huston said, "Your review of 'Treasure' . . . is by far the finest review of a motion picture or of a play that I have ever read in a newspaper." This was not hyperbole; here is a brief excerpt:

> *The Treasure of the Sierra Madre* has greatness; it towers over movies like the Matterhorn, and when the exhilaration from first sight of it subsides, one thinks about it, seeking to separate the component parts that together have created its overwhelming impact. And thinking about this, one finds that one thinks in terms of natural forces, and finally one thinks that its knowledge and acceptance of Nature — human, and God's own creation — is the secret of its might. . . .
>
> The main theme and its contrapuntal embellishment is presented, regarded and photographed directly, explicitly, unsentimentally. . . .
>
> Of course it is magnificently acted, because it is magnificently directed. But out of its vivid gallery emerge two unforgettable, almost epic men: Walter Huston's old prospector, and Alfonso Bedoya's Mexican bandit. They were able to sense fully what John Huston was after and to give it to him, for they are all men of the same size.

In the same box was a fragment of a play Cecelia had begun writing with Beatrice Kaufman in the early forties about a bitter woman trapped in a sterile marriage.

In another box was a small, female leather and canvas golf bag, only

slightly scuffed, probably one Milton had given her, and Cecelia's ukelele, orange silk ribbons still tied to the neck. The Coed must have
brought this along with her to New York in 1921, at around the time she
bobbed her hair, bound her breasts, learned to do the Charleston, and
started smoking Chesterfields. It helped me see her as the saucy little
flapper she must have been. In the bottom of this box was a smaller
version of the torn photograph I'd once seen of fifteen-year-old Cecelia
going off to college wearing a white sailor dress and Alice in Wonderland
hairdo. As for the "bobby socks" she'd once mentioned, these were knee-
length or higher, worn under a pair of hideous, then fashionable mary
jane shoes which had not just one but five or six straps up each leg that
had to be closed with a button hook. The picture suggested why Cecelia
had never allowed me to have the patent leather shoes I'd longed for.
Hers looked like leg irons in a medieval torture chamber.

But the most amazing box, still tied in its original Visigoth twine,
contained a handsome, two-volume edition of Nicolas Rimsky-
Korsakov's *Principes d'orchestration*, published in Paris in 1914 and
bound in dark green watered silk. "Rimsky-Korsakov wrote the book on
orchestration" is a music critics' cliché, and here it was — the actual
book! Bits of music appear on every page to illustrate the French text.
Milton could not possibly have read this work, much as he must have
longed to, because he didn't know any French.

Alongside the *Principes* was a package neatly wrapped in brown paper for fifty years. It contained eight lined composition notebooks written in pencil in Cecelia's unmistakable large, strong hand. My
university-educated, French-speaking, but musically illiterate mother
had painstakingly translated and copied out for Milton the entire damned
two volumes. She must have done it after their marriage; it looked like a
couple of years' work, and certainly could never have been completed
during their four-month courtship. Talk about a labor of love! Only a
young woman positively deliquescent with passion could ever have done
such a thing. Yet she had despised him! Was I not lifelong witness?

* * *

More than a decade would pass before I solved Milton's last puzzle, the riddle of César Franck. "But they'll never find it!" he had said, and for eleven years I couldn't, though scarcely for want of trying. The César Franck oeuvre is not large, and someone with a good musical memory, like my friend Adolph Green, can run through every one of Franck's compositions in his head. He did, and came up empty. So did Arthur Gold and Bobby Fizdale and several other friends, including a noted music patroness and board member of the Juilliard School of Music.

It was my conductor friend Charles Darden, a graduate of the Curtis School of Music and today the foremost interpreter of Scott Joplin's work, who finally solved the mystery. Charles dropped by one August afternoon, sat down at Milton's piano with me, and put two pieces of music on the rack: the familiar third movement of Franck's C Minor Symphony arranged for piano, and "Happy Days Are Here Again." Charles plinked a few notes, and saw it almost immediately. My father hadn't been talking about the melody at all. It was Franck's rhythm, his *syncopation,* that Milton had stolen.

The corresponding feature in both compositions, Darden pointed out, is what musicians call the tie-overs. When a note is tied over from last beat of one measure to the first beat of the next, Charles explained, "so that the fourth, weakest beat of a measure is tied to the strongest beat of the next, you *feel* it, but you don't hear it. And that's syncopation. That's what it *is.*" The syncopation was the whole point. It's what gives Milton's simple tune its tremendous *drive* — and is also why I couldn't figure out how to embroider it on the bathrobe.

"Look!" Charles exclaimed, tapping the sheet music with a muscular brown finger. "The whole piece is built on this little tie-over." He was right. Each page was sprinkled with tie-overs, like arched, amused Milton Ager eyebrows looking out at us from Franck's music itself. Charles totted them up. "In the principal theme of the third movement, that device occurs fourteen times!"

I whooped the good news to Laurel on the phone, and a couple of weeks later received a cassette she'd asked Wray to copy from their CD player. Her penciled note was Scotch-taped to the box.

This is Vivaldi Bassoon Concertos. Listen to 3rd movement of 1st concerto on tape, which is Concerto No. 1 in B flat major, "La Notte." See what you hear! XXX
    L.

What I heard was the same seven notes I'd embroidered on Milton's bathrobe and Laurel had put on his bronze plaque, this time played slow and legato and most beautifully lugubrious as only the bassoon can sound.

Milton's death meant I had lost my collaborator, as well as my father. The only older songwriter I knew of was Irving Berlin, ninety-one years old, and a famed recluse. Mary Ellin told me where to write, and the next thing I knew my phone was ringing.

"Hello, Shana? This is Irving! . . . Your father wrote two great hits. Blockbusters! . . . I don't pay too much attention to how many songs you write, or how popular they are. It's the *blockbusters*, the things that last. Milton's 'Happy Days' will be here always.

"But the really *interesting* one was your mother. Your mother can help you enormously."

"Yes, she can. But my mother's not a musician, you see."

"I'm not a musician either. She knows more about Milton than anybody . . . more than *you* do."

"He felt that the arranger was the forgotten man," I said, "that the arranger's story hadn't been told. And that, I think, was the part of himself that he cared most about."

"Oh, no. Look, arrangers always talk about that, but it isn't true. Look, they're a dime a dozen. They know *music*, but they don't know how to write a tune. Milton knew both."

But he kept coming back to Cecelia. "As a matter of fact, I knew your mother much better than Milton. Milton — he was the best-dressed man around . . . but my feeling about Milton. . . . He was a nice guy. But I can only talk about him as a songwriter. And I think that's the thing *you* oughta talk about. You can just say that he was as good a songwriter as we've had."

"Yes, I will. You know, it's very strange to be Cecelia and Milton's daughter. All the time I was young I had a notion they didn't like each other. I was very wrong. They were devoted. But they had separate lives . . ."

"That's because. . . . Listen, there's a damn good book in your mother's life. She was one of the best *Variety* muggs there are. And she should be very much a part of the story . . . not just because she's your mother."

"No. Because it was an interesting family."

"*Very* interesting. . . . He was not only a great songwriter. He was married to a great woman."

Thinking the compliment might cheer Cecelia up a bit, I called and told her what Irving had just said. But she dismissed it. "That's only because of the fight," she said. "When Ellin ran home and told Irving about it, he took *my side*. In fact, he called me and beseeched me to forgive her!"

"It" turned out to be a 1937 episode at John Frederics in which John felt that Ellin Berlin was speaking to him not as a designer but as a mere millinery salesman, and refused to emerge from his workroom. Cecelia frankly thought Ellin had "carried on as if she were Marilyn Miller on a white horse," but nonetheless attempted to make peace. It was too late, however; Ellin was already marching out in a huff.

How strange! I thought, after Cecelia hung up. She had been so clearly *there*. She was actually *in 1937* as she was telling me the story.

Two days later, ten weeks after Milton's death, Cecelia seemingly had a stroke. Laurel was now in the habit of calling her every morning, and one morning when she didn't picked up the phone, Laurel—who was away in Ohio on business—asked Wray to go check on her. He found her on the floor and took her to UCLA hospital. Nothing more was yet known.

Wray met my plane and, en route to dinner at Victor and Florence's house, where Laurel by now was waiting, he brought me to the hospital. Cecelia was in intensive care, lying flat in a bed with the side rails pulled up. Her hair was down, and she wore a little flowered smock, looked sleepy, and said she was happy I'd come. I kissed her and told her to go to sleep and not worry, I'd be back in the morning.

Cecelia had dined at Dorris Johnson's the previous evening and had seemed a bit unsteady, so Nunnally's daughter and her husband had insisted on driving her home and helping her upstairs. During the night she'd fallen out of bed. Doctors suspected a minor stroke, complicated by a touch of pneumonia from having lain all night in only a thin night-gown. But nothing was certain until she was seen by a team of neurologists in the morning.

My plane had been late, and by the time we got to Victor's, everybody had just sat down and begun eating dinner. Hannah was there, and Florence's sister, and a couple of the Rubenstein children.

Victor rose to embrace me. "Don't get up . . ." I began.

"*I'll* get up!"

Laurel was on her feet, swaying a bit. "*I* took care of the *last* one!" she said. "*I* made the chicken soup! *I* drove on the goddamn freeway five hours every day for two years. And you didn't do *one goddamned thing!* Well — *you* can take care of *this one!*"

Silence. Laurel had never in her life spoken a harsh word to me, or to any of us. Everybody was embarrassed but Laurel, who sat down and resumed eating as if nothing unusual had happened.

We finished dinner as speedily as possible, and the Bentleys dropped me off at the Agers' empty apartment about nine o'clock. I faced a choice of bedrooms. Milton's would have been unbearable, so I made myself several stiff drinks and climbed into Cecelia's bed. On her bedside table was her college copy of Plato's *Republic*, some pages still uncut, others annotated in ink in a young, strong hand, and some lines about old age feebly and I thought perhaps recently underlined in pencil. "For unquestionably old age brings us profound repose and freedom from this and other passions."

I awoke before five A.M. Intensive care would not admit me until eight. I tried to think of someone who cared about Cecelia whom I could call at this hour, and decided on Marlon Brando. He had called me from Tahiti and sent flowers when Harry died, and I wanted to bring him up to date in the thanatology department. His secretary answered, and asked me to hold on. "You know the foam that Marlon's always talking about? Well, the foam man's here now, so I have to go out to the pool and get him."

Brando's private crusade to stave off world starvation was well known to me. Years earlier he'd met an inventor who claimed he could grow algae in seawater and process the resultant foam into sufficient protein to feed all mankind, and Marlon had talked a famously Scrooge-like tycoon into bankrolling the project. When I'd complimented the actor on his powers of persuasion, he'd said, "Wasn't hard. All I had to do was rub his hump with yak butter, and suck on his earlobe a little."

His secretary came back to the phone and said, "Marlon can't talk right now. They've drained the swimming pool and he's in there with the foam man. They've got diving suits and helmets on, and big hoses, and they're spraying the foam on each other." He would call me soon, she promised, and sent Cecelia his love.

At the hospital Cecelia looked better, but they still wouldn't let her sit up, or even give her a pillow. I'd started describing Marlon and the foam man and we were both giggling when three grave-looking physicians in white coats appeared and asked me to step out in the hall.

Ten minutes later they joined me. "Your mother is very lucky. The blood clot is small, and located in a part of her brain that should cause no permanent impairment, physical or mental." The one thing we had to fear, they said, was a second, fatal stroke. Indeed, she had no real symptoms of stroke, save for a subtle condition that only a trained neurologist could detect.

"What's that?"

"We call it *Witzelsucht*."

"What's *Witzelsucht*?"

"Inappropriate laughter."

*   *   *

I visited Cecelia every day until she was ready to come home. One swel-tering afternoon I had just returned from the hospital when the phone rang. I would have done anything to take my mind off my troubles, and the unexpected call from the BBC seemed a godsend. They wanted me to team up with Brendan Gill on a double-dome radio show called *Transatlantic Quiz*, in which we'd be paired off against two British poly-maths, John Julius Norwich and Irene Thomas. Lord Norwich, a writer and essayist, was the son of Diana Duff Cooper. Irene, born a Cockney, had sung in the chorus at Covent Garden, and was a perennial British radio favorite who had won the BBC Brain of Britain contest so many times that the network had finally been forced to name her its Brain Emeritus. The questions proved near-incomprehensible, interminable, and tripartite. The program lasted for the next seven years, during which Brendan and I gradually crept up on and finally actually beat our formi-dable opponents, and all the correct answers which I surprised myself and everyone else by getting were based on things I had read in those six books in the Hotel Salisbury.

By the time Cecelia was ready to come home, Laurel had arranged round-the-clock, live-in nurse/companions. I doubted she even remem-bered her outburst at Victor's, and it would have been cruel to remind her, especially as she had been absolutely right. She *had* done all the work. I resolved to try and be much more helpful with Cecelia, and told Laurel I wanted her and the nurse to visit me in Long Island as often as possible, and would provide first-class tickets.

My purpose in doing this was very clear to me, and Laurel's feelings were not my paramount consideration. I had been told that Cecelia might not live long, and I wanted to make absolutely sure that I treated her very well, so that I would have nothing to reproach myself for, no guilt whatsoever, after she died. Mixed in with this feeling was a deep self-contempt, which I still have today, that I had never told my mother how much I had once feared her, how awful she had once been; how terrible she still was to Laurel and her family. I had never faced Cecelia, never tried to make her face herself, never dared say what I felt. I had avoided it; I had ducked, just as she said, and was and am deeply ashamed. After Milton's death, her grief, her stroke, it was much too late to tell her.

I didn't want to have any more to do with 60 Minutes, I decided. It wasn't just the miserable $600 salary, or the time it took. It was something much more important that I had learned on my book tour. Because my mind was on Milton, it took a while to realize that everywhere I went, people were telling me the same thing. "I wasn't planning to read your book. But I picked up a copy" — here the comments varied — "in a bookstore . . . in the library . . . at my sister's house — and, you know what? It's very good!"

"Why didn't you expect it to be any good?"

The answer was always the same. "Because I watch you on 60 Minutes. Love you, hate him. But why spend $19.95 when I already know what you're going to say?"

The bottom-line effect of playing CBS's house liberal each week in front of forty million people had been to trivialize, and even sabotage, the writer I had spent my life learning to be.

I announced I was not returning to the show during a speech to the Michigan Bar Association, because I knew there would be press coverage, and got home from Detroit to find two messages from Mr. Paley's office. But all he wanted, said the secretary, was to ask me to dinner in Southampton the following night.

We were only four at dinner, and as soon as the Chairman and I were alone I said, "I thought you'd called because I'd quit 60 Minutes."

"You did?" He knew nothing about it. My resignation was not quite the news event I'd supposed. "Why?"

A truthful answer would have been embarrassing, so I said, "I just didn't think it was a good use of my time."

"Oh, yeah? How much were we paying you?"

"Six hundred dollars a week."

"Really!" he exclaimed, sounding just like Jack Benny. After a long pause, he added, "Well, I'm glad *somebody* at that place is minding the store."

On Monday, things got nasty. Don Hewitt, the producer, had the network put out a phony story that I had asked for more money than Jack, though in fact Kilpo and I each got $600. But he was earning about $100,000 a year from his column, and the show was such tremendous advertising for him that he would gladly have done it for nothing, had union rules permitted.

Two weeks after I bailed out of *60 Minutes*, Cecelia and her nurse Charlene flew to New York. A skycap wheeled my mother from the plane to my car with a blanket around her knees and a martini in her hand. I thought she looked weary but good. Charlene was a five foot ten black woman, a former army sergeant who dressed in fatigues, hugged Cecelia a lot, and fed her a diet of grits, pork, and candied yams, which she loved and thrived on. The nurse was experienced and good at her job, and her annual salary was $50,000, "in cash, please." Two years of Charlene precisely used up the nest egg Milton had put together for Cecelia to live on by writing and selling those ten new songs.

Indian summer is the most beautiful time of year in eastern Long Island, and my guests settled happily into the downstairs suite and stayed more than three weeks. Charlene took tender care of Cecelia, bathing and powdering her daily, sprinkling her with cologne and treating her like a tiny doll. Milton, I know, would have been very pleased to see this.

Laurel and I had never disagreed about what an awful mother Cecelia was, but we now found ourselves deeply divided about how sick she was. Laurel insisted she was badly impaired, both mentally and physically. I believed the neurologists' verdict, and found the proof in my experience of living with our mother, watching her on a twenty-four-hours-a-day basis. I think she was suffering grief, terrible boredom without Milton, and some sort of senility or childishness which had been slowly developing in recent years, and which Milton had conspired to hide from the world by in fact taking care of both of them. That is, I think Cecelia may have begun to revert back into childishness — to boomerang back, in fact, from a lifelong position of extreme sophistication — five or even ten years before Milton died, and that Milton had covered up for her. He let her think she was taking care of him, preparing little dishes and so on, but in fact he was watching out for her well-being, her safety and security. That's what the ten new songs had been about.

I also thought she didn't exactly need a *nurse*. On the other hand, Laurel was right: Cecelia could not have lived in that apartment alone. She needed someone to look after her, shop, keep house, and so on, and to make sure she ate properly and did not once again fall out of bed.

In the next eighteen months I made five trips to California. The little flat never changed. The TV was always on, and Cecelia was always seated on the couch, with tangerine sections or other nourishing snacks beside her, seemingly watching it. She was always glad to see me, our conversations were lucid, and she knew exactly what I'd been doing. But the old bite was gone, replaced by an all-pervasive mildness. Seeing her this way was very sad.

Nearly all her friends had stopped coming, except Michael Feinstein. He still visited every week, held her hand, played the songs, stayed an hour or more to chat, and in the warmth of his attention you could almost see her unfurl. Michael agrees that Cecelia wasn't bestroked so much as she was grief-stricken, and bored beyond belief with being alive. He thinks, as I do, that her mind remained sharp. She just quit playing the game.

Kelly was another faithful visitor. I wasn't sure where she lived now. Since Kathy was in college, and traveling in Europe in summer with her boyfriend, it didn't matter. Kelly's life with Steve had paralleled my own; he leaned on her financially and emotionally, and took advantage of her ability to attract interesting friends. One of the most interesting was Cecelia.

"What would you *really* like to do the next time I come?" she once asked Cecelia.

"A picnic would be very nice," my mother murmured, and Kelly next appeared with a beach umbrella, a card table, two folding chairs, and a hamper in the back of her station wagon. They drove to San Vicente Boulevard, which has a wide, parklike strip down the middle, and Kelly set everything up beneath one of the big orange-flowering tropical trees. She put a bottle of chilled Sancerre on the red-checkered tablecloth, unwrapped Cecelia's favorite delicacies, smoked whitefish and deviled eggs, and they had a fine afternoon watching the traffic.

Laurel was still driving the freeways several times a week to see Cecelia and check on Charlene. Victor and Florence too came by, as did Louise. Tommy Thompson stopped in when he could, and always sent me a note. The last one said:

> A couple of nights ago I dropped in on Cecelia, unannounced. . . . She was sipping a little white wine and beside her chair was a bowl of nuts and some fresh apple slices.
>
> Her mind wandered a little now and then, but she was always in focus. We talked about you and she said you were wise to quit *60 Minutes*. During my stay, the phone rang and I answered it. It was Laurel, who had been there earlier in the day. I asked Laurel when you were coming back, and she said, a little snippily, "Who knows?" I told her you were in need of a little getaway time.
>
> That's about all I have to report. I think Cecelia's in good hands, and she probably has some years left in her.

She had about nineteen months.

In Indian summer of 1980, after the tourists had all cleared out, Cecelia and Charlene came back to my house for the last time. My mother was a little smaller, and slower in her movements. But the night Barney

Straus, a nice, presentable, unmarried, rich, Jewish man arrived to pick me up for dinner, Cecelia perked right up, accepted a daiquiri, and held a zippy forty-minute chat with him before we left. Barney's mother was a physician, whom I knew, and Barney flatly refused to believe that Cecelia had even had a stroke.

But that had been a special occasion. Usually Cecelia just sat. She refused the daily walks her doctor had prescribed. I took her for little strolls up and down the driveway, but she always leaned heavily on my arm, or Charlene's; she never walked alone.

One day I came into the kitchen, and Charlene in her army fatigues was sitting on the Napoleonic-style Jimmy Reynolds bench, recovered in its original Roman-striped silk after being redeemed from storage.

"Hiya, Charlene. Where's Cecelia?"

"She takin' a crap."

Such was the flavor of our household.

My mother by then was just waiting to die, but I am certain she was mentally all there. She had been given a cane, but disliked using it. She preferred to steady herself by holding on to furniture, easy in her little apartment, not so easy in my big house.

I had no idea she was still able to climb stairs unaided. But on Charlene's day off, the day before they left, I made a quick trip to the store and came back to discover that, while I was out, Cecelia had come upstairs to my bedroom. In the straw in-box on my desk I found a note, written in her still strong, unmistakable hand.

5:20

Shana!—
    Goodnight, dear
Shana—
    Votre mère.
        Cecelia

My mother and Charlene were flying back to California in the morning, and I'd invited Leif Hope to join our farewell dinner. He is an amusing, endearing man, fond and respectful, and it did not surprise me that Cecelia had always liked him. That evening, our last together before she died, Leif asked Cecelia the question I had never dared.

After dinner, we had moved to the living room and I'd urged Charlene to retire. As a painter with a broad knowledge of music, Leif had spent a great deal of time over the years studying the Gershwin portrait. I did not notice that Leif had gone and got the painting from the maid's room wall, and brought it to Cecelia lying on the couch. He had mixed her a small stinger, the after-dinner drink she preferred, made space for himself on the couch beside her, and propped the painting on her stomach.

"Cecelia, Shana needs to know something, and she's afraid to ask you. *Did* you have a love affair with George Gershwin? Is that what happened? Is that why you put everything in storage?"

I, carrying a tray of dishes to the kitchen, stopped in my tracks. Leif's face was inches from Cecelia's own; no evasion was possible.

Looking him straight in the eye, she said levelly, "No comment."

"How can you say that to your daughter, Cecelia! What does it matter now? Milton is dead. Gershwin is dead. Shana needs an answer. How can you say, 'No comment'? Why do you do that to her?"

Her final reply was a second "No comment." I think of these as my mother's last words.

A few months later Laurel called. Cecelia had had another stroke and was back in the hospital, unconscious. The doctors said it wouldn't be long, only a day or two, and Laurel and I instructed them to use no unusual means to keep her alive. I offered to come out, but said it wasn't necessary. We had already agreed that this time there would be no funeral.

Cecelia Rubenstein Ager, age seventy-nine, died in the small hours of the morning of April 3, 1981, and the doctor telephoned Laurel. My sister buried her alongside Milton, with more grace than Cecelia had ever shown her. For her bronze marker, Laurel chose another set of seven notes:

It was the opening phrase of "My Bridal Veil," the simple 1920 tune Milton had always told us was his personal favorite. "What are the secrets you hold / within each delicate fold," a bevy of bridesmaids dreaming of their own future weddings had sung to the fluttering, stage-wide veil they held aloft while descending a golden stair.

When I next visited the cemetery, Cecelia's marker, newer than Milton's, was still faintly gleaming, and I stood for a time looking down and humming, overcome by the perfect aptness of each of Laurel's choices.

"Happy days are here again," Milton's tablet will cheerfully proclaim down through the years.

"What are the secrets you hold?" Cecelia's tablet will reverberate, unanswered, into eternity.

CLOSING NOTE

Besides the necessity to keep awake,
What is life without the relief of love?
                    — "Executions," *Robert Lowell*

December 1994. I no longer live in the big house behind the apple orchard. One January evening less than two years after my mother's death the telephone rang. An unheated seaside cottage in a cranberry bog beside a pond had just come on the market. I saw it before seven the next morning, and bought it that day. The site, the light, the two prospects of water, and the mixture of sea birds and pond birds were irresistible.

Milton's piano is in the living room, and the four green books are piled on top. Near them is a first-edition score of *Bolero* bound in leather and inscribed in a neat hand, "À chèr Monsieur Milton Ager, M. Ravel." The composer gave it to the Gershwins to bring back to my father in

1928, but for some reason it was never delivered. Michael Feinstein had found it among the family papers and sent it over to Milton just weeks before he died. Michael is thirty-six now, and our foremost interpreter/ scholar of American popular music. To me he is much more than a great singer and pianist; he has become a close friend, "my own heart's darling," as Heathcliff called his beloved, and we visit and talk our hearts out whenever his busy concert schedule permits.

The last fifteen years have seen many more deaths: Mary Stothart, Patrick O'Higgins, Tommy Thompson, Steve Alexander, Tom Prideaux. Today all of them have come to inhabit the same place, along with Harry and the Agers, the place where Tom Prideaux lives: the Past. When I lost Kathy for the last time, in 1987, she joined them there. I mostly live there now too. But I don't hear their voices so clearly any longer, except in dreams.

In the fall of the year Milton died, Kathy enrolled in Guilford College in North Carolina, a small Quaker institution which has a special program for gifted mathematicians, and publishes the only undergraduate journal of mathematics in the United States. Kathy's two papers on topology are still highly regarded. In the spring of 1981, her sophomore year, she told me on the telephone that she and her boyfriend planned to sample each of the world's known hallucinogens; they had been experimenting with LSD for some time. I caught the next plane, took them to lunch, went back with them to a dormitory, and said, "Adam, I don't know about you. You look strong. But Kathy is fragile. I'm not sure she can survive your experiment. And if she doesn't, I want you to know I will hold you responsible."

As one, they got up and walked out of the room. Kathy did not speak to me for two years. Eventually we got back together, and I came to know that Kathy loved me and, more important, she knew that I loved her.

Late one June night in 1983, Laurel called to say that Steve was in the hospital in a coma and was not expected to last the weekend. He had prostate cancer, and Laurel had nursed him during his final months while he'd lived at the Bentleys' house. But he'd forbidden her to tell me or Kathy of his presence. Vanity, she suggested, was his reason: he wanted nobody to see him ill and wasted. I learned much later that after Kelly left him, he had spent a lot of time with Cecelia, doing errands, driving, being helpful, and that she'd rather encouraged him to hang around. Possibly Steve handled his death as he did because he did not want Kelly to hear of his condition. A few months earlier, she had married a good man, Alexander Brook, and now had a life of her own.

The last clear good time I remember having with Kathy was the Tuesday in January 1986 when she drove me in her van to the federal courthouse in downtown Manhattan after visiting me for a few days in Long Island. I'd been in daily attendance at the courthouse for five months, doing research for *The Pizza Connection*, a book anatomizing a grotesquely swollen Mafia drug and money-laundering trial of twenty-two Sicilian-born defendants, each with his own lawyer. I remember the date because, as we approached the Brooklyn Bridge, we switched on the radio and heard the *Challenger* shuttle explode.

Kathy's van had been a college graduation present, and normally she used it to transport rock groups to gigs around the country. A superb driver who did not smoke, drink, or even use caffeine, she had by now driven cross-country ten or twelve times. I don't believe she charged anything for her services; it was 1986, and she and her friends were among the last hippies still around. Her favorite band was the Butthole Surfers, and when they got a gig in Manhattan Beach, Laurel and Wray put up Kathy and the Buttholes for several nights in sleeping bags on their living room floor. Kathy was very comfortable with the Bentleys, and had sometimes dropped off the road to stay with them for long periods, once for more than three months.

Between road tours she lived now in a middle-class section of Brooklyn with a new boyfriend whom I hoped to meet one day, and fervently hoped was better than the last one, who'd worn a safety pin in his ear. She'd been in Brooklyn about a year, and seemed happier than ever before. In November, she'd rhapsodized about her plans for giving their first party. Then in December, just a few days before Christmas 1986, she showed up at the Delmonico heartbroken and distraught. Her boyfriend had asked her to move out. Her presence, he'd told her, was "too depressing to live with."

I had a large, two-bedroom apartment by then, to serve in part as my *Pizza* office, and Kathy moved in with me. She tried to rest and gather her faculties. But rejection by the boyfriend had been so shattering that she could do nothing but sleep all day and play solitaire, so she "wouldn't have to think."

"I would commit suicide, but Kelly would kill me," she wrote in her diary. Her misery was terrible, and for the first time in her life she was willing to see a psychiatrist, a friend of mine. After her first visit, he told me he saw nothing seriously amiss, and she agreed to return the following week.

On February 5, 1987, the day before her second appointment, I drove up to the Bedford Hills Correctional Facility to see a friend who had become indispensable to me, Jean Harris. Our friendship had begun before her trial for murder, and ripened in the prison visiting room while I was interviewing her for a book about her life. Soon Jean had fallen into the habit of telephoning me when she felt the need to talk to someone close, but not too close. The calls came every week or two, and sometimes more often, for the entire time she was in prison. At the start, I'd been the person sustaining her. But somewhere in that marathon, twelve-year sequence of phone conversations our roles had begun to reverse, and I had come to appreciate that it was she whose humor and steady, loving, intelligent friendship were sustaining me. Her life was on hold. Mine was making some sickening twists, and whenever that happened, I held on to her.

Her phone calls were easy to accept; almost always *she* made *me* feel better. But visits to her hellhole were tough, and I made them as infrequently as possible. On the morning of February 5, however, I forced myself to drive up to Bedford Hills one more time. When I got home that evening at dusk, a small crowd had begun gathering under the Delmonico marquee, and a couple of cops were in the lobby. Somebody had just jumped off the roof. It was Kathy. She left no note. PARK AVENUE DEATH LEAP, the papers called it. But, being Kathy, she had been careful to jump off the back.

We buried her in Sag Harbor, and the Kunhardts' eldest son, Philip, now an Episcopal minister, conducted a small graveside service. Her headstone says VALIANT AND FREE.

By October 6, 1990, I was sixty-five years old and eligible for Medicare. Three and a half years had passed since Kathy's death, during which time I had tried and to some extent succeeded in shutting it entirely out of my mind and focusing only on my work. I did after a while get in touch with Vista Del Mar, which had been a leader in the movement for open adoption — a child's right to know the identity of its birth parents. Kathy had never wanted to know; she was always very firm on the matter. But now I wanted to know, and eventually found the kindly social worker, now retired, who had handled her case. It turned out that not only had Steve and I deceived Vista Del Mar about our economic situation; they had been less than entirely forthright with us. The reason Kathy's parents "didn't feel capable of raising a child" — a phrase which might have triggered a certain wariness, a subtle warning signal to any prospective parent not as child-besotted as I — was that one or both of them had been hospitalized for mental illness. Although Kathy was adroit all her life at avoiding any kind of psychiatric diagnosis or therapy, and could outsmart any psychiatrist I've ever met, I suspect she may have been mildly autistic, and perhaps suffered from manic depression as well. After her death Kelly told me that Kathy had talked about suicide to Kelly since her early teens. The peach pits I'd once found in her attic were the residue of her attempts to brew homemade cyanide.

Recently I'd finally begun letting myself think about Kathy, and allowing myself to grieve; soon I was too depressed to get out of bed. I decided to try Prozac, which meant I'd have to find a psychiatrist to prescribe it. A new one had just moved to our remote neighborhood. I was his first patient.

"Tell me something about yourself."

I was telling him about having gone to see a shrink once before, a "lay analyst," not a physician, though thoroughly Freudian and Viennese. When I'd mentioned to her that Steve had three balls, she'd laughed and said, "You mean you were married to a man with three testicles, and you thought there was something the matter with *you!*"

"Stop!" said Dr. S. "Three balls! Don't you realize how unusual that is?"

Sure, I said. "But I know a woman who has four breasts . . ."

"Look," he interrupted, "the sexual organs come in pairs. Women have two breasts, and a few have another pair of vestigial ones, like your friend. Dogs have six or eight; cows have four teats. But *nothing* has three, or five, or seven of anything. Some men do have one testicle, but only because the second one hasn't descended. In the developing embryo, the sex organs of males and females develop from an identical pair of little buds, indistinguishable up to a certain stage. That's why, when something goes wrong in development, some people have both kinds of sex organs: two testicles *and* two ovaries. But nobody has *three!*"

Steve did, I said, and started to describe our years of infertility treatment. Perhaps specialists today actually examine the husbands, but at the Tyler Clinic, nobody had. They'd simply taken our word for it that his general health, like his oft-measured sperm count, was excellent. Probably it never occurred to us to mention his anatomical anomaly; I didn't know how rare it was, and Steve probably figured that having three was slightly better than having two.

Dr. S. spoke again, raising his voice slightly. "*If* your husband really had three testicles, then any embryo fertilized by his sperm would be certain to miscarry early. That is nature's way of preventing the birth of monstrosities, like two-headed calves. Though a sire with three balls would more likely produce a three-headed calf. Three balls is like . . . like *one eye*, for God's sake!"

I rather liked this reference to Polyphemus, the Cyclops I knew from

Greek mythology. In any event, my time was more than up, and Dr. S. was scribbling a prescription for Prozac. "Because you are on Medicare," I heard him saying, though my whirling mind was mostly elsewhere, "I cannot charge you my regular fee. So would $86.06 be acceptable?"

"That would be about right," I said, scrawling a check and staggering out.

The notion that the gods of Olympus amuse themselves by playing tricks on us mere mortals had been familiar to me since reading Bulfinch, back in the Salisbury. And I'd thought myself long since resigned to the workings of the three Fates: Clotho, who held the distaff; Lachesis, who spun the thread of life; Atropos, who cut it off at her whim. But to discover myself the butt of a cosmic joke of this magnitude, played out at this remove in time — hadn't the cruel sisters gone a bit far?

The Prozac helped. I began to feel better. Indeed, I finally felt like starting to write the book I'd put aside eleven years earlier, after Milton's death and Cecelia's stroke; this book.

A year later, on a brief holiday in Paris, I happened to telephone a French cousin whose existence I had not been aware of until Victor had recommended I try to see her on my trip. Nelcya Delanoë was the granddaughter and the sole female descendant of Dr. Eugenia Delanoë, my grandfather Zalkin's sister, the baggy, non-English-speaking traveler who'd turned up briefly at 350 Park Avenue during World War II.

I invited Nelcya to lunch, and met a small, chic woman in her late forties with red-gold hair, lynx furs, and suede boots. She was a professor of American history at the University of Nanterre, and like myself a divorced writer living alone. She had published four books, she told me, three of them pioneering looks at American history from a sophisticated, left-wing European point of view.

But her most surprising book was *La Femme de Mazagan, ou les salines de la mémoire*, a real-life detective story unraveling the hidden history of Nelcya's family by uncovering the true identity of her grand-mother.

We sat in a Paris restaurant for three hours while Nelcya told me the story of her grandmother, my great-aunt. Nelcya was thirty before she discovered that "both my parents, my uncle, my three brothers, and my grandmother had all lied to me about who I was." The secret that Genia was Jewish only began to come to light after Nelcya asked her father if he had any records from Morocco, where the family originated and had lived until several years after Morocco became independent of France, in 1956. Dr. Guy Delanoë gave Nelcya a chest filled with ancient photo-graphs and passionate 1908 love letters exchanged as medical students by Genia and her fiancé, Pierre, a Roman Catholic, including letters in which Pierre asks his future bride to renounce her religion, and she re-fuses. Honor, not piety, compels her. She will not betray her own iden-tity, though she is willing to raise their children in their father's faith. At the bottom of the chest lay Genia's autobiography, *My Thirty Years as a Physician in Morocco*. The book nowhere mentions that she is a Jew. Save for one astonishing outcry in its very last line — "Maroc, Maroc, how I miss my Maroc!" — the book is a discreet, cut-and-dried account of the author's medical practice. But the mysterious last line had triggered Nelcya's long search to unravel Genia's story.

In 1904, having completed her medical education in St. Petersburg, Eugenia came to Paris. Like her girlhood friend Rosa Luxemburg, and her heroine Marie Curie, Genia burned with an overpowering passion to help mankind. She intended to work at the Institute Pasteur, but it soon became clear that first she would have to repeat her medical educa-tion in French. At the famed thousand-year-old medical school at Mont-pelier, Genia met and married a fellow student, Pierre Delanoë, son of a royalist family in St. Denis de la Réunion, an island in the Indian Ocean.

Soon she and Pierre established a maternity hospital at Mazagan, a coastal city west of Casablanca with only seven non-Arab inhabitants. Pierre was often away on public health assignments, but the hospital prospered under Genia's supervision, and even today she is still known throughout Morocco as the doctor who wiped out childbed fever, once the prime cause of death among women. A hospital, a boulevard, and a school have been named for her.

Gradually Genia and Pierre had grown apart, and died apart. Their sons Georges and Guy, born in Mazagan, had spoken Arabic as their first language, and had been raised as Catholics. After attending university in France, they had returned to Morocco to practice their professions. Nelcya's father, a cardiologist, married a prim Swiss Protestant, and their four children were born and raised in Morocco. The family did not move to France until after the long colonial struggle for independence — of which Dr. Guy had been a rare non-Arab supporter — had finally succeeded.

Twenty-two years earlier, when France had fallen to the Nazis, the Vichy government had required all French Jews, even in its colonies, to declare their identity, and soon was cooperating with the Germans in sending them to concentration camps. But Genia's situation was unique: not only did Morocco's King Mohamad V have a long-standing policy of protecting Moroccan Jews, tiny Mazagan with its handful of non-Arabs was so remote that failure to declare oneself would have had no consequences. Nonetheless, Nelcya discovered, after a lifetime of silence Genia had immediately proclaimed herself a Jew, and promptly been barred from her hospital and stripped of her license to practice medicine. She had turned up in our Park Avenue apartment while en route to San Francisco to look for her doctor brother Charles, who had come to the U.S. in the mid-thirties after twenty years' practice in Moscow.

But Genia was not licensed to practice in California, and Victor eventually found her a behind-the-scenes job in a Los Angeles medical laboratory. For five years she had worked and lived alone. During her self-exile she grieved for her children and homeland, and wrote her 1949 book.

Now, in Paris, Nelcya said to me, "But I've been talking far too long about myself. Tell me about your life. Do you have any children?"

"No," I told her, and briefly explained. "Do you?"

"Oh, no! I have known from the time I was a little girl that I would never, ever want to have children."

"But why not?"

"Because I always knew, in my very bones, that I came from a long line of wild, impassioned, unhappy females. It was in our blood, and I was sure I did not want to perpetuate it."

Her answer stunned me. The same fact—our overwrought, becrazed female heritage, the engine that had driven me to waste so much of my life dreaming of bearing and raising a large family of nice "normal" children, people unlike Cecelia and Anzia—had driven Nelcya in exactly the opposite direction; it had made her vow to have no children. Our lives had been opposite, yet they had a kind of symmetry. I might just as readily have followed her path, and spared myself so much agony. Perhaps one would have to have lived my life to understand how healing this realization was.

At bottom we were all the same. Our lives had followed the same pattern. If we could not have love and family, we would have success. Anzia in New York and her remote cousin Genia in Morocco were two of a kind. Nor should we forget Ethel King, the vaudeville cousin with pail and shovel who introduced Cecelia to Milton. She too was one of the wild women, as was her older sister Dr. Hannah, who had attended my birth, and *her* first cousin Viola Kates Stimson, the elderly actress, and her other first cousin Cecelia Rubenstein Ager, and, finally, I suppose, me.

Index